Free Will and Consciousness

A Determinist Account of the Illusion of Free Will

Gregg D. Caruso

LEXINGTON BOOKS
Lanham • Boulder • New York • Toronto • Plymouth, UK

Published by Lexington Books
A wholly owned subsidiary of The Rowman & Littlefield Publishing Group, Inc.
4501 Forbes Boulevard, Suite 200, Lanham, Maryland 20706
www.rowman.com

10 Thornbury Road, Plymouth PL6 7PP, United Kingdom

British Library Cataloguing in Publication Information Available

Library of Congress Cataloging-in-Publication Data
The hardback edition of this book was previously cataloged by the Library of Congress as
follows:

Caruso, Gregg D.
Free will and consciousness : a determinist account of the illusion of free will / Gregg D.
Caruso.
   p. cm.
Includes bibliographical references and index.
1. Free will and determinism. 2. Consciousness. 3. Phenomenology. I. Title.
BJ1461.C37 2012
123'.5—dc23   2011053220

ISBN: 978-0-7391-7136-3 (cloth : alk. paper)
ISBN: 978-0-7391-8440-0 (pbk. : alk. paper)
ISBN: 978-0-7391-7137-0 (electronic)

℮™ The paper used in this publication meets the minimum requirements of American
National Standard for Information Sciences—Permanence of Paper for Printed Library
Materials, ANSI/NISO Z39.48-1992.

Printed in the United States of America

For Elaini and Maya

Contents

Acknowledgments

I began thinking seriously about issues related to free will and consciousness while completing my graduate work in philosophy at the City University of New York. This book represents the culmination of that thinking and is a revision of the dissertation I submitted for my PhD. As a result, *Free Will and Consciousness* has benefited greatly from the vetting it first received from my thesis committee. I am extremely grateful to Michael Levin, David Rosenthal, John Greenwood, Steven Cahn, and Peter Simpson for their expert guidance and support. I am especially indebted to Michael Levin, my dissertation advisor. Michael is the consummate philosopher and his sustained encouragement, open mind, and always insightful feedback greatly improved this book. David Rosenthal also deserves special recognition for his instrumental role in shaping my philosophical thinking. David is a gifted teacher and philosopher and I benefited greatly from my time under his supervision. Thanks are also due to Steven Cahn for contacting Lexington Books on my behalf and encouraging me to turn the dissertation into a book.

Since no philosophical work is ever solely the product of a single individual, I would also like to thank a number of friends, family members, and colleagues. Special thanks to Josh Weisberg, Liz Vlahos, Andrew Hathaway, Jesse Hathaway, Rick Repetti, Bana Bashour, Robert Talisse, Mark McEvoy, Maureen Eckert, Richard Brown, Pete Mandik, Roblin Meeks, Fritz McDonald, Daniel Leafe, and Jarred Blanck for their many helpful conversations over the years. My participation in the CUNY Cognitive Science Symposium and Discussion Group was instrumental in shaping my thinking on consciousness, and the CUNY Free Will Reading Group was where I first rehearsed and developed many of the ideas and arguments contained herein. I would also like to thank James Cruz, John Celentano, Christine Atkins, Andrea Harris, Rob Tempio, Sandra-Turner Vicioso, Vince Lisella, Byron Shaw, and Andrea Rubin for their emotional support and encouragement. I am lucky to have friends and colleagues like you. Special thanks are also due to my editor at Lexington Books, Jana Hodges-Kluck, who did a splendid job in bringing this book to completion.

Finally, this book would have never been possible if it were not for the love, support, and encouragement I received from my family—especially that of my wife, Elaini, and daughter, Maya. Much of the time I spent writing and researching *Free Will and Consciousness* truly belonged to them. I thank you both for your steadfast support and for lifting me up when I needed it most. My deepest thanks also go out to my parents, Louis and Dolores Caruso, my brothers, their families, and Marina and George Kokkinos. Thank you all.

I dedicate this book to Elaini and Maya, to whom I owe more than I can express.

ONE

The Problem of Free Will: A Brief Introduction and Outline of Position

We all naturally take ourselves to be free agents capable of acting in alternative ways by consciously choosing and deciding to follow different courses of action. Indeed, belief in freedom of the will lies at the core of our self-conception and underlies many of our moral, legal, and theological attitudes. When we think of free will we usually think of a kind of personal power to *originate* choices and decisions and thus action. We believe we have free will when "(a) it is 'up to us' what we choose from an array of alternative possibilities and (b) the origin or source of our choices and actions is in us and not in anyone or anything else over which we have no control" (Kane 2002a, 5). Although we sometimes make exceptions for certain subclasses of human behavior, the common assumption remains that most ordinary voluntary actions are freely chosen. A less popular and more radical view, however, maintains that our best scientific theories have the consequence that factors beyond our control produce *all* of the actions we perform and that because of this we do not possess the kind of free will required for genuine or ultimate responsibility (see d'Holbach 1770; Priestly 1788; B.F. Skinner 1971; Edwards 1958; Pereboom 1995, 2001; Strawson 1986; Honderich 1988, 2002a, 2002b). Although few philosophers have historically defended such a *hard* view, this is the position I will defend here.

In this book I will examine both the traditional philosophical problems long associated with the question of free will, such as the relationship between determinism and free will, as well as recent experimental and theoretical work directly related to consciousness and human agency. Although powerful arguments against our ordinary conception of free will have long existed, it is only recently that those arguments have gained additional empirical support. In fact, in recent decades, with de-

1

velopments in the behavioral, cognitive, and neurosciences, the idea that patterns of human behavior may ultimately be due to factors beyond our conscious control has increasingly gained traction and renewed interest in the age-old problem of free will. These developments indicate, for example, that much of what we do takes place at an automatic and unaware level, and that our commonsense belief that our conscious intentions and volitions cause our voluntary actions is mistaken. They also indicate that the causes that move us are often less transparent to ourselves then we might assume—diverging in many cases from the conscious reasons we provide to explain and/or justify our actions. In subsequent chapters I will examine some of these recent scientific findings and I will argue that our commonsense belief in conscious free will is in fact contradicted by empirical evidence. I will further argue that the strong and pervasive belief in free will, which I consider an illusion, can be accounted for through a careful analysis of our phenomenology and a proper theoretical understanding of consciousness. The central goal of this book will therefore be to provide a *determinist account of the illusion of free will*—an account that, in addition to drawing on standard philosophical strategies, emphasizes theoretical work in consciousness studies and empirical findings in the behavioral, cognitive, and neurosciences.

1.1 HARD-ENOUGH DETERMINISM AND THE ILLUSION OF FREE WILL

Few philosophical debates have been waged with greater acrimony than the one over whether we possess free will. In fact, according to one recent history of philosophy, the problem is "perhaps the most voluminously debated of all philosophical problems" (Matson 1987, 158; as referenced by Kane 2002a, 3). The traditional *problem of free will and determinism* comes in trying to reconcile our intuitive sense of free will with the idea that our choices and actions may be causally determined by impersonal forces over which we have no ultimate control. Although there are different ways to state this threat, *determinism*, as it is commonly understood, is roughly the position that every event or action, including human action, is the inevitable result of preceding events and actions and the laws of nature.[1] If determinism is true then every human action is causally necessitated by events and states of affairs that occurred or obtained prior to the agent's existence. But if every action is causally necessitated in this way it would seem no one could have ever acted otherwise. The problem of free will and determinism therefore creates a dilemma of sort. As A.J. Ayer describes it:

> On the one hand, we are inclined to believe that all spatio-temporal processes, and therefore also human actions, are governed by natural

laws; and from this we are inclined to infer that given the initial circumstances whatever actually happens could not have happened otherwise. On the other hand, all our moral assessments of our own and other people's conduct and all our legal practice depend on the assumption that people are responsible for their acts; but this seems to imply that, even given the existing circumstances, they could have acted otherwise. But these conclusions are mutually contradictory. It has been shown, then, either that there is some flaw in this reasoning, or that at least one of the premises of one or other of these arguments is false. (1969, 14)

Historically, philosophers have attempted to resolve this dilemma in one of three ways. These are represented by the three main positions on the problem of free will and determinism: *libertarianism, determinism,* and *compatibilism.*

These positions can be defined by how they answer two main questions: whether all events are determined or not—*determinism* versus *indeterminism*—and whether freedom can coexist with determinism or not—*compatibilism* versus *incompatibilism. Libertarians,* for example, are incompatibilists who defend a form of indeterminist free will. That is, libertarians maintain that free will is at odds with determinism—if determinism is true, free will is impossible—but they also maintain that at least some of our choices and actions are free in the sense that they are not causally determined. *Determinists* (or *hard determinists*), on the other hand, are incompatibilists who deny the existence of free will—they maintain that all human behavior, like the behavior of all other things, arises from antecedent conditions given which no other behavior is possible. The third position, that of *compatibilism* (or *soft-determinism*), tries to reconcile free will with causal determinism. Compatibilists maintain that the problem of free will and determinism is a pseudo-problem that can be solved (or dissolved) once we acknowledge that moral freedom (the kind of freedom required for responsibility) does not require the denial of determinism.

Beyond these three main categories are a number of subcategories. Libertarianism, for example, may be broken down into *agent-causal* and *event indeterminist* versions. These two accounts differ as to the ontology of causation. Agent-causal accounts posit *agents* as uncaused causes of their own behavior where an *agent* is to be viewed as a substance and not an event. Event indeterminist accounts, on the other hand, insist that only *events* can be causes and eschew any discussion of other entities such as substances (see ch. 2 for details). Compatibilist approaches also vary on how they define the requirements of compatibilist freedom and how they respond to the standard incompatibilist argument. *Hierarchical* and *mesh accounts,* for example, make different demands than *classical compatibilism.* And defenders of "conditional" analyses of "could have done otherwise" respond to incompatibilism differently than do defenders of *charac-*

ter examples and *Frankfurt-style examples* (see ch. 3 for details). Beyond these subcategories are a number of *hybrid* and *successor views* (see Kane 2002a). Chief among these are the hybrid position of *semi-compatibilism*, which maintains that moral responsibility is compatible with determinism but free will is not (e.g., Fischer and Ravizza 1998), and such successor views to hard determinism as the positions of Galen Strawson (1986, 1994b, 2002), Ted Honderich (1988, 2002a, 2002b), Derk Pereboom (1995, 2001, 2002), and myself.

My overall position, though similar to classical hard determinism, is not identical. For this reason I prefer to call it *hard-enough determinism*: the thesis that all human choice and action, and the underlying neural and psychological processes that give rise to them, are part of a causally determinate system (or "near-determined")[2] such that no human action is free (appropriately understood). *Hard-enough determinism* differs from *hard determinism* in that it leaves open the possibility that there may be some indeterminism in the universe, perhaps at the microlevel, but it maintains that any such indeterminism is screened out at levels sufficiently low not to matter to human behavior. Although the standard Copenhagen interpretation of quantum mechanics has been taken by many to undermine the thesis of universal determinism (see Hodgson 2002), I believe serious determinist concerns still remain. I maintain that even if there are real metaphysical quantum indeterminacies they are of such a vanishing magnitude as to cancel out before reaching the required neural level (see also Honderich 1988, 2002a, 2002b). Furthermore, I agree with Galen Strawson and other critics that libertarian free will is an impossibility *whether or not* determinism is true (see Strawson 1986, 1994b, 2000; Dennett 1984; Honderich 1988; Pereboom 2001). Hard-enough determinism therefore shares with classical hard determinism two main claims: (1) that free will—in what Strawson (1986) calls the "true-responsibility entailing" sense—is incompatible with determinism, and (2) there is no such incompatibilist or libertarian free will. Keeping in mind, then, this proviso about quantum mechanics, I will, for the most part, drop the "enough" in what's to follow. That is, whenever I refer to my position as "hard determinism" from here on out, this should be understood as really referring to "hard-enough determinism" as defined above.[3]

In arguing for hard determinism, I will take two different approaches. My first, more traditional approach can be found in chapters 2 and 3 where I discuss compatibilism and libertarianism. In negative fashion, if I can establish that both positions fail for various reasons this would be sufficient to establish the two main theses of hard(-enough) determinism. My second, more novel approach is contained in chapters 4-7 where I argue that there are good empirical reasons for doubting the existence of free will; reasons that go beyond the simple acceptance of macrolevel causal determinism. These reasons largely have to do with consciousness and what recent discoveries in the behavioral, cognitive, and neurosciences tell us about it. I will argue that the work of Benjamin Libet (1985), Daniel Wegner (2002), John Bargh (1990, 1994, 1997, 2008), Timothy Wilson (2002), and others, threaten many of our centrally held presuppositions about freedom and autonomy. For example, neuroscientific discoveries about the timing of conscious processes and their relationship to underlying neural processes suggest that consciousness does not perform the sort of executive function we typically think. More specifically, these findings raise questions about the role our conscious intentions, volitions, and willings play in the initiation and control of voluntary behavior. Additional findings in psychology and social psychology on *automaticity* and the *adaptive unconscious* raise further concerns about the role and function of consciousness. These findings reveal that the higher mental processes that have traditionally served as quintessential examples of free will—such as goal pursuits, evaluation and judgment, reasoning and problem solving, interpersonal behavior, and action initiation—can and often do occur in the absence of conscious choice or guidance (Bargh and Ferguson 2000, 926). They also reveal just how "wide open" (Jarrett 2008) our internal psychological processes are to the influence of external stimuli and events in our immediate environment, without knowledge or awareness of such influence. In arguing against free will, then, I will focus on both traditional concerns surrounding determinism and indeterminism, and, more importantly, on empirical discoveries in the behavioral, cognitive, and neurosciences.

Complementing this defense of hard determinism from a cognitive science point of view, another focus of mine, indeed my primary focus, will be explaining the phenomenology surrounding our *subjective feeling of freedom*.[4] An implication of hard determinism is that our feeling of freedom—which includes, but is not limited to, the feeling that we are free agents capable of self-determination, origination, and the ability to do otherwise—is an illusion. Although I believe this to be true, I do not think it's enough to simply state this as an implication of one's theoretical position. Since I take our feeling of freedom to be undeniable, I acknowledge an obligation to address it directly. Although it has been a longstanding tradition of determinists to claim that our feeling of free will is an illusion, there have been surprisingly few positive accounts given of how the illusion actually arises.[5] I believe this has created a major obstacle in the way of accepting the thesis of determinism (in both its *hard* and *hard-enough* forms). If the obstacle can be removed I believe progress can be made. Hence, one of the primary goals of this book is to argue that our subjective feeling of freedom, as reflected in the first-person phenomenology of agentive experience, is an illusion created by certain aspects of our consciousness. So after working to establish that our ordinary conception of free will is in fact an illusion in chapters 2-4, I then proceed to give a novel account of just how that illusion is created in chapters 5-7. I present my illusionist account using one leading theory of consciousness—the *higher-order thought* (or HOT) theory of consciousness as developed by David Rosenthal (2005a). The HOT theory will not only provide a theoretically useful and accurate account of *state consciousness*—that is, an account of why certain mental states are conscious and not others—but it will also prove useful in interpreting many of the empirical findings in the behavioral, cognitive, and neurosciences, as well as provide an explanation of those aspects of our phenomenology that give rise to the illusion of free will.[6]

In presenting my illusionist account, I will focus primarily on four key aspects of our phenomenology:

1. The *apparent* transparency and infallibility of consciousness—i.e., the feeling that we have immediate, direct, and infallible access to our own mental states and processes.
2. The *feeling* that our intentional states arise spontaneously and are causally undetermined (in contrast (say) to our sensory states, which are experienced as caused by states of the world).
3. The *feeling* of *conscious will*—i.e., the feeling that we consciously cause or initiate behavior directly through our conscious intentions, decisions, and willings.
4. And our *sense* of a *robust, unified Self* who is the willful author of behavior.

I will argue that each of these phenomenological components plays an important role in generating our sense of free will but that by combining the theoretical framework of the HOT theory with empirical findings in the behavioral, cognitive, and neurosciences we can come to see that each is an illusion. In fact, the HOT theory, I maintain, is particularly well suited to explain away the phenomenology in a way that preserves the phenomenological appearances. I will argue that the illusion of free will is created by the particular way our higher-order thoughts make us conscious of our mental states and how our sense of self is constructed within consciousness. I will discuss the apparent transparency and infallibility of consciousness in chapter 5, the apparent spontaneity of our intentional states along with our feeling of conscious will in chapter 6, and self-consciousness and our sense of agency in chapter 7. My account of our subjective feeling of freedom, if successful, will preserve and explain the phenomenological data (something I believe all accounts of free will must do) while simultaneously revealing why it does not support a corresponding belief in free will.

1.2 FREEDOM AND DETERMINISM: DEFINING THE PROBLEM

The problem of free will revolves around the difficulty in reconciling our first-person folk-psychological account of ourselves with our scientific understanding of the world.[7] The fundamental problem is that we are faced with two distinct images of ourselves-in-the-world, each vying for our allegiance, and each telling us something different about the possibility of human freedom (see Sellars 1963; Flanagan 2002; P.F. Strawson 1962; Nagel 1986; Bok 1998; Blackburn 1999). According to the one image, we, as persons or agents, are free to make certain choices and perform certain actions. As Manuel Vargas writes:

> [W]e see ourselves as having genuine, robust alternative possibilities available to us at various moments of decision. We may even see ourselves as agent-causes, a special kind of cause distinct from the non-agential parts of the causal order. Moreover, we tend to think of this picture of our own agency as underwriting many important aspects of human life, including moral responsibility. How we think about a range of social issues (crime and punishment, addiction, and even issues such as homelessness), and the social policies we construct around them, in part depend on the presumption of this picture of agency. (2007, 127)

This ordinary conception of human action—which is reflected in our personal experience, reactive attitudes (P.F. Strawson 1962), folk theories of human agency, religious and theological doctrines, and beliefs about moral responsibility—attributes to agents a high degree of autonomy. It tells us that when we make a conscious choice or perform a voluntary act, alternative possibilities lie open before us, and one of those possibilities is made actual by what we do. According to this *personal* or *practical* standpoint, when an agent is confronted with two or more incompatible courses of action he or she engages in a process of deliberation (weighing the considerations for and against the several alternatives involved), chooses among the alternative possibilities, and then acts or not on the basis of that choice. It's also part of our belief, and ultimately what's in question, that this process is "ultimately up to us." That is, we all experience, as Galen Strawson puts it, a sense of "radical, absolute, buckstopping *up-to-me-ness* in choice and actions" (2004, 380). We typically feel that we are not causally determined to do just the thing we do. This feeling of *up-to-me-ness*, of self-determination, is ultimately what underlies our feeling of freedom. It suggests that the origins or source of our actions are in us and not in something else over which we have no control—"whether that something else is fate or God, the laws of nature, birth or upbringing, or other humans" (Kane 2002a, 5).

We all subjectively feel that it's *ultimately up to us* what we choose and how we act, and that we could have chosen or acted otherwise than we in fact did. When we look within ourselves, at our ability to deliberate and make choices, and our subsequent ability to act on those choices, we *feel* ourselves to be directly aware of our freedom. This strong sense of freedom leads us to believe we have free will. As Corliss Lamont states the intuition:

> One of the strongest supports for the free choice thesis is the unmistak-
> able intuition of virtually every human being that he is free to make the
> choices he does and that the deliberations leading to those choices are
> also free flowing. The normal man feels too, after he has made a deci-
> sion, that he could have decided differently. That is why regret or
> remorse for a past choice can be so disturbing. (1967, 3)

Surrounding the notion of free will is a cluster of other concepts. These concepts are largely given to us by our folk-psychological understanding of human action. Included in this cluster are notions such as: *autonomy, origination, self-determination, self-control, reasons-sensitivity,* and, once again, the *ability to do otherwise.* Our understanding of human freedom is intimately tied to these notions; in fact, they largely define it. I will be discussing these concepts at great length in what's to follow. The prob-lem, however, is that a number of these concepts are threatened by a competing image of ourselves-in-the-world.

This competing image arises when we begin to realize just how pro-foundly the world influences us in ways previously unknown. Some-thing happens to our familiar picture of ourselves and other persons when, as Kane writes, "we view ourselves from various *impersonal, objec-tive* or *theoretical* perspectives (Nagel 1986: 110)" (2002a, 5). From the perspective of the laws of nature, for example, it would seem that our choices and actions are part of the flow of the physical world and hence subject to the same deterministic laws of nature as all other physical objects and events. Classical physics provides us with an apparently ac-curate and comprehensive account of the macrolevel workings of matter and energy in space-time that is completely deterministic.[8] There is no reason to think we are immune from these deterministic laws. Even if we allow some indeterminacy to exist at the microlevel of our existence — the level studied by quantum mechanics — there would still remain, as Hon-derich puts it, *determinism-where-it-matters* (2002a, 5). "At the ordinary level of choices and actions, and even ordinary electrochemical activity in our brains, causal laws govern what happens. It's all cause and effect in what you might call real life" (2002a, 5). Hence, if every macrolevel event and state of affairs is causally determined by antecedent conditions, and human choices and actions (and the agents that give rise to them) are just macrolevel events and states of affairs, then all human choices and ac-tions are causally determined as well.

It's easy to see, then, how our personal or practical standpoint be-comes threatened once we move to the theoretical perspective of causal determinism. Human choice and action would be, if causal determinism were true, *as* determined as the rest of the physical world. In fact, the rubber really meets the road when one considers things from the perspective of the mind/brain. If the fundamental principles of classical physics hold true at the level of the brain (a bio-*physical* organ), and one were willing to accept a naturalistic account of the mind according to which all mental states are identical with brain states—or at least strongly correlated with brain states—then human freedom would immediately be threatened. If our choices, actions, and mental states are simply part of the flow of the physical world, and the thesis of causal determinism is true (or true enough), then there would appear to be no break in the causal chain leading from initial environmental input to eventual behavioral output. If the mind/brain works according to the basic principles of classical physics, it's hard to see how there can be any free will.[9]

Our personal or practical conception gets further challenged when we consider it in relation to recent advances in psychology, sociology, and neuroscience. As Robert Kane writes:

> [D]evelopments in sciences other than physics—in biology, neuroscience, psychology, psychiatry, social and behavior sciences—have convinced many persons that more of their behavior is determined by causes unknown to them and beyond their control than previously believed. Of particular significance among these scientific developments is the growing knowledge of genetics and physiology, of biochemical influences on the brain, including the susceptibility of human moods and behavior to drugs and biochemical sources of psychiatric disorders. (2002a, 33)

These too are worries over determinants but unlike the previous family of concerns they do not presuppose any particular account of physics.[10] These determinants range from genes to upbringing, heredity to culture, habitual likes and dislikes to electrochemical activity in the brain, early childhood experiences to unconscious motives and other psychological springs of action of which we are unaware. The more we learn about these determinants, the more "they threaten our self-image and cause a corresponding crisis in human thinking (Farrer 1967, Kenny 1978)" (Kane 2002a, 5). That is, the more we learn that much of our character and behavior is influenced by hereditary and environmental factors (Pinker 2002; Ridley 2003), or by subtle chemical imbalances in our brains (Sternberg 2010), or that our thoughts and behavior can be covertly influenced by social conditioning (Waller 1990; Double 1991), or that much of our day-to-day life may be guided by unconscious automatic processes (Bargh 1997; Bargh and Chartrand 1999; Bargh and Ferguson 2000), the more our personal/practical standpoint (including our belief in free will) becomes threatened.

The problem of free will and determinism, then, comes in trying to reconcile these two competing conceptions of the world. As stated earlier, there are essentially three options. One could argue that the conflict is more apparent than real—this is the approach compatibilism takes. The remaining two options involve challenging certain core assumptions of one or another of these conceptions. Libertarians, for example, attempt to defend our intuitive sense of agency by postulating that the laws of classical physics do not have universal application when it comes to human behavior, and that the more specific forms of determinism do not threaten free will. Hard determinism, on the other hand, maintains that our best scientific theories do indeed indicate that every human choice and action results solely and exclusively from factors and determinants outside our control, and because of this we lack the kind of free will and responsibility ordinarily assumed. Which of these options is correct, then, will ultimately depend on two questions: Can our folk-psychological conception of our own and others' behavior be reconciled with determinism? And, if not, can a plausible account of libertarian freedom be made sense of and defended in light of our best scientific theories?

With the problem now stated, I will proceed, after one aside, to arguing that hard(-enough) determinism is the only justified option.

1.3 A WORD ABOUT MORAL RESPONSIBILITY

It is important that I end this introduction with a few comments about moral responsibility. Although discussion of moral responsibility and related notions is unavoidable, the primary focus of this work will be on the metaphysics of free will, how it relates to the philosophy of mind, and the cognitive psychology behind our subjective feeling of freedom. Some may find this unsatisfying since, as they see it, such concerns constitute *the* problem of free will and determinism (e.g., Stace 1952; P.F. Strawson 1962; Vargas 2007, 128). Many philosophers reject the thesis of hard determinism because they believe it threatens certain centrally-held moral, legal, and theological beliefs and attitudes—most notably, those associated with moral responsibility, praise and blame, reward and punishment, and such concepts as sin, redemption, merit, and duty. It is commonly held that the existence of free will is a necessary condition for moral responsibility—i.e., that unless one is free to do otherwise, he cannot be justly held responsible for his actions any more than he can be held responsible for his date of birth or eye color. I will not question this assumption here.[11] I will follow tradition and assume that the kind of free will under discussion is the kind that would make us truly or ultimately responsible for our actions "in such a way as to be truly and *sans phrase* deserving of (moral) praise and blame for them" (Strawson 2010, vi). In fact, I acknowledge that accepting hard determinism involves relinquishing the idea that we are *ultimately* responsible for who we are and what we do. For some, this implication is reason alone for rejecting determinism—since, they argue, it would have dire consequences for morality, society, our legal system, and how we interact with each other.

In fact, there seems to be a "quiet consensus" among philosophers that "morality and moral responsibility stand or fall together" (Waller 2004, 427). Peter van Inwagen, for example, writes that "If there is no free will, then morality as it is ordinarily conceived is an illusion" (1990, 394). C.A. Campbell, a fellow libertarian, likewise asserts that denial of justly deserved praise and blame would destroy "the reality of the moral life" (1957, 167; as quoted by Waller 2004, 427). This kind of thinking is not limited, however, to libertarians. The compatibilist Ishtiyaque Haji (1999, 2002b) has argued, for example, that in a deterministic world we would be bereft of any "moral anchors," that is to say, moral deontic normative statuses like those of being morally right, wrong, or obligatory.[12] Some have even gone so far as to claim that the denial of free will would increase anti-social behavior (Baumeister, Masicampo, and DeWall 2009; Vohs and Schooler 2008) and even threaten to destroy the entire social fabric of society (Smilansky 2000; Perlovsky 2010).

Although I acknowledge the importance of these issues, I believe the rejection of hard determinism on the grounds that it will have such dire consequences is misguided (in my mind at least) for two reasons. First, to reject determinism *because* of its implications is not an argument *for* free will, it is simply a statement of the importance of the issue. It addresses only the *desirability* of a belief in free will, not whether the belief is true or false. And wishful thinking does not make it so. In fact, allegiance to "ought implies can" and the assumption that morality requires free will has driven many philosophers to desperate strategies. Libertarians, for example, "have postulated miracle-working faculties that empower individuals to do what they ought to do" in a desperate attempt to save moral reality (Waller 2004, 431). A good example of this would be Immanuel Kant's reasons for embracing libertarianism. Kant (1788) famously held that despite the lack of evidence in support of agent-causal libertarianism—which, in his view, is required for moral responsibility—we must nonetheless postulate that we possess such freedom to uphold the validity of the moral law.[13] In a similar fashion, van Inwagen (1983) embraces libertarianism despite his own conclusion that "free will remains a mystery" (2000) because, he argues, if determinism were true we could not then be responsible for our actions—something he finds obviously false and unacceptable. Yet there seems to be something wrong, as Saul Smilansky argues, with "the claim that there is a conclusive case for the direct obviousness of the existence of libertarian moral responsibility (i.e., libertarian-free-will-assuming moral responsibility), despite the lack of a case for such direct obviousness as to the existence of libertarian free will" (1990, 29). I would argue, instead, that one must deal with the metaphysical issue of free will first and then let the chips fall where they may. We should not let our desire to preserve certain moral, legal, and theological concepts, no matter how useful they may be, dictate metaphysics. If it turns out that there is no free will, then it may well turn out that moral responsibility does not exist either. Whether or not this conclusion is troubling we cannot reject it simply based on its unpleasantness.

Secondly, it's unclear whether relinquishing moral responsibility *would* have the dire consequences some predict. Pereboom (2001, 2002), for example, has defended the view that morality, meaning, and value remain intact even if we are not morally responsible, and furthermore, that adopting this perspective could provide significant benefits for our lives. Pereboom, perhaps more than any other philosopher, has explored the implications of *living without free will* (see also Waller 1990; Honderich 2002b). He has expended a great deal of time and energy, more than I could offer here, exploring concerns over moral reform and education, crime prevention and detention, interpersonal relationships and how we treat others, and our reactive attitudes of indignation, guilt, gratitude, love and repentance. In very persuasive fashion, he argues that life without free will and responsibility would not be as destructive as many people believe. Prospects of finding meaning in life or of sustaining good interpersonal relationships, for example, would not be threatened (2001, ch.7). Although severe punishment (such as the death penalty) and retributivism would be ruled out, preventive detention and rehabilitation programs would be justified (2001, ch.6). He even argues that relinquishing our belief in free will might well improve our well-being and our relationships to others since it would tend to eradicate an often destructive form of "moral anger."[14]

Although I tend to agree with Pereboom's overall assessment of life without free will, I will not attempt to defend these claims here. Such concerns go beyond the scope of this work. As I've stated, I am primarily interested in the relationship between consciousness and free will and what recent developments in the behavioral, cognitive, and neurosciences can tell us about human agency. Given that all inquiries must be limited, I will therefore focus my attention on the two tasks outlined earlier: arguing for hard determinism and providing an illusionist account of our subjective feeling of freedom. These are lofty goals in themselves and more than enough to strive for in a single work.

NOTES

1. Traditional *scientific* determinism maintains that the state of the universe at any given time is wholly and unequivocally determined by the state of the universe at prior times and the laws of nature. Such determinism is sometimes illustrated by the thought experiment of *Laplace's demon*—an all-knowing intellect that given knowledge of all past and present facts, and the laws of nature, would be able to foresee the future down to the smallest detail. This idea was first given expression by the French mathematician and scientist Pierre Simon Laplace: "We may regard the present state of the universe as the effect of its past and the cause of its future. An intellect which at a certain moment would know all forces that set nature in motion, and all positions of all items of which nature is composed, if this intellect were also vast enough to submit

these data to analysis, it would embrace in a single formula the movements of the greatest bodies of the universe and those of the tiniest atom; for such an intellect nothing would be uncertain and the future just like the past would be present before its eyes" (1814, 4). Although this conception of determinism represents the traditional way of understanding the problem of free will and determinism, there have been other related and historically important threats. For example, divine foreknowledge has, for many, posed as much a threat to free will as natural laws. As Robert Kane writes: "Many theologians through the centuries have believed that God's power, omniscience, and providence would be unacceptably compromised if one did not affirm that all events in the universe, including human choices and actions, were foreordained and foreknown by God. But many other theologians argued, with equal force, that if God did in fact foreordain or foreknow all human choices and actions, then no one could have chosen or acted differently, making it hard to see how humans could have ultimate control over their actions in a manner that would justify divine rewards and punishments. In such cases, the ultimate responsibility for good and evil deeds, and hence responsibility for evil, would devolve to God—an unacceptable consequence for traditional theists" (2002a, 35). I will not discuss such theological threats to free will here, but for a comprehensive and illuminating guide to the contemporary literature on theological fatalism see Linda Zagzebski (2002). Instead I will focus on threats to free will from the most relevant human and natural sciences—i.e., versions of macro-level causal determinism (a variant of the natural law determinism outlined above) and psychological/neurological determinism.

    2.   Honderich's preferred term (see 1988, 2002a, 2002b).

    3.   Kane (2002a, 27-32) maintains that classical hard determinism consists of three theses: (1) free will (in the strong sense required for ultimate responsibility and desert) is not compatible with determinism; (2) there is no free will in this strong sense because (3) all events are universally determined by natural causes (i.e., universal determinism is true). My position, like other successor views, accepts (1) and (2) but remains noncommittal about (3). I leave it to the scientific community to work out the final interpretation of quantum mechanics. I maintain, however, that even if the current orthodox interpretation wins the day, there are still three good reasons to think (1) and (2) hold true: (a) from what we can tell thus far, human behavior appears as determined as the rest of the macrolevel universe (see below and ch.2); (b) even if indeterminism did sometimes have macrolevel effects on human behavior it would be of no help to believers in free will since such indeterminism would not enhance, but would only diminish, freedom and responsibility (see ch.2); lastly, and perhaps most importantly, (c) besides abstract worries and general concerns over macrolevel determinism, recent developments in the behavioral, cognitive, and neurosciences appear to threaten many of our core presuppositions about freedom and autonomy (see ch.4-7).

    4.   The phrase "subjective feeling of freedom" is here meant as a catchall for a number of different first-person experiences to be identified and discussed in subsequent chapters.

    5.   One recent exception is Daniel Wegner's much discussed account in *The Illusion of Conscious Will* (2002). See chapters 6 and 7 for details as well as ways in which my account differs from his. See also Galen Strawson (1986).

    6.   Rosenthal himself uses his theory to account for certain subjective aspects of our feeling of freedom (see 2002a, 2002b, 2003). Although he anticipates a good deal of what I wish to argue, there are some differences in focus, emphasis, and application of the HOT theory. There are also more substantive differences. One, which I can mention at the outset, is that Rosenthal appears to be a compatibilist and therefore cannot be viewed as denying the existence of free will. He claims, for example, "Acting freely consists not in our volitions being uncaused, but in those volitions fitting comfortably within a conscious picture we have of ourselves and of the kinds of things we characteristically want to do" (2002a, 219). I instead will use the HOT theory to argue for the

stronger thesis of hard(-enough) determinism. It's my contention that Rosenthal does not take the application of his own theory far enough.

7.   Robert Kane sets the problem up a little differently—though, I believe, in a fashion consistent with the set-up here. He claims the problem of free will arises when humans reach a certain higher stage of self-consciousness about how profoundly the world may influence their behavior in ways of which they were unaware (1996, 95-96; 2002a, 4).

8.   In the classical physics of Newton, Maxwell, and Einstein, the material universe develops over time in accordance with physical laws that are functional in form, so that the state of the universe at any given time is uniquely determined by the state of the universe at prior times and the laws of nature. Einstein, for example, writes: "Everything is determined, the beginning as well as the end, by forces over which we have no control. It is determined for the insect as well as the star. Human beings, vegetables, or cosmic dust, we all dance to a mysterious tune, intoned in the distance by an invisible piper" (1929, 117).

9.   To be clear, I do not assume that a materialist account of the mind or the claim that the brain functions according to the principles of classical physics are anywhere near established. I realize that one must defend both of these claims, and I will do so in chapter 2. In chapter 2, I will argue that one must accept a materialist/physicalist account of the mind if they wish to preserve mental causation. And I will argue that quantum mechanics, a challenge to classical physics and the first half of the conjunction, is irrelevant here since the wet-wear of the brain appears to rule out the possibility of indeterminacy existing at the required neuronal levels. (Furthermore, even if, per impossible, such indeterminacy were capable of reaching the macrolevel, it would still be unable to preserve the kind of responsibility-entailing freedom required of free will.)

10.   I am here using the term *determinant* rather widely, to cover anything in any category that can be appealed to in a causal explanation. A determinant is something that has a role in causing or determining an outcome.

11.   Although I do not question this assumption, some philosophers have. John Fisher and Mark Ravizza, for example, have argued for something they call *semi-compatibilism* (see Fischer 1994; Ravizza 1994; Fischer and Ravizza 1998). According to semi-compatibilism, moral responsibility is compatible with determinism (since it does not require the power to do otherwise), while freedom (which does require the power to do otherwise) is not compatible with determinism.

12.   For a discussion of such views, and an argument to the contrary, see Trakakis (2007).

13.   Kant declared 'freedom of the will' to be one of only three metaphysical problems which lie beyond the power of the human intellect—the other two intractable problems were God and immortality. The problem for Kant was that the Newtonian science of his day was completely deterministic and he naturally felt this was incompatible with freedom of action; yet he also believed that without freedom of action there could be no moral responsibility and no ethics. Hence, as Kane describes: "Kant held that we must believe in an undetermined free will because it is presupposed by our practical reasoning and our moral life. But Kant also believed that science and theoretical reason could not explain how an undetermined free will was possible. We had to believe it on faith" (2002d, 19).

14.   Other philosophers have made similar arguments. Waller, for example, has argued that "morality—morality of almost any variety one favors—can survive and flourish in the absence of moral responsibility" (2004, 428; see also 1990). Trakakis likewise argues that "all of our central moral notions, and not merely some of them, can be reconciled with the hard determinist outlook—though such reconciliation . . . will be possible only after the moral notions in question have, at least to some degree, been reconceived" (2007, 16).

TWO

Against Libertarianism

The debate over whether we possess free will is often a debate over intuitions, presuppositions, and starting points. Whether we hold as primary our intuition that at least some of our choices and actions are free, or whether we instead take as primary the widely held scientific supposition that the world is causally closed under the physical laws of nature, will often determine what we think about free will. Nowhere is this struggle over the primacy of our intuitions clearer than in the debate between determinists and libertarians. Libertarians, while holding to our commonsense belief in free will, also maintain the incompatibility of determinism and human freedom. Given these starting points, libertarians believe in the existence of a traditional antideterminist (or incompatibilist) free will. That is, libertarians maintain that given the same antecedent conditions at a particular time, t, and the same laws of nature at t, an agent remains undetermined and has the power to choose from branching paths that are metaphysically open—i.e., it is up to the agent what the world will look like after t. Put differently, keeping all the laws and antecedent conditions the same, the agent *could have done otherwise* than they in fact did do at time t; they were not causally necessitated to do just the thing they did.

Of course, defining libertarian freedom and accounting for libertarian freedom are two different things. Historically, libertarians have been faced with the daunting task of answering what Robert Kane calls the *Intelligibility Question* (2002a, 22; 1996, 13; 2002b, 414): Can one make sense of a freedom or free will that is incompatible with determinism? Is such an incompatibilist freedom coherent or intelligible, or is it, as many critics contend, essentially mysterious and terminally obscure? The challenge of the Intelligibility Question comes in trying to reconcile not determinism and free will but *indeterminism* and free will. If free will is not compatible with determinism, it does not seem to be compatible with indeterminism either. As Timothy O'Connor asks, "Why doesn't the assumption of indeterministic factors in the causation of behavior amount to the injection of mere randomness?" (2000, 23). Hence, the task of the libertarian is to give a plausible account of incompatibilist (and indeterminist) freedom that does not make the agent's actions and choices appear arbitrary, capricious, random, irrational, uncontrolled, or inexplicable. As Kane writes:

> It is one thing for libertarians to put forth arguments for incompatibilism or to point out flaws in compatibilist accounts of free agency (as they have often done); it is quite another to give a positive account of the libertarian free agency that will show how such a free will can be reconciled with indeterminism and how it is to be related to modern views of human behavior in the natural and human sciences. (2002a, 23)

Unfortunately for libertarians, giving an intelligible account of incompatibilist freedom has proven difficult. Traditionally, libertarian theories have fallen into two broad categories: *agent-causal theories* and *event indeterminist theories*. In this chapter, I will examine both and argue that neither succeeds in providing a plausible positive account of libertarian free will (although each fails for different reasons).

The first half of this chapter will focus on traditional *agent-causal* accounts of free will. In discussing agent-causation (hereafter abbreviated as AC) it will be important to spell out the metaphysical commitments of the position—some of which are rather radical.[1] As we will see in section 2.1, AC requires not only a rejection of determinism but an appeal to sui generis kinds of agency and/or causation. Although different AC theorists describe the commitments of the theory differently, they all acknowledge causal powers and/or entities that are not causally closed under the physical laws of nature. By positing an agent who is exempt from physical laws and irreducible to the more basic physical constituents of the body, AC sacrifices certain widely held metaphysical and scientific assumptions. In particular, AC relinquishes the principles of physical causal closer and atomistic physicalism (see sec. 2.1). Peter Unger, for example, has argued that libertarian freedom requires giving up the principle that: "Wholly composed of such mindless physical parts as electrons, you are a being whose powers are all physical powers, physically deriving from the powers of your parts and their physical arrangements" (2002, 1). I will show that on both weak and strong versions of the theory, "agent causation requires an ontology on which persons are enduring, ineliminable substances that are in *some* robust sense more than the sum of the constituents of their bodies" (O'Connor 2002, 341).

Although many libertarians are convinced that AC is the only way to explain how acts that are undetermined can be free, I will argue that AC is an implausible and incoherent theory. Not only would the reality of AC be inconsistent with a scientific and naturalistic worldview, but, I maintain, the concept of agent-causation is itself incoherent. Although the latter criticism is far more devastating if true, the former is not insignificant. In fact, it's easy to view the metaphysical commitments of AC as sufficient reason for rejecting the theory. I strongly disagree with the AC theorist's willingness to sacrifice certain intuitions rather than others. As they sometimes say, one person's *modus ponens* is another's *modus tollens*! The agent-causal theorist reasons that since our belief in free will is primitive and non-negotiable, and since physical causal closure and physicalism prevent there being any free will, we should give up physical causal closure and physicalism.[2] The hard-determinist, on the other hand, starts from the assumption of physical causal closure and a physicalist account of the mind and argues that we should give up our belief in free will. I will argue that these moves are not equally justified. I maintain that not only do we have a *prima fascia* reason to preserve physical causal closure and physicalism, but in giving up these commitments AC accounts of human behavior become incoherent.

A number of critics have questioned the coherence of AC, but I will focus, for the most part, on AC's inability to account for mental causation. By introducing the issue of mental causation into the equation the number of intuitions being juggled is increased. On the flip side, the number of acceptable options decreases. Agent-causation, which requires either substance dualism or radical emergentism, becomes unacceptable and implausible once we realize that not only does it require us to give up important metaphysical and scientific assumptions, but it also fails to account for mental causation—a necessary condition for free will. I will argue that AC theories are ultimately caught in a dilemma: To make sense of free will, they need to preserve mental causation; yet, to preserve mental causation, they must relinquish the ontology of AC and accept *some form* of mind-brain physicalism. This is an untenable position for a libertarian. If they want to make sense of the basic conception of agent-causation, they must posit "a *sui generis* form of causation by an agent that is irreducible (ontologically as well as conceptually) to event-causal processes within the agent" (O'Connor 1995a, 7). On the other hand, to make sense of mental causation (a necessary condition for free will), libertarians must relinquish the anti-naturalist metaphysics that make agent-causation possible. Either way AC cannot give us a plausible and consistent account of libertarian freedom. Not only are the metaphysical commitments of AC inconsistent with our scientific worldview, the theory itself is incoherent. It makes mental causation, and by extension free will, impossible.

Event indeterminist theories, on the other hand, take a different approach. These theories attempt to make undetermined free actions intelligible "without postulating *sui generis* kinds of agency or causation that cannot be spelled out in terms of events or states of affairs involving the agent" (Kane 2002a, 23). That is, instead of appealing to a scientifically intractable agent and a unique form of causation, these accounts stick to the basic metaphysics of event causation. Event indeterminist theories have their own set of problems, however. In examining such theories, it's important to distinguish two varieties: (1) *simple indeterminist* theories, and (2) *causal indeterminist* (or *event-causal*) theories. As Timothy O'Connor describes the difference, *simple indeterminist* theories maintain that "free agency doesn't require there to be any sort of causal connection (even of an indeterministic variety) between the agent and his free actions"; while *causal indeterminist* (or *event-causal*) theories maintain that agents cause their "free actions via [their] reasons for doing so, but indeterministically" (1995a, 7). In the following, I will examine both *simple* and *event-causal* indeterminist theories, paying special attention to Robert Kane's (1996, 1999, 2002b) promising and much discussed version of the latter. Although I maintain Kane's account is superior to simple indeterminism, in the end I argue that all event indeterminist theories fail to answer the Intelligibility Question—that is, they fail to reconcile free will with indeterminism. On all such accounts, the agent's actions and choices, I maintain, become arbitrary, capricious, random, irrational, uncontrolled, and inexplicable.

In section 2.1, I lay out and discuss the metaphysical commitments of AC. In section 2.2, I introduce the problem of mental causation and explain why AC theories are unable to preserve a causal role for the mind. I also discuss recent attempts at preserving libertarian freedom via quantum theoretical accounts of the mind and argue that these too fail. In section 2.3, I conclude with a detailed examination of Robert Kane's event-causal (or *teleological intelligibility*) theory.

2.1 AGENT-CAUSAL ACCOUNTS OF FREE WILL

Agent-causal libertarians maintain that AC is a simple reflection of our commonsense understanding of human agency. An *agent* is someone with the capacity to perform *actions*. In this sense, whenever we perform meaningful, purposive actions we are agents. We do things like turn the stereo on, make coffee, write an email, and tell a joke. These are actions that we perform and they're unlike *mere happenings*. Mere happenings are events that involve us—like growing hair and fingernails, sweating on a hot day, and sneezing—but differ from actions in that they are not *voluntary* or *intentional*. No one in the free will debate denies this kind of agency—they instead differ on the kinds of accounts they give of it and over whether such agency is free or causally determined. The hard-determinist maintains that the actions agents perform are causally determined by antecedent conditions, which themselves are outside the control of the agent.[3] Compatibilists, while acknowledging that agents are determined, nonetheless believe that they possess enough "control" to ground free will and moral responsibility. Libertarians, on the other hand, maintain that agents are sometimes self-determining beings, causally undetermined by antecedent conditions. Although there are different ways to spell out the libertarian account of agency, I will start by focusing on traditional agent-causal accounts. The most prominent AC theorists have included the eighteenth-century Scottish philosopher Thomas Reid (1788, 1895), and such contemporary philosophers as C.A. Campbell (1957, 1967), Roderick Chisholm (1964a, 1966, 1976a, 1976b, 1995), Richard Taylor (1966, 1992), Randolph Clarke (1993, 1996, 2002, 2003), and Timothy O'Connor (1995b, 1996, 2000, 2002).

Common to all AC accounts is the belief that an intelligible notion of an agent's causing an event can be given according to which the kind of causation involved is fundamentally distinct from the kind that obtains between events. The traditional notion of event causation assumes that all caused events are causally necessitated by prior events (or that all events that are caused are caused or necessitated by prior events). For an event (or set of events), a, to be the cause of another event, b, means that a causally necessitates b; or that a is causally sufficient for b happening. This means that a cannot happen without b necessarily following. The agent-causal theorist shuns the notion of causal necessity because they believe it's incompatible with human freedom. So instead of appealing to event causation, the AC theorist introduces a new type of causation, *agent-causation*, to account for human agency and freedom.

According to this notion of agent-causation, it's the *agent* himself that causes, or initiates, free actions. And the *agent*, which is the cause of his/her own free actions, is a *self-determining being*, causally undetermined by antecedent events. Agent-causal theorists differ over whether they believe we should view all intentional actions as agent-causal in nature or just some intentional actions. But at a minimum, AC is viewed as a necessary condition for an action's being free.[4] The following quote by Richard Taylor does a good job summing up the basic position:

> The only conception of action that accords with our data is one according to which people . . . are sometimes, but of course not always, self-determining beings; that is, beings which are sometimes the causes of their own behavior. In the case of an action that is free, it must be such that it is caused by the agent who performs it, but such that no antecedent conditions were sufficient for his performing just that action. In the case of an action that is both free and rational, it must be such that the agent who performed it did so for some reason, but this reason cannot have been the cause of it. (1992, 51)

Roderick Chisholm, another leading defender of AC, further elaborates this notion of self-determination when he writes: "If we are responsible, and if what I have been trying to say [about agent causation] is true, then we have a prerogative which some would attribute only to God: each of us, when we act, is a prime unmoved mover. In doing what we do, we cause certain events to happen and nothing—or no one—causes us to cause those events to happen" (1964a, 32). Timothy O'Connor prefers the expression "not wholly moved movers" (2000, 67) but the point is similar: according to AC, the agent must be the cause of his action but himself not causally necessitated to perform just that action—i.e., the agent must be a kind of uncaused cause creating *ex nihilo*. This is what separates AC accounts from other accounts of human agency.

Given that agent-causal libertarians are incompatibilists, they define human freedom in terms of the agent's ability to act counter-causally—which they view as inconsistent with determinism. The libertarian notion of freedom states that an action is free *if and only if* the agent has the ability to behave in a purposive, non-random fashion that is not determined by neurophysiological structure, physical laws, or any other factors (meaning, of course, causally sufficient determining factors). This definition contains both a positive and a negative constraint. The negative constraint stipulates that the agent must not be wholly determined by conditions that they themselves do not control. Thomas Reid puts the negative point as follows:

> If, in any action, he had power to will what he did, or not to will it, in that action he is free. But if, in every voluntary action, the determination of his will be the necessary consequence of something involuntary in the state of his mind, or of something in his external circumstances, he is not free; he has not what I call the liberty of a moral agent, but is subject to necessity. (1895, 2:599)[5]

So negatively stated, the agent has to be free from determination by his neurophysiology or any other internal or external (i.e., "involuntary") circumstances. But as Reid and other AC theorists are quick to point out, it's not enough to simply introduce some indeterminism into the system. In addition to the claim that the agent must be undetermined, the AC theorist must also accord to the agent some positive power. To avoid randomness and to preserve purposive behavior, AC theorists typically maintain that you need to introduce an *agent causal power*; a causal power possessed by the agent to either directly cause their own actions or to initiate a causal sequence that results in an action. Turning again to Reid, the positive notion of *agent as cause* is captured in the following sentiment: "I consider the determination of the will as an effect. This effect must have a cause which had power to produce it. . . . If the person was the cause of that determination of his will, he was free in that action, and it is justly imputed to him, whether it be good or bad" (1895, 2:602). Elsewhere he puts the point as follows: "I grant, then, that an effect uncaused is a contradiction, and that an event uncaused is an absurdity. The question that remains is whether a volition, undetermined by motives, is an event uncaused. This I deny. The cause of the volition is the man that willed it" (1895, 1:88). This directly introduces the notion of *agent as cause*. It also reiterates the point made earlier that the agent must be viewed as a *prime unmoved mover*, or as a not wholly moved mover.

The reason why the agent, or self, *has to be* a prime unmoved mover is that this is the only way to avoid both horns of a dilemma commonly touted by both libertarians and determinists. Many libertarians who give AC accounts of free will accept the premises of the following dilemma: If determinism is true, human choices and actions are not free since they are determined by antecedent causes; but if simple indeterminacy is true, human actions are also not free since they would then be random and chaotic. As Taylor writes:

> Only the slightest consideration will show . . . that [the] simple denial of determinism has not the slightest plausibility [of preserving free will]. For let us suppose it is true, and that some of my bodily motions—namely, those that I regard as my free acts—are not caused at all or, if caused by my own inner states, that these are not caused. We shall thereby avoid picturing a puppet, to be sure—but only by substituting something even less like a human being; for the conception that now emerges is not that of a free person, but of an erratic and jerking phantom, without any rhyme or reason at all. . . . There will never be any point in asking why these motions occur, or in seeking any explanation of them, for under the conditions assumed there is no explanation, they just happen, from no causes at all. (1992, 48)

He goes on to argue:

> It is . . . obvious that our data cannot be reconciled to the theory of simple indeterminism. I can deliberate only about my own actions; this is obvious. But the random, uncaused motion of any body whatever, whether it be a part of my body or not, is no action of mine and nothing that is within my power. I might try to guess what these motions will be, just as I might try to guess how a roulette wheel will behave, but I cannot deliberate about them or try to decide what they shall be, simply because these things are not up to me. Whatever is not caused by anything is not caused by me, and nothing could be more plainly inconsistent with saying that it is nevertheless up to me what it shall be. (1992, 50-51)

Agent causation, therefore, is presented as a way to split the horns of this dilemma. As Taylor puts it, "The theory of agency avoids the absurdities of simple indeterminism by conceding that human behavior is caused, while at the same time avoiding the difficulties of determinism by denying that every chain of causes and effects is infinite" (1992, 52). The causal chains leading to actions, on this view, have beginnings, and they begin with the agents themselves. Later I will examine one leading *event-causalist* account of libertarian freedom—an account that avoids acknowledging agents as causes independent and separate from event causation—to see if it can somehow avoid this dilemma. For the moment, though, it's important to acknowledge that most AC theorists introduce their position as an alternative to simple indeterminism, and therefore willingly embrace the unique commitments of agent-causation.[6]

Although AC theorists differ on a number of key points, the vast majority accept the following four principles:

1. It's the *agent* himself that causes, or initiates, free actions.
2. The notion of causation involved is fundamentally different from event causation.
3. The *agent*, who is the cause of his/her own free actions, is a self-determining being, causally undetermined by antecedent events. And,
4. The *agent* is ontologically irreducible to purely physical parts, constituents, and events.

Libertarians believe this last commitment is necessary to make sense of (1) thru (3). The AC theorist could not, for example, accept any account of agency that reduces the causal mechanisms involved down to "brute" physical events. The AC notion of the *self as agent* requires an ontologically robust notion of the "self." Different agent causal theories describe the ontological status of the "self" differently, but all dismiss the determinist's hypothesis of a complete causal explanation based on a correlation of mental events with brain events. The reason why they *must* do so is that if all mental events are identical to brain events, or even if all mental events are fully determined by brain events, there would be no place for free will to enter the causal picture since brain events are presumably physical events that are causally determined by antecedent conditions. Plus, *even if* such brain events were *not* fully determined, the AC theorist (as we've just seen) denies that simple indeterminism of events would be strong enough to support freedom. Given their *own* commitments then, AC theorists are forced to widen their ontology beyond that of physical events.

Some AC accounts view the *self* as a nonmaterial/nonphysical substance (Foster 1991; Eccles 1994; Swinburne 1986); other accounts view the self as a radically emergent entity (O'Connor 2000; Hasker 1999; Sternberg 2010); others still view the self simply as an unexplained mystery (Taylor 1966, 1992). Whether an emergent systems feature, Cartesian soul, or mystery, the self is here regarded as primitive and basic. In recent years, for example, John Eccles, John Foster, and Richard Swinburne have all argued for neo-Cartesian forms of dualism. Modern readers might find such appeals to dualism outdated but if one were attempting to free the agent from determination by physical (including neurophysiological) factors, one could do no better than to free the agent from the physical realm altogether. Embracing substance dualism allows the AC theorist a way to satisfy the negative requirement outlined above. Since these agent-causal powers are presumably possessed by a non-physical, mental substance, they would be free from determination by physical laws. *Of course there still remains the possibility of another set of laws, non-physical laws, that govern the mental realm such that the agent would be causally determined by these,* but dualists, when they take the trouble to address this possibility, usually simply stipulate that there are no such laws! Although I think this problem is more serious than the dualist usually acknowledges, for the sake of argument let's grant them that the mental realm is not causally determined. Given this proviso, freeing the agent from the physical realm is one way to make sense of the claim that the agent is not determined by neurophysiological structure, physical laws, or any other determining factors. Since the most likely determining factors are physical ones, dualism holds out a *possible* theoretical and ontological foundation for the commitments of AC.

Those AC theorists who find traditional dualism implausible, on the other hand, typically appeal to the notion of *emergence*—the idea that the mind emerges from the functioning of the brain and nervous system. The notion of emergence, however, has been employed with a variety of different meanings, and it is therefore necessary to clarify exactly which *type* of emergence is required for AC. Robert Van Gulick (2001) has recently discerned ten varieties of the concept of emergence. Some of these varieties are benign and need not cause ontological concern to most physicalists, while others are highly controversial and run counter to certain centrally held physicalist principles. For the sake of brevity, I will only differentiate three types of emergence—hopefully this will be sufficient to bring out the needed contrast. First, there is the ever-popular *epistemic conception of emergence.* According to epistemic emergence: *P* emerges from properties or constituent components *a, b, c, . . .,* if you cannot predict the presence of *P* from the presence of *a, b, c, ...* Note, however, that this is much too weak for AC, since *P* could be determined by, or even identical to, *a, b, c, . . .,* even though nobody did or could recognize this. A second type of emergence, which we can call *modest kind (or system features) emergence,* maintains that a system's feature *P* is emergent in the sense that the system exhibits different features than its constituent components *a, b, c, . . .,* or their joint presence. The basic idea is that the whole has properties or features that are *different in kind* from those of its parts. For example, a piece of cloth might be purple in hue even though none of the molecules that make up its surface could be said to be purple. Or water might have the properties of transparency and liquidity even though none of the constitutive molecules do. As John Searle describes this form of emergence (which he labels *emergent1*):

> Suppose we have a system, *S,* made up of elements *a, b, c. . .* For example, *S* might be a stone and the elements might be molecules. In

general, there will be features of *S* that are not, or not necessarily, features of *a, b, c. . . .* For example, *S* might weigh ten pounds, but the molecules individually do not weigh ten pounds. Let us call such features "system features." (1992, 111)

The problem with this kind of emergence is that it is again too weak to support AC. Although the whole exhibits features that are different in kind from those of its parts, *modest* emergent system features may nonetheless be determined by the features of their parts, their mode of combination, and the law-like regularities governing the features of their parts. Hence, if *P* is inevitably present when *a, b, c,* . . . are, perhaps by metaphysical necessity, we still do not get the indeterminacy AC requires.

Most AC theorists therefore embrace a kind of *radical emergence.* Although there are different ways to state even this thesis, we can say, in general terms, that something is *radically emergent* if and only if the whole has features that are both: (1) different in kind from those of its parts, and (2) of a kind whose nature and existence is not necessitated by the features of its parts, their mode of combination, and the law-like regularities governing the features of its parts (Van Gulick 2001). Whether or not there are any cases of radical emergence is controversial and highly questionable. John Searle, after distinguishing between what he calls *emergent1* (e.g., modest emergence) and *emergent2* (e.g., radical emergence) writes:

A feature *F* is emergent2 iff *F* is emergent1, and *F* has causal powers that cannot be explained by the causal interactions of *a, b, c* . . .If consciousness were emergent2, then consciousness could cause things that could not be explained by the causal behavior of the neurons. The naive idea here is that consciousness gets squirted out by the behavior of the neurons in the brain, but once it has been squirted out, it then has a life of its own. It should be obvious . . . that on my view consciousness is emergent1 but not emergent2. In fact, I cannot think of anything that is emergent2, and it seems unlikely that we will be able to find any features that are emergent2, because the existence of any such features would seem to violate even the weakest principle of the transitivity of causation. (1992, 112)

Accepting radical-kind emergence would be, as Van Gulick points out, "conceding that there are real features of the world that exist at the system or composite level that are not determined by the law-like regularities that govern the interactions of the parts of such systems and their features" (2001, 18). Doing so would require abandoning the atomistic conception, which is typically embraced by mainstream physicalism. That is, radical emergence would require giving up at least one of the following core principles of atomistic physicalism (Van Gulick 2001):

AP1. The features of macro items are determined by the features of their micro parts plus their mode of combination. (In a slogan: Micro features determine macro features.)

AP2. The only law-like regularities needed for the determination of macro features by micro features are those that govern the interaction of those micro features in all the contexts, systemic or otherwise.

By challenging atomistic physicalism, radical emergentism, like dualism, challenges one of our most centrally held scientific and metaphysical assumptions. As Van Gulick writes:

The notion that causal powers might exhibit radical-kind emergence merits special attention since it poses perhaps the greatest threat to physicalism. If wholes or systems could have causal powers that were radically emergent from the powers of their parts in the sense that those system-level powers were not determined by the laws governing the powers of their parts, then that would seem to imply the existence of powers that could override or violate the laws governing the powers of the parts; i.e., genuine cases of what is called 'downward causation' (Sperry, 1983; 1991; Kim, 1992; 1999; Hasker, 1999) in which the macro powers of the whole 'reach down' and alter the course of events at the micro level from what they would be if determined entirely by the properties and laws at that lower level. (2001, 19)

The notion of radical emergence (and by extension the concept of *down-ward causation*) is troubling precisely because it challenges our belief in *physical causal closure*.[7] It is in this respect that radical emergent causal powers would "pose such a direct challenge to physicalism, since they would threaten the view of the physical world as a closed causal system; i.e., the idea that nothing outside the physical causally affects the course of the physical events (Kim, 1990; 1999)" (Van Gulick 2001: 19). Not surprisingly, though, the features that make radical emergence so threatening to physicalism are the very ones that make it attractive to AC emergentists like William Hasker (1999) who invoke emergence in support of ontological dualism. As Hasker writes:

The most plausible example we have seen of an emergent2 [i.e., radically emergent] property is libertarian free will, and it seems clear that this cannot be a property that consists of properties of, and relations between, the parts that make up a system of objects. If we are to include libertarian free will as an attribute of persons, it seems we shall need to recognize persons, or minds, or souls, as unitary subjects, not analyzable as complexes of parts . . . this means we shall have to acknowledge the existence of minds as *emergent individuals*. (1999, 178)

Hasker's position, which he calls *emergent dualism*, maintains that the radical emergence required for libertarian free will is an emergence not of properties but of a new *substance*. According to Hasker, "[I]t is not enough to say that there are emergent properties here; what is needed is an *emergent individual*, a new individual entity which comes into existence as a result of a certain functional configuration of the material constituents of the brain and nervous system" (1999, 190). In other words, when a substance S has a certain functional configuration—for instance, when a nervous system reaches a sufficient degree of complexity—then a new substance S' comes into existence, which is capable of initiating events. This new substance would be "endowed, as we take it be, with libertarian freedom," and able to "cause things that could not be explained by the causal behavior of the neurons" (1999, 190).

Whether or not dualism or radical emergentism make sense as metaphysical theories, and whether or not they can preserve libertarian free will, are questions I will explore in the following section. For the moment, it is important to acknowledge the truly radical nature of these commitments. In fact, some libertarians find it hard to put forth their theory with "complete comfort...and not wholly without embarrassment" (Taylor 1992, 53). Taylor, when laying out his account of AC, admits that it involves some "rather strange metaphysical notions that are never applied elsewhere in nature." As Taylor, himself, puts it:

> Now this conception of activity, and of an agent who is the cause of it, involves *two rather strange metaphysical notions that are never applied elsewhere in nature*. The first is that of a *self* or *person*—for example, a man—who is not merely a collection of things or events, but a self-moving being. For on this view it is a person, and not merely some part of him or something within him, that is the cause of his own activity. Now, we certainly do not know that a human being is anything more than an assemblage of physical things and processes that act in accordance with those laws that describe the behavior of all other physical things and processes. Even though he is living being, of enormous complexity, *there is nothing, apart from the requirements of this theory*, to suggest that his behavior is so radically different in its origin from that of other physical objects, or that an understanding of it must be sought in some metaphysical realm wholly different from that appropriate to the understanding of nonliving things. (1992, 52; italics added)

The second "strange metaphysical notion" referred to by Taylor is the rejection of our ordinary understanding of event causation discussed above:

> Second, this conception of activity involves an extraordinary conception of causation according to which an agent, *which is a substance and not an event*, can nevertheless be the cause of an event. Indeed, if he is a free agent then he can, on this conception, cause an event to occur—namely, some act of his own—without anything causing him to do so. This means that an agent is sometimes a cause, without being an antecedent sufficient condition. (1992, 52; italics added)

Taylor admits, however, that this conception of the causation of events by things that are not events is, in fact, so different from the usual philosophical conception of a cause that "it should not even bear the same name, for 'being a cause' ordinarily just means 'being an antecedent sufficient condition or set of conditions.'" Instead, then, of speaking of agents as *causing* their own acts, Taylor suggests "it would perhaps be better to use another word entirely, and say, for instance, that they *originate* them, *initiate* them, or simply that they *perform* them" (1992, 52). At this point one could hardly be blamed, I think, for viewing these commitments as a *reductio* of AC. Libertarians, nonetheless, believe that while the theory requires us to accept a worldview at odds with physicalism and our ordinary conception of causation, our strong (and, for the libertarian, *more primitive*) belief in free will requires that we do so. For libertarians, the existence of free will is a phenomenological given (see ch.5). Hence, the data of experience should be preserved at all costs. If we want to preserve our intuitive and pretheoretical sense of free will, argues the libertarian, then we need to accept the requirements of AC—however "strange" they may be.

The AC theorist, and libertarians in general, take human agents to enjoy a kind of freedom not compatible with a purely mechanistic account of human psychology. Thus they hold that, at least in normal circumstances, the agent has a genuine power of choice whose operation is not constrained by prior physical or psychological conditions and which enables him to exercise *ultimate control* over his/her actions. This ultimate control, this power to choose from branching paths that are metaphysically open, is what underlies ascriptions of moral responsibility to agents. According to this notion of ultimate control, or what we might simply call *absolute agency*, it's the agent that causes or initiates their own actions, and no antecedent conditions were sufficient for them performing just that action. In endorsing AC, these theorists maintain that they are simply endorsing the commonsense view that agents are self-determining beings who ultimately control their own actions, who are capable of deciding what to do between alternative courses of action, and that because of this they are morally responsible for those actions.

According to libertarians, we hold agents morally responsible because we believe they are the ultimate arbiters of what they do. We believe that *because* they could have refrained from acting, or could have acted in a different way, agents are free and morally responsible for the actions they perform. As Taylor writes:

> [T]his conception fits what people take themselves to be; namely, beings who act, or who are agents, rather than beings that are merely acted upon, and whose behavior is simply the causal consequence of conditions that they have not wrought. When I believe that I have done something, I do believe that it was I who caused it to be done, I who made something happen, and not merely something within me, such as

one of my own subjective states, which is not identical with myself. If I believe that something not identical with myself was the cause of my behavior—some event wholly external to myself, for instance, or even one internal to myself, such as a nerve impulse, volition, or whatnot—then I cannot regard that behavior as being an act of mine. (1992, 51)

If the belief in libertarian agent-causation has the backing of common-sense at all, I believe it gets it from the way we experience our own actions. Our strong *feeling of freedom* is an essential element in our ordinary experience of decision-making—that is, in our deliberations, choices, and actions, we typically experience a conscious feeling of freedom. As Simon Blackburn points out, "Consciousness of freedom seems closely allied to any kind of consciousness at all" (1999, 82).

To this extent, the phenomenology of agentive experience does strongly support a libertarian agent-causal conception of freedom. For whenever we are conscious of having to make a decision, it seems that we cannot help but think of the outcome as resting with us rather than as already fixed by prior conditions. Of course, as John Foster remarks:

This does not mean that we never feel under any pressure to choose in one way rather than another, much less that we are wholly indifferent to the promptings of our own desires. But it does mean that we feel the final decision to be in our own hands; that whatever the external pressures or internal promptings, we feel it is ultimately up to us whether we yield to them or not. (1991, 267)

This feeling of ultimate control and self-determination is an important part of our phenomenology. And as Foster further elaborates, even if reason and our better judgment tell us that we shouldn't act in a particular way, we still *feel* as though we have the power the do so:

This is so even when the case in favour of a particular decision is overwhelming. Thus, taking account of both my self-interest and my moral duty, I now recognize an overwhelming case against jumping out of the (second-floor) window. None the less, I feel that I have the power to do it; and not just the power to do it *if I choose*, but the power, irrationally and gratuitously, *to choose in that way*. (1991, 267)

This brings out another requirement of AC. The agent may be influenced by reasons, character traits, moral principles and the like, but they *cannot* be wholly determined by them. This must be so, according to the AC theorist, because the agent must be undetermined, and potential determinants include both physical and psychological factors. Libertarians argue that this requirement is further supported by our phenomenology, since we typically feel as if we're free to act irrationally and against our better judgment *at will*.

Of course the fact that decisions *feel* free in no way *proves* that they *are* free. As I will argue in subsequent chapters, phenomenology is not always a reliable guide to reality. In fact, the main aim of this work is to argue that this feeling of freedom is illusory. It may well be true that we cannot live our lives without feeling free, that our subjective feeling of freedom is an essential element of our conscious decision-making process. It may also be true that from a practical, first-person perspective we have to live our lives often assuming the libertarian perspective. It does not follow from this, however, that from a more objective, third-person perspective we cannot come to see that this feeling of freedom is an illusion, a chimera of our consciousness. Of course the burden falls on me to show that such libertarian freedom does not exist. The remainder of this chapter will be an attempt to move one step closer to establishing that conclusion. If I can show that the kind of agency entailed by AC is incoherent and implausible, I will have cut down one major reason for believing such freedom exists. If I can further explain (as I hope to in later chapters) the phenomenology surrounding agentive experience in a way that does justice to the phenomenological datum while at the same time explaining *why* it's illusory, I will have erased whatever temptation remains for accepting the metaphysical commitments of AC. As Taylor, himself, writes:

> One could hardly affirm such a theory of agency with complete comfort, however, and not wholly without embarrassment, for the conception of agents and their powers which is involved in it is strange indeed, if not positively mysterious. In fact, one can hardly be blamed here for simply denying our data outright, rather than embracing this theory to which they do most certainly point. Our data . . . rest upon nothing more than fairly common consent. These data might simply be illusions. (1992, 53)

Taylor's honesty here is refreshing! I would go further, however, and propose that: *if* a plausible illusionist account of the phenomenological data can be given, *and* AC turns out to be incoherent and implausible, we *should indeed* conclude that the data (and with it the existence of free will) is an illusion.

2.2 THE PROBLEM OF MENTAL CAUSATION

Normal intuitions tell us that certain mental events cause, and are caused by, certain physical events. I desire a beer and believe there's one in the refrigerator so off the couch and into the kitchen I go. The combination of my desire for a beer and my belief that there's one in the refrigerator, which are mental events, seem to cause my ensuing movements, which are physical events. The notion of mental causation typified in these examples is basic to our understanding of human behavior. We all believe that our beliefs, desires, choices, and deliberations causally affect our behavior. The existence of psychophysical causal relations is seldom seriously questioned. In fact, some have argued that to deny such relations would be tantamount to saying that not one intentional action has ever been performed (e.g., Malcolm 1968). The causal efficacy of the mental is not something we are readily willing to give up. Jerry Fodor powerfully writes, "[I]f it isn't literally true that my wanting is causally responsible for my reaching, and my itching is causally responsible for my scratching, and my believing is causally responsible for my saying, . . . if none of that is literally true, then practically everything I believe about anything is false and it's the end of the world" (1990, 156). There are serious questions concerning human agency and cognition that rely on the fact that mental causation is real, and not just illusory. Both libertarians and determinists alike typically agree on this. Libertarians, however, *must* preserve our intuitive sense of mental causation if they want to preserve free will—for without mental causation there would be no way to account for *agency* and all events would become mere happenings.

Libertarians, I maintain, need to preserve the distinction between *voluntary* and *involuntary* behavior. Crudely defined, a voluntary action is one that has as its immediate cause some internal psychological state—or mental state—like a belief, desire, or decision. An involuntary act, on the other hand, is one that has as its immediate cause either an external event (or state of affairs) or an internal *non-mental* state of the body. Put differently, voluntary actions are caused by intentional states with intentional content whereas involuntary behavior is not. So as not to beg the question, I'll leave out any appeal to the notion of *control* in defining this distinction and instead rely simply on immediate causal origin. That said, preserving the voluntary/involuntary distinction along with mental causation is imperative if the libertarian wants to preserve most of what our folk-psychological and scientific theories of human behavior tell us. For if there were no mental causation there would be no voluntary action, hence there would be no *agency* at all since there would be no distinction between *actions* and *mere happenings*. This is wholly unacceptable. Independent of worries over human freedom one should still want to preserve the existence of mental causation. Both our folk-psychological and scientific theories presuppose the existence of mental causation in describing and accounting for human behavior. If it turned out that there were no genuine cases of psychophysical causal interaction, almost everything we believe about human beings would turn out to be false.

It would appear, then, that libertarians should be committed to preserving mental causation because without it the notion of agency—and the distinction between actions and mere happenings—is lost. Giving an account of how psychophysical causation is possible, however, has proven to be a difficult task. Jaegwon Kim writes that, "not only has this problem played a pivotal role in shaping doctrines concerning the mind-body problem, but also it has often been the rock on which many mind-body theories have foundered" (1979, 31). I would dare to add that the problem of mental causation is also the rock on which many theories of free will founder. Libertarians often think that simply giving a plausible account of how free will is possible—one that simply establishes internal coherence—regardless of whether it's empirically or theoretically warranted, is enough. Although I believe there are serious problems regarding the internal coherence of AC, *even if* internal coherence were established, giving a plausible account of free will that makes mental causation impossible or intractable would be equivalent to throwing the baby out with the bathwater.[8] If AC theorists want to account for free will they have to address the problem of mental causation straight on.

The difficulty AC theorists face is that in embracing substance dualism or radical emergentism they essentially make it impossible to account for mental causation. The main challenge to mental causation is one that arises from the principle, embraced by most physicalists, that the physical domain is *causally closed*. The principle of physical causal closure states that the causes and effects of all physical events are themselves physical. As Kim defines the principle:

> Pick any physical event, say, the decay of a uranium atom or the collision of two stars in distant space, and trace its causal ancestry or posterity as far as you would like; the principle of causal closure of the physical domain says that this will never take you outside the physical domain. Thus, no causal chain involving a physical event will ever cross the boundary of the physical into the nonphysical. (1996, 147)

One could then state the principle of causal closure as follows: If x is a physical event and y is a cause or effect of x, then y, too, must be a physical event. Another way to state the principle is to say that if a physical event has a cause at time t, it has a physical cause at t. It follows then from physical causal closure that we would never need to go outside the physical domain to explain the occurrence of a physical event. This principle of physical causal closure is commonly assumed in scientific theorizing; in fact, one could argue that it's indispensable to scientific reasoning. If accepted, however, one could present a devastating argument against all AC accounts of human agency.

The kind of argument I have in mind was initially developed by Kim (1989, 1993b, 1998, 2005) and recently taken up by David Papineau (2002). It stems from what Kim calls the "causal exclusion problem." Kim directs his argument against the nonreductive-physicalist position that mental events and properties are distinct from, yet either "supervenient on," wholly "realized by," or "emergent from" physical events and properties. He argues that all such non-reductive views fail to coherently account for the causal efficacy of the mental, assuming two rather plausible principles: that there are no causal factors beyond the physical (i.e., physical causal closure), and that mental causes do not systematically overdetermine events caused by physical factors. Kim's argument, if successful, forces one to embrace either an outright identity between mental events and physical events, or to move toward a more robust sort of dualism. Embracing dualism, however, would entail giving up on physical causal closure. And, as I'll argue now, this additionally leaves one unable to account for the causal efficacy of the mental. Either way then, if what I wish to argue is correct, the ontology embraced by agent-causation leaves mental causation unaccounted for.

The fundamental problem facing both substance dualism and radical emergentism is the following. If the mental is fundamentally distinct from the physical, either because it's a unique substance or because it has radically emergent causal powers not determined by lower-order physical properties and relations, then the mental could not affect the course of physical events without violating the causal closure of the physical (Kim 1990, 1999). Thus, the AC theorist seems forced to choose between two unsatisfactory alternatives: (a) give up the causal closure of the physical, or (b) regard the mental as epiphenomenal (at least qua the physical domain). I will argue that neither alternative is promising since neither alternative is capable of accounting for mental causation. And this failure, I maintain, provides a fatal blow to the position.

Papineau's argument, like Kim's, is also based on the need to preserve mental causation. He calls his argument the "causal argument," and putting aside all complications for the moment, it can be stated as follows: "Many effects that we attribute to conscious causes have fully physical causes. But it would be absurd to suppose that these effects are caused twice over. So the conscious causes must be identical to some part of those physical causes" (2002, 17). This argument, like Kim's, assumes physical causal closure and the denial of systematic overdetermination. To appreciate the full force of this argument, imagine a case of mental-to-physical causation, a case where we would normally attribute a bodily movement to some conscious mental cause. Take, for example, my walking to the corner because I want to get a cup of coffee at the deli. In cases like this it's assumed that my want, or a combination of my want and a belief that I can get coffee at the deli, is the cause of my physical behavior, the movements entailed in my walking to the corner. If we add to this picture, however, the plausible assumption that the cause of this physical behavior can be described in purely physical terms, we end up with a problem. Either my behavior is causally overdetermined, caused by both my conscious want and by purely physical causes, or these conscious causes are identical to some part of these physical causes. Since we're rejecting systematic overdetermination, it seems we're left with a mind-brain identity as the only plausible solution.

Let's look at this Kim-Papineau argument in more detail. The argument can be broken down into three premises. The first claims:

(1) At least some conscious mental states have physical effects.

This is simply the assumption that mental causation exists. It's the assumption that there are psychophysical causal relations, that my mental states—like my beliefs, desires, deliberations, and decisions—at least sometimes have physical effects. As I've already argued, this assumption should not be given up and must be defended by libertarians. In addition, the two leading alternatives—*pre-established harmony* and *epiphenomenalism*[9]—have very counterintuitive implications. Since both the hard-determinist and the libertarian maintain the existence of mental causation, and since defenders of free will like the AC theorist cannot maintain the existence of free will without also maintaining the existence of psychophysical causal relations, I'll take premise (1) as given.

Premise two is simply the assumption of physical causal closure. As stated earlier, it's this premise that creates the real problem. As Papineau states it:

(2) All physical effects are fully caused by purely *physical* prior histories.

With regard to mental causation, the idea is that the behavioral effects of conscious mental causes, like my walking to the deli because I want a cup of coffee, will always have fully physical causes. The thought behind premise 2 is that "such physical behaviour will always be fully caused by physical contractions in your muscles, in turn caused by electrical messages traveling down your nerves, themselves due to physical activities in your motor cortex, in turn caused by physical activity in your sensory cortex, and so on" (Papineau 2002, 18). This premise is the one AC theorists typically deny. Denying the premise, however, has its own pitfalls. If one denies physical causal closure, thereby cutting the mental free from the physical, they're ultimately stuck with the impossible task of explaining how psychophysical causal interaction is even possible. In the following section I'll examine the difficulties that come in giving up the principle of physical causal closure, but for the moment let's see what happens if we accept the principle and add to it one more plausible assumption.

Both Kim and Papineau maintain that we should rule out systematic overdetermination with regard to mental causation. Although the overdetermination of certain effects may be recognized in special causal circumstances, like the death of a man who simultaneously falls off a building and is shot, this does not seem to be the appropriate model for mental causation. Causal relations support counterfactuals. And although it may make sense in the case of the man dying to say that even if one of the causes were absent the man still would have died, it doesn't seem appropriate to say the same for the bodily effects of conscious causes. For with the man dying, it's at least plausible that even if he hadn't been shot the fall would have killed him, and vice versa. But the problem is that it is highly implausible to say, when I raise my arm intentionally, that, even if I hadn't decided to raise my arm I still would have, or alternatively, even if my neurons hadn't been firing I still would have raised my arm. It only makes sense to say the physical effect, the raising of my right arm, is caused by both my conscious decision and the firing of my neurons if the causes were identical. Otherwise the appropriate counterfactuals don't seem to hold.

So if we add a final premise to the argument, one that rules out overdetermination, some form of mind-brain identity seems to follow. We can state the premise as follows:

> (3) The physical effects of conscious causes aren't always overdetermined by distinct causes.

The combination of these three premises entails a mind-brain identity of one form or another. Premises (1) and (2) tell us that certain bodily effects have both a conscious mental cause and a physical cause. Premise (3), however, tells us that these bodily effects do not have two distinct causes. To avoid a contradiction, we must conclude the following:

> (4) The conscious occurrences mentioned in (1) must be identical with some part of the physical causes mentioned in (2). (Papineau 2002, 18)

Of course this conclusion is still rather weak. As it stands now it does not tell us what exactly is being identified, *properties* or *events*. It also doesn't tell us whether what's being identified should be viewed as *token* or *type* identities. This conclusion leaves open a host of physicalist positions. Kim's version of the argument was of course designed to argue against all versions of nonreductive physicalism (see 1989, 1993a, 1993b, 1998). The conclusion I'm defending, however, is more inclusive. One could, for example, maintain a nonreductive token identity between events like Donald Davidson (1970, 1993) or a version of psychophysical type-identity like that developed by D.M. Armstrong (1966, 1968, 1977) and David Lewis (1966, 1972). I'm going to leave all such possibilities open. If this argument establishes the minimum conclusion that to preserve mental causation one must accept *some* form of a mind-brain identity, without specifying the details of such an identity, that would be sufficient to rule out all versions of agent-causation.[10]

Challenges to Physical Causal Closure

Since premise (2) is the crucial premise let me address some potential challenges to it. Critics of determinism and critics of physicalism often attempt to turn the tables by arguing that since physical causal closure cannot be decisively proven one need not assume it. This to me is bad theorizing. In theorizing what matters is the usefulness, fruitfulness, coherence, and success of a position. Its sheer unprovability counts for very little against it.

Let's focus for the moment on dualist versions of AC since they're the prime example of what you get when you give up on physical causal closure. (Although I will be focusing on dualism, most of what I'll have to say can also be applied to radically emergentist versions of AC since these too require a violation of physical causal closure.) In embracing dualism the AC theorist denies premise (2) of the Kim-Papineau argument. In accepting an ontology that recognizes both physical and nonphysical substances, and maintains that mind and matter are two independent, mutually irreducible domains that causally interact, the AC theorist denies that all physical events have completely physical causes. On this thesis, certain physical events, presumably neurophysiological events in the brain, are (at least sometimes) caused by a nonmaterial mind. Positing such psychophysical causal interaction between distinct substances may be the most effective way to avoid the conclusion of the previous argument, but it also creates a host of new problems.

Ever since the time of Descartes, it has been objected that substance dualism ultimately founders over its inability to explain how, even in theory, the two domains can causally interact. One recent writer put the problem this way:

> [S]uppose someone dips his toe into a swimming pool to test the water. The cold water quickly cools the skin on his toe, and changes the temperature of the nerve endings that are "scattered" there. Then some sort of electrical charge flows up the nerve, jumping across various gaps between one nerve and the next. Perhaps there are stages in which the electrical event causes some chemical change, which in turn causes a suitable electrical event in the next nerve. This purely physical chain of events eventually reaches some part of the brain. Here is where the trouble begins. How does it make the last step, the one that gets it from the physical apparatus of the nervous system, and into the mind? . . . [T]he last step cannot be electrical in nature. No electrical event can causally influence the mind—it's not a physical object. Nor can the last step be chemical, thermal or mechanical. Each of these requires a physical object. How does the body finally influence the mind? How does all the electrical and chemical activity in the nervous system finally bring about that distinctive feeling of cold that reveals that the water is too chilly for swimming? Many philosophers would say that this alleged causal connection is simply inconceivable. (Feldman 1986, 202-203).

The causal connection in the other direction—that from mind to brain—is equally difficult to understand. The objection here is essentially a conceptual one—how, on purely conceptual grounds, are we to understand how a non-physical substance can causally interact with a physical substance? Since the categories are, *ex hypothesi*, mutually exclusive, it's hard to comprehend how such causal interaction is even conceptually possible. If the mental lacks all physical properties, and vice versa, how can the one causally affect the other? How does the mind bring about change in the brain without possessing physical properties? Any posited point of causal contact would seem to be ruled out.[11]

In addition to this conceptual objection, there are also two important empirical objections to interactive substance dualism. The first is simply an empirical defense of physical causal closure. Although not decisive, it claims that as a matter of empirical fact, the cause of any bodily event is always some other physical event. As Michael Levin states the objection:

> [T]he anti-dualist presses what appears to be the empirical fact that for every physical event *e* involving a human body, there is some preceding physical event which is *the* cause of *e*. As far as anyone knows there are no gaps in the sequence of bodily events to be bridged by a mental event, or into which a mental event might slip. There is no physical event whose cause is mental, in the dualist's intended sense. (1979, 82)[12]

Our scientific understanding of the human body has progressed sufficiently for this to be an empirically warranted assertion. Of course no amount of empirical evidence will ever *prove* that the physical domain is causally closed. However, since the assumption of physical causal closure provides invaluable pragmatic advantage, inference to the best explanation would suggest that *even* in cases where a physical cause currently eludes detection, it's still wise to posit such a cause. Given the practical significance of the principle, along with its empirical support, the burden of proof falls on the dualist to show, persuasively, that the assumption is false.

A dualist could argue, I imagine, that we should maintain the principle when it comes to inanimate physical properties, events, and states of affairs, but deny the principle when it comes to psychophysical causal interaction. But what motivation do we have for accepting such a proposal? The strength of the principle comes in its universality. If we were to accept a bifurcated account of the universe, one that had one set of rules for all inanimate physical objects and a different set of rules for human behavior, we would in essence be placing human behavior beyond the realm of scientific investigation. Even more troubling, the fundamental physical laws of nature—the laws used to explain and predict the behavior of inanimate physical objects—would *themselves* be undermined since their apparent universality would be questioned. The fundamental laws of physics presuppose the causal closure of the universe. To posit gaps in the causal structure would be to posit violations in the physical laws. The AC theorist can't have it both ways. Either the laws hold universally or they don't. This is an important point, for while repudiating the causal closure of the physical world, dualists often shrink from contesting the validity of the laws of physics, not realizing that this is contingent on the presumption of causal closure. This brings us to our last main objection.

In addition to an empirical defense of physical causal closure, there is a more decisive argument that can be mounted against interactive dualism. It has been argued that any hypothesis proposing that non-physical minds exist, and that such minds play an active role in influencing physical events, requires the violation of fundamental physical laws (D.L. Wilson 1976, 1995, 1999; Papineau 2002). In particular, it is argued that it violates the law of the conservation of energy. This objection goes all the way back to Leibniz (1898) who objected that Descartes' interactionism was predicated on an overly lax conception of the fundamental conservation principles of physics. Energy conservation states that energy can neither be created nor destroyed. The fundamental problem then facing the dualist is the following: "If immaterial mind could move matter, then it would create energy; and if matter were to act on immaterial mind, then energy would disappear. In either case energy. . .would fail to be conserved. And so physics, chemistry, biology, and economics would collapse" (Bunge 1980, 17). Daniel Dennett spells out the difficulty in more detail:

> Let us concentrate on the returned signals, the directives from mind to brain. These, *ex hypothesi*, are not physical; they are not light waves or sound waves or cosmic rays or streams of subatomic particles. No physical energy or mass is associated with them. How, then, do they get to make a difference to what happens in the brain cells they must affect, if the mind is to have any influence in the body? A fundamental principle of physics is that any change in the trajectory of any physical entity is an acceleration requiring the expenditure of energy, and where is this energy to come from? It is this principle of conservation of energy that accounts for the physical impossibility of 'perpetual motion machines', and the same principle is apparently violated by dualism. This confrontation between quite standard physics and dualism has been endlessly discussed since Descartes' own day, and is widely regarded as the inescapable and fatal flaw of dualism. (1991, 35)

Michael Levin vividly drives the difficulty home with an example:

> Originally my leg, which has mass w, is motionless. Then it moves distance d. Enough work was done to move a mass w a distance d. Where did the energy come from? It is an empirical fact, the law of the conservation of energy, that energy had to come from somewhere, and not only does it come from some preceding physical event, no immaterial substance could possibly supply mechanical energy. The mind can apply no physical force to the leg, while the contraction of the hamstring muscle supplies just the right amount—and the bodily event just *is* the motion of an object of mass w through distance d. Thus the contraction of the muscle is *the cause* of e. If there were non-physical

causes of physical events, the energy in the universe would increase. (1979, 85)

Since the fundamental laws of physics rule out any such increase in energy, they too rule out the hypothesis of interactive dualism. Since it would be foolish to give up the law of the conservation of energy, an empirically justified principle, to accommodate the hypothesis of interactive dualism, a hypothesis that is itself controversial, one could view this as a refutation of the position.

One last thing about physical causal closure. The AC theorist might object that the principle of physical causal closure is equivalent to determinism and therefore begs the question against him. Although in the end these two principles may come to the same thing with regard to human events, conceptually they are distinct. The principle of physical causal closure simply states that any physical event that has a cause must have a physical cause. It says nothing about the causal necessity of physical events. An indeterminist, for example, could maintain that the cause of a particular physical event, y, is another physical event, x, yet maintain that x indeterministically caused y. In fact, many forms of libertarianism maintain just that. Such event-causalist libertarians shun the "strange metaphysical commitments" of AC in favor of accounts built on indeterministic physical event causation. Now this conception of *indeterminist event causation* may itself be problematic—for the reasons to be discussed in the last section—but it's not incoherent. Hence, physical causal closure is not conceptually equivalent to determinism.

One Last Challenge: The Quantum Mind

Before I turn to event-causalist accounts of free will to see if they fare any better, I would like to consider one last attempt to make sense of traditional AC. Some AC theorists who accept substance dualism meekly defend their position, claiming that by exploiting the loophole of quantum-mechanical uncertainty the non-material mind is capable of influencing matter without violating basic physical laws (Eccles 1970, 1994; Beck and Eccles 1992). This, however, is mistaken (see D.L. Wilson 1999). Let us consider for the moment some possible means of mind-brain interaction. Some basic neuroscience is required here. Given our best understanding of how the nervous system works, conscious mental functions such as volition would somehow have to produce action potentials (nerve impulses) in neurons. Such action potentials are signals that transmit information along axons and, in most neurons, initiate the process of synaptic transmission of a chemical signal to follower (postsynaptic) cells. These action potentials are necessary to bring about muscle contractions, which in turn produce all behavior, from simple movements to coordinated actions and speech.

Since I'm a philosopher and not a neuroscientist, let me cite an authority on the ways in which such action potentials could be produced:

> Action potentials are produced by opening sodium channels in neuronal membranes, which allow the movement of sodium ions across the membrane. Action potentials also involve potassium channels, but we can ignore that complexity for the purpose of this analysis. The flux of sodium ions through the sodium channels produces a voltage change across the membrane. The resulting action potential self-propagates along the axon. The sodium channels are voltage-gated in that they can be opened by changes in the voltage across the membrane. Other channels, such as those at the synaptic connections between neurons, can indirectly induce an action potential by allowing ions to move across the membrane, which alters the voltage, and thereby induces the opening of the voltage-gated sodium channels that produce the action potential. (D.L. Wilson 1999, 186)

The question then becomes, could a non-physical mind trigger an action potential in one or more of these ways within the limits of quantum-mechanical uncertainty, or in a way that would otherwise avoid violating physical laws—such as energy conservation? Biologist David L. Wilson (1999) has argued that this cannot be done. One way to bring about an action potential would be by opening enough voltage-sensitive sodium channels to trigger an action potential directly. The problem with this, argues Wilson, is that the opening of sodium channels through direct conformational change requires energy. And, as Wilson points out, "That requirement of energy, if met by a non-physical mind, would violate the first law of thermodynamics (energy would be created)" (1999, 187).

A second alternative is for mind to open sodium channels by altering the voltage across the membrane. This voltage change would trigger the opening of voltage-gated sodium channels. As Wilson describes:

> A voltage gradient is a potential-energy gradient, and thus, in the simplest case, would require the expenditure of energy to modify. Such modification might occur, for instance, by moving charges. Enough positive charges on the inside of the membrane could be moved toward the membrane, and/or enough negative charges away from the membrane, to depolarize to threshold. (1999, 197)

The problem with this possibility is the following. A nerve cell typically generates an action potential when its axon hillock region has a membrane potential that reaches threshold, an area that would contain a number of voltage-gated sodium channels. Wilson has shown, however, that just modifying the voltage gradient over a single channel, a much smaller area than an axon hillock, requires too much energy to be "hidden" under the uncertainty principle. His calculations show that the maximum possible time period for such an energy increase, as allowed by the uncertainty principle, would be too brief to allow for any ion flow. From this he concludes:

> Given our knowledge of neurophysiology, actions at the level of quantum mechanical uncertainty do not appear to be adequate to generate action potentials by the above mechanisms. It would thus appear that a non-physical mind, which generated action potentials by supplying the energy necessary either to directly open sodium channels or to indirectly open such channels by altering voltage gradients, would violate the first law of thermodynamics. (1999, 187-188)

He further considers synaptic transmission, both presynaptic and postsynaptic, as other possible ways for a non-physical mind to influence brain and concludes that they suffer similar problems.

Furthermore, there appears to be no obvious way, consistent with what is currently known of neurophysiology and neurochemistry, for such a non-physical mind to bring about volitional acts by altering brain events only at a level within quantum-mechanical uncertainty (D.L. Wilson 1999; Tegmark 1999). Max Tegmark (1999) argues that in systems as massive, hot, and wet as neurons of the brain, any quantum entanglements and indeterminacies would be eliminated within times far shorter than those necessary for conscious experience. Tegmark presents calculations to suggest that any macroscopic quantum entanglement in the brain would be destroyed in times of the order of 10(-13) to 10(-20) seconds; far short of what would be required for consciousness. The time scale in typical experiments about consciousness—attention, decision, short-term recall—are generally on the scale of 10(-3). In addition, the model of synaptic vesicle release presumed by Beck and Eccles (1992) is not a likely or reasonable model given our current knowledge of the mechanism of synaptic transmission (Söllner and Rothman 1994; Jahn and Sudhof 1994; Matthews 1996; D.L. Wilson 1999).

Beyond the seemingly necessary violation of physical laws, there appears to be one further problem with the current proposal. As Wilson describes it:

> Even were a minimal interference, under the uncertainty principle, shown to be possible, it would not allow a non-physical mind to influence brain without the violation of physical laws because any event occurring within quantum-mechanical uncertainty are required to be random. The patterned firing of action potentials in neurons that appear to be required by volitional actions would be highly non-random. (1999, 195)

It seems we are once again back to the dilemma discussed earlier: If determinism is true, human choices and actions are not free since they are determined by antecedent causes; but if simple indeterminacy is true, human actions are also not free since they would then be random and chaotic. The introduction of a non-physical mind as the mechanism that causes the patterned firing of action potentials in neurons was meant to avoid simple indeterminism and randomness. The AC theorist introduced such an entity to account for purposive, meaningful action. This runs counter, however, to the proposal that such causal interaction takes place within quantum-mechanical uncertainty. Events related to collapse of a wave function, or events occurring under quantum mechanical uncertainty, occur randomly. If the AC theorist attempts to defend the position that the mind-brain interaction takes place within quantum-mechanical uncertainty, they are confronted with a new dilemma: *either the firing of action potentials occurs randomly, in which case the main appeal of AC is lost; or it occurs non-randomly, in which case the appeal to quantum-mechanical uncertainty is undermined.* Either way, the AC theorist is unable to turn to quantum-mechanical uncertainty as a way to preserve libertarian free will.

So far there seems to be no account of dualistic interaction that doesn't entail some violation of physical laws. Most would take this as an irremediable flaw of the theory. Dualists, however, would probably welcome this conclusion. The appeal of dualism to many is that it frees the mind from determination by physical laws. That's exactly what the interactive substance dualist openly embraced when he decided to give up on physical causal closure. But his enthusiasm for his position does not make it any more plausible.

One last thing. Thus far I have been assuming the traditional "Copenhagen interpretation" of quantum mechanics according to which there exists at the smallest level of the universe a measure of irreducible indeterminism. I have done so in an attempt to show that *even if* we grant such indeterminism, AC accounts are unable to make sense of libertarian free will. One should be aware, however, that there are respectable accounts of quantum mechanics that are thoroughly deterministic (e.g., Bohm 1952a, 1952b, 1984, 1986; Bohm and Hiley 1993)—and these accounts have recently gained some traction in the scientific community (see Holland 1993; Durr et al. 2004; Barbosa and Pinto-Neto 2004; Sanz and Borondo 2007; Sanz 2005; Albert 1994). On the traditional interpretation, quantum mechanics is taken to reveal three main features of subatomic particles: indeterminacy, non-locality, and observer-participation. But, as one contemporary philosopher writing on free will points out, "This interpretation might be false and the behavior of subatomic particles might be deterministic" (Ross 2006, 129). I have no way of knowing which interpretation will ultimately win out. And since I do not want to defend a deterministic interpretation of quantum mechanics, I will simply state an additional empirical constraint on any libertarian account of free will. *If the standard interpretation of quantum mechanics turns out to be false, those accounts of libertarian free will that depend upon the existence of quantum indeterminacy would be empirically falsified.* This empirical constraint does not affect any of the arguments given thus far—if I'm correct, all AC accounts fail regardless of whether or not quantum indeterminacy exists. Nonetheless, the truth or falsity of the traditional interpretation remains a strong empirical constraint on those libertarians who wish to defend a scientifically acceptable (or, at least, scientifically consistent) account of libertarian freedom.

2.3 NATURALIZED LIBERTARIANISM: IS ANYONE UP FOR A ROLE OF THE DICE?

If all AC accounts are bound to fail, is there any other way to make sense of libertarian freedom? As Peter Ross writes, "Traditionally, libertarianism has rejected the attempt to fit ourselves as free agents into the natural world characterized by science" (2006, 130). He goes on to point out, however, that over the past three decades philosophers like Robert Kane (1996, 1999, 2002b) have developed libertarianism in new ways, striving to naturalize it. These newer versions of libertarianism attempt to "avoid the mystery of a scientifically intractable agent" (Ross 2006, 133) and claim to offer accounts of libertarian freedom that are scientifically innocuous. The problem, however, is that "a naturalized libertarianism continues to face the serious challenge of addressing how libertarian freedom, in holding that indeterminacy is sometimes sufficient for control, makes sense at all" (Ross 2006, 130). Kane himself recognizes this problem and calls it the *Intelligibility Question* (1996, 13; 2002b, 414). As Kane expresses the problem:

> The threat to free will posed by this Intelligibility Question does not come from determinism, but from its opposite, *indeterminism*: if free will is not compatible with determinism, it does not seem to be compatible with indeterminism either. An event that is undetermined might occur or not occur, given the entire past. So whether or not it actually occurs, given its past, would seem to be a matter of chance. But chance events are not under the control of anything, hence not under the control of the agent. How then could they be free and responsible actions? If a different choice might have occurred given exactly the same past, then exactly the same deliberation, the same thought processes, the same prior beliefs, desires, and other motives—not a sliver of difference—that led to an agent's favoring one option (say, choosing to vacation in Hawaii rather than Colorado), might by chance have issued in the opposite choice instead. If such a thing happened, it would seem a fluke or accident, like an uncontrolled quantum jump in the brain, not a rational, free, or responsible action. (2002b, 415)

As Ross further describes the challenge:

> It is crucial to libertarianism that it doesn't hold that just any indeterminacy is sufficient for control. This claim would render libertarian freedom rather blatantly unintelligible. Instead, the libertarian claims that

indeterminacy *in a certain context* is sufficient for control. The tradition-al libertarianism filled out the context (to the extent that this was pos-sible) in terms of a scientifically intractable agent. Naturalizing libertar-ianism amounts to offering a naturalistic context. And the fundamental problem for naturalized libertarianism is whether it makes sense to think that there is a naturalistic context in which indeterminacy is suffi-cient for control. (2006, 130)

How, then, do these so-called naturalized versions of libertarianism an-swer the Intelligibility Question?

Robert Kane attempts to do so with his co-called *Teleological Intelli-gibility* (TI) theory. TI theories try to make undetermined free actions intelligible in terms of reasons and motives, intentions and purposes, without invoking extra entities or special forms of causation. As Kane writes:

What prompted me to begin thinking about free will issues thirty years ago was a growing dissatisfaction with the standard responses to this intelligibility problem on the part of defenders of incompatibilist or libertarian free will. Libertarian responses invariably followed a certain pattern. Since agents had to be able to act or act otherwise, given exact-ly the same prior psychological and physical history (as indeterminism seems to require), some 'extra (or special) factors' had to be introduced over and above the normal flow of events in order to explain how and why agents acted as they did. . . . But, whatever form they have taken, extra factor strategies have tended to reinforce the widespread view that notions of free will requiring indeterminism are mysterious and have no place in the modern scientific picture of the world. More im-portantly, as I see it, extra factor strategies give only the appearance of solving the problems of indeterminism, while creating further prob-lems of their own. (2002b, 415)

I agree with Kane's assessment of extra factor strategies for all the rea-sons outlined above. Kane's own TI theory—which is a *causal indetermin-ist* (or *event-causalist*) theory—is, as he puts it, an attempt "to see how far one can go in making sense of libertarian freedom without appealing either to sui generis kinds of agency or causation" (2002b, 416). If Kane were successful in providing an intelligible account of libertarian free-dom, one that avoided such extra (or special) factors, such an account would need to be taken seriously. Since Kane's theory is the most promis-ing naturalized account out there, and the most discussed, I will examine it carefully.

Before we can understand Kane's proposal it is necessary that we understand his incompatibilist requirement of Ultimate Responsibility. According to Kane, for an agent to be free they must satisfy the require-ment of *Ultimate Responsibility* (UR).

UR: To be ultimately responsible for an action, an agent must be responsible for anything that is a sufficient reason (condition, cause, or motive) for the occurrence of the action. (2002b, 407)

If, for example, a choice issued from, and can be sufficiently explained by, an agent's character and motives (together with background conditions), then to be *ultimately responsible* for the choice, the agent must be at least in part responsible, by virtue of choices and actions voluntarily performed in the past, for having the character and motives he or she now has. As Kane understands UR, it is incompatible with determinism. That is, ultimate responsibility for an action requires either that the action not be causally determined or, if the action is causally determined, that any determined cause of it result (at least in part) from some action by that agent that was not causally determined.[13] UR therefore requires some indeterminacy and some ability to control the formation of our own character and motives. If we are to be to any degree *creators of our own wills*, argues Kane, some actions in our lifetime must be *will-setting* and not already will-settled. At these moments, we must be able to go in different directions willingly. Actions are "willing-setting" when "the wills of agents (their motives and purposes) are not already 'set one way' *before* they act, but rather the agents set their wills one way or the other in the performance of the actions themselves" (2002b, 412). Although UR does not require that we could have done otherwise for *every* act performed, it *does* require that we could have done otherwise (in an incompatibilist sense) with respect to *some* acts in our past life histories by which we formed our present character. Kane calls such "regress-stopping" actions, *self-forming actions* (SFA) or *self-forming willings* (SFW). Hence, UR requires indeterminism, but indeterminism does not have to be involved in all acts done "of our own free will." Only those choices or acts in our lifetime by which we make ourselves into the kinds of persons we are (i.e., SFA) have to be undetermined.

How, then, does Kane make sense of the idea that event indeterminacy is sometimes sufficient for control (i.e., in cases SFA) without making such actions unintelligible? According to Kane, in cases of SFA (or will-setting)—e.g., situations of deep moral conflict—there is tension and uncertainty in our minds about what to do. He theorizes that:

[T]his is reflected in appropriate regions of our brains by movement away from thermodynamic equilibrium—in short, a kind of stirring up of chaos in the brain that makes it sensitive to micro-indeterminacies at the neuronal level. The uncertainty and inner tension we feel at such soul-searching moments of self-formation would thereby be reflected in the indeterminacy of our neuronal processes themselves. What is experienced personally as uncertainty corresponds physically to the opening of a window of opportunity that temporally screens off complete determination by influences of the past. (2002b, 417)

Kane appears to locate quantum indeterminacy at a particular point in deliberation involving a conflict of values (e.g., egoistic and altruistic values), and asks us to imagine that in such conflict circumstances there is a "kind of stirring up of chaos in the brain that makes it sensitive to micro-indeterminacies at the neuronal level." According to Kane, the uncertainty we experience from conflicting desires—for example, the desire to continue on to work and the desire to stop and help a person in need—"corresponds physically" with metaphysical indeterminacy at the neuronal level. Being torn due to such conflicts creates chaotic conditions that amplify quantum indeterminacy so that its effects percolate up—i.e., are manifested at the level of individual neurons, and then at the level of neural networks (Kane 1996, 128-130). As Kane puts it in his book *The Significance of Free Will*:

> These [moral] conflicts create tensions that are reflected in appropriate regions of the brain by movement further from thermodynamic equilibrium, which increases the sensitivity to micro indeterminacies at the neuronal level and magnifies the indeterminacies throughout the complex macro process which, taken as a whole, is the agent's effort of will. (1996, 130)

Thus, Kane's view is that the indeterministic noise experienced during "soul-searching moments of self-formation" (somehow) creates the conditions in which quantum indeterminacies can be amplified and manifested in our deliberative processes.

Leaving aside the speculative nature of this proposal for the moment, how does this amplification of the effects of quantum indeterminacy preserve voluntary, intentional, rationally motivated behavior? Here, I believe, is where Kane is at his most original. He argues that under these conditions the choice (either way) will *not* be "inadvertent," "accidental," "capricious," or "merely random" *because* it will be *willed* by the agent either way, done for *reasons* either way which the agent then and there endorses. In these self-forming actions, whichever way the agents choose, they will have succeeded in doing what they were trying to do *because they were simultaneously trying to make both choices*. For Kane, remember, cases of "will-setting or self-forming actions occur at those difficult times of life when we are torn between competing visions of what we should do or become" (2002b, 416-417). Perhaps we are torn between doing the moral thing or acting from ambition, or between egoistic or altruistic motives, or between present desires or long-term goals. According to Kane, "When we do decide under such conditions of uncertainty, the outcome is not determined because of the preceding [neuronal] indeterminacy—and yet it can be willed (and hence rational and voluntary) either way because, in such self-formation, the agents' prior wills are divided by conflicting motives" (2002b, 471). Kane provides the following example:

Consider a businesswoman who faces a conflict of this kind. She is on
the way to a meeting important to her career when she observes an
assault taking place in an alley. An inner struggle ensues between her
moral conscience, to stop and call for help, and her career ambitions
that tell her she cannot miss this meeting. She has to make an effort of
will to overcome the temptation to go on to her meeting. If she overcomes this temptation, it will be the result of her effort, but if she fails,
it will be because she did not *allow* her effort to succeed. And this is due
to the fact that, while she wanted to overcome temptation, she also
wanted to fail, for quite different and incommensurable reasons. When
agents, like the woman, decide in such circumstances, and the indeterminate efforts they are making become determinate choices, they *make*
one set of competing reasons or motives prevail over the others then
and there *by deciding*. . . . Their acts are "will-setting." (2002b, 471)

According to Kane, then, the neuronal indeterminacy that accompanies
the woman's uncertainty satisfies the incompatibilist demand for undetermined action, nonetheless the action is still intelligible *because* it will be
willed by the woman either way, done for *reasons* either way—moral conviction if she turns back, ambitious motives if she goes on. Even though
the outcome of the businesswoman's deliberation is indeterminate, it is
backed by reasons *since* each of the competing courses of action is.

   Although this proposal avoids the "extra factors" and "strange metaphysical commitments" of AC, it's unclear whether it answers the Intelligibility Question. What, for example, warrants Kane's use of intentional
language when he says the businesswoman "makes" one set of competing reasons or motives prevail over the others by "deciding"? Or that she
either "overcomes" her temptation to go on to her meeting through an
"effort of will" or "allows" herself to give in? In what sense is this woman
deciding or *overcoming* anything? Recall that AC theorists typically argue
that libertarian freedom requires not only a *negative constraint* (i.e., some
indeterminism) but a *positive constraint* (i.e., a causal power possessed by
the agent to either directly cause their own action or to initiate a causal
sequence that results in an action). By doing away with "extra entities or
special forms of causation," Kane is unable to accommodate this positive
constraint—since he is left only with event indeterminacy (presumably
carried out by "micro-indeterminacies at the neuronal level"). In what
sense can we say that a random quantum event at the neuronal level is an
act of deciding or *effort of will*? The agent, in this situation, cannot be responsible for causing such an event—since, as Taylor says, "whatever is
not caused by anything is not caused by me." It doesn't matter that these
indeterminacies percolate up as part of a chaotic system, as Kane proposes, for the ultimate outcome is still the result of a random event.[14]
Kane, it would appear, is guilty of the precise thing he set out to avoid—
i.e., the ultimate outcome of the woman's internal conflict, if it were a
result of quantum indeterminacy, "would seem a fluke or accident, like

an uncontrolled quantum jump in the brain, not a rational, free, or responsible action" (Kane 2002b, 415).

To help make this problem more vivid I would like to introduce a case where the quantum indeterminacy is located outside the agent (although everything else remains the same as Kane's example). Let's imagine that Louis is a middle aged man who is currently feeling down because his wife recently left him. To get his mind off things he decides to spend the afternoon making a doghouse for his companion Philo. Louis takes out his power tools and gets to work cutting the necessary pieces. Now, in the process of cutting the wood Louis is overcome with a strong urge to harm himself. (Perhaps he thinks this is a good way to get back at his ex.) In this situation, Louis desires *both* to cut the wood so as to finish Philo's doghouse and to injure himself. An inner struggle ensues and Louis is confronted with an important life choice. He is, at that very moment, undecided. Now let's imagine that in the process of cutting the wood a random quantum event causes the blade to jump, cutting off two of his fingers. Did Louis "freely cause" his injuries? Did he "decide" or "make" this event happen? In no way can we say that Louis *caused* or *controlled* the outcome since no one causes or controls quantum events! Hence, it would be counterintuitive to call this a *free act.* Yet Kane cannot easily explain why the example of the businesswoman is an example of libertarian freedom while this is not. Even though the outcome is indeterminate—as it was in the businesswoman case—it *is* nonetheless backed by reasons since each of the competing courses of action is something Louis wanted to do. Whatever the outcome, Louis would have succeeded in doing what he was trying to do *because* he was simultaneously trying to cut the wood and harm himself.[15]

According to Kane's theory, "the felt indeterminacy and reasons backing of deliberative outcomes is necessary and sufficient for control (1996: 133-135, 141; 1999: 174-176)" (Ross 2006, 131). The Louis example satisfies both of these conditions. Louis, clearly in the throes of a soul-searching moment, experiences uncertainty and inner tension. He is conflicted by his competing desires and *feels* as though branching paths are metaphysically open before him. Phenomenologically, then, he satisfies the first condition—felt indeterminacy. He also satisfies the second condition because he has reasons backing either outcome. Whatever happens, Louis wanted it to happen. Kane, of course, is likely to argue that such "external" or "accidental" indeterminacies are irrelevant and that what is needed is a *correspondence* between experienced indeterminacy and micro-level indeterminacy at the neuronal level. It's unclear, however, why indeterminacy at the neuronal level is required for this correspondence! Kane's proposal requires only a correspondence between experienced (or phenomenological) uncertainty and "the opening of a window of opportunity that temporarily screens off complete determination by influences of the past." This correspondence, I maintain, is met in my example. What difference does it make that the (posited) quantum indeterminacy is located at the neuronal level and not, say, the micro-level of the saw blade? The uniqueness of Kane's theory comes in his locating the indeterminacy at a crucial *temporal* moment in the deliberative process— i.e., at the moment when one is confronted with a difficult life choice and is uncertain about what to do. It is the *temporal* location of the indeterminacy that matters, not its spatial location. It might be scientifically relevant where Kane posits the required indeterminacy—since, empirically, certain hypotheses will be more plausible than others—but philosophically it's irrelevant where the indeterminacy occurs. As long as the phenomenological indeterminacy experienced during the deliberative process is accompanied by metaphysical indeterminacy, and there are reasons backing the alternative outcomes, both of Kane's singly necessary and jointly sufficient conditions for control are satisfied.

Now, for the sake of argument, let's change the case so that the posited indeterminacy occurs back at the neuronal level. According to Kane, indeterminate efforts of will are complex chaotic processes in the brain involving neural networks that are globally sensitive to quantum indeterminacies at the neuronal level (see 1996, 130). Elaborating on the businesswoman example, Kane provides a little more detail about how this might work in cases of SFA:

> Imagine that in such conflicting circumstances, two competing (recurrent) neural networks are involved. (These are complex networks of interconnected neurons in the brain circulating impulses in feedback loops of a kind generally involved in high-level cognitive processing.) The input of one of these networks is coming from the woman's desires and motives for stopping to help the victim. If the network reaches a certain activation threshold (the simultaneous firing of a complex set of "output" neurons), that would represent her choice to help. For the competing network, the inputs are her ambitious motives for going on to her meeting, and its reaching an activation threshold represents the choice to go on. (2002b, 419)

Kane's proposal, then, is that the "stirring up of chaos in the brain" ultimately creates two competing neural networks that reflect our competing choices. The amplification of the micro-indeterminacies at the neuronal level make the outcome of our deliberation indeterminate, yet intelligibility is maintained since the indeterminacy "occurs in the physical basis of the interaction among neurally realized goal-directed states which express our values" (Ross 2006, 131). One should notice, however, that there really are two proposals here. The first is an empirical proposal regarding the chaotic amplification of indeterminacy in the brain. The second is a philosophical response to the Intelligibility Question. Regardless of the empirical merits of the first proposal, it is the second proposal that I am here questioning. Kane maintains that "when either of the pathways 'wins' (that is, reaches an activation threshold)," this amounts to a genuine example of *choice* (2002b, 419). This is because, *whatever the outcome*, it will be done for *reasons* which the agent then and there endorses. It's Kane's concept of *choice* and, consequently, his answer to the Intelligibility Question that is unconvincing. The problem is that whichever set of competing reasons prevails (or "wins" out) is ultimately an arbitrary and capricious matter. No meaningful explanation can be given for *why* the businesswoman ultimately chooses one option over the other. Kane, himself, admits, "To be sure, with such 'self-forming' choices, agents cannot control or determine which choice outcome will occur *before* it occurs, or else the outcomes would be predetermined after all" (2002b, 420). Kane does not think this is a problem, but it's hard to see how intelligibility is preserved on such an account.

Kane tries to reconcile the arbitrariness of indeterminacy with libertarian freedom as follows:

> An ultimate arbitrariness remains in all undetermined SFAs because there cannot in principle be sufficient or overriding *prior* reasons for making one set of competing reasons prevail over the other. . . . [However] the absence of an explanation of the difference in choice in terms of prior reasons does not have the tight connection to issues of responsibility one might initially credit it with...None of [the conditions necessary and sufficient for responsibility] is precluded by the absence of an explanation of the difference in choice in terms of prior reasons. (1999, 176-177)

Putting aside the apparent question-begging nature of this response, there is a more significant problem. As some critics have pointed out, Kane, *at best*, only shows that indeterminacy is *consistent* with responsibility and control, *not* that it is sufficient for responsibility and control (see Ross 2006). Kane's argument is only that indeterminacy does not *preclude* control. Whether or not Kane is correct, this approach is vulnerable to the following objection raised by Peter Ross:

> The libertarian must render intelligible the idea that there is a context for indeterminacy where it is *sufficient* for control, not just one where it is consistent with control. Kane's approach involves enriching this context through the inclusion of the reasons backing of deliberative outcomes. But the question then becomes whether this inclusion allows us to understand Kane's claim of sufficiency by smuggling in the satisfaction of compatibilist sufficient conditions for control while pointing to an indeterminacy which, irrelevant to sufficiency for control, merely plays the role of satisfying the incompatibilist intuition that indeterminacy is necessary for control. (2006, 132)

The worry seems to be that the kind of naturalized libertarianism offered by Kane is, as Galen Strawson puts it, "a covert compatibilism with an idle incompatibilist premise dangling subjoined" (1986, 32). Kane's posited indeterminacy satisfies his incompatibilist intuitions, but it plays no clear role in sufficiency for control. When it comes to explaining control, Kane focuses primarily on the reasons backing of deliberative outcomes and other compatibilistic conditions. Control, on Kane's account, essentially comes down to the agent being motivated by various wants, desires, and values—and the outcome, whatever it ends up being, be backed by reasons the agent there and then endorses. No indeterminist control is imparted to the agent as it is in AC accounts. For this reason, Randolph Clarke, a fellow libertarian, has argued: "[A]n event-causal libertarian view adds no new types of causes to those that can be required by a compatibilist account, and hence the former appears to add nothing to the agent's positive power to determine what he does" (2002, 374). Clarke argues that causal indeterminist theories like Kane's provide "leeway" for choice, but no more control over actions than compatibilists offer—and more control, argues Clarke, is needed for libertarian freedom and responsibility. O'Connor (2000) presents a similar argument against Kane. He argues that positing causal indeterminism in the triggering of an action isn't enough—a successful account of libertarian freedom "must further explain how it could be *up to the agent* which option is realized" (2000, 24; italics added).[16] Indeterminacy may open the door for libertarian freedom, but it does not explain the control needed to carry out such freedom.[17]

An additional problem with Kane's conception of control comes in his conception of *wanting to act on certain reasons more than any others.* According to Kane, "an agent *wills* to do something at time t just in case the agent has reasons or motives at t for doing it that the agent wants to act on more than he or she wants to act on any other reasons (for doing otherwise)" (1996, 30). *Wanting more* also figures prominently in Kane's so-called plurality conditions for free will (see Clarke 2002). Kane's conception of wanting more gives the impression that some control is maintained by the agent. Clarke, however, argues that Kane's notions of wanting more does not help to address the problem of control because:

> An agent's wanting more to act on certain reasons is, on Kane's view, brought about *by* her performing a SFW, by, for example, her making a certain choice. Hence it cannot contribute to the active control that the agent exercises, for this . . . is a matter of what brings about the choice or other action, not of what the choice or other action brings about. (2002, 371)

Control, argues Clarke, should involve a kind of active directedness—an active attempt to produce certain outcomes. Wanting more, as Kane construes it, cannot contribute to such active directedness since the agent's wanting more is brought about *by* performing a SFA. Wanting more, as Kane construes it, plays no role in *bringing about* the choice or action—hence, it cannot contribute to the active control libertarians believe in.

Nor does it seem to contribute to the rationality of free choices or help explain *why* the agent makes the choice they do (see Clarke 2002, 383 fn.39). As Clarke points out, "the rationality of a choice is a matter of the normative strength of the reasons *for which* the agent makes the choice" (2002, 384). Kane's understanding of wanting more provides no account of such normative reasons for choice and action.

Let me make one last point concerning intelligibility. A key component of Kane's account of SFA, remember, is the agent's simultaneous attempt to bring about inconsistent courses of action. For example, in cases of moral conflict like that of the businesswoman the agent tries to make the moral choice (e.g., stop and call for help) and at the same time tries to make the self-interested choice (e.g., continue on to the meeting). This "doubling" of effort is what allows Kane to say that the agent endorses, hence *wills*, either outcome. Although I did not question this notion of simultaneous efforts of will earlier, it's unclear whether it makes any sense. As Clarke argues:

> This doubling of efforts of will introduces a troubling incoherence into cases of moral (and prudential) choice. There is already present, in such a case, an incoherence in the agent's motives. This type of conflict is common and no apparent threat to freedom. Indeed, libertarians often maintain . . . that such motivational conflict is *required* for freedom. However, to have the agent actively trying, at one time, to do two obviously incompatible things raises serious questions about the agent's rationality. This additional incoherence may thus be more of a threat than an aid to freedom. (2002, 372)

Kane's whole account—not only of SFA but of libertarian freedom in general—rests on the coherence of indeterminate efforts of will. Yet, how are we to understand an agent that is *actively* and *simultaneously* trying to bring about two inconsistent ends? When an agent is confronted with a difficult moral choice—like whether they should accept the sexual advances of a stranger or stay faithful to their spouse—it's easy to imagine the agent experiencing a conflict of desires. But to say that in such a situation the agent is actively willing *both* the moral choice to stay faithful to their wife *and* the choice to give in to their temptation makes the agent appear irrational. Such simultaneous but inconsistent efforts of will amount to the agent willing P and $\sim P$ at the same time. Not only is this of dubious coherence, it is far from the model of rationally guided behavior we were promised. (Furthermore, it's worth reiterating just how counterintuitive this is as an account of "overcoming temptation." Try explaining to your wife that you *actively willed* (hence *tried*) sleeping with a stranger but was unsuccessful because the competing neural network "won" out—the result of an indeterminate event!)

For all the reasons just discussed, Kane's account fails to make intelligible event-indeterminism. It does not satisfactorily answer the very Intelligibility Question it set out to tackle. Although it does improve upon simple indeterminist accounts—i.e., accounts that simply posit indeterminism in the triggering of an action—in the end, the agent's choice, whatever it ends up being, remains arbitrary, capricious, and uncontrolled.

In addition to Kane's failure to address the intelligibility issue, I believe the account suffers from several other difficulties. The first regards the empirical question of whether the effects of quantum indeterminacy are manifested in neural processes. Not only would Kane's theory be subject to the empirical constraint outlined at the end of the previous section, it would also be subject to a more stringent empirical constraint: *If quantum indeterminism is shown not to exist at the appropriate neuronal level, then Kane's account (and any other libertarian accounts that depend upon the existence of such neuronal indeterminacy) would be empirically falsified.* Kane's theory depends not only on the traditional interpretation of quantum mechanics, but quantum indeterminacies existing at the appropriate level of neuronal activity. This makes Kane's theory (at least this component of it) a testable hypothesis. I have already argued, however, that David Wilson and Max Tegmark's calculations suggest that such indeterminacy is extremely unlikely. The burden of proof therefore falls on Kane to show not only the existence of micro-level neuronal indeterminacy but the chaotic amplification of such indeterminacy in the brain. Kane's account, recall, posits that chaotic conditions amplify quantum indeterminacy so that its effects percolate up to the level of neural networks. It's worth considering, however, just how demanding the theory's commitments are. As Manuel Vargas points out:

> [N]ot only do agent mental processes have to turn out to be indeterministic, but they must also be indeterministic in a very particular way. If multiple mutually exclusive aims did not cause the brain to go into a chaotic state the theory would be disproved. If it turned out that neurological systems weren't sensitive to quantum indeterminacies the theory would be disproved. If it turned out that neurological systems were sensitive to quantum indeterminacies, but not sufficiently sensitive to amplify quantum indeterminacies in a way that affects the outcome of choice, this too would disprove the theory. These are not marginal or insubstantial bets about what brain science will reveal to us. (2007, 143)

Given the precise nature of Kane's account, I find his appeal to quantum indeterminacy as a way to salvage libertarian freedom empirically implausible. There is currently no support for the claim that micro-level indeterminacies are capable of reaching the level of neural networks in the way Kane's theory demands.

A second concern has to do with Kane's claim that indeterminism is only required for self-forming actions. If the only actions (or willings) that are undetermined are SFA (or will-settings), does this preserve *enough* freedom? Kane's account does not seem to preserve the rich sense of freedom we all feel. Most of us believe that the majority of our voluntary actions and choices are free (in an undetermined way), not just those that happen at crucial moments of character formation and moral conflict. Furthermore, what reason do we have for thinking that SFA are capable of stirring up quantum chaos while everyday mundane choices are not? Why think that when I'm standing in the aisle at the supermarket unsure which toothbrush to buy my mind is determined by previously fixed character traits and deterministic neuronal processes, but when I'm confronted with a choice between stopping to help someone in need or proceeding on to work my indecision is capable of moving me "away from thermodynamic equilibrium"? Why not think that *even in cases* of deep moral conflict my decisions are the result of previously determined character traits and determined brain activity? I see no reason for acknowledging two different realms of voluntary action—one that is not determined by antecedent conditions (SFA) and one that is (all those actions that proceed from SFA). Kane has no reason, other than to preserve some sense of incompatibilist freedom, for positing this more limited realm of undetermined action.

At this point, I imagine, Kane is likely to appeal to phenomenology. In several places, Kane claims that in self-forming actions the feeling that branching paths are metaphysically open is "a neural sensitivity" to the amplified effects of quantum indeterminacy (see 1996, 130-133; 1999, 164). Kane seems to think that since the *feeling of indeterminacy* is so strong in SFA, it *must* be accompanied by real metaphysical indeterminacy—whereas, "By contrast, when we act from predominant motives or settled dispositions, the uncertainty or indeterminacy is muted" (2002b, 417). Kane's theory, therefore, relies heavily on introspective evidence—as do all libertarian accounts. As Ross writes:

> Introspection does seem to indicate that when we struggle with a conflict of values, branching paths are metaphysically open. Whatever the metaphysics turns out to be, we experience ourselves as undeterminedly and directly forming the particular intention which causes our action. Thus we feel that we could have done otherwise (in the same circumstances) if we had formed a different intention. This feeling of freedom is a type of introspective state—that is, it represents a mental state rather than the world—and this type of introspective state provides evidence in favor of libertarian freedom . . . [Not only does Kane appeal to such introspective evidence], all libertarians assign introspective evidence some role, for it is our feeling of metaphysically open branching paths that is the raison d'être of libertarian freedom. It is the first-person perspective that at least seems to give self-formation meaning. (2006, 134-135)

Kane, in fact, goes so far as to argue that introspective evidence is capable of trumping our present inability to address the Intelligibility Question.[18]

Although I agree with Kane's basic description of the phenomenology, there is no reason to believe that experienced indeterminacy is *actually* accompanied by metaphysical indeterminacy. Perhaps the indeterminacy experienced during SFA is only epistemological indeterminacy? I will argue in subsequent chapters that our introspective phenomenology is not reliable and does not support the libertarian conclusion. For the moment, though, I will settle for another empirical constraint—this one expressed by Ross.

> The Libertarian claims that the best explanation of our feeling that there are metaphysically open branching paths is that we become aware of an absence of sufficient mental causes. A specific question for research is whether this is the best explanation. If psychologists were to provide an alternative explanation which not only indicates that there are sufficient mental causes even in ordinary cases where our introspection indicates otherwise, but also offers a model explaining the illusion of their absence, this would undermine any naturalized libertarianism. (2006, 139)

Psychological research into the accuracy of introspection therefore provides another powerful empirical constraint.[19] If evidence in the behavioral, cognitive, and neurosciences shows (as I believe it does) that the best explanation of our introspective phenomenology is not the one Kane and other libertarians provide, then the main support for the libertarian position will be undermined (even falsified).

In this chapter I have discussed two main libertarian approaches—*agent-causation* and *event-causal indeterminism*—and argued that both are bound to fail. Kane's version of event-causal indeterminism avoids appealing to sui generis kinds of agency and causation but ultimately fails to address the Intelligibility Question. The theory also depends upon at least two empirically questionable assumptions: the quantum amplification of micro-level indeterminacies, and the trustworthiness of introspective phenomenology. *Simple event indeterminism*—which posits significant indeterminism in the triggering of an action but without imparting any causal role to the agent or their reasons for action—is even worse off than Kane's account. Since it does not even attempt to make intelligible undetermined actions, it is directly confronted by the following dilemma: If determinism is true, human choices and actions are not free since they are determined by antecedent causes; but if simple indeterminacy is true, human actions are also not free since they would then be random and chaotic. Kane attempts to improve on simple indeterminism by introducing his TI theory and the reasons backing of deliberative outcomes, but if what I've argued here is correct, Kane does not deliver on his promise to resolve the intelligibility issue while making libertarianism a scientifically respectable position. In the end, Kane imparts no more control to agents than simple indeterminism or compatibilism; whichever set of competing reasons prevails (or "wins" out), on Kane's account, remains an arbitrary and capricious matter.

AC theories, on the other hand, at least give the impression of maintaining intelligibility since they attempt to split the horns of the above dilemma by introducing a scientifically intractable agent and a sui generis notion of causation. Yet these accounts are even less appealing. Not only are the metaphysical commitments of AC inconsistent with our scientific worldview, the theory makes mental causation impossible. Given the fact that most agent-causal theorists reject event indeterminism for its inability to address the Intelligibility Question, traditional AC accounts are confronted with their own dilemma: If they want to avoid randomness and maintain intelligibility, they must accept (according to AC) metaphysical commitments that make mental causation impossible; but if they instead attempt to preserve mental causation (a necessary condition for free will), they must accept a naturalistic worldview that makes AC impossible. Either way, AC fails to make sense of libertarian freedom. Given the Kim-Papineau argument and my defense of physical causal closure, agent-causal theorists are confronted with an impossible task. If they give up physical causal closure, as the theory requires, there's no way for them to account for mental causation. If, on the other hand, they attempt to preserve and make sense of mental causation, they are forced to relinquish the ontology of AC and accept *some form* of mind-brain physicalism. The failure of AC to account for mental causation, I maintain, is not just an epistemic limitation on our current understanding of how the mind works, it's an in-principle failure of the position.

NOTES

1. Following common practice, I will hyphenate expressions like "agent-causation" and "agent-causal" when talking about AC theories to indicate that a special kind of relation is intended.

2. In section 2.1 we'll see that agent-causal theorists view libertarian freedom as incompatible with physical causal closure and any strong mind-body correlation. According to AC, these commitments lead to either determinism (which all libertarians consider incompatible with free will), or simple event indeterminism (which agent-causal theorists *in particular* consider incompatible with free will).

3. It would do us all well to recognize that hard-determinists want to preserve the voluntary/involuntary distinction along with the action/mere happenings distinction, as do all other positions. Some have maintained that if hard-determinism were true all human behavior would turn out to be involuntary. This is mistaken. The notion of action is here defined in terms of intentional action. And it should be pointed out that the concept of action is distinct from that of free action. The question of whether an action is free is different from whether it is voluntary. There can be intentional actions—i.e., voluntary actions—that are not free. Some compatibilists have confused the issue by equating free actions with voluntary actions.

4. Some, such as Richard Taylor, maintain AC as a feature of all intentional actions. The more common view, held by most agent-causal theorists, is that being caused by an agent is a necessary feature of *freely* chosen activity. That is to say, while some of our actions may be agent-causal in nature others may not, and there may be possible forms of intentional activity that lack it altogether. Whether or not AC is best viewed as an account of intentional action in general, or as applying to only a subclass of intentional action, one thing is clear: *all* AC theorists view it as a necessary condition for *free* action. In what's to follow, I'll focus exclusively on AC as an account of free action.

5. As quoted by O'Connor (2000, 44).

6. For good AC arguments against simple indeterminism, see O'Connor (2000, ch.2) and Clarke (2002). *Simple indeterminism*, as O'Connor defines it, is "the thesis that agent control is noncausal in nature" (2000, 24). Simple indeterminist theories (e.g., Ginet 1990, 2002; McCann 1998) posit significant indeterminism in the triggering of an action in such a way that very different actions are causally possible in those circumstances. Unlike *event-causal* (or *causal indeterminist*) theories, however, simple indeterminism imparts no causal role to the agent's reasons for action—i.e., simple indeterminism maintains that "free agency doesn't require there to be any sort of causal connection (even of an indeterministic variety) between the agent['s reasons] and his free actions" (O'Connor 1995a, 7). Because of this, critics charge that these theories fail to account for the relation of reasons to action and are unable to account for the causal role of agents in the control of free actions (see Clarke 2002). Clarke, for example, writes: "Two main problems arise for libertarian accounts of this sort. . . . The first concerns control. Performing an action, even acting unfreely, is exercising some variety of active control over one's behavior; acting freely is exercising an especially valuable variety of active control. A theory of action, whether of specifically free action or not, ought to say what the pertinent variety of control is or in what it consists. . . . The second main problem concerns rationality. Acting freely is acting with a capacity for rational self-governance and determining, oneself, whether and how one exercises that capacity on a given occasion. Hence it must be possible for a free action to be an action performed for a certain reason, an action for which there is a rational explanation" (2002, 357-358). Clarke argues that simple indeterminist theories (or what he calls *noncausal* theories) fail to offer an adequate account of both control and rational explanation. O'Connor, commenting on Ginet's version of simple indeterminism, likewise writes: "The fact that free actions have uncaused volitions at their core is prima facie puzzling. If it is uncaused, if it is in no sense determined to occur by anything at all, then it is not determined to occur by me in particular. And if I don't determine it, then it's not under my control" (2000, 25).

7. For an argument that "downward causation" is ultimately an incoherent concept, see Jaegwon Kim (1992, 1999).

8. A number of critics have questioned the internal coherence of AC (see C.D. Broad 1952; Searle 2001a; Kane 1989, 1996; Clarke 1995b; van Inwagen 2000; Walter 2001; Ginet 2002). One of the main criticisms has to do with the intelligibility of the AC claim that the agent's reasons for acting play either no causal role in agent-causation (e.g., O'Connor 1995b, 2000) or only a probabilistic or indeterminate role (e.g., Clarke 1993, 1996). Critics question how well these theories account for the relation of reasons to action. As one critic notes, "If free decisions are not caused by *anything but* the agent himself, then they are also not caused by reasons. Therefore, they are not intelligible" (Walter 2001, 262). Other critics have argued that free will and indeterminism are incompatible *even if* our acts or their causal antecedents are the product of agent causation—i.e., the concept of agent causation is entirely irrelevant to the problem of free will (van Inwagen 2000). Van Inwagen's makes a persuasive case that AC does not deliver on its promise to make indeterminism compatible with free will. Although I believe there are serious, even fatal problem with AC as an account of libertarian freedom, I will instead take a different approach in attacking AC. I maintain that if, *per impossible*, AC were coherent and able to reconcile indeterminism with libertarian

freedom, it would still fail to account for mental causation and would be contrary to naturalism and other important philosophical and scientific commitments.

9. According to *pre-established harmony* the mind and body do not causally interact. The mind has no influence over the body. The appearance of interaction is due to a pre-established harmony created by God. That is, although the mind and body don't actually interact, God has created them such that they run on separate but parallel tracks. The appearance of interaction is the result of the constant co-occurrence of certain mental events with physical events pre-established by God. *Epiphenomenalism* maintains that physical events cause mental events but that mental events never cause physical events. As Papineau writes: "Epiphenomenalism . . . would require us to deny many apparently obvious truths, such as that my conscious thirst caused me to fetch a beer, or that my conscious headache caused me to swallow an aspirin" (2002, 22).

10. Let me say something here about the concept of *supervenience*. Some philosophers who give up on dualism and radical emergentism have turned instead to the concept of supervenience as a way of accounting for mental causation, while at the same time maintaining the primacy of the physical and the reality of the mental (e.g., Davidson 1970, 1993; Sosa 1984; Kim 1984a). It's important to note, however, that whatever the merits of supervenience as an account of mental causation, *it would be of no use to the AC theorist*. The thesis that the mental is supervenient on the physical is roughly the claim that the mental character of a thing is wholly determined by its physical nature. Three ideas have come to be closely associated with supervenience: (1) *Property covariation*, which claims if two things are indiscernible in base properties, they must be indiscernible in supervenient properties; (2) *Dependence*, which holds that supervenient properties are dependent on, or determined by, their subvenient bases; and (3) *Non-reducibility*, that property covariation and dependence involved in supervenience can obtain even if supervenient properties are not reducible to their base properties. It's the first two conditions that rule out supervenience as an acceptable alternative for AC theorists. For more on the concept of supervenience and the various ways the covariation and dependency relations have been defined, see Kim (1984b, 1987, 1990). (I would argue that supervenience suffers from many of the same difficulties just examined (see Kim 1993b). I personally favor a functional reductive type-type identity theory like that developed by D.M. Armstrong (1966, 1968, 1977) and David Lewis (1966, 1972, 1980). Essentially, it's the same kind of account recently accepted by Kim (1998) and David Braddon-Mitchell and Frank Jackson (1996). One need not accept this form of functionalism, however, to accept the argument I have here presented against AC. All I want to argue here is that to preserve mental causation one must accept a mind-brain identity theory *of one form or another*.)

11. Radical emergence suffers from its own related problem with "downward causation" (see Kim 1992, 1999). The challenge for those who wish to embrace radical emergence is to explain how the *emergent substance* or *individual* is causally significant without violating the basic causal laws that operate at the lower levels.

12. Immediately preceding this passage, Levin points out: "The notion of '*the* cause' of an event has a sufficiently wide preanalytic currency to justify invoking it here. When we say that event *c* is the cause of event *e*, we mean that *c* contains all the necessary conditions for *e*, and that, given *c*, *e* had to occur. . . . A *description* of *c* will refer to only some of *c*'s traits, and this has led some philosophers to suppose that 'the cause' of an event is simply the most distinctive causally relevant preceding event. This is mistaken: *c* itself is the (entire) preceding event, although it may be the cause only in virtue of some of the descriptions it satisfies. Understood thus, a given event has only one cause" (1979, 81). This rules out the possibility of causal overdetermination. A point just argued.

13. According to Kane, "If this were not so, there would have been nothing we could have *ever* done to make ourselves different than we are—a consequence, I believe, that is incompatible with being (at least to some degree) ultimately responsible

(UR) for what we are" (2002b, 408). For more on the incompatibility of UR and determinism, see Kane (1996).

14. Kane would insist that the indeterminacies percolate up as part of the agent's self-system, hence are hers. But since they are nonetheless random, even if they are "hers" in this sense, what she does is still the result of a random event.

15. In response, Kane will probably say that the quantum event occurred inside the woman's self-system, whereas the man's quantum event occurred in the saw. Although true, the randomness of both events, which they have in common, seems much more important to the status of what happens than where the events happen. See below.

16. According to O'Connor, "Even though the causal indeterminist account allows for the real possibility of different courses of action, any of which would be 'controlled' by the agent in the minimal sense of being an 'outflow' of the agent, it's not 'up to the agent,' something he 'has a choice about,' just which potential cause will be efficacious in any given instance and so which action will actually occur" (2000, 29).

17. There may be another concern here as well. If Kane's account of control comes down to the agent being motivated by various wants, desires, and values, it's unclear whether these antecedent motivational states are themselves causally determined by prior life choices and settled dispositions. In a correspondence with Clarke, he appears to suggest that they are (see Clarke 2002). This would mean that in cases of SFA, the competing motivations that make up the agent's indecision (and represent his indeterminate effort of will) are *themselves* determined by antecedent sufficient conditions. If this is what Kane has in mind, it's unclear whether this is consistent with his demand for Ultimate Responsibility. Although the efforts of will that precede self-forming actions (and self-forming willings) must be actions for which the agent is ultimately responsible, it is allowed (it seems) that the efforts themselves be causally determined. Clarke has argued that this leads to a regress problem of sorts. "If the account of the freedom of an effort of will requires that the effort itself result from a prior free effort, then a vicious regress looms" (2002, 373).

18. Kane, for example, write: "I agree that if the physical description of these events were the only legitimate ones, then free will would look like nothing more than chance or probability. When neuroscientists describe it in physico-chemical terms, all they would get are indeterministic chaotic processes with probabilistic outcomes. In short, when described from a physical perspective alone, *free will looks like chance*. But the physical description is not the only one to be considered. The indeterministic chaotic process is also, experientially considered, the agent's effort of will; and the undetermined outcome of the process, one way or the other, is, experientially considered, the agent's choice. From the free willist point of view, this experiential or phenomenological perspective is also important; it cannot simply be dispensed with" (1996, 147).

19. Ross, in fact, claims "psychological research into the accuracy of introspection is the *most* powerful empirical constraint for the problem of free will" (2006, 134; italics added).

THREE

Against Compatibilism

I just argued that libertarian agent-causal accounts of freedom are philosophically and scientifically unacceptable because they are unable to preserve mental causation, a necessary condition for free will, and because they sacrifice important and well-founded scientific and metaphysical assumptions. In making my case against libertarianism, I also argued that: (1) To preserve psychophysical causation, some form of mind-brain physicalism (or materialism) must be accepted; and (2) Quantum mechanical indeterminacy, besides being unable to preserve purposeful free action, is irrelevant to the issue of free will since the wet-wear of the brain appears to rule out the possibility of such indeterminacy existing at the required levels. These two conclusions go a long way in establishing my thesis of hard(-enough) determinism. If we accept a materialist or physicalist account of the mind according to which all mental states are identical with brain states (or at least strongly correlated with brain states), and we agree that the fundamental principles of classical physics hold true at the level of the brain (a bio-physical organ), then we must conclude that the mind/brain is part of a deterministic system—whether or not there is indeterminacy elsewhere in the universe.

Of course, accepting determinism with regard to human agency does not alone establish my core claim—namely, that free will is an illusion—but it does bring us closer. If libertarian freedom does not exist, then we can at least conclude that one type of freedom (libertarian freedom) is an illusion. This victory, however, would be an empty one if libertarian freedom were not the kind of freedom we cared about. Hence, the goal of this chapter is to defend an incompatibilist understanding of freedom. Incompatibilists maintain that free will is at odds with determinism and that the two cannot be reconciled—if determinism is true, free will is impossible. Compatibilists (or soft-determinists), on the other hand,

59

maintain that our ordinary, folk-psychological notions of freedom and moral responsibility are completely consistent with the acceptance of determinism.[1] My thesis of hard-enough determinism is an incompatibilist one since it maintains that all human choice and action, and the underlying physical and psychological processes that give rise to them, are part of a causally determinate system such that no human action is free (properly understood). Although I find the libertarian position unacceptable on the whole, I do share with the libertarian two key tenets: (a) that if determinism is true (or true-enough) with regard to human agency, free will is an illusion; and (b) that the kind of freedom people care about—the kind that matters—is libertarian agent-causal freedom.

In this chapter, I challenge the claim that compatibilism reflects our pretheoretical beliefs and I present existing results and experimental evidence in social psychology to argue against the compatibilist thesis. In section 3.1, I spell out the compatibilist position and briefly discuss the standard incompatibilist argument—the so-called consequence argument. I also consider a number of traditional compatibilist replies and argue that they all face serious objections. In section 3.2, I then take a closer look at the folk psychology of free will and argue that, contra the compatibilist, recent empirical research by Shaun Nichols, Joshua Knobe, and others, reveals that our folk-psychological intuitions are essentially incompatibilist and libertarian in nature. I conclude in section 3.3 by examining the phenomenology of agentive experience and argue that it further undermines the compatibilist thesis. This chapter will represent my main reasons for rejecting compatibilism although I will raise additional concerns in the next chapter as well.

3.1 COMPATIBILISM AND THE CONSEQUENCE ARGUMENT

There are many different ways to state the compatibilist position but I will here focus on what some have called classical compatibilism (e.g., Watson 1975; Kane 2002a). According to classical compatibilism, as long as we do something we want to do—something we choose to do—and we are not constrained or impeded in any way, we are acting freely. Put in terms of the voluntary/involuntary distinction, we can say that free actions are those we do voluntarily, whereas unfree actions are those we do involuntarily (appropriately qualified).[2] Classical compatibilists typically maintain that "A physical barrier or even an internal compulsion or addiction can be an impediment to action; but when one acts simply because one wants to, one is not being impeded from acting otherwise. Hence, one is expressing one's freedom by doing what one wants" (Berofsky 2002, 182). A number of well-known philosophers have held versions of this position, including Thomas Hobbes (1654), David Hume (1743), John Stuart Mill (1860), W.T. Stace (1952), A.J. Ayer (1954), Moritz

Schlick (1939, 1966), Donald Davidson (1973), and Michael Levin (2004, 2007). Levin, for example, maintains that compatibilism rests, essentially, on three explicative definitions:

The Freedom clause: "Freedom" means "doing what you want to."

The Responsibility clause: "Agent A is responsible for action X" means "X happened because A wanted X to happen."

The Power clause: "A could have done otherwise" means "A would have done otherwise, had he wanted to." (2004, 426)

Levin acknowledges that these definitions need polishing, but they provide a good starting point for understanding the compatibilist position.

Classical compatibilism argues that the traditional free will debate is a "pseudo-problem," the product of a series of conceptual or terminological confusions. It maintains that, when the relevant terms are rightly understood, there is no inconsistency in holding to both free will and causal determinism. Levin, for example, maintains that "The Freedom clause certainly seems to capture the everyday meaning of 'free'" (2004, 426). Furthermore:

[T]he Freedom clause reconciles freedom with universal causal determinism. Under it, the causes of individual thoughts and actions may trace back to the Big Bang and certainly precede the birth of anyone now alive, yet still everyone acts freely every day. And this point of logic needs no explicit discussion of determinism generally, or genes, upbringing, environment, laws of nature, quantum mechanics, chaos dynamics or divine foreknowledge. (2004, 426)

W.T Stace likewise argues that if we accept the compatibilist definition, "then free will certainly exists, and the philosopher's denial of its existence is seen to be what it is—nonsense" (1952, 385). Compatibilists argue that free action is to be distinguished from unfree action not by the absence of causes, as incompatibilists insist, but rather by the type of causes at work. That is, free actions are caused by our desires, wants, or willings, whereas unfree actions are not.[3] As long as the action is caused by the inner psychological states of the agent, and is not externally or internally constrained or impeded, the action is free on this account.

A.J. Ayer, in his essay "Freedom and Necessity" (1954), defends this compatibilist definition by making a distinction between "causes" and "constraints." In contrast to traditional views that contrast freedom with causation—such that an agent who is caused to do something is not held to be acting freely—Ayer defines freedom in terms of constraint, such that anyone who is acting in the absence of constraint is considered to be acting freely.[4] In illustrating the distinction between cause and constraint, Ayer uses the example of a kleptomaniac and compares him to that of a "normal" man. The kleptomaniac, argued Ayer, is not free because he is constrained (or compelled) to steal. Even if the kleptomaniac resolved not to steal and told himself that he would pass up the merchandise, his compulsion would take over and in a sense force him to go against his desires. Since the kleptomaniac could not have done otherwise, even if he had wanted to, he is not free. On the other hand, argues Ayer, a normal man who steals is unconstrained and thus is acting freely. This leads Ayer to conclude:

> If this is correct, to say that I could have acted otherwise is to say, first, that I should have acted otherwise if I had so chosen; secondly, that my action was voluntary in the sense in which the actions, say, of the kleptomaniac are not; and thirdly, that nobody compelled me to choose as I did: and these three conditions may very well be fulfilled. When they are fulfilled, I may be said to have acted freely. (1954, 282)

According to Ayer, then, someone is free just in case, if they chose to do otherwise, they would have. This definition claims to reconcile freedom and causal determinism since it does not require one's actions to be uncaused or undetermined, just unconstrained. Ayer's basic idea is that causation, which is not freedom-undermining even in its deterministic forms, is often confused with compulsion or coercion, which is freedom-undermining.[5]

Some compatibilists add to this basic classical definition a further requirement—i.e., that there be an appropriate "mesh" or "hierarchal integration" between one's first-order and second-order desires (e.g., Frankfurt 1971; Dworkin 1970a, 1970b; Neely 1974). Some argue that this is needed to further distinguish between compulsives and so-called normals. Take, for example, the case of a degenerate or habitual gambler. According to Levin:

> No simple account in terms of preferences can tell their whole story, since even though a compulsive gambler placing a bet is doing what he wants, plainly he differs from normals. A plausible suggestion is that despite doing what he wants, he also wants, impotently, not to want what he wants; he wants not to want to gamble. Normals by contrast accept their desires. They eat when hungry and don't bemoan their getting hungry every few hours. A gambler does bemoan his urge to bet the rent and his yielding to it: he will hate himself tomorrow, and however much he wins he will be spurred to keep going until he loses. Yet despite these misgivings he bets, opening a gap between his preference and what he wants his preference to be. The tenacity of his preference thwarts his freedom, because he wants to banish or muffle it yet cannot do so. (Levin 2004, 430)

To exclude compulsives, then, many modern compatibilists define freedom as acting from desires you approve of or do not deplore. The compatibilist would argue that the compulsive in the above example has two desires: to gamble and to cease desiring to gamble. He satisfies one, the gambling desire, but not the other, the desire to suppress the desire to gamble. Contrary to normals, compulsives (like Ayer's kleptomaniac and Levin's degenerate gambler) are moved contrary to their higher-order desires or "volitions." Hence, for compatibilists "Analysis of compulsion and weakness of will into a first-order desire plus a higher-order desire about that desire refines the core idea of freedom as doing what one wants" (Levin 2004, 430).

Compatibilists that adopt such second-order or hierarchical theories maintain that the sort of freedom required for responsibility is essentially a function of an appropriate "mesh" or connection between an agent's choices or action and her other actional constituents like desires and preferences (see Haji 2002a, 210).[6] Harry Frankfurt (1971), in his seminal article "Freedom of the Will and the Concept of a Person," asserts that one essential difference between persons and creatures is to be found in the structure of persons' wills. Persons, unlike simpler animals and young children, are able to form second-order desires and "have the capacity for reflective self-evaluation that is manifested in the formation of second-order desires" (1971, 7)—desires to have or not to have various first-order desires. Simplifying quite a bit, Frankfurt maintains that free will and responsibility require that we assess our first-order desires and form "second-order volitions" about which of our first-order desires should move us to action. The first-order desires that move us to action are free, according to Frankfurt, when they conform with our second-order volitions—i.e., when we have the will (first-order desires) we want to have (second-order desires). When this occurs we "identify" with our wills.[7] Similarly, Dworkin's (1988) theory of personal autonomy appeals to the distinction between second-order and first-order desires. Dworkin proposes that a person is autonomous "if he identifies with his desires, goals, and values, and such identification is not influenced in ways which make the process of identification in some way alien to the agent" (1988: 61). The key idea behind these accounts is that when an agent reflects critically on a first-order desire and gives higher-order approval of that desire, the agent identifies with his will and hence is free and responsible.[8]

Although hierarchical accounts are, in many ways, an improvement over classical compatibilism, they remain compatibilist since they define free will in terms of conformity (or "mesh") between desires at different levels without requiring that desires at any level be undetermined. As Levin writes, "According to compatibilism, to be sure, minding or accepting one's desires is as much an effect of past causes as the desires themselves. Still, so long as nothing (including the agent himself) stops the agent from doing what he wants, he acts freely" (2004, 430). The question, then, is whether compatibilists are correct in thinking that free will and causal determinism can be reconciled in this way. Although many find compatibilism attractive since it allows us to "have our cake and eat it too" (Levin 2004, 433), many critics argue that the compatibilist conception of freedom is incoherent and that instead of solving the problem it only camouflages it (e.g., Taylor 1992; Hospers 1950a, 1950b; Kane 1996; Pereboom 1995, 2001). A long line of distinguished philosophers agree with Immanuel Kant when he says:

> It is a wretched subterfuge to seek to evade [the problem of determinism and freedom] by saying that . . . the actions of the human being, although they are necessary by their determining grounds which precede them in time, are yet called free because the actions are caused from within, by representations produced by our own powers, whereby desires are evoked on occasion of circumstances and hence actions are produced at our own discretion. (1788, 216-217)

The real question, critics insist, is whether or not our wants and desires are themselves caused. Since compatibilists have to concede that they are, because they accept or assume determinism,[9] critics charge that it does not preserve real freedom.[10] It is incoherent, they argue, to claim that an action is both free and causally determined. If the inner psychological states that determine our choices and actions are themselves causally determined, how can free will be preserved? As Brand Blanshard writes, "The real issue, so far as the will is concerned, is not whether we can do what we choose to do, but whether we can choose our own choice, whether the choice itself issues in accordance with law from some antecedent" (1958, 21). For reasons such as these, William James famously labeled compatibilism a "quagmire of evasion" (1884, 149) and Anscombe said it is nothing more than "so much gobbledygook" (1971, 146).

Compatibilists, nonetheless, insist that whether or not our inner psychological states are causally determinism is irrelevant. What is of real importance, they argue, is that the agent does as he/she wants (or that the agent's first-order desires conform to his second-order "volitions").[11] The only freedom that matters, according to compatibilism, is the ability to guide our conduct by means of our own wants and desires. As Levin puts it:

> An agent's wants can be effects of factors beyond his control, indeed preceding his birth, and the action they lead to be free, so long as the action is an effect of the wants. The sources of his wants don't matter; freedom is consistent with any account of those sources, including fully deterministic ones. Thus, my daily jog may well be a product of my genes, upbringing and current environmental stimuli, none of which I had a say in, yet I jog of my own free will since I jog because I want to (whatever caused that want). Genes, upbringing and environment produced a desire to exercise, and that desire—not kidnappers, not a gust of wind—caused me to move along the running track . . . I acted freely when I jogged yesterday, says compatibilism, insofar as I did what I wanted, and there, pending refinements, the analysis ends. (2004, 426)

Compatibilism believes that this is the appropriate definition of freedom since it accords with our everyday common usage. They maintain that our folk-psychological or commonsense notions of freedom and moral responsibility are completely consistent with determinism. They insists that in ordinary language freedom essentially means doing as we want to do, not some libertarian notion of freedom. They also insist that our ordinary conception of responsibility is perfectly consistent with determinism. What matters, compatibilists contend, is whether or not the agent acted voluntarily, not whether the action is determined by upbringing, heredity, personal psychology, brain chemistry, or the environment. This, they maintain, fits with our ordinary usage, and for most classical compatibilists common usage is the appropriate criterion for deciding how these notions should be defined (see, for example, W.T. Stace 1952; Ayer 1954; Levin 2004; Baumeister 2008; Perry 2010).

Levin, for example, writes: "Use fixes meaning, and 'free' is used of actions flowing from preference" (2004, 427). Stace goes further and maintains that "The [problem of free will and determinism] is merely verbal, and is due to nothing but a confusion about the meanings of words. It is what is now fashionably called a semantic problem" (1952, 383). He goes on to argue that the dispute can be resolved by examining what people ordinarily mean by 'free' and 'responsible.' He writes: "common usage is the criterion for deciding whether a definition is correct or not. And this is the principle which I shall apply to free will" (1952, 383). Ayer likewise maintains that the compatibilist definition must reflect our ordinary notion of freedom.

> It is indeed obvious that if we are allowed to give the word 'freedom' any meaning that we please, we can find a meaning that will reconcile it with determinism: but this is no more a solution of our present problem than the fact that the word 'horse' could be arbitrarily used to mean what is ordinarily meant by 'sparrow' is a proof that horses have wings. (1954, 278)[12]

Other compatibilists, although less explicit about the need to comport with ordinary usage and our folk-psychological intuitions, nevertheless maintain that the compatibilist conception of freedom and its cognates corresponds "to what laypersons generally mean when they distinguish free from unfree action" (Baumeister 2008, 14).

The obvious question, then, is whether the compatibilist is correct in assuming that our ordinary understanding of free will is a compatibilist one. Do people generally believe free will is compatible with their own inner psychological states being causally determined? I believe the answer is no, but I will explore this question more fully in the following section where I turn to empirical research in social psychology for support. Before doing so, however, I would briefly like to look at one of the more traditional incompatibilist arguments. There are a number of arguments against compatibilism but perhaps the most famous and direct incompatibilist argument is the so-called Consequence (or Modal) Argument (see Ginet 1966, 1980, 1983, 1990; van Inwagen 1975, 1983, 2000; Wiggins 1973; Lamb 1977). This is widely regarded as the best argument for the incompatibility of free will and determinism. It attempts to establish the conclusion that, if determinism is true, then it is never up to us how we act. Since this argument has been exhaustively discussed by others, and since those who are not yet convinced by it are unlikely to be persuaded by anything I have to say, I will only outline the argument and some possible replies before moving on to an alternative line of attack.

Although there are many different formulations of the consequence argument, we can follow van Inwagen in stating the basic idea as follows: "If determinism is true, then our acts are the consequences of the laws of nature and events in the remote past. But it is not up to us what went on before we were born; and neither is it up to us what the laws of nature are. Therefore, the consequence of these things (including our present acts) are not up to us" (1983, 16). According to the consequence argument, if it's not up to us whether certain things happen, then neither is it up to us whether the consequence of those things happen. Van Inwagen calls this the No-Choice Principle. Essentially it claims: If we have no control over certain things, then we do not have control over the consequences of those things, either. As van Inwagen points out, it is not up to us what went on before we were born, nor is it up to us what the laws of nature are—we simply have no control over those things. Hence, if we have no control over the laws and the past, and they have the consequence that we will act a certain way, then we have no control over how we act. This is a very powerful argument.

The consequence argument can be viewed as part of a more general incompatibilist argument. This standard incompatibilist argument can be stated as follows:[13]

1. The existence of alternative possibilities (or the agent's power to do otherwise) is a necessary condition for acting freely.
2. Determinism is not compatible with alternative possibilities (it precludes the power to do otherwise).
3. Therefore, determinism is not compatible with acting freely.

The consequence argument can be seen as a defense of premise (2), the crucial premise, since it maintains that, if determinism is true, the future is *not* "open" but is rather the consequence of the past (going back before we were born) and the laws of nature. According to the consequence argument, if determinism is true we lack genuine alternative possibility (and hence the ability to do otherwise) since, as William James puts it, "Possibilities that fail to get realized, are, for determinism, pure illusions; they never were possibilities at all" (1884, 151). The determination of an action, it is argued, renders an agent powerless to perform any alternative action. Hence, our belief that there is more than one choice we *can* make, more than one action we *can* perform, and more than one future which is *within our power* to bring about, must be an illusion if determinism is true. [14]

Compatibilists have a number of replies to this argument. The standard compatibilist reply has been to accept premise (1) but deny premise (2). Classical compatibilists typically grant that the agent's power to do otherwise is a necessary condition for acting freely, but deny that determinism precludes this power. In arguing against premise (2), classical compatibilists usually maintain that terms like *can, power*, and *ability* should be given a *conditional* or *hypothetical* analysis. They maintain that when we say that an agent *can* (i.e., has the *power* or *ability* to) do something, we mean that the agent *would* do it *if* the agent wanted (desired or chose) to do it. According to classical compatibilism, this type of conditional analysis fits common usage and allows us to see how the power and freedom *to do otherwise* can be reconciled with determinism. If the power to do otherwise means only that you *would have done otherwise if you wanted or desired*, so the argument goes, it would be consistent with determinism since it would not require changing the past or violating laws of nature. To say "you could have done otherwise" would only amount to the counterfactual claim that you would have done otherwise, if (contrary to fact) the past (or the laws of nature) had been different in some way. Conditional analyses of this type have been defended by the likes of G.E. Moore (1912), A.J. Ayer (1954), Aune (1967), Nielsen (1971), Lehrer (1980), and Levin (1979, 2004, 2007). [15]

On this compatibilist line, alternative possibilities and an agent's power to do otherwise are perfectly consistent with determinism. There are things you *can* do, even though the laws and the past have the consequence that you don't do them. The compatibilist accepts that you can't make the laws and the past be different, but nonetheless believes there are certain things you *can* make happen, such that, in a counterfactual situation where you do make those things happen, the laws or the past *would* have been different. Simply put, the compatibilist position maintains that it is *possible* for an agent to do *A* at time *t*, if and only if it is in the agent's *power* to do *A* at *t*. In turn they insist that this notion of *power* should be interpreted in a *conditional* or *hypothetical* way: An agent has the *power* to do *A* means the agent *would* do *A* if the agent *wanted, desired*, or *chose* to do it. Hence, it doesn't matter on this conditional analysis whether the agent's wants or desires are themselves determined.

Although this is an interesting and sophisticated way to counter the incompatibilist argument, there is growing agreement among philosophers that it fails. [16] In fact, some compatibilists have even abandoned conditional analyses, insisting that if compatibilism is to succeed it must find an alternative strategy (e.g., Lehrer 1976; Audi 1974; Berofsky 1987, 2002). The compatibilist Bernard Berofsky, for example, surveys the leading attempts to reconcile determinism with the ability to do otherwise and concludes: "The rebuttal of [the incompatibilist] position based on a hypothetical analysis of power is a failure" (2002, 198). He comes to this conclusion for a number of reasons but I will here focus on two. One early criticism of the conditional analysis was raised by C.A. Campbell (1951). As Berofsky describes it:

> Campbell (1951), the Scottish libertarian, challenged several underlying assumptions of the analysts with a lucidity equal to the best of their own practitioners. With respect to the hypothetical analysis, he observed that its truth is at best a necessary condition of the sort of freedom that is essential to moral responsibility. Campbell thereby reminded the analysts of the danger of divorcing the practice of philosophical analysis from the contexts that generate a concern in the issues. It is surely true that in everyday ascriptions of freedom, we often mean nothing more than that the agent would have acted differently had she chosen. But if she has no control over her choices, we would not hold her morally responsible. Thus, for moral responsibility, it must be the case that one could have chosen otherwise. (2002, 182)

Campbell also argues that it would not be enough to acknowledge the legitimacy of this demand but contend, as G.E. Moore does (1912, 93), that we are just insisting that the agent would have chosen differently had he made a different prior choice (see Berofsky 2002). A compatibilist could argue, for example, that one *does* have the ability to choose otherwise but in a conditional or hypothetical sense. Berofsky provides the following example: "an alcoholic could have chosen to refrain from alcohol yesterday because she would have if only she had not earlier chosen to resume drinking with the knowledge that she would likely become addicted" (2002, 183). Campbell, however, insists that the re-application of the hypothetical analysis at the level of choice or will is problematic. This is because the analysis lacks plausibility when the antecedent of the conditional whose consequence is "she would have chosen differently" refers to remote causal origins of choice. As Berofsky argues, "It may be true that I would have chosen differently had I been educated in a different way or had I been exposed to people with different personalities; but these facts do not imply that I, a person educated in a certain way and exposed to the people I was actually exposed to, now could have chosen differently" (2002, 182). For this analysis to be plausible, the antecedent of the conditional must refer to conditions the agent has some "ultimate control" or "authentic agency" over. The problem, however, is that determinism seems to leave no room for such authentic agency. Although there are different ways to define this somewhat amorphous idea, according to one prominent view, "an agent is morally responsible for her behavior only if the antecedent actional elements, like her values, desires, or beliefs that cause that behavior, are 'truly her own'; they are not, for example, the product of direct, surreptitious implantation" (Haji 2002, 202). There are many who argue, however, that if determinism is true, this "authenticity" condition can never be met because our spring of action is ultimately the product of events long before our births and hence products of external sources over which we have no control (see G. Strawson 1986; Kane 1995, 1996; Pereboom 1995, 2001).[17]

Another main criticism of the conditional or hypothetical analysis is that it appears to lead to a *regress problem* (see C.D. Broad 1952; Chisholm 1964b, 1966; Lehrer 1964). C.D. Broad, for example, defended incompatibilism by pointing out that it is possible to raise the question "But could the person have chosen differently?" at any level. To continually answer this question by re-applying the hypothetical analysis would lead to an infinite regress. As Berofsky describes the problem:

> If we demand that the person could have chosen differently, and we suppose that this power is constituted at least by the fact that she would have done so had she made a different prior choice, we must also demand that the person have been able to execute a different prior choice. It is then clear that the strategy of the hypothetical analysis fails, for no matter how often it is re-applied, it will never suffice to capture all relevant choices. There will always be a dangling choice over which, for all we know, the agent never had control. (2002, 183)

The problem for the compatibilist is that, having made my choice and acted upon it, the question remains: could I have chosen otherwise or not? As Taylor writes, "Here the [compatibilist], hoping to surrender nothing and yet to avoid the problem implied in the question, bids us not to ask it; the question itself, he announces, is without meaning" (1992, 45). According to the compatibilist, to say that I could have done otherwise means only that I would have done otherwise, if those inner states that determined my action had been different; if, that is, I had decided or chosen differently. But to ask whether I could have chosen or decided differently is, for the compatibilist, only to ask whether, had I decided to decide differently, or chosen to choose differently, or willed to will differently, I would have decided or chosen or willed differently. And this, as Taylor points out, "*is* unintelligible nonsense" (1992, 45). Taylor, however, goes on to argue:

> But it is not nonsense to ask whether the cause of my actions—my own inner choices, decisions, and desires—are themselves caused. And of course they are, if determinism is true, for on that thesis everything is caused and determined. And if they are, then we cannot avoid concluding that, given the causal conditions of those inner states, I could not have decided, willed, chosen, or desired other than I, in fact, did, for this is a logical consequence of the very definition of determinism. Of course we can still say that, if the causes of those inner states, whatever they were, had been different, then their effects, those inner states themselves, would have been different, and that in this hypothetical sense I could have decided, chosen, willed, or desired differently—but that only pushes our problem back still another step [italics added]. For we will then want to know whether the causes of those inner states

were within my control, and so on ad infinitum. We are, at each step, permitted to say "could have been otherwise" only in a provision sense—provided, that is, that something else had been different—but must then retract it and replace it with "could not have been otherwise" as soon as we discover, as we must at each step, that whatever would have to have been different could not have been different. (1992, 45-46)

It would seem that the compatibilist conception of *could have done otherwise* amounts to nothing more than the little "could" that "would" but can't so won't! The problem is that instead of reconciling determinism with the ability to do otherwise, the conditional interpretation merely pushes the problem back one step causing a regress. On this analysis, to say that *I could have done otherwise* means *I would have done otherwise if I wanted (or chose) to*. This only invites the obvious question: Do I have the freedom or ability to want (or choose) differently? For the compatibilist argument to work it would have to show that the *ability to want otherwise* is itself compatible with determinism; and here the conditional interpretation will not help.

Although I believe these objections are fatal, some compatibilists attempt to salvage hypothetical analyses by appealing to second-order or hierarchical accounts to make sense of the ability to want or choose otherwise. As Berofsky notes:

Some compatibilists select the antecedent condition of the hypothetical not because the person has control over its occurrence, but rather because the condition is supposed to reflect origination in the self. If a free agent is one who determines her own actions, and this is interpreted to mean that she does what she does because she wants to [and doesn't mind wanting to], then a case exists for analyzing the freedom to have done otherwise as "She would have done otherwise if she had wanted to." To be self-determined is to be determined by one's own desires. (2002, 187)

This seems to be what Levin has in mind when he writes:

I suggest that the worry that we are unfree because our actions are caused by desires (caused by genes and environment) in effect treats all desires as compulsions, external forces pushing the self where it doesn't want to go. This idea is plainly incoherent, since the self cannot *want* to resist desires without having (further) desires of its own. Do the self's own desires, if caused, coerce it? But then the self must have a further desire to fight its own desires, . . . and a regress is under way. This regress is stopped by identifying the self, metaphorically, with the desires and thoughts it is customarily said to have, or, less metaphorically, with whatever entity—brain or soul—those desires and thoughts are states of. Whatever their origin, your desires can't push you around, since they pretty much *are* you. Compulsions are felt as alien because they work against the bulk of other desires, hence are necessarily exceptional. (2004, 431)

For some compatibilists it makes perfect sense to talk about a want or desire to be "freely" chosen—in hierarchical terms, you want something "freely" if you want it because you want to want it, or don't mind wanting it. That is, hierarchical theorists will replace "acting from desire" with a superior candidate for self-determination, "perhaps acting from 'deepest desire' or 'desire arising from careful, rational, and independent reflection'" (Berofsky 2002, 187). Does this, however, save conditional analyses? I maintain that it does not.

Whatever advantage hierarchical accounts have in distinguishing compulsive desires from normal desires, such accounts cannot be employed here to salvage hypothetical analyses. For one, hierarchical accounts, though an improvement over classical compatibilism, have their own set of problems (see Haji 2002a; Slote 1980; Watson 1975, 1987). Furthermore, in taking this approach, "The defender of the hypothetical analysis would then rest her case against the infinite regress argument on the primacy of self-determination (understood in her terms) over power" (Berofsky 2002, 187).[18] This, however, is unsatisfying for two reasons. First:

> [I]f the power to be able to want (even deeply) otherwise is not important, why bother to insist upon a hypothetical analysis of freedom of action? Why say that a free agent is one who could have done otherwise, that is, one who would have done otherwise if he had wanted (deeply) to, if one regards self-determination, even in the absence of the power to do otherwise, as sufficient for freedom on the level of desire? Is not the position inherently unstable? (Berofsky 2002, 187-88)

In fact, some compatibilists indeed respond by saying that power at either level is unnecessary. These compatibilists maintain that the power to do otherwise is not a necessary condition for freedom and responsibility (e.g., Frankfurt 1969). This brand of compatibilism abandons the conditional analysis of 'can' and instead rest its entire case on the sufficiency of hierarchical accounts of self-determination to preserve freedom and responsibility (more on this approach in a moment). Secondly, hierarchical accounts seem to lead to their own regress problem (see Watson 1975; Shatz 1985; Friedman 1986; Christman 1991; Zimmerman 1981). As Haji writes:

> For an agent to be morally responsible by virtue of the conformity between his will and a second-order volition, V1, V1 must be freely willed. But for V1 to be freely willed, there must be conformity between V1 and some higher order volition, V2, which must in turn be freely willed and so requires a yet higher order violation, and so forth. (2002a: 212)

To arbitrarily stop the regress by appealing to some more basic conception of self-determination (one, for example, that simply requires an appropriate mesh between two levels of desires or some chosen set of desires), would be to once again fall victim to the previous objection. For these and other reasons, I reject the conditional analysis of power as a satisfactory response to the consequence argument.[19]

As an incompatibilist, I am persuaded by the consequence argument. I understand, however, that compatibilists will continue to insist that their definitions of *can*, *freedom*, and *power* fit with our folk-psychological theories and our commonsense usage of the terms. Despite what I have just argued, many compatibilists continue to believe that the spirit, if not the letter, of hypothetical analyses of power and freedom can be defended (e.g., Lewis 1981; Falk 1981; Audi 1993; Peacocke 1999; Levin 2004, 2007). For these compatibilists, one need not have *ultimate* control over his inner psychological states; all that is required for freedom is that one act voluntarily (or that one's first-order desires conform to one's second-order "volitions"). The compatibilist will insist that the consequence argument (and with it the regress objection) is flawed since it requires too much, or that the challenge it presents can be met with a proper understanding of 'could have done otherwise.' For the compatibilist, it is irrelevant whether our wants, desires, and choices are causally determined—in fact, they are willing to grant that they are—all that matters is that the agent does as he/she wants (appropriately understood). Incompatibilists will disagree, and it is here that the compatibilists/incompatibilist debate reaches its traditional stalemate. In the end, then, everything seems to come back to the fundamental question: *Which definition of free will, the compatibilist or incompatibilist one, actually fits best with folk psychology? What do people ordinarily mean when they talk of free will?*

Before I attempt to answer this question, I should also point out that there is another possible reply to the incompatibilist argument. Because of the various problems with conditional analyses, many contemporary compatibilists take an alternative approach. Instead of arguing against premise (2) by means of conditional analyses, some compatibilists—such as Harry Frankfurt (1969) and Daniel Dennett (1984)—have decided to question premise (1). These compatibilists attack the basic assumption upon which the incompatibilist argument rests—i.e., that the existence of alternative possibilities (or the agent's power to do otherwise) is a necessary condition for acting freely. Although compatibilists have historically been willing to grant that freedom requires the power to do otherwise, a growing number of contemporary compatibilists now deny this. Although this approach has the advantage of avoiding highly contested and problematic conditional analyses, it sacrifices, I believe, a crucial component of our ordinary notion of freedom. Most of us believe that when we deliberate, make choices, and act, we could have done other than what we did do. We also believe that this ability or power is an essential component of our freedom. To give up on alternative possibilities and the agent's power to do otherwise is, I believe, to give up on free will. For this very reason, this approach has been attacked by both compatibilists and incompatibilists alike (e.g., Widerker 1995a, 1995b, 2002; Kane 1985, 1996; Ginet 1996; Goetz 2005; Lamb 1993; Shatz 1997; Dworkin 1986; Audi 1991). Levin, for example, speaks for many classical compatibilists when he maintains that "freedom requires the ability to do otherwise" and writes: "Emphatically, [classical] compatibilists seek to preserve freedom in its full robust sense, which includes moral responsibility and the power to do other than we do . . . These ideas belong to our ordinary conception of ourselves, leaving any account of freedom that rejects them of little interest" (2004, 425). Incompatibilists further complain that many of the examples used to argue that agents can be free and responsible without being able to do otherwise, either beg the question or don't prove what they claim to (e.g., Widerker 1995a, 1995b, 2002; Kane 1985, 1996; Shatz 1997; Ginet 1996).

There are generally two types of arguments given in the compatibilist literature for denying premise (1)—the requirement that an agent acted freely, or of his own free will, only if the agent had alternative possibilities open to him, or could have done otherwise. The first kind of argument appeals to what has been called "character examples" (see Shatz 1997); the second kind appeals to what have come to be known as "Frankfurt-style examples"—named after Harry Frankfurt, who introduced the first example of this kind in his influential article "Alternative Possibilities and Moral Responsibility" (1969).

One of the best known arguments that appeals to *character examples* comes from Daniel Dennett (1984).[20] Dennett argues against premise (1) of the standard incompatibilist argument (the "could have done otherwise" requirement), offering as a counterexample the case of Martin Luther. According to Dennett, when Martin Luther famously said, "Here I stand. I can do no other," upon finally breaking with the Roman Catholic Church, he meant "that his conscience made it *impossible* for him to recant" (1984, 133). Dennett argues that, even if we assume that Luther was literally right about this—i.e., he could not then and there have done otherwise because his act was determined by his character and motives— this would not matter to Luther's free will or responsibility. According to Dennett, "[Luther's] declaration is testimony to the fact that we simply do not exempt someone from blame or praise for an act because we think he could do no other" or because we think his act was determined by his character (1984, 133). In fact, Dennett argues, we often praise the actions of individuals who are so good that in certain spheres they just cannot do the wrong thing. Dennett says of himself, for example, that he cannot be induced to torture someone for a thousand dollars:

I claimed it would not be possible to induce me to torture someone *for a thousand dollars.* Those who hold dear the principle of "could have done otherwise" are always insisting that we should look at whether one could have done otherwise in *exactly* the same circumstances. I claim something stronger; I claim that I could not do otherwise even in any roughly similar case. I would *never* agree to torture an innocent person for a thousand dollars. It would make no difference, I claim, what tone of voice the briber used, or whether or not I was tired and hungry, or whether the proposed victim was well illuminated or partially concealed in shadow. I am, I hope, immune to all such offers. (1984, 133-134)[21]

From these character-based examples, Dennett concludes that neither free will nor moral responsibility require alternative possibilities or the power to do otherwise; and hence neither requires the falsity of determinism.[22]

Although "character examples," like Dennett's Luther example, have undeniable appeal, they do not provide conclusive evidence that free will does not require alternative possibilities and hence that free will is compatible with determinism (see Kane 1985, 1996; Shatz 1997; Ekstrom 2000; van Inwagen 1989). Kane, for example, has argued that it may be true that Luther's "Here I stand" might have been a morally responsible act done "of his own free will," even if he could not have done otherwise at the time he performed it and even if his act was determined by his then-existing character and motives. But this would be true *only* to the extent that one could assume other things about the background of Luther's action that made him responsible or accountable for it—namely, that he was responsible by virtue of earlier choices and actions for making himself into the kind of person he now was, with this character and these motives, and that he could have done otherwise with respect to at least some of those earlier acts (Kane 2002a, 16; 1996, 37-40). If this were not so, argues Kane, there would have been nothing he could have *ever* done to make himself different than he was—a consequence that is difficult to reconcile with the claim that he is morally responsible for being what he is.

According to Kane and other critics, if Luther's affirmation did issue inevitably from his character and motives at the time it was made, then his moral accountability for it would depend on whether he was responsible *for being the sort of person he had become at that time.*

Those who know something about Luther's biography know about the long period of inner turmoil and struggle he endured in the years leading up to that fateful "Here I stand." By numerous difficult choices and actions during that period, Luther was gradually building and shaping the character and motives that issued in his act. If we have no hesitation in saying that he was responsible for the final affirmation, I think it is because we believe that he was responsible through many past choices and actions for making himself into the kind of man he then was. And, if this is so, the question of whether Luther could have done otherwise shifts backwards from the present act to the earlier choices and actions by which he formed his character and motives. If he is ultimately accountable for his present act, then at least some of these earlier choices or actions must have been such that he could have done otherwise with respect to them. (1996, 39-40)

If this were not the case, then what he was would have never truly been "up to him" because *nothing he could have ever done would have made any difference to what he was* (see Kane 1985, 1996). Kane's point is that we want to be responsible not just for our actions but also for our wills, that is for the very reasons that motivate our desires. And we can have this Ultimate Responsibility (UR) only if we could have done otherwise with regard to some choices or actions in our life histories.[23] If Kane is correct, then Dennett's examples do not conclusively establish the falsity of premise (1). We may still require the ability to do otherwise for those choices or actions that are responsible for the formation of our character (see also Shatz 1997; van Inwagen 1989; Ekstrom 2000; Russell 2002).[24]

Turning, then, to the other main attempt to refute premise (1), we come to the highly contrived scenarios known as Frankfurt-style cases. Although a precursor can be found in John Locke (1689), examples of this kind were originally developed by Frankfurt (1969) with the intent of undermining what he called the *Principle of Alternative Possibilities* (PAP): "[A] person is morally responsible for what he has done only if he could have done otherwise" (1969, 829). Although there are numerous versions of Frankfurt-style examples in the literature, such examples typically involve a controller who can make an agent do whatever the controller wants (perhaps by direct control over the agent's brain). The controller will not intervene, however, if the agent is going to do on his own what the controller wants. Frankfurt argues that if the controller does not intervene because the agent performs the desired action "for reasons of his own," the agent can then be morally responsible (having "acted on his own") even though the agent literally could not have done otherwise (because the controller would not have let him) (1969, 838). Here is a particular version of a Frankfurt-style case. Suppose Jones is in a voting booth deliberating about whether to vote for Barack Obama or John McCain. After reflection, he chooses to vote for John McCain and does vote for John McCain by marking his ballot in the normal way. Unbeknownst to him, Black, a conservative neurosurgeon working with the Republican Party, has implanted a device in Jones' brain which monitors Jones' brain activity. If he is about to choose to vote Republican, the device simply continues monitoring and does not intervene in the process in any way. If, however, Jones is about to choose to vote, say, Democratic, the device triggers an intervention that involves electronic stimulation of the brain sufficient to produce a choice to vote for the Republican (and a subsequent Republican vote is cast). Proponents of such examples maintain that because Black did not intervene in this case, it seems intuitive to say Jones "acted on his own" or "for reasons of his own," as Frankfurt puts it, and so Jones is responsible for his choice and action even though he could not have done otherwise.

Although many contemporary compatibilists consider Frankfurt-style examples to be a refutation of PAP, there are also many critics that argue that these examples do not refute every relevant form of PAP and do not show that moral responsibility and free will are compatible with determinism (Ekstrom 2002; van Inwagen 1978, 1983; Kane 1985, 1996; Lamb 1993; Widerker 1995a, 1995b, 2002; Ginet 1996; Copp 1997; Wyma 1997). Since the literature on Frankfurt-style examples has grown too large for me to do justice to it here, I will simply mention a few reasons for being skeptical of such examples and then move on to other matters. The first thing to note, as even some compatibilists are quick to point out, is that "most cases are not Frankfurt cases" (Perry 2010, 95). It's hard to imagine that such a contrived scenario could establish the sweeping conclusion that PAP has been absolutely refuted. Even Dennett, who endorses Frankfurt's analysis of these cases, believes this strategy (of attempting to refute PAP) is "insufficiently ambitious" (1984, 132). As Dennett points out:

> Although *he* takes his counterexamples to show that the 'could have done otherwise' principle—which he calls the principle of alternative possibilities—is irremediably false, his counterexamples are rather special and unlikely cases, and they invite the defender of the principle to try for a patch: modify the principle slightly to take care of Frankfurt's troublesome cases. (1984, 132)

In fact, this is exactly what a number of incompatibilists have done—they have modified PAP or introduced closely related principles to get around the kinds of concerns involved in Frankfurt-style cases (see, for example, van Inwagen 1978, 1983; Widerker 2002).[25]

A number of other critics have argued that the intuition Frankfurt and others have, that agents are morally responsible in such examples, begs the question against those who believe free will is incompatible with determinism (Kane 1985, 51; 1996, 142-145; Widerker 1995a, 1995b; Ginet 1996; Wyma 1997; Ekstrom 1998, 2002). This objection can be put in the form of a dilemma: either the proponents of Frankfurt-style examples are presupposing the truth of causal determinism (in which case they are begging the question against the incompatibilist) or they are presupposing the truth of indeterminism (in which case they are wrong in assuming the agent could not have chosen otherwise). To see how this objection works, consider the Frankfurt-style example just introduced. In the example, an inclination on the part of Jones to choose to vote for Obama serves as a sign for Black to intervene. An inclination to choose to vote for

McCain, on the other hand, can also serve as a sign for Black not to intervene. Let us suppose that Black's monitoring mechanism is programmed so that if Jones were to show an inclination to choose to vote for McCain, then this inclination would be a sign that Jones would do what Black wants him to do, namely, to choose to vote for McCain, and the mechanism would not intervene. Before we can judge, however, whether Jones is responsible for his actual choice (and subsequent action), we need to know more about the metaphysical presuppositions of the example. The question to ask is whether proponents of Frankfurt-type cases are assuming that causal determinism is true in the scenario. If they are, they seem to be begging the question against the incompatibilist for the following reason. If Jones's showing an inclination to choose to vote for McCain is causally sufficient for choosing to vote for McCain (or is regularly associated with something that is causally sufficient for this choice), then Jones's inability to vote for Obama is due to the assumption of determinism, not Black's counterfactual control mechanism. As Laura Ekstrom writes:

> [If causal determinism is assumed in the scenario,] then the counterfactual intervener is entirely *superfluous*, for agents in deterministic scenarios cannot do otherwise than act just as they do and could not ever have acted or decided otherwise. It is a mistake, then, for the [incompatibilist] to grant that the agent in a Frankfurt-style scenario is responsible . . . [F]or the compatibilist to assume that the agent is morally responsible under the assumption of determinism is question-begging in a context in which the relation between moral responsibility and alternative possibilities is at issue. (2002, 311)

If, on the other hand, proponents of Frankfurt-style examples are assuming indeterminism—maintaining instead that the inclination to choose to vote for McCain is *not* a sufficient causal condition of choosing to vote for McCain—then Black's monitoring of Jones's intentions cannot be said to remove the ability to *choose* otherwise. Under the assumption of indeterminism, critics argue, it is false that Jones could not choose otherwise—because even though the inclination to choose to vote for McCain occurs, Jones (libertarians maintain) could still *choose* to vote for Obama. With Jones free to choose to vote for Obama, however, the example fails to undermine PAP.

Although there have been attempts to respond to this objection by proponents of Frankfurt-style cases (e.g., Fischer 1999b, 2002a, 2002b; Hunt 2000; McKenna 2003), I do not believe they succeed in avoiding begging the question against the incompatibilist (see Goetz 2005). Stewart Goetz sums the problem up nicely in the following quote:

> [Frankfurt-style examples create] the appearance that it is Black's device, which is in the alternative sequence of events, that makes it the case that Jones is not free to choose otherwise. This appearance is *illuso-*

ry because without the obtaining of causal determinism in the actual
sequence of events, the device cannot prevent Jones from making an
alternative choice, and with causal determinism in the actual sequence
of events it is not the device that prevents Jones from making an alternative choice. In short, if Jones is not free to choose otherwise, it is
because of the occurrence of causal determinism in the actual sequence
of events and not because of Black's device in the alternative sequence.
Therefore, it is wrong to conclude that Jones is morally responsible
even though he is not free to choose otherwise. (2005, 85)

In the end, I believe both character-based examples and Frankfurt-style
examples fail to show that premise (1) of the standard incompatibilist
argument (or PAP) is not required for free will and responsibility. Of
course, as with conditional analyses, some compatibilists will disagree.
Ultimately, then, the question once again comes down to folk psychology—i.e., whether or not our ordinary, folk-psychological notions of freedom and moral responsibility require the ability to do otherwise.

Incompatibilists (like myself) insist that, *pace* Frankfurt and Dennett,
our ordinary notions of free will and responsibility actually do require
the ability to do otherwise. Furthermore, we maintain that our folk
psychology is essentially incompatibilist in that it views determinism as
being at odds with the existence of alternative possibilities and the
agent's ability to do otherwise. I maintain that instead of being a reflection of our pretheoretical beliefs, compatibilism is a complex philosophical position—one that is defended by sophisticated philosophical moves.
This, I believe, is witnessed by the compatibilist replies to the consequence argument discussed above. As Thomas Pink writes, "Compatibilism is not something naturally believed, but something that has to be
taught—by professional philosophers, in philosophy books, and through
philosophy courses" (2004, 43). I agree with Robert Kane that:

> [M]ost ordinary persons start out as natural incompatibilists. They be-
> lieve there is some kind of conflict between freedom and determinism;
> and the idea that freedom and responsibility might be compatible with
> determinism looks to them at first like a 'quagmire of evasion' (William
> James) or 'a wretched subterfuge' (Immanuel Kant). Ordinary persons
> have to be talked out of this natural incompatibilism by the clever
> arguments of philosophers. (1999, 217)

Although I believe "we come to the table, nearly all of us, as pretheoretical incompatibilists" (Ekstrom 2002, 310), I *am* a philosopher—and philosophers are not always the best guide to our pretheoretical beliefs! In
fact, both sides claim to reflect our ordinary, folk-psychological intuitions. How, then, can we move beyond the traditional stalemate? I propose that we examine our folk-psychological intuitions and judgments
empirically. The debate between compatibilists and incompatibilists ultimately comes down to who is right about our folk-psychological intui-

tions; and this, I maintain, is an empirical issue. The recent *experimental philosophy* movement proposes that we can shed new light on traditional philosophical problems by empirically studying our pretheoretical intuitions and judgments (see Knobe and Nichols 2008). This approach, I believe, can be especially helpful in the free will debate where both sides lay claim to commonsense. In the following section, then, I will present existing results and experimental evidence in social psychology that reveals that our folk-psychological intuitions are essentially incompatibilist and libertarian in nature.

3.2 THE FOLK PSYCHOLOGY OF FREE WILL

Philosophers have long argued that our folk psychology is inherently incompatibilist (e.g., Kane 1999; G. Strawson 1986), but only recently has the issue been explored empirically. Shaun Nichols (2004, 2006a), for example, has argued that recent work in developmental psychology on the understanding of agency in infants and toddlers indicates that young children deploy a notion of agent-causation. Nichols uses existing results as well as his own experimental data to support this claim. Appealing to the work of Meltzoff (1995) and Johnson (2000; Johnson, Slaughter, and Carey 1998; Johnson, Booth, and O'Hearn 2001), Nichols first argues that developmental research indicates that from a very early age children regard agents as distinctive and causal—"They quantify over agents, and they locate in the agent a causal power to produce an action" (2004, 482). This, however, is not yet enough to prove children are employing a libertarian notion of agent-causation. Children might regard agents as causes and also expect such causal activity to fit comfortably into a deterministic framework. Unfortunately for the compatibilist this does not seem to be the case. Nichols (2004), through some simply designed experiments, reveals that children also regard agents as having the robust capacity to do otherwise. According to agent-causal theories, an agent is an agent-cause of a given action only if the agent could have *not* caused it, that is, only if the agent *could have done otherwise*. Nichols's experiments indicate that children deploy just such a notion of agent-causation.

In one experiment, Nichols placed children in one of two conditions to investigate whether they regard agents as having the capacity to do otherwise.[26] Those in the *agent* condition (condition 1) witnessed an agent exhibit motor behavior; those in the *object* condition (condition 2) witnessed an object move. For instance, children in the agent condition were shown a closed box with a sliding lid. The experimenter said, "See, the lid is closed and nothing can get in. I'm going to open the lid." The experimenter then slid the lid open and touched the bottom. Children in the object condition were shown the same closed box with a ball resting on the lid; the experimenter then slid the lid open and the ball fell to the bottom. The children were asked whether the agent/object had to behave as it did after the lid was open, or whether it could have done something else instead. The results were very clear. Every single child said the person could have done something else and nearly every child rejected this option for the thing. In a second experiment, both children and adults were presented with cases of moral choice events (e.g., a girl steals a candy bar) and a physical event (e.g., a pot of water comes to a boil), and they were asked whether, if everything in the world was the same right up until the event occurred, the event *had* to occur.[27] In this setting, both adults and children were more likely to say that the physical events had to occur than that the moral choice events had to occur. According to Nichols, this provides evidence that the folk have an indeterminist concept of free choice on which agents *could have done otherwise*.

A compatibilist, of course, might object that this data is open to alternative compatibilist interpretations. Nichols, however, considers several alternative interpretations of the data and concludes:

> Given the results of the above experiments, I suggest, as a tentative hypothesis, that children regard agents as having the capacity to have done otherwise in a way that can't merely be reduced to a conditionalized analysis. The above experiments hardly rule out all the possible alternative interpretations. No small set of experiments could do that. But the evidence certainly fits the indeterminist interpretation. And there's not (yet) any evidence against it. On the contrary, the available evidence provides support for the claim that children embrace both claims of the agent-causal account. Apparently children think that an agent is a causal factor in the production of an action. They also seem to think that when an agent produces an action, he could have done otherwise, and moreover, that when an agent makes a moral choice, he was not determined to choose as he did. (2004, 488-489; see also 2006b)

I agree with Nichols that the data is best interpreted in an incompatibilist way, and to see why let us once again examine the leading alternative interpretation. According to the standard compatibilist approach, when people claim that an agent *could have done otherwise*, what they really mean is a tacitly conditionalized 'would' statement: i.e., the agent *would have done otherwise* if the conditions had been different. With regards to the present study, the compatibilist might say that when the children claimed that the agent *could have done otherwise*, they were only claiming that the experimenter *would have done otherwise* under different conditions. It is, no doubt, difficult to rule this possibility out completely. Nonetheless, I believe there are several reasons for not favoring this interpretation of the data. For one, as Nichols points out, "The contrast with the *thing*-case goes some distance to rebutting this interpretation. For nearly all the children said that the ball *had* to do as it did, but of course, children understand that the ball *wouldn't* have touched the bottom under different conditions, e.g. if the experimenter had turned the box over as he opened the lid" (2004, 486). If the children were deploying a conditionalized understanding of 'could have done otherwise,' one would expect that they would apply it to both *agent* and *thing* cases alike. Since they don't apply it in the *thing* case, I believe there is at least *prima facie* reason to think that they're not applying it in the *agent* case either.[28]

Secondly, as I pointed out in the previous section, there are serious philosophical problems with such conditional analyses and even some compatibilists have argued it does not successfully preserve free will or reflect our intuitive understanding of 'could.' Thirdly, and perhaps most importantly, one could turn the tables and ask: What psychological evidence do compatibilists have that people *actually* interpret *could have done otherwise* in this conditional way? The compatibilist provides us with a philosophically sophisticated interpretation of *could have done otherwise*, but what reason do we have for believing that people *actually* employ such a notion? It is simply not enough to present a *possible* interpretation of what *might* be going on. I contend that the compatibilist has to make a *plausible* case that people *actually* view matters in this way. There is, however, little empirical support for this conclusion. Quite to the contrary, Nichols (2006b) has recently conducted a pilot study that suggests just the opposite. In the study, 75 undergraduates were given the following vignette:

> On 4/13/2005, Bill filled out his tax form. At precisely 10:30 AM, he decided to lie about his income. But of course he didn't have to make this decision. Bill could have decided to be honest.

The subjects were then asked to judge whether a sentence sounded right or wrong (on a scale of 3 to -3). One group got the following sentence, modeled on conditional analyses:

> Bill could have decided to be honest at 10:30, 4/13/2005, but only if some things had been different before the moment of his decision.

The other group got the following sentence, modeled on unconditional analyses:

> Bill could have decided to be honest at 10:30, 4/13/2005, even if nothing had been different before the moment of his decision.

The results were telling. Subjects were more likely to judge that the unconditional sentence sounded right. They gave higher ratings for the sentence modeled on unconditional analyses than for the one modeled on conditional analyses. Although I think further studies here would be helpful, I agree with Nichols that "this helps to shore up the philosophical consensus that conditional analyses do not reflect the folk notion of *could have done otherwise*" (2006b, 306).[29]

Further support for the claim that people regard free will and choice as indeterminist can be found in experiments Nichols and Joshua Knobe

(2007) recently conducted. Nichols and Knobe presented adult subjects with a questionnaire that described both a determinist universe (A) and an indeterminist universe (B), described as follows:

> The key difference . . . is that in Universe A every decision is complete-ly caused by what happened before the decision—given the past, each decision *has to happen* the way that it does. By contrast, in Universe B, decisions are not completely caused by the past, and each human deci-sion *does **not** have to happen* the way that it does.[30]

After the description was read, subjects were asked, "Which of these universes do you think is most like ours?" The vast majority of subjects (over 90%) answered that the *indeterminist* universe (Universe B) was most like ours. Nichols and Knobe conclude that, since the only feature of the universe that is indeterminist is choice, the data indicates that people are committed precisely to the idea that choice is indeterminist. In a second study designed to test the folk-psychological notion of moral re-sponsibility, subjects were read the same descriptions of Universes A and B and were asked: "In Universe A [the deterministic universe], is it pos-sible for a person to be fully morally responsible for their actions?" Most subjects (86%) said "no." These results are especially telling because they further reveal an incompatibilist theory of moral responsibility.

Nichols and Knobe did, however, find exceptions to this conclusion. They found that there are certain experimental contexts in which subjects do express compatibilist judgments. Nahmias et al. (2006) have also re-ported such findings. But with regard to these cases, Nichols and Knobe write:

> Our hypothesis is that people have an incompatibilist theory of moral responsibility that is elicited in some contexts but that they also have psychological mechanisms that can lead them to arrive at compatibilist judgments in other contexts . . . [The] data show that people's re-sponses to questions about moral responsibility can vary dramatically depending on the way in which the question is formulated. When asked questions that call for a more abstract, theoretical sort of cogni-tion, people give overwhelmingly incompatibilist answers. But when asked questions that trigger emotions, their answers become far more compatibilist. (2007, 105-106)

In fact, Nichols and Knobe found support for the hypothesis that when people are confronted with a story about an agent who performs a moral-ly bad behavior, this can trigger an immediate emotional response, and this emotional response can play a crucial role in their intuitions about whether the agent was morally responsible. On their view, "most people (at least in our culture) really do hold incompatibilist theories of moral responsibility." It's just that, "in addition to these theories of moral re-sponsibility, people also have immediate affective reactions to stories about immoral behavior" (2007, 109). In fact, those experimental paradigms which elicit compatibilist responses generally share an interesting feature: they ask participants to consider concrete cases, often a type guaranteed to provoke affective responses. When subjects are offered questions that call for more abstract, theoretical cognition—questions that rely less on emotional reactions to immoral behavior—subjects markedly exhibit incompatibilist theories of moral responsibility. When, for example, Nichols and Knobe asked the abstract question whether anyone could be "fully morally responsible" in a deterministic universe, subjects tended to say "no."[31] This reveals that the compatibilist claim, that according to folk psychology moral responsibility is *completely* compatible with determinism, is simply mistaken.

Of course a compatibilist could object to the way Nichols and Knobe formulate their main question, but ultimately I believe this objection fails. The question Nichols and Knobe asked is whether we can be "fully" responsible in a deterministic universe. To this, most subjects (86%) say "no." Levin (in correspondence) objects that the implicature is that "fully responsible" is something other than "responsible." According to Levin, "since the subject does not see that something extra, and is only ready to agree that we are responsible, he denies that we can be fully responsible." Although I cannot rule this possibility out completely, I find it highly unlikely. For one, these are rather robust results. It's hard to believe that 86% of participants were thrown by the addition of "fully." Furthermore, compatibilists still need to explain why roughly 95% of respondents describe Universe B (the one in which human decision making was indeterministic) as the one most like ours. On the plausible assumption that participants believe free will is absent in Universe A (the deterministic universe) and that responsibility requires free will, these findings are exactly what one would expect. Secondly, what is this "extra," apparently mysterious, conception of responsibility which agents are mistaking for ordinary, run-of-the-mill responsibility? What are the conditions of satisfaction for this type of responsibility, and why not think these are the conditions people ordinarily demand for responsibility? Compatibilists cannot beg the question here by assuming that the only acceptable or meaningful conception of responsibility is one that is *not* libertarian or incompatibilist. Thirdly, *even on this interpretation*, these results show that at least one form of responsibility is inconsistent with determinism—a conclusion that is, I maintain, troubling in itself. Lastly, and perhaps most importantly, subsequent studies have shown that similar incompatibilist responses were given when they were simply asking whether such people "should still be morally blamed" (Roskies and Nichols 2008). Hence, it does not appear that the incompatibilist response is an artifact of the way the question is phrased (see Sarkissian et al. 2010).

Incompatibilist intuitions about moral responsibility have also been documented and discussed by a number of other philosophers and psychologists (see Monterosso, Royzman, and Schwartz 2005; Vargas

2005, 2006a, 2006b; Feltz, Cokely, and Nadelhoffer 2009; Sarkissian et al. 2010). For example, Sarkissian et al. (2010) have recently extended the findings of Nichols and Knobe beyond their own qualification that "at least in our culture" most people hold incompatibilist theories of moral responsibility. Sarkissian and colleagues have recently conducted a cross-cultural study examining intuitions about free will in subjects from the United States, Hong Kong, India, and Colombia. Their results reveal a striking degree of cross-cultural convergence. In all four cultural groups, the majority of participants said that (1) our universe is indeterministic and (2) moral responsibility is not compatible with determinism. These results appear to rule out the possibility that the original findings of Nichols and Knobe reflect some idiosyncratic property of contemporary Western culture, and instead point to "some more fundamental truth about the way people think about human freedom" (Sarkissian et al. 2010, 346).

In another recent study conducted by Monterosso, Royzman, and Schwartz (2005), participants were asked to complete questionnaires designed to examine the tendency of scientific explanations of undesirable behaviors to mitigate perceived culpability. Participants were presented with four vignettes depicting personally or socially undesirable behavior and were given two different *explanation-types* for each behavior: *physiological* and *experiential*. Monterosso and his colleagues found that physiological explanations of behavior tend to undermine responsibility attributions significantly more than experiential explanations that appeal to the agent's history or experience. For example, when a physiological (e.g., neuro-chemical) explanation of a particular action was given, subjects were less likely to blame the agent than when experiential explanations were given. In addition, physiologically explained behavior was more likely to be characterized as "automatic," and willpower and character were less likely to be cited as relevant to the behavior. In commenting on these findings, Manuel Vargas predicts: "If this trend holds . . . what we should expect to find . . . is that when underlying physiological features are emphasized (e.g., Ajay's brain chemistry) this will lead to exculpatory judgments more frequently than cases that ignore these aspects and instead focus on what deliberation was like for the agent" (2006a, 250). The findings of Monterosso and his colleagues definitely point in this direction.[32] Yet how could a compatibilist explain this? In theory, if compatibilism were correct about our folk psychology we shouldn't find this. Compatibilism maintains that our folk-psychological notions of free will and moral responsibility are compatible with determination by antecedent conditions—which, in theory, should include determination by neuro-chemical brain activity. If free will and antecedent determination are compatible, then why would explanations of behavior based on physiological causes diminish or undermine ascriptions of moral responsibility? The simplest and most obvious answer is that the folk view certain types of deterministic explanations as incompatible with moral responsibility—more specifically, physiological explanations disincline the folk to ascribe responsibility.

If all this research is correct, this is bad news for compatibilism since the whole compatibilist project is an attempt to reconcile causal determinism with our commonsense understanding of free will. I think Vargas says it best when he writes:

> First, these results yield something of a victory for incompatibilists. Incompatibilists need not—indeed they generally do not—deny that there are conditions under which we operate with compatibilist notions of abilities. What incompatibilists maintain is free will and moral responsibility (in some important sense(s)) are incompatible with determinism. For compatibilism to be a meaningful position, it must hold that there is *no* important sense in which free will and moral responsibility are incompatible with determinism. However, if Nichols' data are correct, contra to what traditional compatibilists have claimed, we really do imagine ourselves to be agents with genuine, metaphysically robust alternative possibilities available to us. Moreover, we really do—at least in moments of cool, abstract consideration—tend to favor an alternative possibilities requirement on moral responsibility. On the plausible assumption that these senses are important—and minimally, they are important for our self-conception—it turns out that compatibilism is dead wrong about there being no important sense in which free will and moral responsibility are incompatible with determinism. (2006a, 243-244)

If it turns out that our common sense intuitions regarding free will are wholly or largely libertarian and indeterminist, the compatibilist project comes crashing down. No longer can the compatibilist maintain that their (re)definition of free will reflects (or is equivalent to) our ordinary conception, nor can they appeal to our folk-psychological intuitions as unequivocal support for their position. If ordinary folk are pretheoretical incompatibilists who believe in indeterminist free will, then compatibilists are no longer justified in affirming that their theory elucidates our *ordinary* conception of freedom and its cognates.[33]

Additional Folk-Psychological Commitments

In addition to the above results, a closer examination of our folk metaphysics (our collective commonsense intuitions regarding metaphysical matters) reveals other libertarian commitments. Paul Bloom, a developmental psychologist, has persuasively argued that young children have a number of philosophically ill-mannered commitments. In his fascinating book, *Descartes' Baby* (2004), he presents several studies that reveal that a major component of our folk psychology (at least in the West) is our belief in dualism—the belief that the mind is fundamentally different from the brain. According to Bloom, the belief in dualism comes naturally to children and this dualistic worldview persists in adulthood. Accordingly, "we are dualists who have two ways of looking at the world: in terms of bodies and in terms of souls. A direct consequence of this dualism is the idea that bodies and souls are separate. And from this follows certain notions that we hold dear, including the concepts of self, identity, and life after death" (2004, 191). This widespread belief in dualism provides further proof that our folk psychology is inherently libertarian (especially agent-causal) and not compatibilist. Belief in dualism fits nicely with belief in agent-causal powers, and many agent-causal theories adopt dualist metaphysics (e.g., Foster 1991; Eccles 1994; Swinburne 1986). In many ways, these two beliefs go hand-in-hand. Bloom, in fact, suggests that the belief in indeterminist free will is another piece of this central dualistic worldview.[34]

If compatibilists are going to insist that our folk-psychological intuitions are inherently compatibilist, they should focus not only on intuitions about moral responsibility—which, again, are often incompatibilist (Nichols 2004; Nichols and Knobe 2007)—but also take account of intuitions like these. Our folk psychology reveals a robust folk metaphysics, and it would be disingenuous of compatibilists to focus only on those intuitions that support (or sometimes support) their position while ignoring those that don't. There is reason to think that folk-psychological dualism plays a major role in intuitions and ascriptions of moral responsibly. In the study conducted by Monterosso and his colleagues, we saw that physiological explanations of behavior tend to undermine responsibility attributions significantly more than experiential explanations. Monterosso, Royzman, and Schwartz speculate that this might have to do with an underlying commitment to dualism in ordinary person perception. They write:

> Put together, these three propositions—(1) mind (soul) and body are two separate entities capable of independently affecting human behavior; (2) behavior is voluntary and "owned" by the self only insofar as it flows from the mind and soul; (3) alternative, independently plausible, and non-contradictory accounts of human action can undercut each other—may elucidate why, in our vignettes, when a physiological explanation was given, there was a tendency for participants to view the body as the cause of the behavior, and motivations as less relevant, with the result that the behavior was perceived as less voluntary...More generally, in viewing the mind and body as two mutually exclusive attributional suspects (as opposed to alternative levels of analysis), the stage is set such that advances in the physiological behavioral sciences progressively shrink what is left to attribute to the intentional agent. (2005, 155)

Given the plausibility of this hypothesis, compatibilists cannot ignore the folk-psychological acceptance of dualism. If Bloom and others are correct, dualism is a major part of our folk psychology, and any account of our folk-metaphysical conception of free will needs to take into account and make sense of these other metaphysical commitments. Here compatibilism fails.

3.3 THE PHENOMENOLOGY OF FREEDOM

Why are our folk-psychological notions of freedom and responsibility incompatibilist and libertarian? There are a number of possible reasons. For one, the folk concept is pre-scientific, hence unencumbered by deterministic presuppositions. Children appear to acquire folk-psychological theories about free will and moral responsibility pretty early on. At such an early stage of development, the child is not hampered by scientific theories and need not reconcile personal experience with a scientific understanding of the world. In addition, there are probably developmental and social reasons for why our folk-psychological notions persist even after we become acquainted with scientific claims about determinism. Bloom and Weisberg, for example, have recently argued that:

> [The] developmental data suggest[s] that resistance to science will arise in children when scientific claims clash with early emerging, intuitive expectations. This resistance will persist through adulthood if the scientific claims are contested within a society, and will be especially strong if there is a non-scientific alternative that is rooted in common sense and championed by people who are taken as reliable and trustworthy. (2007, 997)

Bloom and Weisberg use this hypothesis to explain why people continue to believe in such non-scientific posits as dualism, creationism, and the existence of supernatural entities. It is natural, however, to apply this analysis to the problem at hand. If, as Nichols's research indicates, agent-causal intuitions about human agency emerge early in childhood, one reason why they might persist (despite exposure to scientific claims to the contrary) is that we live in a society where scientific claims about determinism are contested with regard to human behavior and where non-scientific alternatives are rooted in common sense and championed by reliable and trustworthy people.

In addition to the above suggestion, there is perhaps a more fundamental reason why we find the belief in incompatibilist freedom so compelling. I maintain that our phenomenology strongly supports an incompatibilist, libertarian, essentially agent-causal conception of free will. My thesis is that our folk psychology is inherently incompatibilist because such incompatibilism is experientially encoded in us (cf. Bayne 2008; Foster 1991; Ginet 1990; Pink 2004; Searle 2001a). In subsequent chapters I will attempt to explain *why* we experience ourselves as possessing libertarian freedom, but for the moment I will simply say that *if* we experience ourselves as having incompatibilist freedom this is, at least *prima facie*, important in shaping our pretheoretical beliefs. Although other factors may be relevant, it's natural to think that our phenomenology plays a major role, perhaps the central role, in shaping our pretheoretical beliefs about human agency and free will. If true, compatibilists cannot simply neglect or dismiss the nature of agentive experience. The important question, then, is whether or not we actually experience ourselves as exercising incompatibilist freedom—and here, I believe, our phenomenology is rather definitive.[35]

From a first-person point of view, we feel as though we are *self-determining agents* who are capable of acting *counter-causally*.[36] The phenomenology of volitional agency includes (at a minimum) a feeling of being undetermined by antecedent events, a feeling of origination and self-determination, and a feeling that one could have done otherwise. Put more inclusively, we all experience, as Galen Strawson puts it, a sense of "radical, absolute, buckstopping *up-to-me-ness* in choice and actions" (2004, 380). This feeling of *up-to-me-ness*, I maintain, is inherently libertarian in nature. It includes, for example, an experience of the *self-as-cause*, where the self is perceived largely as libertarians describe. From the first-person perspective, the phenomenology of agency presents in experience "a self that is an apparently embodied, apparently voluntarily behaving, agent" (Horgan, Tienson, and Graham 2003, 323). Horgan and colleagues have argued, for example, that "your phenomenology presents your own behavior to you as having *yourself as its source*, rather than (say) presenting your own behavior to you as having your own occurrent mental events as its source" (2003, 325). If true, our phenomenology reveals a sense of *self* that does not fit with compatibilist metaphysics. As Tim Bayne writes:

> I am not at all convinced that we ever experience ourselves as homunculi, strictly speaking, but I do think there is something to the idea that in acting we experience ourselves as *things*—as substances rather than bundles. Bundle theories of the self might be correct as accounts of the self's ultimate nature, but they do not seem to have much going for them as accounts of how the self is represented in agentive experience. It's not just that the experience of the self is neutral on the question of whether or not the self is a bundle—instead, it seems to be flatly inconsistent with such a view. (2008, 194)

In addition to experiencing a robust sense of self, we also perceive ourselves to be uncaused causes. When I perform a voluntary act, like reaching out to pick up my coffee mug, I feel as though it is *I*, myself, that causes the motion. We feel as though we are self-moving beings that are causally undetermined by antecedent events. As C.A. Campbell asks:

> Why do human beings so obstinately persist in believing that there is an indissoluble core of purely self-originated activity which even he-

redity and environment are powerless to affect? There can be little doubt, I think, of the answer in general terms. They do so, at bottom, because they feel certain of the existence of such activity from the immediate practical experience of themselves. (1967, 41)

Although this sense of *self*-agency (where the self is viewed as a thing/ substance capable of acting *ex nihilo*) may be an illusion, it is important that we acknowledge it as a phenomenological datum—one that is inconsistent with a belief in determinism. Agentive experience, I maintain, supports the kind of libertarian agent-causal position discussed in the previous chapter, not the compatibilist position.

Additionally, my feeling of *up-to-me-ness* is directly connected to my feeling of being able to have done otherwise. When we deliberate and make choices, and then go ahead and act on those choices, we *feel as though we could have decided or acted otherwise than we in fact did*. I take this feeling (along with the feeling of self-agency) to be the driving force behind the libertarian argument for free will. A compatibilist, of course, would offer a conditional analysis of could-have-done-otherwise here, but if what I've argued thus far is correct, this analysis is philosophically unsound and psychologically unjustified.[37] Additionally, it does not fit with our phenomenology. As one leading libertarian describes our experience:

> [W]e feel the final decision to be in our own hands; that whatever the external pressures or internal promptings, we feel it is ultimately up to us whether we yield to them or not . . . This is so even when the case in favour of a particular decision is overwhelming. Thus, taking account of both my self-interest and my moral duty, I now recognize an overwhelming case against jumping out of the (second-floor) window. None the less, I feel that I have the power to do it; and not just the power to do it if I choose, but the power, irrationally and gratuitously, to choose in that way. (Foster 1991, 267)

A conditional analysis of could-have-done-otherwise does not suitably capture this feeling. It is not as though we feel that if things had been different then we would have done otherwise. We actually feel as though we have the power to choose in a way that is not causally determined by antecedent events and conditions. Compatibilists have traditionally neglected phenomenology, focusing instead on the semantic analysis of the expression 'could have done otherwise.' This, however, is unfortunate. By focusing almost exclusively on a semantic solution to the problem of determinism, compatibilists have failed to take seriously the nature of agentive experience. And to the extent that agentive experience is important, and prima facie it is, compatibilists end up missing the mark.

I have here presented a number of arguments against the compatibilist thesis. In section 3.1, I spelled out the compatibilist position, presented the standard incompatibilist argument, and critically discussed the common compatibilist replies. Although I find the consequence argument convincing and the standard compatibilist replies philosophically unsound, the compatibilist/incompatibilist debate has traditionally been a war of intuitions. To help advance the debate beyond its current stalemate, I proposed that we examine our pretheoretical intuitions empirically. In section 3.2, I then presented existing results and experimental evidence in social psychology to argue against the compatibilist thesis. I argued that the findings of Shaun Nichols, Joshua Knobe, and Monterosso and his colleagues reveal that our folk-psychological intuitions are essentially incompatibilist and libertarian in nature. Although we might occasionally express compatibilist judgments—especially in cases of moral choice events that trigger emotional reactions—the findings suggest that our more abstract, theoretical reasoning is overwhelmingly incompatibilist. If correct, this yields something of a victory for incompatibilists. No longer can the compatibilist maintain that their definition of free will reflects (or is equivalent to) our ordinary conception, nor can they appeal to our folk-psychological intuitions as unequivocal support for their position. If ordinary folk are pretheoretical incompatibilists who believe in indeterminist free will, then compatibilists are no longer justified in affirming that their theory elucidates our *ordinary* conception of freedom and its cognates. I concluded in section 3.3 by arguing that the phenomenology of agentive experience further undermines the compatibilist thesis. The fact that we perceive ourselves to be self-determining agents capable of acting counter-causally is wholly inconsistent with a corresponding belief in determinism. The only avenue left for the compatibilist, then, is to defend a *revisionist* account of free will—one that proposes we accept a definition that deviates from our ordinary conception (e.g., Vargas 2005, 2007). To do so, however, would be to undermine the very goal of compatibilism. To give up our *ordinary* conception of freedom for a revisionist one would be to admit that what we ordinarily think of as free will *cannot* be reconciled with determinism.

NOTES

1. There is another position, *semi-compatibilism*, that maintains that although free will is *not* compatible with determinism, moral responsibility is (see Fischer 1999a, 1999b; Fischer and Ravizza 1998). According to Fischer, we are responsible if our decision-making mechanisms could have responded otherwise in a compatibilist sense—i.e., they would have responded otherwise to other inputs. Although I will not be discussing this position directly, I believe semi-compatibilism is subject to many of the same criticisms I will be presenting against compatibilism.

2. When I say 'appropriately qualified' I mean to include the traditional compatibilist proviso that free actions entail the absence of *constraints* or *impediments* preventing us from doing what we want, will, or choose. These are usually meant to include physical restraints, lack of opportunity, duress or coercion, physical or mental impair-

ment, and the like. In the following, I will drop this qualification (when appropriate) for the sake of brevity.

3. W. T. Stace, for example, defines free will as follows: "Acts freely done are those whose immediate causes are psychological states in the agent. Acts not freely done are those whose immediate causes are states of affairs external to the agent" (1952, 385).

4. In this way, Ayer's definition can be seen as an extension of Moritz Schlick's: "Freedom means the opposite of compulsion; a man is free if he does not act under compulsion, and he is compelled or unfree when he is hindered from without in the realization of his natural desires. Hence he is unfree when he is locked up, or chained, or when someone forces him at the point of a gun to do what otherwise he would not do. This is quite clear, and everyone will admit that the everyday or legal notion of the lack of freedom is thus correctly interpreted, and that a man will be considered quite free...if no such external compulsion is exerted upon him" (1939, 150). Ayer, however, adds to Schlick's list the concept of internal compulsion/constraint.

5. I should point out that not everyone is convinced that the freedom-undermining compulsion that Ayer discusses is as limited as he thinks. John Hospers (1950a, 1950b), for example, has argued that psychoanalysis shows that in both "normal" and "abnormal" cases there is deep inward compulsion by unconscious psychic forces, and this factor counts against the distinction that the compatibilist makes. He writes: "Is it true that all acts, though caused, are free as long as they are not compelled in the sense which he specifies? May it not be that, while the identification of 'free' with 'uncompelled' is acceptable, the area of compelled acts is vastly greater than he or most other philosophers have ever suspected?" (1950a, 389).

6. For this reason, some theorists also refer to these types of accounts as "mesh theories"—a term first introduced by Fischer and Ravizza (1998, 185) and later adopted by Haji (2002a). Mesh theories, which form an influential class of new compatibilist theories that go beyond classical compatibilism, can be further divided into a number of subclasses (see Haji 2002a). The most widely discussed of mesh theories are the hierarchical theories of motivation of Gerald Dworkin (1970b), Harry Frankfurt (1971), Wright Neely (1974), and others. Additional mesh theories not to be discussed here include "valuation" theories, such as that of Gary Watson (1975), and Susan Wolf's "reason view" (1990). For a good survey of these various mesh accounts, see Haji (2002a).

7. Haji (2002a) points out, however, that Frankfurt has offered several different accounts of the notion of identification (see 1987, 1988, 1992a, 1992b, 1993, 1994a). In one work, for example, he proposes that one identifies with a first-order desire when one has an unopposed second-order volition to act in accordance with it, and one judges that any further deliberation involving other higher order desires about the matter would result in the same decision (see 1987). But, as Haji writes: "In recent essays, Frankfurt appeals to a distinction between passivity and activity with regard to one's desires in order to explain identification. He says that the desires with which a person has identified are 'wholly internal to a person's will rather than alien to him; that is, he is not passive with respect of them' (1992b: 8). Further, 'insofar as a person's will is affected by considerations that are external to it, the person is being acted upon. To that extent, he is passive. The person is active, on the other hand, insofar as his will determines itself' (1994b: 437)" (2002a, 211). In addition to the variation in how identification has been defined, philosophers have further criticized Frankfurt's account(s) of identification on a number of different grounds (see Haji 2002a; Slote 1980; Watson 1987). There is the concern, for example, that identification can be "engineered" in such a fashion that the agent, contrary to the implications of hierarchical accounts, is not morally responsible (Haji 2002a, 212). Watson complains that "Frankfurt's distinctions illuminate the problem of compulsive desires, but fail to cope with problems about the genesis of one's second-order attitudes. For example, might not the citizens of the Brave New World have effective second-order volitions? Phenomena such as 'brainwashing' and 'indoctrination' seem to require a different treatment from compulsive desires" (1982, 7; see also Slote 1980). Haji further worries that hierarchical

accounts like Frankfurt's are too internalist; "they are insufficiently sensitive to how one acquires one's springs of action" (2002a, 212). Although I believe there are potential problems with Frankfurt's account(s) of identification, I will set aside such worries here and focus instead on more general concerns with the compatibilist approach.

8.   Another concern I will not address here has to do with how first- and second-order desires are perceived. Some critics have argued that hierarchical accounts rest on the unwarranted assumption that the agent's "real self" is to be identified with the cluster of his higher order volitions and those lower order elements selected by them (Haji, 2002, 212; Thalberg, 1989; Berofsky, 1995).

9.   Most compatibilists accept determinism. Michael Levin, for example, writes: "Compatibilists usually agree that free will does require behavior at least to be determined, since you cannot freely do what is beyond your control, and what happens causelessly, randomly, is beyond anyone's control" (2004, 425). And W.T. Stace, writes: "The only reasonable view is that all human actions, both those which are freely done and those which are not, are either wholly determined by causes, or at least as much determined as other events in nature" (1952, 385). For those compatibilists who may not themselves accept determinism, they at least assume the truth of determinism for the sake of argument since they are trying to show that it is compatible with freedom and responsibility. An example of such a pro tem compatibilist is David Lewis in "Are we free to break the laws?" (1981).

10.   Richard Taylor, for example, argues that soft determinists are committed to the following three claims: "(1) that the thesis of determinism is true, and that accordingly all human behavior, voluntary or other, like the behavior of all other things, arises from antecedent conditions, given which no other behavior is possible—in short, that all human behavior is caused and determined; (2) that voluntary behavior is nonetheless free to the extent that it is not externally constrained or impeded; and (3) that, in the absence of such obstacles and constraints, the causes of voluntary behavior are certain states, events, or conditions within the agent himself; namely, his own acts of will or volitions, choices, decisions, desires, and so on" (1992, 44). He goes on to argue that these three claims are inconsistent (see 1992).

11.   For the sake of brevity, when it is not of importance, I will drop this additional refinement of the compatibilist conception of doing as one wants.

12.   Ayer at least seems to maintain this in "Freedom and Necessity" (1954). Ironically, in his later work, *Metaphysics and Common Sense* (1969), Ayer backs away from his earlier claim that compatibilism reflects our ordinary sense of freedom. He write: "In common with many other philosophers I used to hold that . . . the antithesis between the claims of free will and determinism was illusory, but in so far as this is a question of what people actually believe, I now think it more likely that I was wrong" (1969, 238-239). He goes on to say that the issue of what ordinary people think about freedom and responsibility is "indeed a matter for a social survey"—a challenge I will take up in section 3.2. He nonetheless speculates that "I should however expect it to indicate that if it were shown to them that a man's action could be explained in causal terms, most people would take the view that he was not responsible for it" (1969, 239).

13.   See Kane (2002a, 11).

14.   Robert Kane (1996) has argued that his condition of *Ultimate Responsibility* (UR) is also incompatible with determinism. Recall that for Kane, ultimate responsibility for an action requires either that the action not be causally determined or, if the action is causally determined, that any determined cause of it result (at least in part) from some action by that agent that was not causally determined. According to Kane, "If this were not so, there would have been nothing we could have *ever* done to make ourselves different than we are—a consequence, I believe, that is incompatible with being (at least to some degree) ultimately responsible (UR) for what we are" (2002b, 408). For more on the incompatibility of UR and determinism, see Kane (1996).

15.   David Hume was perhaps the first to propound a conditional analysis of freedom in *An Enquiry Concerning Human Understanding*: "By liberty, then, we can only mean a power of acting or not acting according to the determinations of the will; that

is, if we choose to remain at rest, we may; if we choose to move, we also may. Now this hypothetical liberty is universally allowed to belong to everyone who is not a prisoner and in chains" (1743, 104). Even earlier Thomas Hobbes had expressed a similar sentiment: "For he is free to do a thing, that may do it if he have the will to do it, and may forbear, if he have the will to forbear" (1654, 240).

16. See C. A. Campbell (1951, 1957), Broad (1952), Ginet (1995), Austin (1956, 1966), Chisholm (1964b, 1966), van Inwagen (1983), and Lehrer (1964, 1966, 1968). For a good overview of these arguments, see Kane (1996) and Berofsky (2002).

17. Compatibilists typically reject the demand for "ultimate control" or "authentic agency," either because they find the concept incoherent or because they believe it is not required for free will and responsibility. As an incompatibilist, however, I maintain that a plausible account of the concept can be given and that the demand for such authenticity represents a real challenge for compatibilism. For more on this line of attack, see the articles cited above as well as my discussion of "character-based examples" further below. (Also see below for my reply to a possible compatibilist alternative based on hierarchical compatibilism.)

18. As Levin, himself, notes, "Crude compatibilism stops [the traditional] regress by flatly denying that desires are free. Hierarchical compatibilism . . . modifies this denial by counting desires caused by higher-order desires as free, but does not rescind it, since acts caused by undesired hierarchies of desires also count as free" (2007, 435 fn.8).

19. There are additional arguments that I have not discussed here. Keith Lehrer (1966), for example, presents "a simple and apparently devastating argument" (Berofsky 2002, 191) against all conditional analyses of power, whether it be the power of human beings or inanimate objects. Lehrer argues that no matter what C is, "If C, then S X's" cannot mean "S can X," for the former is compatible with "S cannot X." It would be the case that S cannot X if both (a) C were not present and (b) the absence of C rendered S incapable of doing X (see Berofsky 2002: 191). For more details see Lehrer (1966). For a reply to Lehrer, see Aune (1967). For Lehrer's reply see (1968).

20. Much of this paragraph mirrors Kane's discussion of Dennett's argument (see 2002a, 15).

21. Susan Wolf (1990) likewise draws our attention to individuals who are so good that in certain spheres they just cannot do the wrong thing. Both Wolf and Dennett maintain that, in such cases, since one's inability derives from one's own nature, not the machinations of some external force, the individual is free and responsible. Wolf and Dennett part ways, however, on the status of people who do the wrong thing. See Berofsky (2002, 190).

22. One criticism that I will not consider here has to do with the way Dennett spells out the relationship between responsibility and character. Paul Russell, for example, writes: "The view that Dennett defends is that in the realm of responsibility, what really interests us is what an action reveals about the character of the agent. More specifically, what we want to know is what we can *expect* from the agent in the *future* (1984: 137-38)" (2002, 245). Russell, however, complains that "This view is plainly at odds with our ordinary moral assumption that agents are no less responsible for out-of-character action than for action that is in character" (2002, 246).

23. In a similar fashion, Martha Klein (1990) has argued "that one of the things which disqualifies an agent from blameworthiness is his not having been responsible for the causes of his decisions or choices" (1990, 51). This conviction commits us, she says, to a *U-condition* for agent accountability; the condition that "agents should be ultimately responsible for their morally relevant decisions or choices—'ultimately' in the sense that nothing for which they are not responsible should be the source of their decisions or choices" (1990, 51). Klein's interpretation of the basic rationale behind the U-condition is that if agents' acts are caused by factors for which they are not responsible, it is not obvious how they can be responsible for acting as a result of those factors (1990, 50). Dennett, of course, would reply by maintaining that we do not need to be "absolute agents" capable of self-creation ex nihilo. According to Dennett, it is a

false dilemma to suggest that either we are "a completely self-made self, one hundred per cent responsible for its own character" or we are "mere dominos" in the causal chain (1984, 100, 156-157). In response to Dennett, however, Paul Russell has argued: "According to the U-condition theorist, this general line of reply entirely misses the point. It is not denied that agents may possess some relevant capacity to be 'reason-responsive' and to revise and alter their character on the basis of reflection. We might well be able to distinguish agents of this kind from individuals who lack these capacities (as new compatibilism suggests). Nevertheless, all this only postpones the fundamental difficulty. While our beliefs and desires may be subject to self-monitoring activities of various kinds, it remains true that these activities are themselves conditioned by factors that are not of the agent's own making. Reflection on this process, therefore, strips away our confidence that we are truly 'self-creators' *even in the normal case*. For this belief to be sustained, we must presuppose some power to undertake 'self-forming actions' that enable us to be the (ultimate) origin of our character and conduct" (2002, 244).

24. It should be noted that this type of criticism is not only unique to the incompatibilists cited above. The compatibilist Robert Audi (1991) has also emphasized the importance of responsibility for *character* as well as for individual actions. Audi's view allows him to concede the point Kane is making about a need for the power to do otherwise, but he is also one of those compatibilists who offers a conditional analysis of the power to do otherwise (1974, 1993) rather than denying its importance for responsibility.

25. Van Inwagen (1978, 1983), for example, has developed what John Fischer (2002b) has called the "divide and conquer" strategy of responding to Frankfurt-style examples. Van Inwagen argues that proponents of these cases are not sufficiently precise in specifying what the relevant agent is morally responsible for. As Fisher describes it: "We typically hold individuals morally responsible for various items, including actions, omissions, and consequences (envisaged either as 'particulars' or more coarsely individuated 'universals'). Van Inwagen's contention is that (in the Frankfurt-style cases and elsewhere) there is no one item of which it is true both that there is no alternative to it and that the agent is morally responsible for it. . . . Van Inwagen's diagnosis of the confusion of the proponent of the Frankfurt-style cases is that he is (perhaps implicitly) thinking of one sort of item when he is focusing on moral responsibility, and another when he is focusing on alternative possibilities" (2002b, 283). Van Inwagen essentially distinguishes four principles linking responsibility and alternative possibilities. (PAP): A person is morally responsible for what he has done only if he could have done otherwise. (PPA): A person is morally responsible for failing to perform a given act only if he could have performed that act. (PPP1): A person is morally responsible for a certain event-particular only if he could have prevented it. And (PPP2): A person is morally responsible for a certain state of affairs only if (that state of affairs obtains and) he could have prevented it from obtaining. Van Inwagen contends that (PPA), (PPP1), and (PPP2) cannot be refuted by Frankfurt-style cases. See van Inwagen (1978, 1983) for more details. For a criticism of van Inwagen, see Fischer (2002b). For what I believe to be a good reply to a number of Fisher's key points, and a solid defense of a number of objections to Frankfurt-style examples, see Ekstrom (2002). See also Widerker (2002) for additional responses to a number of new Frankfurt-style examples and a defense of a more limited version of PAP for at least one kind of moral responsibility—moral blameworthiness.

26. The mean age of participants was 4 years, 10.5 months. All of the children were at least three years old. This is important since some of the experiments required participants to answer counterfactual questions—and studies have shown that three-year-olds are good at answering simple counterfactuals questions, and four-year-olds can answer even somewhat complicated counterfactual questions (Harris, German, and Mills 1996; German and Nichols 2003).

27. Participants were required to answer comprehension questions correctly before proceeding.

28. A compatibilist could argue that the participants were employing two different senses of 'could have done otherwise'—intuitively distinguishing between doing something because one wants to (understanding that the wants themselves are causally determined) and events caused in other ways. A more plausible interpretation, however, is that the participants were employing an indeterminist conception of choice according to which the agent's actions were causally undetermined. Given the additional results to be discussed below (i.e., Nichols 2006b), I believe the burden of proof falls on the compatibilist to show that this is not the case.

29. Michael Levin (in correspondence) has objected that the formulation of the first sentence is unfair because the compatibilist does not hold that if Bill could have done otherwise things would have been different; he holds that if Bill had done otherwise things would have been different. Although Levin is certainly correct about the compatibilist's claim, I nonetheless think the formulation of the first sentence adequately captures the spirit of the conditional analysis. The choice between the two sentences is relatively clear. Subjects are essentially being asked to choose between two different interpretations of 'could have done otherwise': one that says Bill's ability to do otherwise requires that some things had been different before the moment of his decision (e.g., he had been raised in a different way, exposed to different people, or somehow had acquired a different set of motivational states); the other says, keeping everything the same up until 10:30 AM on 4/13/2005, Bill could have nevertheless decided otherwise. Since subjects overwhelmingly choose the latter, I believe this provides strong evidence against the compatibilist interpretation. I imagine, though, that a compatibilist could nonetheless defend something like the following alternative interpretation. They could agree that Bill could have been honest, even if nothing had been different, but maintain that the following counterfactual still holds true: *Even if nothing had been different*, Bill would have been honest if Bill had wanted to be honest (see Levin 2007, 452-455). Note, however, that this interpretation still requires the counterfactual ability to want otherwise. That is, for Bill to have wanted to be honest at precisely 10:30 AM on 4/13/2005, contrary to fact, he would have had to have been in a different set of motivational states (which, of course, still requires that "some things had been different before the moment of his decision"). I therefore conclude that these results provide *prima facie* evidence against the compatibilist interpretation. If compatibilists want to continue to maintain that conditional analyses reflect our folk intuitions, it now falls on them to provide empirical support for such a view.

30. This is only a portion of what was read to the subjects. Subjects were given further descriptions of Universes A & B. See Nichols and Knobe (2007) for more details.

31. Manuel Vargas (2006a) agrees with Nichols and Knobe that we hold incompatibilist theories of moral responsibility and points out that we need to keep our folk conceptual metaphysics separate from our pragmatic practices: "I am inclined to think that the Nichols and Nichols and Knobe evidence helpfully illuminates a perpetual challenge for working out the metaphysics of moral responsibility: distinguishing our genuine 'theoretical beliefs' (roughly, folk conceptual metaphysics) regarding moral responsibility from the pragmatic dimensions of holding people responsible. There are plenty of good pragmatic reasons for us to hold one another responsible, and for us to assume that a person is morally responsible, especially when they have brought about some strongly undesirable consequence. Indeed, the phenomenon of apparent overascription of culpability is familiar to legal scholars, and there is no reason to doubt that something similar is happening in the context of moral responsibility…The difficulty of reading our metaphysics off of our practices is that we run into the difficulty of distinguishing between the pragmatic elements of our practices and the underlying theoretical beliefs that make up the folk metaphysics concerning the practice" (2006a, 246-47).

32. They write, for example, "the stage is set so that advances in the physiological behavioral sciences progressively shrink what is left to attribute to the intentional agent" (2005, 155).

33. Vargas himself favors what he calls a *revisionist* approach, which attempts to combine the folk conceptual analysis of incompatibilism with the metaphysical minimalism of compatibilism (see 2005, 2006b, 2007). He believes that such an approach avoids many of the strongest objections leveled at both incompatibilism and compatibilism while picking up many of their chief advantages. Such a revisionist project, however, is very ambitious, and remains a goal rather than a theory. I also imagine that most compatibilists would not welcome such a project—see, for example, Perry (2010). Most compatibilists do not see themselves as offering a revisionist account of moral freedom (the freedom required for moral responsibility). On the contrary, they see themselves as elucidating the full concept, the whole meaning, of what is ordinarily conveyed by talk of 'freedom' and 'responsibility.' For my present purposes, then, I need not comment further on this revisionist project—but for a good critical discussion, see Fischer, Kane, Pereboom, and Vargas (2007). All I wish to establish here is that our folk-psychological conception of free will is an incompatibilist one. This corresponds to what Vargas calls the *descriptive* or *diagnostic* project, and on this central issue Vargas agrees that folk free will is incompatible with determinism (see 2006b, 2007). This conclusion, I maintain, undermines the traditional compatibilist project.

34. One could debate, however, the direction of causation between the two beliefs. For example, Nichols and Bloom appear to differ over this issue. Nichols writes, "While I agree with Bloom that people are intuitive dualists, I have a different view of the direction of causation. Bloom indicates that the belief in immortality and free will are consequences of a prior commitment to dualism. I would maintain that the situation is revered. We believe in dualism because we have intuitions of immortality and free will. That is, dualism is embraced because it fits with other aspects of our intuitive worldview, included the intuition that actions aren't determined and that we exist past biological death" (2006b, 319). For my present purposes, I need not take a stand on this issue. I am here simply concerned with making the case that our folk psychology is essentially indeterminist and incompatibilist.

35. In claiming that our phenomenology is overwhelmingly incompatibilist and libertarian in nature, I do not mean to imply that compatibilists cannot account for *certain features* of agentive experience (cf. Grunbaum 1953). Hierarchical accounts, for example, do a good job capturing the difference between acting on wants I approve of and acting on wants I disapprove of. Clearly the drug addict and kleptomaniac experience their actions differently than a person who acts on wants they do not mind having. This, however, is not the only, or even the most important, aspect of agentive experience.

36. As Vargas writes, "We tend to think of ourselves as having a powerful kind of agency, of the sort described by various libertarian accounts. That is, we see ourselves as having genuine, robust alternative possibilities available to us at various moments of decision. We may even see ourselves as agent-causes, a special kind of cause distinct from the non-agential parts of the causal order" (2007, 127).

37. "Philosophically unsound" for the reasons discussed in the previous section— e.g., the objections of C.A. Campbell (1951), Broad (1952), Berofsky (2002), and Lehrer (1964, 1968, 1980). "Psychologically unjustified" because compatibilists have failed to provide empirical evidence showing that people *actually* employ such a notion—in fact, to the contrary, Nicholas (2006b) provides *prima facie* evidence that conditional analyses do not reflect the folk notion of *could have done otherwise*.

FOUR

Consciousness and Free Will (I): Automaticity and the Adaptive Unconscious

I would now like to shift gears and begin to examine the relationship between consciousness and free will. There are a number of different positions one can take on the importance and role of consciousness in the free will debate, but at a minimum we can distinguish three main categories (Pink 2009). First, there are those who appeal to consciousness, especially the supposed consciousness we have of our own freedom, as evidence for the reality of free will. Secondly, there are those (like myself) who argue that a proper understanding of consciousness actually reveals that free will is an illusion. Lastly, there are those who simply maintain that consciousness is irrelevant to the free will debate. Of this last group, Thomas Pink writes:

> [M]any philosophers, especially in the English-language tradition, have taken the view that the question of free will has nothing to do with consciousness. For them the free will problem is about the correct semantic analysis of the expression 'could have done otherwise'; and such an analysis is to be provided simply by considering concepts or sentence meanings, without any reference to consciousness or experience. (2009, 296)

I maintain that this last approach is unacceptable because it fails to address several important questions. Any comprehensive theory, whether arguing for or against the existence of free will, needs to ask itself: Is consciousness necessary for free will? If so, what role does consciousness play in the exercise of free will? Furthermore, what percentage of our day-to-day lives are controlled and guided by unconscious states and processes? And do unconsciously caused actions threaten free will?

Those who wish to defend free will without any reference to conscious-ness (as many compatibilists attempt to do) fail to grasp the importance of these questions.[1]

Nowadays, the main threat to free will comes, not from abstract wor-ries over determinism or the conceptual analysis of concepts, but from scientific discoveries in the behavioral, cognitive, and neurosciences that suggest that *conscious free will* (or simply *conscious will*) is an illusion. Compatibilists have to either make room for these discoveries or chal-lenge their validity. They cannot, as they have traditionally done, simply sidestep the issue (see Sie and Wouters 2010). According to classical com-patibilism, we are free so long as we do what we *want* and are not exter-nally constrained or impeded. Compatibilists, however, seldom address whether such wants need to be conscious. They also fail to address whether or not their understanding of *control* and *ability* require con-sciousness. More sophisticated accounts of compatibilism, like *hierarchical accounts* and *mesh accounts*, suffer from similar problems. According to Frankfurt's hierarchical theory (1971, 1988), an agent is morally respon-sible *if and only if* it has a desire to act upon the desire that is its will. In his classic example, an unwilling addict who gives in to his overpowering urge to take a drug could not be said to want the drug-taking desire to be his will, and thus, is not a responsible agent. By contrast, a willing addict counts as responsible because he both *wants to take the drug* and he *wants the desire to take the drug to be his will*—i.e., both his lower- and higher-order desires are in agreement. The requirement of hierarchical integra-tion, however, is again *ambiguous* with regard to conscious and uncon-scious mental states. Do both our higher- and lower-level wants and desires need to be conscious for us to satisfy the required integration? Can one desire be conscious and the other not? What if we consciously *believe* our higher and lower desires are in agreement (and hence, there is the *appearance* of integration) but we are actually unaware of other uncon-scious mental states—states that *if conscious* would cause cognitive disso-nance? Furthermore, do hierarchical accounts assume infallible knowl-edge of our own minds? If so, is this defensible? If not, does this mean that third parties are equally good or perhaps better judges of whether or not we are acting freely?[2]

These are questions compatibilists must satisfactorily answer—and they must answer them in a way that is compatible with both our ordi-nary understanding of free will and what we now know about the uncon-scious mind. Until the compatibilist answers these questions he has no way of dealing with the growing realization (which will be the focus of this chapter) that our *conscious selves* may not be in the driver's seat.

In the past there have been those who have attacked compatibilism by appealing to a Freudian or psychoanalytic understanding of the uncon-scious mind (see Freud 1901; Hospers 1950a, 1950b, 1958). Freud, for example, "considered human behavior to be determined mainly by biological impulses and the unconscious interplay of the psychic forces those impulses put into motion" (Bargh and Chartrand 1999, 462). Since the individual was described as usually unaware of these intrapsychic struggles and of their causal effects on his or her behavior, Freud denied the existence of free will. In a similar fashion, John Hospers (1950a, 1950b) has argued that compatibilism is founded on a superficial view of being *compelled*. According to Hospers, compatibilists proceed as though all compulsion were external, but in fact psychoanalysis shows that there is deep inward compulsion. "What is not welcome news," Hospers maintains, "is that our very acts of volition, and the entire train of deliberations leading up to them, are but facades for the expression of unconscious wishes, or rather, unconscious compromises and defenses" (1950a, 390-91). Hence, according to Hospers: "We talk about free-will, and we say, for example, the person is free to do so-and-so if he can do so *if* he wants to—and we forget that his wanting to is itself caught up in the stream of determinism, that unconscious forces drive him into the wanting or not wanting to do the thing in question" (1950a, 392).

The argument I wish to make here, however, is significantly different than those of Freud and Hospers. My argument will be based, not on an outdated Freudian account of the unconscious, but on a modern understanding of what we can call the *adaptive unconscious* (Wilson 2002). I will argue that automatic and unconscious processes—which control far more of our day-to-day lives than previously believed—create a problem for compatibilism (and defenders of free will generally) because they undermine our folk-psychological understanding of free will and moral responsibility. I maintain that to whatever extent unconscious cognitive states and processes determine our actions, to that extent our actions fail to be free.

4.1 IS CONSCIOUSNESS NECESSARY FOR FREE WILL?

Let me begin by examining whether consciousness is necessary for free will. *Prima facie* it is. The folk-psychological concept of free will concerns the individual and actions that are under the individual's *active control.* We believe that we have the *power/ability* to act or not act in certain ways. The debate over free will typically focuses on whether or not the individual is an autonomous agent who, at least some of the time, is able to *choose* how to act from among multiple possible options. But does it make sense to allow for free will to be exercised unconsciously? I do not believe such a concept fits with our ordinary understanding of free will. When we say that an action is free, we typically mean (among other things) that it was the result of a voluntarily choice, *consciously willed.* Conscious will is seen as an essential aspect of free will (see Wegner 2002). As Hospers writes, "What people want when they talk about freedom, and what they hold to when they champion it, is the idea that the *conscious* will is the master of their destiny: 'I am the master of my fate, I am the captain of my soul'—and they surely mean their conscious self, the self that they can recognize and search and introspect" (1950a, 395). We seem to assume, almost on an axiomatic level, that for an action to be free consciousness must be involved in *intention and goal formation*. Meaningful, purposeful action seems "to aim towards a goal, as if pulled teleologically from the intention through to the intended effect" (Haggard 2005, 292). If there is no conscious intention to act one way or another, if there is no conscious will or volition involved, it's hard to see how the action can be considered free.

This is supported by the fact that we do not hold people responsible (or *as* responsible) for actions they did not consciously will or intend to do. We do not, for example, generally hold people responsible for involuntary actions or actions they performed while sleepwalking. We would not, for example, hold someone with Tourette's Syndrome responsible for a verbal outburst at an inappropriate moment (say at a funeral) precisely because the outburst was not consciously willed or under the conscious control of the agent. The same outburst by someone without Tourette's would, of course, be viewed differently. Since the conscious self has no control over such behavior, and there is no conscious intention present, we do not view the individual as the willful author of the act. The same is true for sleepwalking. Sleepwalking (also called *somnambulism* or *noctambulism*) is a parasomnia or sleep disorder where the sufferer engages in activities that are normally associated with wakefulness while he or she is asleep or in a sleep-like state. In some severe cases of somnambulism people have been known to perform very complex actions, including rearranging furniture, cooking meals, walking around their neighborhood, and even driving. Given that sleepwalking is a parasomnia manifested by automatism, we do not usually hold people responsible for actions performed while in such a state. In fact, there have been several reported cases of people committing murder while sleepwalking. In trials involving these cases, the defendants have pleaded not guilty on the grounds that they were not aware of what they were doing and hence not in control. Such defenses have often been successful, in part because *conscious intent* is one of the legal standards used for judging premeditation.[3]

If one were to hold that consciousness is *not* required for free will, he would have to allow for the possibility of a fully free, autonomous, and responsible somnambulist, yet to do so would be to depart dramatically from our ordinary understanding of free will. Although minimal awareness may still be present in cases of somnambulism, the kind of consciousness we typically associate with control, authentic agency, and self-determination is missing. In fact, to see just how important the assumption of *conscious will* is to our understanding of free will, try imaging an automaton—someone who lacks conscious awareness *altogether*—but who possesses free will. The difficulty, or perhaps even impossibility, of imagining such a being reveals just how important consciousness is to our ordinary conception of free will. For this reason, I do not believe it makes sense (at least not under any normal conception of freedom) to call actions that are performed automatically and unconsciously—actions that are not consciously controlled, guided, and willed—free actions. In fact, as David Hodgson points out, it is widely assumed that "in significant choices we are consciously aware of experiences, thoughts (including thoughts in which we attend to *beliefs*), and/or feelings, that provide *reasons* . . . for one or more of the available alternatives" (2005, 6). It is intuitive to think that consciousness is required for the kind of *reason-sensitivity* we typically associate with free will (see Searle 2000, 2001a; Hodgson 2005). In addition, as Bargh and Ferguson point out, "Willfulness is assumed to reside in consciousness, and, therefore, a lack of conscious involvement in a process implies it was not willed" (2000, 925-26; see also Bargh 1989, 1996, 1997).

Consciousness appears necessary for purposeful intentional action because it is assumed that consciousness is needed for the *executive control and guidance* required for free will. Timothy O'Connor, for example, claims that "This appears to follow from the very way in which active power has been characterized as structured by motivating reasons and as allowing the free formation of executive states of intention in accordance with one of the possible courses of action represented to oneself" (2000, 122). It is widely assumed (whether correctly or incorrectly) that consciousness is the source of intentional action and that without it *we*, our conscious selves, are not *in the driver's seat*—i.e., we lack the kind of authorship associated with agency.[4] The *up-to-meness* that we associate with 'freedom' applies to *intentional agency*—i.e., to things we can intentionally do or refrain from doing—but such agency seems missing when consciousness is absent. As Sean Spence notes, "The 'purposeful' acts which arise without consciousness seem either futile and ill-conceived (e.g., in somnambulism, fugue, and delirium) or mundane and repetitive (as in driving along a familiar route, or performing a simple manual task" (1996, 86). The fact that we do not view the actions of automatons or those performed while sleepwalking as free indicates that our folk-psychological understanding of free will requires conscious awareness. Since the executive control of consciousness is absent in such cases we do not ascribe freedom to the subject.

Further evidence that this assumption is essential to our folk-psychological doctrine can be found in a recent study by Stillman, Sparks, Baumeister, and Tice (2006; as reported in Baumeister 2008). They had participants rate scenarios that varied systematically along several dimensions. Participants rated people's actions as freest when, among other things, their choices were made after conscious deliberation. More specifically, participants rated people's actions as freest when their choices were made after conscious deliberation, when their actions went against external pressure rather than going along with it, and when people acted against their short-term self-interest. Baumeister concludes, "Thus conscious, rational choice and self-control seem to be integral parts of what people perceive as free" (2008, 16). Additional studies have found similar results.

Phenomenology is also relevant here. The fact that we experience ourselves as exercising *conscious will* is important because consciousness "provides the medium for the experience of free will, and beliefs pertaining to the latter" (Spence 1996, 78). Daniel Wegner (2002, 2003), for example, has recently demonstrated just how important the experience of conscious will is to the first-person phenomenology of agency. According to Wegner, "perhaps the most basic principle of the sense of will is that conscious thoughts of an action appearing just before an act yield a greater sense of will than conscious thoughts of an action that appear at some other time—long beforehand or, particularly, afterwards" (2002, 70). Actions that are not proceeded by relevant conscious intentions and thoughts typically feel more automatic and less willed. The importance of Wegner's work comes in his discovery that the first-person experience of agency can be dissociated from the actual causes of behavior—i.e., people may cause an action but experience no sense of agency or authorship, or they may experience themselves as causing an action that was actually triggered by external forces. With regard to the former, Wegner has documented a number of cases of *automatisms*—i.e. cases when we lose the experience of agency while performing voluntary actions (2002, ch.4).[5] On the other hand, Wegner has also demonstrated that individuals can *feel* they willfully performed an action that was actually performed by someone else when conditions suggest their own conscious thought may have caused the action (Wegner and Wheatley 1999).[6] This strongly suggests that the *perception* of conscious will (rather than actual conscious initiation of action) is essential to our experience of freedom. According to Wegner, "The [conscious] intentions we have to act may or may not *be* causes, but this doesn't matter, as it is only critical that we *perceive* them as causes if we are to experience conscious will" (2002, 65).[7] The fact that consciousness plays an essential role in our experience of free will is important because our *beliefs* regarding free will are inextricably entwined with the way we *experience* our actions. Our phenomenology, I maintain, plays a major role, perhaps the central role, in developing our pretheoretical intuitions. And it seems that both our phenomenology and our pretheoretical beliefs support the claim that, "Free will presumes that consciousness and choice intercede in the causal flow of events" (Brown 1996, 35).

This consciousness-requirement, though, is not only part of our folk psychology it is also widely assumed by philosophers and psychologists.

John Bargh (2008) has argued that in the field of psychology the primacy of conscious will is essentially a meta-assumption. Philosophers likewise give primacy to consciousness. This is most notable with libertarian agent-causal accounts, but is also true of other philosophical accounts. John Searle's *indeterminist* defense of free will, for example, is predicated on an account of what he calls *volitional consciousness*.[8] According to Searle, consciousness is essential to rational, voluntary action. He boldly proclaims: "We are talking about conscious processes. The problem of freedom of the will is essentially a problem about a certain aspect of consciousness" (2000, 9). Searle argues that to make sense of our standard explanations of human behavior, explanations that appeal to reasons, we have to postulate "an entity which is conscious, capable of rational reflection on reasons, capable of forming decisions, and capable of agency, that is, capable of initiating actions" (2000, 10).

David Hodgson (2005) presents a similar defense of free will. Like Searle he argues that free will exists in conscious voluntary action. He sets out to defend what he calls "A Plain Person's Free Will." In particular, he defends the *plain person's* intuition that a free action is determined by the conscious subject him/herself and not by external or unconscious factors. He puts forth the following *consciousness requirement* (which he believes is a requirement for any intelligible account of indeterministic free will): "[T]he transition from a pre-choice state (where there are *open alternatives* to choose from) to a single post-choice state is a conscious process, involving the interdependent existence of a subject and contents of consciousness." For Hodgson, this associates the exercise of free will with consciousness and "adopts a view of consciousness as involving the interdependent existence of a self or subject and contents of consciousness" (2005, 4). In the conscious transition process from pre- to post-choice, Hodgson maintains, the subject grasps the availability of alternatives and knows-how to select one of them. This, essentially, is where free will gets exercised.[9] For Hodgson, it is essential to an account of free will that subjects be considered as capable of being *active*, and that this activity be reflected in the contents of consciousness. He writes: "Again, this is intelligible and plausible: indeed, it is widely accepted that voluntary behavior is active conscious behavior" (2005, 5). Whether or not Searle and Hodgson's indeterminist defenses of free will succeed (I believe they do not),[10] I believe they get one very important thing correct: an essential, perhaps non-negotiable component of our everyday conception of free will holds that consciousness must play a role in the causing of "free" actions.

One might begin to think that this assumption is only held by libertarians, but it's important to recognize that it is also widely held by compatibilists. Some compatibilists have recently argued that free will is a product of evolutionary processes (e.g., Dennett 2003; Baumeister 2005, 2008). A number of prominent philosophers and psychologists now point to the evolution of complex cognitive processes as evidence of freedom. The evolutionary processes that seem to be of most importance, however, processes that distinguish *us* from other creatures and organisms that lack free will, include conscious deliberation, decision-making, self-regulation, and plasticity. Roy Baumeister, for example, writes:

> My thesis is that free will can be understood in terms of the different processes that control human action and that, indeed, these differences correspond to what laypersons generally mean when they distinguish free from unfree action. To discuss free will in terms of scientific psychology is therefore to invoke notions of self-regulation, controlled processes, behavioral plasticity, and *conscious decision-making*. (2008, 14; italics added)

Baumeister proposes that the defining thrust of human psychological evolution was selection in favor of cultural capability—i.e., the ability to live together in societies. He writes:

> That process might well have included a new, different way of controlling behavior, whose purpose was enabling the beast to function in a complex, information-based society. The hallmarks of this new form of behavioral control include personal responsibility, conscious deliberation, invoking abstract rules and principles to guide actions, autonomous initiative, and a capacity to resist urges that have earlier evolutionary roots but that may be incompatible with civilized life. (2008, 16)

I am not here concerned with the truth or success of this account. Rather, I am simply interested in showing the importance these evolutionary accounts of freedom place on consciousness. Baumeister himself concludes that, "Conscious, controlled, and self-regulated processes seem likely to be important aspects of what people understand as free will" (2008, 18).

The compatibilist commitment to the primacy of consciousness can also be seen in more traditional accounts. Since compatibilists maintain that freedom of the will is compatible with determinism, what ultimately distinguishes *free actions* from *unfree actions* cannot be that one is caused and the other uncaused. Compatibilists instead maintain that an action is free if it is determined by *certain kinds of causes* and not others. What kinds of causes count as relevant for free will? Traditionally, compatibilists have pointed to the inner psychological states of the agent. Actions that have as their proximate causes external states of affairs—or internal, non-psychological states—are not considered free. What is of upmost importance to the compatibilist is that a *choice* or *volition* be part of the causal sequence. But do such choices and volitions need to be conscious? It would be hard to make sense of the compatibilist position if we allowed unconscious causes to count here as relevant. Unconscious "choices" are presumably involved in cases of sleepwalking, yet it would be counterintuitive to attribute free will to somnambulists. It cannot be, then, that *all* we care about is that the agent is unconstrained (as a Hobbesian compatibilist might say) or that his actions flow from his character (as a Humean might say). It's easy to imagine an example where a somnambulist is unconstrained and behaves in a way consistent with his character—e.g., cleaning the house or making himself a snack in the middle of the night. What we care about, then, and what most compatibilists presumably care about, is that our choices are the result of deliberation, that they are in line with our other wants and desires, that they are sensitive to reasons, and that they are willed. It is hard to see how deliberation that results in choice, or choice that is willed, can fail to be conscious. Although many compatibilists leave the importance of consciousness unstated, others are more explicit. For example, compatibilist hierarchical and mesh theories often require a conscious reflective process. As Henrik Walter describes this reflective process:

> An act—using an easily understood everyday intuition also employed in the courts of justice—is attributable to a person, if she has reflected upon it. The capacity for reflection means to weigh reasons for an action against its consequences and competing motives and to relate it to one's own person. Many compatibilists consider this production process to be the central component of any theory of free will: "Processes of free will are personal processes (involvement of the whole structured person) based on motivation conflicts that go through hierarchically ordered recursive loops and to a certain degree consciously represented personality instances" (von Cranach and Foppa 1996, p. 342). (2001, 263)[11]

Whether or not the requirement of conscious, executive control is tenable, the assumption is an important one. Anyone who defends an account of free will that makes consciousness inessential has to admit that they have abandoned the standard definition of free will.

The assumption that consciousness is necessary for free will is both widespread and plausible. Even those who refuse to enter into the debate over whether a conscious decision is necessary for free will—such as Roediger, Goode, and Zaromb (2008)—have to conclude "that the notion of unconscious volition is quite far removed from a straightforward conception of free will" (2008, 210). This is all I wish to establish. My aim here has simply been to establish the depth and importance of this assumption. Those theorists who attempt to defend a notion of free will that *does not* require consciousness must therefore realize that their conception is not compatible with our folk-psychological intuitions or the commonplace assumptions of most philosophers and psychologists. Of course one could defend a *revisionist* definition of free will, but to do so would be to relinquish one of the most important claims of compatibilism—that their definition corresponds "to what laypersons generally mean when they distinguish free from unfree action" (Baumeister 2008, 14).

One last point. Recall that Monterosso and his colleagues (2005) found that different kinds of explanations have significant effects on the perceived culpability of actors. They found that physiological explanations of inappropriate behavior mitigate responsibility attributions significantly more than experiential explanations. Consistent with these findings, I hypothesize that the more an individual sees an action or behavior as the result of processes outside the conscious control of the agent, the less willing they are to hold the agent at all responsible. In fact, this fits to a large degree with what Monterosso and his colleagues found: "[P]articipants were more likely to characterize the blame mitigation they indicated as having been due to the behavior being 'automatic' when the explanation was physiological as opposed to experiential, and this was true even controlling for ratings of culpability" (2005, 150-151). When participants judged the antecedent to be mitigating of blame, they were more likely to attribute their judgment to the actor's behavior having been automatic. Even though these studies were done with physiological explanations and not explanations involving unconscious psychological processes, I believe the fact that participants mitigated blame based on the perceived automaticity of the action reveals something important. There seems to be a direct correlation between ascriptions of moral responsibility and the perception that a behavior is "automatic"—i.e., the more one views a behavior as automatic (i.e., outside the conscious control of the agent) the less likely one is to ascribe moral responsibility. In fact, when a behavior was characterized as "automatic," willpower and character were less likely to be cited as relevant to the behavior. I am willing to predict that the kinds of explanations given below—explanations based on automatic, unconscious processes—would likewise mitigate ascriptions of blame.

Monterosso and his colleagues write, "the stage is set such that advances in the physiological behavioral sciences progressively shrink what is left to attribute to the intentional agent" (2005, 155). I would extend the threat of scientific explanations to include those that explain sophisticated, high-level behavior in terms of automatic, deterministic, unconscious processes. In fact, the psychologist John Bargh writes "it is hard to escape the forecast that as knowledge progresses regarding psychological phenomena, there will be less of a role played by free will or conscious choice in accounting for them" (1997, 1).[12] The question, then, is to what extent do our conscious wills control our actions and how pervasive are automatic and unconscious processes?

4.2 AUTOMATICITY AND THE ADAPTIVE UNCONSCIOUS

Recent research has revealed that unconscious cognitive processes control far more than we previously thought. John Bargh has gone so far as to argue that much of everyday life—thinking, feeling, and doing—is automatic in that it is "driven by current features of the environment (i.e., people, objects, behaviors of others, settings, roles, norms, etc.) as mediated by automatic cognitive processes of those features, without any mediation by conscious choice or reflection" (1997, 2). These unconscious processes can be placed into essentially two categories: lower-level cognitive processes—or what I will call *sub-mental* processes—and higher-level mental processes. The discovery of both types of cognitive processes are a threat to human freedom since it reveals that there is more to our choices, judgments, preferences, and actions than we are consciously aware of. In fact, some theorists have even come to question whether we *ever* have direct veridical access to the cognitive processes involved in evaluation, judgment, problem solving, and the initiation of behavior (e.g., Nisbett and Wilson 1977). Other researchers have gone so far as to suggest that the unconscious mind does virtually *all* the work and that consciousness is largely epiphenomenal (e.g., Velmans 1991; Wegner 2002). Though not everyone is prepared to relegate conscious thought to the epiphenomenal refuse heap, there is, as Timothy Wilson writes, "more agreement than ever before about the importance of nonconscious thinking, feeling, and motivation" (2002, 5).

Recent research into the *automaticity* of higher mental processes has provided compelling evidence for the determinism of those processes (see Bargh and Ferguson 2000; Bargh and Chartrand 1999). This research has revealed that social interaction, evaluation and judgment, problem solving, and the operation of internal goal structures can all proceed without the intervention of conscious acts of will and guidance.[13] Automaticity refers to control of one's internal psychological processes by external stimuli and events in one's immediate environment, often without knowledge or awareness of such control—as such, "automatic phenomena are usually contrasted with those processes that are consciously or intentionally put into operation" (Bargh and Williams 2006, 1). Reference to "nonconscious" or "unconscious" cognitive processes is now commonplace in the scientific, psychological, and philosophical literature.[14] It is traditionally assumed that processes that can occur without conscious involvement are paradigm examples of deterministic processes. This, in fact, is the traditional conception of determinism in cognitive and social-cognitive science (see Bargh 1989, 1996; Bargh and Ferguson 2000). As Bargh and Ferguson point out:

> According to this standard perspective . . . the complexity and the abstract, protracted nature of the kinds of mental processes and social

behavior that social-cognitive research has recently discovered to operate and occur without conscious, aware guidance have bestowed an
unprecedented legitimacy to the traditional conception of determinism.
(2000, 926)

Just as the earlier realization that figural synthesis in vision (e.g., Neisser
1967) can be accomplished without conscious decision-making implied
that the process was causally determined, the discovery of nonconscious
higher-level processes likewise indicate that they are determined. If what
I argued in the previous section is correct and conscious will is necessary
for freedom, the discovery that higher-level cognitive processes can be
carried out unconsciously threatens both libertarian and compatibilists
conceptions of free will. Libertarianism would be threatened because
such processes would be considered determined and hence unfree. Compatibilism would be threatened because it would face the daunting (and I
believe impossible) task of reconciling a plausible understanding of free
will with this kind of determinism by unconscious processes.

Many contemporary compatibilists ignore developments in the behavioral, cognitive, and neurosciences that purport to challenge our ideas
of free will and responsibility. Maureen Sie and Arno Wouters (2010)
believe this is because compatibilists simply view these developments as
additional support for determinism. Compatibilists appear to reason, "If
free will and determinism are compatible, the alleged support of determinism by the results of the [behavioral, cognitive, and neurosciences] cannot pose a threat to free will" (Sie and Wouter 2010, 123). The problem
with this response, however, is that it ignores the specific character of the
new compatibilist answer to the incompatibilist challenge. As Sie and
Wouter point out, "The new compatibilist approach is based on the idea
that personal responsibility is grounded not in our assumed ability to
choose otherwise, but in our ability to decide and act on the basis of
reasons" (2010, 123). Following the lead of P.F. Strawson's (1962) *reactive
attitudes* and Frankfurt's (1969) *hierarchical view*, many contemporary
compatibilists sidestep the whole issue of the compatibility of the freedom to do otherwise with the thesis of determinism. Instead of trying to
preserve *counterfactual* freedom, which they are willing to give up on,
these so-called *new compatibilists* focus instead on *reasons-responsiveness*
(e.g., Wallace 1994; Wolf 1981; Fischer and Ravizza 1998; Raz 2006). As
Sie and Wouter describe: "According to new compatibilism the ultimate
justification of our practices of responsibility lies in our ability to act for
reasons. Roughly, the idea is that we are responsible for what we do
because we are the kind of beings that can figure out what to do and
respond correspondingly" (2010, 125).[15] Joseph Raz, for example, maintains that individuals are only truly in control of their actions when they
are guided by reason, and individuals are only persons when they recognize and intend to act on the values which their reason allows them to

realize (2006, 3). Gary Watson likewise argues that the quintessential feature of willfulness is an individual's ability to evaluate, which requires reason (1975, 1987). For Watson, what's important is the active state of using reason to identify courses of action that are independently valuable and worthy of pursuit.

Ironically, though, it is precisely our ability to act for *conscious reasons* in relation to all the factors that influence us—including those we are not aware of—that the behavioral, cognitive, and neurosciences focus on. As we will now see, the assumed compatibilist connection between free will, on the one hand, and conscious rational choice, planning, evaluation, and self-control on the other, is seriously questioned by findings in the behavioral, cognitive, and neurosciences. Compatibilists are therefore wrong not to address and feel challenged by these recent scientific developments. I maintain, *this* form of determinism (i.e., determinism by unconscious processes and unnoticed features of the environment) truly threatens *all* senses of free will. Compatibilists cannot easily accommodate the insight that most of our everyday life is determined by automatic processes triggered by external cues.

The Adaptive Unconscious

Let's begin with a discussion of the adaptive unconscious. Timothy Wilson (2002) has used the term *adaptive unconscious* to describe the pervasive, adaptive, and sophisticated cognitive processes that occur without our conscious control or awareness. As Wilson describes the adaptive unconscious:

> The mind operates most efficiently by relegating a good deal of high-level, sophisticated thinking to the unconscious, just as a modern jetliner is able to fly on automatic pilot with little or no input from the human, "conscious" pilot. The adaptive unconscious does an excellent job of sizing up the world, warning people of danger, setting goals, and initiating actions in a sophisticated and efficient manner. It is a necessary and extensive part of a highly efficient mind. (2002, 6)

Wilson, however, makes an important point of saying that the adaptive unconscious is not the same as the Freudian psychoanalytic one. As Malcolm Gladwell describes the difference:

> The adaptive unconscious is not to be confused with the unconscious described by Sigmund Freud, which was a dark and murky place filled with desires and memories and fantasies that were too disturbing for us to think about consciously. This new notion of the adaptive unconscious is thought of, instead, as a kind of giant computer that quickly and quietly processes a lot of the data we need in order to keep functioning as human beings. (2005, 11)

Whereas Freud's view of the unconscious was largely based on the notion of repression, the modern view of the adaptive unconscious holds that "a lot of the interesting stuff about the human mind—judgments, feelings, motives—occur outside of awareness for reasons of efficiency, and not because of repression" (Wilson 2002, 8).[16] The mind is here viewed as a wonderfully sophisticated and efficient tool—far more efficient than any computer. An important source of the mind's power "is its ability to perform quick, nonconscious analyses of a great deal of incoming information and react to that information in effective ways" (Wilson 2002, 15-16). Our mind can interpret, evaluate, and select information that suits our purposes, even while our conscious mind is otherwise occupied. This distinction lies at the heart of recent dual process models of the mind (see Chaiken and Trope 1999; Cohen, Dunbar, and McClelland 1990; Posner and Snyder 1975).

For Wilson, the term "adaptive unconscious" is meant to convey that nonconscious thinking is an evolutionary adaptation.

> The ability to size up our environments, disambiguate them, interpret them, and initiate behavior quickly and nonconsciously confers a survival advantage and thus was selected for. Without these nonconscious processes, we would have a very difficult time navigating through the world. . . . This is not to say that nonconscious thinking always leads to accurate judgments, but on balance it is vital to our survival. (2002, 23-24)

One should not be surprised at the adaptive advantage of relegating such high-level mental activity to the unconscious. To quote Wilson again: "Consciousness is a limited-capacity system, and to survive in the world people must be able to process a great deal of information outside of awareness" (2002, 8). The basic processes of perception, memory, and language comprehension, for example, are all sub-mental cognitive processes that are inaccessible to conscious awareness—quite possibly because they evolved before consciousness did (Wilson 2002, 8). The adaptive unconscious, however, is not limited to such sub-mental processes. A full list of higher-level mental processes that can occur without the intervention of conscious deliberation, choice, and guidance, would include (but not be limited to): evaluation and judgment, reasoning and problem solving, social interaction, processing of stereotypes, the operation of internal goal structures, and the initiation of action.[17]

Before getting to these higher-level functions, let me first say something about the importance of sub-mental nonconscious processes. It is relatively uncontroversial now to view certain lower-level (or sub-mental) functions of the human mind—such as perceptual processing and language comprehension—as operating outside the reach of consciousness. These processes are typically viewed as inaccessible to consciousness. The cognitive psychologist George Mandler writes, for example,

"There are many systems that cannot be brought into consciousness, and probably most systems that analyze the environment in the first place have that characteristic. In most of these cases, only the products of cognitive and mental activities are available to consciousness" (1975, 245). As Neisser points out, "The constructive processes [of encoding perceptual sensations] themselves never appear in consciousness, their products do" (1967, 301). Recent research has made it increasingly clear that the majority of our perceptual and sensorial information is processed by modules that are cognitively closed off to consciousness. We have no conscious awareness, for example, of the processes that form perceptual representations, that bind the various sensory modalities, and that process visual, auditory, tactile, olfactory, and gustatory information. Consciousness only has access to the products of such processes, not to the processes themselves. Other cognitive systems that are not available to conscious experience include processes that control memory formation and storage, facial feature analysis, deep syntactic structure, affective appraisals, computational processes, language production systems, and many kinds of action systems.[18]

One should not underestimate the importance of these lower-level, or sub-mental, processes. Compatibilists may not feel threatened by these nonconscious processes, but this is partly because they fail to realize the close tie of these processes to behavior. The sub-mental nonconscious processes that monitor our environment can have significant effects on behavior—effects that we are unaware of and do not consciously control, will, or intend. Sophisticated behaviors can be automatically triggered and guided through the perception-behavior link (see Chartrand and Bargh 1999a; Bargh and Chartrand 1999; Bargh, Chen, and Burrows 1996; Dijksterhuis and van Knippenberg 1998). There is now evidence that submental perceptual processes can trigger higher-level mental processes, and subsequently sophisticated patterns of behavior, in a completely unconscious and automatic way. As Chartrand and Bargh describe:

> The existence of an automatic, unintended, and passive effect of perception on behavior has important ramifications for whether social behavior can occur nonconsciously and without intention. If the effect of perception on behavior is automatic, then direct environmental causation of social behavior could be produced in a two-step process. The first would involve automatic (i.e., not effortful or consciously guided) perceptual categorization and interpretation of social behavior (environment to perception), with this perceptual activation continuing on to activate corresponding behavioral representations (perception to behavior). In this way, the entire sequence from environment to behavior would occur automatically, without conscious choice or guidance playing a role. (1999a, 894)

If the perception-behavior link, through the kind of two-step process just outlined, can automatically and unconsciously trigger and guide sophisticated patterns of behavior, compatibilists should be sure not to treat these unconscious perceptual processes lightly. To be clear though, the fact that our perceptual mechanisms and processes occur outside of conscious awareness does not itself cause a problem for free will. Rather, it is the potential effects these processes can have on higher-level mental processes (and subsequently on behavior) that causes the problem.

Let me turn, then, directly to those higher-level unconscious processes that are more troubling to defenders of free will. Let me begin with an interesting experiment conducted by Antoine Bechara and his colleagues (1997). Bechara et al. had participants perform a gambling task in which behavioral, psychophysiological, and self-account measures were obtained in parallel. The gambling task was designed to simulate real-life decision-making in the way it factored in uncertainty, rewards, and penalties. Participants were given four decks of cards, a loan of $2000 facsimile U.S. bills, and asked to play so as to win as much money as possible. In the experiment, turning each card carries with it either a reward or penalty. For example, turning cards in decks A and B carries an immediate reward of $100, while turning cards in decks C and D brings a reward of only $50. However, cards in decks A and B carry a higher penalty than cards in decks C and D. The game is set up so that playing from the disadvantageous decks (A and B) leads to an overall loss, while playing from the advantageous decks (C and D) leads to an overall gain. The players, however, have no way of predicting when a penalty will arise in a given deck, no way to calculate with precision the net gain or loss from each deck, and no knowledge of how many cards they must turn to end the game.

Bechara et al. found that participants began to choose advantageously before they consciously realized which strategy worked best. He found that after about 10 cards participants began to generate anticipatory skin conductance responses (e.g., their palms began to sweat) whenever they pondered a choice that turned out to be risky, before they knew explicitly that it was a risky choice. At about the same time (around 10 cards) they began to avoid decks with large losses. It wasn't until much later, at about 80 cards, that they were able to explain why decks C and D were better in the long run. And it wasn't until about 50 cards—forty cards after the gamblers started generating stress responses to the risky decks—that they were able to say they had a "hunch" that something was wrong with those decks. Bechara et al. conclude: "The results suggest that, in normal individuals, nonconscious biases guide behavior before conscious knowledge does" (1997, 1293). Without the help of such biases, they maintain, overt knowledge may be insufficient to ensure advantageous behavior. They argue that "the automatic responses we detected are evidence for a complex process of nonconscious signaling, which reflects access to records of previous individual experience" (1997, 1295). There appears to be two parallel (though, perhaps, interacting) processes going on here: one conscious and one unconscious. As Malcolm Gladwell puts it:

> What does this Iowa experiment tell us? That in those moments, our brain uses two very different strategies to make sense of the situation. The first is the one we're most familiar with. It's the conscious strategy. We think about what we've learned, and eventually we come up with an answer. This strategy is logical and definitive. But it takes us eighty cards to get there. It's slow, and its needs a lot of information. There's a second strategy, though. It operates a lot more quickly. It starts to kick in after ten cards, and it's really smart, because it picks up the problem with [decks A and B] almost immediately. . . . It's a system in which our brain reaches conclusions without immediately telling us that it's reaching conclusions. (2005, 10)

This experiment provides some insight into the power and role of the adaptive unconscious. It reveals how high-level, sophisticated behavior—like choosing cards from a deck—can be guided by automatic, unconscious assessments of our environment.

Most of us assume that our decisions and actions are guided by conscious executive control. We assume that we are consciously and systematically processing incoming information in order to construe and interpret our world and to plan and engage in courses of action. This assumption, I've argued, plays a major role in our folk-psychological understanding of free will and responsibility. Experiments like this, however, reveal how questionable this assumption is. Here you have an example of a quick and efficient unconscious process that appraises risk—one that is not guided by conscious will, deliberation, or choice. Participants begin generating stress responses to the risky decks and start favoring the advantageous decks about forty cards before they are able to even report a "hunch" of what is going on, and about seventy cards before they are able to verbalize why decks C and D are better in the long run. It seems "Our conscious mind is often too slow to figure out what the best course of action is, so our nonconscious mind does the job for us and sends us signals (e.g., gut feelings) that tell us what to do" (Wilson 2002, 36). Why does the adaptive unconscious detect and figure out what's going on well before the conscious mind does? Precisely because consciousness is a limited-capacity system, and "to survive in the world people must be able to process a great deal of information outside of awareness" (Wilson 2002, 8).

It has long been argued that consciousness is a limited-capacity system (e.g., Kahneman 1973; Miller 1956; Posner and Synder 1975), but recent studies on "ego depletion" conducted by Baumeister and his colleagues have demonstrated just how limited our conscious self-regulatory capacities are (Baumeister et al. 1998; Muraven, Tice, and Baumeister 1998; Muraven and Baumeister 2000). In a series of experiments, Baumeister et al. (1998) found that an act of conscious self-control in one domain seriously depletes a person's ability to engage in self-control in a subsequent, entirely unrelated domain. Baumeister and his colleagues used the term ego depletion to refer to this state of reduced self-regulatory powers or self-control stemming from prior exertion.[19] They consistently found that people performed relatively poorly at almost any self-control task if they had recently performed a different self-control task. Baumeister et al. found, for example, that resisting the temptation to eat chocolates and cookies caused people subsequently to give up faster on difficult puzzle problems. They also found that ego-depletion resulting from acts of self-control interfered with subsequent decision making by making people more passive. Muraven and colleagues (1998) likewise found that after people tried to control their emotional responses to a film, their physical stamina was reduced. In another study, they found that trying to suppress an experimentally activated thought of a white bear caused people to be subsequently less successful at resisting laughing while watching a funny film. Subsequent studies have found similar results with regard to consumers, dieters, and impulsive spending (see Novemsky et al. 2007; Vohs and Heatherton 2000; Vohs and Faber 2007).

Ego depletion has been found to occur not only with self-control but with conscious choice too. Baumeister et al. (1998) found, for example, that a preliminary act of personal choice and responsibility caused a similar decrement in persistence at a difficult task. Recent findings by Vohs et al. (2008) have likewise found choice to be depleting. In four different studies they found that making a series of choices led to poorer self-control on subsequent, unrelated tasks, as compared with just thinking about items or answering questions about them without making choices among them. According to Baumeister, "The fact that effortful choice uses the same resource as self-control links two main forms of free will and supports the idea that they share a common underlying mechanism" (2008, 17). It seems that initial exertions of conscious self-control and choice in one sphere led to poorer performance on subsequent tests in other spheres. The implication of all these findings, according to Baumeister, is that the first task used up some resource that was then no longer available to enable people to perform well on the second task. Baumeister has proposed that conscious choice, active response, self-regulation, and other volitions may all draw on a common inner resource (Baumeister et al. 1998; Baumeister, Heatherton, and Tice 1994; Baumeister 2002, 2008). It seems that the conscious self expends some limited resource, akin to energy or strength, when it engages in acts of volition. Whatever this common inner resource turns out to be, our capacity for conscious self-regulation (or active volition generally) is severely limited.[20] When the limited resource is depleted, self-control fails and decision making is impaired.

What does this all mean for free will? Baumeister concludes, "Our research on ego depletion provides one way to understand why free will is at best an occasional phenomenon" (2008, 17). Baumeister, himself, believes that a more limited understanding of free will can still be preserved, but these finds are truly troubling for anyone who understands free will in terms of conscious will. Bargh and Chartrand write:

> Given one's understandable desire to believe in free will and self-determination, it may be hard to bear that most of daily life is driven by automatic, nonconscious mental processes—but it appears impossible, from these findings, that conscious control could be up to the job. As Sherlock Holmes was fond of telling Dr. Watson, when one eliminates the impossible, whatever remains—however improbably—must be the truth. (1999, 464)

If the conscious mind is not up to job, if our reserves of conscious "power" are so easily depleted, then we can only reason that the bulk of self-regulatory behavior is carried out nonconsciously. Ego depletion helps make vivid the fact that consciousness is a limited-capacity system. It also indicates, as Baumeister admits, that conscious will is "at best an occasional phenomenon." How occasional is still an empirical question, but the more we learn about the adaptive unconscious the less it seems free will and conscious choice play the prominent role we once thought.[21]

Perhaps no one has done more to reveal the pervasiveness of automatic, nonconscious processes than John Bargh and his colleagues. Bargh has even gone so far as to argue that most of a person's everyday life is determined not by their conscious intentions and deliberate choice but by mental processes that are put into motion by features of the environment and that operate outside of conscious awareness and guidance (e.g., Bargh and Chartrand 1999, 462; Bargh 1997). According to Bargh, our ability to exercise conscious, intentional control is actually quite limited— and contrary to what is typically assumed, most moment-to-moment psychological life must occur through nonconscious means if it is to occur at all. Bargh and Chartrand (1999) identify three different mechanisms that produce automatic, environmental control: an automatic effect of perception on action, automatic goal pursuit, and a continual automatic evaluation of one's experience. They conclude that these various nonconscious mental systems "perform the lion's share of the self-regulatory burden, beneficently keeping the individual grounded in his or her current environment" (1999, 462). They playfully call this the unbearable automaticity of being. Bargh provides a wealth of empirical support for this conclusion, some of which I will now report.

4.3 THE UNBEARABLE AUTOMATICITY OF BEING

Experiments carried out by Bargh, Chen, and Burrows (1996) found that when trait constructs were nonconsciously activated during an unrelated task, what is known as priming, participants were subsequently more likely to act in line with the content of the primed trait construct. In one experiment, participants were primed on the traits of either rudeness or politeness (or neither) using a scramble-sentence test in which they were told to form grammatical sentences out of short lists of words. Participants were exposed to words related to either rudeness (e.g., rude, impolite, obnoxious), politeness (e.g., respect, considerate, polite), or neither (in the control condition). Participants were told that after completing the test, they were to go tell the experimenter that they were done. When they attempted to do so, however, the experimenter was engaged in a staged conversation. Bargh and his colleagues wanted to see if participants would interrupt. What they found was astonishing: among those primed for "rudeness" 67% interrupted, among those primed for "politeness" only 16% interrupted, and for the control group, 38% interrupted.[22] In addition, during an extensive post-experiment debriefing, none of the participants showed any awareness or suspicion of the possible influence of the scramble-sentence test on their interrupting behavior.[23] This is a vivid demonstration of how our actions—in this case, whether or not to interrupt—can be influenced in ways that fall well outside conscious awareness. The mere priming of certain words was enough to influence behavior directly and automatically. And this apparently happened without any conscious will—for as Daniel Wegner points out, in cases like these "it is difficult to maintain that the person had a conscious intention to behavior as he or she was seen to behave" (2002, 129).[24]

In a second experiment, Bargh and his colleagues (1996) found similar results with stereotype activation. In the experiment, participants were primed (once again using the scrambled-sentence paradigm) with either words related to the elderly stereotype (e.g., Florida, old, gray, sentimental, wrinkle) or with words unrelated to the stereotype. Bargh and his colleagues found that participants primed with words related to the elderly-related stereotype subsequently behaved in line with the stereotype. Participants were instructed to work on a scrambled-sentence task as part of what they believed was a language proficiency experiment. After completing the task, participants were thanked, partially debriefed, and sent on their way. At this point experimenters surreptitiously recorded the amount of time the participant took to walk down the corridor after exiting the laboratory room. Participants primed with the elderly stereotype walked more slowly down the hallway than did those who had not been primed with the stereotype. And after a complete debriefing, no participant expressed any knowledge of the relevance of the words in the scrambled sentence task to the elderly stereotype. Furthermore, no participant believed that the words had an impact on his/her behavior. This lack of awareness—and the apparent lack of conscious intention—is what make these cases so interesting. Hence, this experiment once again confirms the presence and power of automatic, nonconscious effects on behavior—in this case, on walking speed.[25]

Additional experiments conducted by Dijksterhuis, Bargh, and Miedema (2001) have also shown that such automatic effects on behavior hold for another central feature of the elderly stereotype—forgetfulness. They found that participants primed with the elderly stereotype subsequently could not remember as many features of the room in which the experiment was conducted as could control participants. The automatic activation of the elderly stereotype was enough to directly and nonconsciously prompt memory loss. Similar nonconscious behavioral effects of automatic stereotype activation have been found in experiments conducted by Dijksterhuis and van Knippenberg (1998). In one experiment, Dijksterhuis and van Knippenberg primed participants with the stereotype of professors; presumably a positive stereotype that includes intelligence traits. When the participants were then given a series of questions from a Trivial Pursuit game, they answered more items correctly than did participants given no professor prime. In a second experiment, participants were primed with the stereotype of soccer hooligans; a negative stereotype. As predicted, the primed participants exhibited decreased performance on the general knowledge trivia. According to Dijksterhuis and van Knippenberg, this is evidence that perception can automatically and nonconsciously evoke complex behavioral patterns. The activation, for example, of the trait intelligent (by priming a stereotype that contains this trait) leads to the activation of a set of concrete behavioral representations stored under it: "e.g., to concentrate on a problem, to adopt an analytical approach, to think systematically about possible solutions" (1998, 867). Merely priming a stereotype—i.e., unconsciously getting someone to think about a kind of person—leads to complex overt unintentional behavior in line with the activated stereotype. Through the perception-behavior link, the behavior is automatically triggered and carried out without conscious will or intention.[26]

These findings are troubling because they reveal how easily our behaviors can be guided by our stereotypes. The environment can automatically and unconsciously trigger a stereotype, which in turn can cause us to behavior in certain unintended ways.[27] All of this can happen without any conscious guidance or will. Bargh and Chartrand write:

> In real life, stereotypes aren't triggered by lists of words but by skin color, gender characteristics, and other easily detected features of group members (Brewer, 1988)—in other words, by the actual presence of the person being stereotyped. The effect of stereotypes on behavior

could therefore create—entirely nonconsciously—a "self-fulfilling prophecy" (e.g., Rosenthal & Jacobson, 1968; Snyder, Tanke, & Berscheid, 1977) by causing the perceiver to behave in line with stereotypic expectations, to which the stereotyped person might well respond in kind. (1999, 467-468)

Bargh conducted additional studies that found this to be true with stereotypes about African American males. In one experiment, when white participants were subliminally presented with faces of young African American males, they subsequently acted with greater hostility to a mild provocation when compared with the control condition (Bargh, Chen, and Burrows 1996).[28] In another experiment, the same subliminal priming manipulation was used but participants were then asked to play a potentially frustrating game of "Catch Phrase," in which the object was to get their partner to correctly guess a specific word by giving clues (Chen and Bargh 1997). Chen and Bargh hypothesized that those subliminally primed with the African American faces would exhibit hostile behavior which in turn would cause a kind of self-fulfilling prophecy to occur. This is exactly what they found:

> As predicted, the partners of participants who had earlier been subliminally primed with African American faces manifested greater hostility than the partners of those who had not been primed. Most important, the primed participants themselves rated their partners as being more hostile than did nonprimed participants. For the primed participants, their own hostile behavior, nonconsciously driven by the content of their stereotype of African Americans, caused their partners to respond in kind, but the primed participants had no clue as to their own role in producing that hostility. (Bargh and Chartrand 1999, 467)

This is an excellent example of how (in principle) unconscious stereotypes—through our own unintended actions—can cause stereotype-consistent behavior in the stereotyped person. Given these experiments, there should be little doubt that sophisticated social behavior can be triggered and guided automatically by features of the environment. The social interactions modeled in these experiments are analogous to our day-to-day social interactions.

In addition to these cases, a number of other automaticity phenomena, in which behavior is automatically triggered and guided in the absence of conscious awareness, have been found. Winkielman, Berridge, and Wilbarger (2005), for example, have conducted a series of experiments that reveal that: (a) emotions—defined as affective reactions, such as "liking" and "disliking"—can occur unconsciously; and (b) such unconscious affective reactions (or emotions) can guide behavior in ways we are not consciously aware of and hence do not consciously will or intend (see also Berridge and Winkielman 2003). In their first experiment, thirsty participants were subliminally presented with happy, neutral, or angry faces. They were then asked to rate their own subjective emotion on a 10-point hedonic scale. They were also presented with a pitcher of fruit-flavored drink and asked to pour themselves as much as they wanted, to drink it, and to evaluate it. Winkielman and colleagues found that those thirsty participants who had been subliminally exposed to happy facial expressions subsequently evaluated the fruit-flavored drink more favorably and also drank substantially more of it (up to 50% more) than did neutral-primed participants. Those who had been shown the angry face drank least of all. In addition, participants reported no conscious awareness of any intervening change in their subjective emotion. These finds are quite remarkable since they provide evidence that an unconscious affective (or emotional) reaction can control actual consumptive behavior in a real-life situation.[29] Similar unconscious effects on behavior were found in a second experiment that measured participants' willingness to pay for the fruit-flavored beverage.[30]

Given the importance we typically place on the conscious control and guidance of voluntary actions, experiments like these should be disturbing to defenders of free will. These participants were given a pitcher of fruit-flavored drink which they could physically interact with, pour and consume, however they wanted. They were "free" in a compatibilist sense to pour as much as they wanted and consume as much as they wanted. Despite the fact that these are voluntary acts, many would be troubled by the influence these subliminal images exert on behavior and the lack of conscious control over the emotions and subsequent choices. People are frightened by the idea that their unconscious minds can be influenced, without their awareness, to respond to such subliminal images. If conscious intention, control, and guidance of behavior is a folk-psychological requirement for free will, then it's easy to see the problem. These individuals are completely unaware of what's causing them to behave as they do—they are unaware of subliminal effects on their emotions, and they are unaware of the effects their emotions have on their behavior. Unconscious environmental stimuli trigger unconscious affective states, and through these unconscious affective states our behavior is unconsciously caused. This is a problem because our folk-psychological understanding of free will and moral responsibility find such cases of automaticity (or unconsciously caused action) troubling.

Experiments like these reveal how subtle environmental influences—influences we are unaware of—have the power to affect us in ways that we do not consciously will or intend. Every day, in a multitude of ways, unconscious environmental determinants are acting on us, triggering various behaviors. Contrary to our subjective experience and folk-psychological theories, many of our behaviors occur automatically, determined by causes far removed from our awareness. For example, it has been empirically shown that people automatically imitate the postures, facial expressions, and speaking styles of others—what is known as *mim-*

icry or the *chameleon effect* (Chartrand and Bargh 1999a; Giles, Coupland, and Coupland 1991)—and that behavioral patterns can be activated by incidental stimuli such as mundane physical objects and unnoticed features of the environment (Kay et al. 2004; Williams and Bargh 2008; Dutton and Aron 1974). The fact that we remain completely unaware of these environmental effects on behavior is troubling to our ordinary sense of free will which presupposes a kind of conscious executive control over our behavior. As Christian Jarrett writes in his aptly titled "Mind Wide Open":

> From the effects of mirrors and the subliminal presentation of happy faces, to the sight of a briefcase and the power of mimicry, the range of factors influencing our behavior without us realizing it is overwhelming. Taken together, the research undermines the notion that our conscious selves are in control, and points instead to a sophisticated nonconscious mind, wide open to outside influences as the real source of our decision making. (2008, 294)

We fail to realize just how *wide open* our unconscious minds are, and how easily our decision making is influenced by unnoticed environmental determinants.

Take for instance Kay, Wheeler, Bargh, and Ross' famous briefcase experiment (referenced above by Jarrett). In a classic study on the influence of mundane physical objects on situational construal and competitive behavioral choice, Kay et al. asked subjects to participate in a financial game. Kay and his colleagues found that those who sat at a table with a briefcase strategically placed on it played the game far more competitively and selfishly than did participants who sat near a backpack. The mere presence of a briefcase, which is presumably associated with business, is enough to trigger behavioral dispositions associated with business. This occurred, as with earlier experiments, without the participants' awareness of the relevant influence. When probed in post-experiment interviews, none of the participants were aware of any aspect of the physical environment that may have influenced their playing strategies. Additional studies conducted by Kay et al. showed that exposure to other objects common to the domain of business (e.g., boardroom tables) increased both the likelihood that an ambiguous social interaction would be perceived as less cooperative (Study 2) and the amount of money that participants proposed to retain for themselves in the "Ultimatum Game" (Study 3). This is just one demonstration of how incidental, environmental stimuli (e.g., briefcases, business suits, or boardroom tables) can nonconsciously influence the degree to which behavioral dispositions (e.g., competitiveness) are expressed.

In another interesting set of experiments, Williams and Bargh (2008) found that the simple act of holding a hot or cold cup of coffee can directly affect *temperament* (e.g., whether we act "warmly" or "coldly") and *personality impressions* (e.g., whether we rate others as "warm" or "cold" people). There appears to be a direct link between physical warmth (and coldness) and emotional "warmth" (and "coldness"). The first of two studies involved a group of 41 undergraduates who were taken by elevator to a fourth floor room. During the elevator ride a research assistant, who was unaware of the study's hypotheses, handed the test subject either a hot cup of coffee or a cold iced coffee to hold while the researcher filled out a short information form on a clipboard. The drink was then handed back. When participants arrived on the fourth floor they were asked to assess the traits of another person. Williams and Bargh found that contact with a cup of hot coffee led individuals to rate a random person as warmer and friendlier than did contact with a cup of cold coffee. In a second study, done under the guise of a product-evaluation test, it was found that participants holding a hot (versus cold) therapeutic pack used to treat muscle aches were more likely to choose a gift for a friend instead of for themselves—an emotionally "warmer" response.[31] This research demonstrates that physical temperature can affect our behavior, temperament, and perception of others in dramatic ways *without us noticing.* Experiencing physical warmth (or coldness), for example, can increase (or decrease) feelings of interpersonal "warmth."

It is even possible for emotional states like attraction to be triggered by features of the environment automatically and unconsciously. Psychologists have known for years that attraction is more likely to happen when people are aroused, be it through laughter, anxiety, or fear. This is known as the *misattribution of arousal paradigm* and it occurs when arousal arises for one reason but receives another cognitive label (see Baumeister and Bushman 2008; Cantor, Zillmann, and Bryant 1975). Social psychologists often use the misattribution of arousal paradigm to determine if people really understand what makes them act the way they do (see Schachter and Singer 1962). The most famous experiment using the misattribution of arousal paradigm was conducted by Dutton and Aron (1974). In the experiment, male passersby between the ages of 18-35, and unaccompanied by women, were contacted either on a fear-arousing suspension bridge or a non-fear-arousing bridge by an attractive female interviewer who asked them to fill out a questionnaire. The suspension bridge was a 5-foot wide, wobbly, swaying bridge suspended 230 feet above rocks and shallow rapids. About halfway across the bridge, test subjects (the single men) were approached by the attractive woman who asked them to fill out a survey. She also gave them her phone number to call if they had any further questions. The experiment was repeated upriver on a bridge that was wide and sturdy. The real experiment was to see which group of men were more likely to call the woman. Dutton and Aron found that the subjects on the fear-arousing bridge rated the woman more attractive and were more likely to attempt post-experimental contact with the interviewer. They were even more likely to ask the interviewer out on a date. The reason for this is that the men on the fear-arousing suspension bridge misattributed their arousal (i.e., fear) from the suspension bridge for arousal (i.e., attraction) for the woman.[32] Unconsciously, fear got their attention and aroused emotional centers in the brain (e.g., spikes in amphetamines, dopamine, and norepinephrine) which also play a big role in sexual attraction. These men confused their physiologically aroused state for one that was brought on by sexual attraction. This is just one example of how arousal from one situation—say walking across a shaky bridge versus a stable one—could intensify a subsequent emotional state without us realizing. It appears that feelings as basic as whom we find attractive are influenced, often heavily, by our environment in ways we do not and perhaps cannot easily understand.[33]

Examples abound of how incidental environmental stimuli, like holding a hot cup of coffee, can unconsciously and automatically affect behavior. Friedman and Elliot (2008), for example, have found that visual exposure to sports drinks, relative to a spring water control condition, led to greater persistence on physical tasks without participants exhibiting any awareness of the effect that viewing the sports drink had on their subsequent behavior. Friedman and Elliot conclude that their findings provide support for the notion that physical objects can alter athletic performance outside of conscious awareness (2008, 749). Lerner, Small, and Loewenstein (2004) have further shown how the decisions we make in the present are influenced by emotional hangovers from the past, without us realizing it. Lerner and colleagues demonstrated this by showing student participants one of three film clips chosen to provoke sadness (*The Champ*), disgust (*Trainspotting*), or a neutral emotion (a *National Geographic* special). They found that students shown the disgusting clip were subsequently willing to pay less for a highlighter set than viewers of the neutral clip, consistent with the idea that disgust triggers a desire to avoid taking in anything new. By contrast, viewers of the sad clip were willing to pay more than those in the neutral group, probably because sadness triggers the implicit goal of changing one's circumstances. Levine, Morsella, and Bargh (2007) have even found evidence suggesting that incidental stimuli can instigate actions that run counter to one's current goals and directly cause the expression of undesired actions. All of this research is unnerving because it reveals that the range of factors influencing our behavior without us realizing it is overwhelming. Holding a hot cup of coffee, seeing the picture of a sports drink, watching a certain movie, standing on a suspension bridge, or sitting next to a briefcase can cause us to behavior in ways we are unaware of and do not consciously intend. In our day-to-day lives we fail to realize just how powerful these unconscious forces are and how pervasive the adaptive unconscious actually is.

The fact that mundane and incidental features of the environment can affect our behavior in ways we are unaware of is troubling enough, but what about behaviors that are driven by goals and motivation? Here, one might think, conscious deliberation, choice, and guidance are necessary. Most theories of goal pursuit, both folk-psychological and scientific, emphasize conscious choice and guidance of behavior on a moment-to-moment basis. As Chartrand and Bargh point out:

> Many current models of motivation and goal pursuit continue the tradition of maintaining continuous, conscious choice and guidance of behavior—directed by the individual's chronic intents and desires—as the cornerstone and foundation of self-regulation (e.g., Bandura, 1977, 1986, 1997; Mischel, 1973). This view has intuitive appeal. We are often cognizant of deliberating among various desires and wishes and choosing which goals to actually pursue. We often consciously engage in goal-directed action and then carefully evaluate our subsequence performance. Thus, intuition tells us that the goal pursuit sequence is available to conscious awareness, and many current theories of motivation reflect and support this (Bandura, 1986; Cantor & Kihlstrom, 1987; Carver & Scheier, 1981; Deci & Ryan, 1985; Locke and Latham, 1990). (2002, 13-14)

We think of people as active agents in the world with purposes and goals they want to attain. We think that most of our voluntary actions and responses to the environment in the form of judgments, decisions, and behavior are "determined not solely by the information available in that environment but rather by how it relates to whatever goal we are currently pursuing" (Bargh and Chartrand 1999, 468). The question, though, is whether goal-directed behavior can occur outside of conscious awareness. Is it possible for goal-directed behavior to occur automatically and without conscious guidance? Bargh and his colleagues have shown that it can (see Bargh 1990, 1997; Bargh et al. 2001; Chartrand and Bargh 1996, 2002; Bargh and Chartrand 1999; Bargh and Gollwitzer 1994).

Bargh's auto-motive goal-directed model (1990) maintains that mental representations of goals can become activated without an act of conscious will, such that subsequent behavior is then guided by these goals within the situational context faced by the individual. According to Bargh, no conscious intervention, act of will, or guidance is needed for this form of goal pursuit. On the auto-motive goal-directed model: (a) goal structures can be activated directly by relevant environmental stimuli, and (b) goals, once activated, produce the same outcomes whether they are put in motion by consciously made choice or through external stimuli. More specifically:

> The model holds that although many of the goals an individual pursues are the result of conscious deliberation and choice, conscious choice is not necessary for goal activation and operation. In addition to the deliberate mode of activation, goals and intentions also can be started in motion by environmental stimuli. First, the model assumes that intentions and goals are represented in memory in the same way

that social attitudes, constructs, stereotypes, and schemas are represented. Second, because constructs and stereotypes are capable of being
automatically activated by relevant environmental stimuli, goal representations should have this capability as well. With repeated and consistent choice (i.e., activation) of a particular goal in a certain social
situation over time, the representation of that goal may become directly
and automatically linked in memory to the representation of that situation. The goal will eventually come to be nonconsciously activated
within the situation, independently of the individual's conscious purposes at that time. (Chartrand and Bargh 2002, 15)

In this way, situational features in the environment can automatically
activate goals frequently associated with them in the past, and these goals
can then operate to guide information processing and behavior without
conscious intervention at any point in the sequence. Although it may be
hard to reconcile this with our intuitive sense of conscious control, there
is now substantial evidence that individuals frequently pursue goals that
they are not aware of having.

In a series of experiments, Bargh et al. (2001) found that goals having
to do with achievement and cooperation can be activated outside of
awareness and then operate nonconsciously to guide self-regulation effectively. In their first experiment, they primed participants (or not) with
the goal of performing well. In an initial task, participants were given a
"word search" task in which synonyms of achievement (e.g., win, compete, strive, succeed) were presented as a way to prime the achievement
goal. Bargh and his colleagues found that those participants that had
been primed with the achievement goal significantly outperformed the
control (nonprimed) condition—e.g., they worked harder and scored
higher on a subsequent verbal task. In a second experiment, participants
were primed (or not) with the goal to behave cooperatively. They were
then asked to play a fishing game in which they had to choose between
behaving competitively and maximizing profits, through keeping most
or all of the fish caught on each trial, or behaving cooperatively and
replenishing the stock of fish in the lake. They found that those participants in the prime-condition exhibited more cooperative behavior and
were more likely to return fish to the common resource. Importantly, in
both experiments the participants were not only unaware that these goals
had been activated but they were also unaware of their operation—even
though they behaved in ways to attain the goals. Numerous other cases
of automatic goal pursuit have been reported (see Spencer at el. 1998;
Chartrand and Bargh 1996, 2002; Bargh and Chartrand 1999; Moskowitz
et al. 1999; Bargh and Gollwitzer 1994).[34]

Importantly, the research on automatic goal pursuits shows it to display the same features as conscious goal pursuit—e.g., flexibility, persistence, effects of success and failure on mood, information processing,
memory storage, social behavior, and task performance (see Bargh and

Ferguson 2000; Bargh et al. 2001). Experiments conducted by Bargh et al. (2001), for example, found that nonconsciously activated goals demonstrate the same qualities of persistence over time toward the desired end state, including overcoming obstacles in the way. In one experiment, Bargh and his team nonconsciously activated the high-performance-goal and then had participants work on a relatively uninteresting and intellectually demanding word search task. During the task, participants were interrupted by a power failure for a lengthy period of time. After the power was resumed, those whose high-performance-goal was nonconsciously activated (but interrupted) were more likely to opt for returning to the "boring" task than control participants, who preferred instead the intrinsically more attractive alternative (a "cartoon-human rating" task). This demonstrates that nonconsciously pursued goals are also "associated with high commitment, because the person goes back to the task to see it completed (i.e., attain the goal)" (2001, 1023). These and other studies confirm that nonconsciously activated and operating goals not only produce higher performance, they exhibit all the same qualities as conscious goal pursuits. This may seem counter-intuitive, but given that consciousness is a limited capacity system "it makes sense that even complex self-regulatory goals can operate automatically and efficiently, without needing to be instigated and then guided by expensive acts of will and choice" (Bargh and Chartrand 1999, 473).

Let me end this section by briefly mentioning perhaps the most disturbing findings yet having to do with the adaptive unconscious. Thus far I have focused primarily on research from psychology and social psychology, but perhaps the biggest threat to our ordinary conception of conscious will comes from findings in neuroscience. Work by Benjamin Libet and others now suggests that our sense of conscious will—understood as consciously initiated action—is not only severely limited but illusory (cf. Libet et al. 1983; Libet 1985; Haggard and Eimer 1999; Haggard, Newman, and Magno 1999; Wegner 2002; Sirigu et al. 2004; Soon et al. 2008; Jeannerod 1997, 2006; Pockett 2006; Matsuhashi and Hallett 2008). An empirical understanding of how the brain causes behavior and where consciousness fits into the picture has recently emerged, and this research suggests that consciousness comes too late in the neuropsychological sequence to either initiate or control ongoing voluntary behavior. Marc Jeannerod, for example, has accumulated evidence that ongoing actions are generally controlled by unconscious processes, with the subject's consciousness being kept informed (if indeed it is informed at all) only after the event—"and then more as a professional courtesy than anything else" (Pockett, Banks, and Gallagher 2006, 4; see Jeannerod 1997, 2006).

Libet and his colleagues have further shown that the initiation of a spontaneous voluntary act appears to begin in the brain unconsciously, well before one is even aware of the intention to act. In their groundbreaking working on the neuroscience of movement, Libet et al. (1983) investigated the timing of brain processes and compared them to the timing of conscious will in relation to self-initiated voluntary acts and found that the conscious "urge, intention or decision" to move came before the actual movement, but *after* the start of the brain activity leading up to it. More specifically, they found that the conscious intention to move came 200 milliseconds before the motor act, but 350-400 ms after *readiness potential*—a ramplike buildup of electric activity that occurs in the brain and precedes actual movement. If Libet's findings are correct, this means that we only become conscious of our will *after* we begin to do something. Some people have taken Libet's discovery as a direct empirical refutation of free will, but since I will be discussing this research at length in chapter 6, along with criticisms and alternative interpretations, I will leave a fuller discussion of its implications until then. Here I will simply say that, interpretations aside, Libet's findings suggest that our conscious selves do not cause and initiate spontaneous voluntary behavior (see ch.6 for more details).

4.4 IMPLICATIONS FOR FREE WILL

In this chapter I have attempted to do two main things. The first is to establish that conscious will, control, and guidance are both a folk-psychological and, for many philosophers and psychologists, theoretical requirement for any intuitive sense of free will. The second is to argue that empirical findings in the behavioral, cognitive, and neurosciences seriously question our intuitive assumption that our conscious selves are in the driver's seat. We have seen that social interaction, evaluation and judgment, reasoning and problem solving, the processing of stereotypes, the operation of internal goal structures, and the initiation of voluntary behavior can all proceed without the intervention of conscious acts of will and guidance. We have also seen how one's internal psychological processes are wide open to the influence of external stimuli and events in one's immediate environment without knowledge or awareness of such control. Such automaticity can occur in a number of different ways, including the automatic effect of perception on action, automatic goal pursuit, and a continual automatic evaluation of one's experience. In this way, the higher mental processes that have traditionally served as quintessential examples of free will—such as goal pursuits, judgment, evaluation, interpersonal behavior, and action initiation—can and often do occur in the absence of conscious choice or guidance.

Just what role consciousness plays and what functions it serves is something I will explore further in the next few chapters. But since consciousness is an extremely limited-capacity system and a late evolutionary add-on, it should not be surprising that the adaptive unconscious performs the lion's share of the self-regulatory burden. This goes contrary to our commonsense beliefs and threatens our sense of free will, but to survive in our complex world people must be able to process, analyze, and react to a great deal of information outside of awareness. The conscious mind is a slow, serial processing system and does not seem up to the task of processing parallel streams of information quickly and efficiently. The adaptive unconscious, on the other hand, is an extremely powerful, pervasive, and efficient tool. As Bargh and Chartrand write:

> [A]utomatic evaluation of the environment[, for example,] is a pervasive and continuous activity that individuals do not intend to engage in and of which they are largely unaware. It appears to have real and functional consequences, creating behavioral readiness within fractions of a second to approach positive and avoid negative objects, and, through its effect on mood, serving as a signaling system for the overall safety versus danger of one's current environment. All of these effects tend to keep us in touch with the realities of our world in a way that bypasses the limitations of conscious self-regulation capabilities. (1999, 475-476)

It is a great biological boon, then, for our unconscious minds to be able to monitor our environment, react quickly, take in and appraise information, and guide our goal-directed behavior without conscious involvement and guidance. Of course, as Dutton and Aron's (1974) experiment and the literature on misattribution shows, the unconscious mind is not infallible—mistakes can happen—but the adaptive unconscious is, on the whole, an extremely efficient, affective, and useful tool. In fact, there is a growing body of evidence suggesting that evaluations, judgments, and choices made quickly and/or unconsciously are actually more reliable than those made after lengthy deliberation (Dijksterhuis 2004; Dijksterhuis et al. 2006; Dijksterhuis and van Olden 2006; Wilson and Schooler 1991; Bargh 2008; Gladwell 2005). Recent research from Dijksterhuis (2004), for example, has shown that better decisions are made when a person is distracted while making them than when able to devote total conscious attention and deliberation to the process. These findings are controversial only if one assumes that free will or conscious processes are required for such decision-making. [35]

What conclusions can we draw at this point about free will? Well, if we are to understand free will in terms of conscious will—which I think we should, since this is the kind of free will ordinary folk care about—then I believe we have to draw some troubling conclusions. As Malcolm Gladwell writes:

> The results from these experiments are, obviously, quite disturbing. They suggest that what we think of as free will is largely an illusion: much of the time, we are simply operating on automatic pilot, and the way we think and act—and how well we think and act on the spur of

the moment—are a lot more susceptible to outside influences than we realize. (2005, 58)

Such results are disturbing precisely because they undermine our intuitive sense of conscious control. Bechara et al.'s card game experiment reveals just how effectively and quickly the adaptive unconscious works. Baumeister's findings on ego depletion show just how limited our consciousness self-regulatory capacity is. All the experiments on stereotype and trait activation reveal how environmental factors—factors we are often oblivious to—can affect our social behavior directly, automatically, and without conscious intention. Bargh's auto-motive goal-directed model (1990) and his experimental findings on automatic goal pursuit show that goal-directed behavior need not be initiated or guided by conscious choice or deliberation. Lastly, Libet's work on the timing of conscious will and brain processes indicates that we do not consciously cause or initiate our voluntary behavior (see also ch.6). Taken together, all of this research undermines the notion that our conscious selves are in control, and points instead to a sophisticated nonconscious mind, wide open to outside influences, as the real source of our decision making (Jarrett 2008, 294).

Now, a compatibilist may still attempt to argue that "free will" can be preserved despite these findings—that is, one may grant that for every psychological effect (e.g., behavior, emotion, judgment, etc.) there exists a set of causes that uniquely lead to that effect, but nonetheless maintain that freedom can be preserved. In response to this, I would say three things. First, I would reiterate the arguments of chapter 3. Not only are there philosophical problems with the various compatibilist attempts to reconcile free will and determinism, but empirical studies in social psychology reveal that our folk-psychological intuitions are essentially incompatibilist and libertarian in nature. Those studies, I believe, are sufficient to show that compatibilism, at best, is working with a *deviant* or *revisionist* conception of free will. Secondly, I would further argue that if compatibilists want to defend their position in light of these findings, they need to work out a set of answers to the questions I presented at the beginning of this chapter. Until they present a developed account of the importance, or rather *unimportance* of conscious control, it's hard to judge the merits of the position. I would argue that the picture I have here attempted to paint of the adaptive unconscious goes beyond simple determinism to argue that the bulk of our day-to-day lives are controlled by unconscious processes. This, I believe, is more threatening than normal determinist arguments because it suggests we do not possess the kind of conscious executive control we typically assume. To the extent that our actions are controlled by automatic and unconscious processes, which I acknowledge is an empirical matter, it would seem free will is an illusion.[36] To think otherwise would be to assume a conception of free will that is drastically different from our folk-psychological notion. For the compatibilist to once again redefine the notion of free will so as to make it fit with the empirical data on automaticity and the adaptive unconscious would require a more drastic departure from folk psychology than such commonsense theories can handle.

Take, for instance, the average person's reaction to the controversial practice of subliminal advertising. Putting aside questions of whether, and to what extent, such advertising was ever actually used, we know that subliminal images can have a dramatic effect on behavior—witness the experiment conducted by Winkielman, Berridge, and Wilbarger (2005) which used subliminal priming. The reason why people are so troubled by prospects of subliminal advertising is that they view it as an unacceptable means of control and manipulation. Subliminal advertising, it is thought, circumvents our "free will" since it directly affects our behavior in an automatic and unconscious way. Many have opposed the practice as unethical on these very grounds. Notice, however, that a compatibilist should have no problem with subliminal advertising, since in the end the agent does as they *want* or *desire*. One could even image the agent identifying with their first-order desires, hence fulfilling the requirement of hierarchical integration. It should not matter, then, that our want or desire is causally determined by subliminal images since, according to compatibilism, *all* of our inner psychological states are causally determined. It shouldn't matter *how* our want or desire came about. Most people, however, would feel just the opposite. To think that a particular want, desire, or choice (e.g., to buy a particular soft drink) is caused by subliminal advertising (e.g., images quickly flashed on a movie screen), frightens us because it undermines our sense of conscious control. People are frightened by the idea that their unconscious minds can be influenced, without their awareness, to respond to subliminal advertisements. Such worries demonstrate just how out of step the compatibilist position is with our ordinary intuitions. It also reveals the kinds of difficulties it faces in trying to account for automatic processes. The concerns ordinary people have about subliminal advertising extend to *all* cases of automaticity, since there is no principled difference between actions that are supraliminally and subliminally triggered and controlled (see Bargh 1992). In both cases the individual is completely unaware of the environmental stimuli's influence on behavior. If one case of automaticity threatens free will, so too should the other. Whether it's a subliminal image or an incidental physical object, if one's internal psychological processes are controlled by external stimuli and events in the world without knowledge or awareness of such control, our ordinary sense of free will is undermined.[37]

Lastly, since I am primarily concerned with phenomenology and the nature of agentive experience, compatibilist concerns once again seem irrelevant. A central component of our belief in free will is the feeling that we are causally undetermined. Our actions do not seem, from a first-person point of view, to be causally determined in the way other events are. Our phenomenology clearly supports a libertarian agent-causal conception of free will. Phenomenologically, that is, we feel that our conscious selves are uncaused causes. Although one cannot deny that we experience many of our actions in this way, it should be clear from the data presented here that this sense of free will is an illusion. Contrary to our subjective experience, many of our behaviors occur automatically, determined by causes far removed from our awareness. Although our subjective phenomenology gives us the strong sense, difficult to overcome, that our conscious will is the source of our behaviors, judgments, and goal pursuits, we are often unaware and do not experience all of the unconscious influences acting upon us. Our internal psychological processes can be determined by external stimuli and events in one's immediate environment without knowledge or awareness of such control. We may not feel causally determined but this is because we remain unaware of these myriad determinants. What we do not experience in our day-to-day lives are the multitude of unconscious influences that determine exactly what we think, feel, and act.

Although the existence of libertarian freedom is an illusion, as the evidence here and elsewhere shows, the *phenomenological feeling of libertarian free will* (i.e., the feeling that we are capable of self-determination and our actions are causally undetermined) is very real. It is just as real for those who deny its existence as those who affirm it. This is why I will spend the next three chapters trying to explain the cognitive causes of this illusion. I will argue that the illusion of free will is due to the way we experience our own minds and the misleading nature of consciousness. In particular, I will argue that the illusion is due to four key phenomenological features of consciousness; all of which trick us into believing that we have (incompatibilist) free will and are capable of acting counter-causally. On my proposal, contrary to Dennett's (2003) suggestion that freedom evolves, it is actually the illusion of freedom that has evolved with the rise of consciousness and self-consciousness (see Wegner 2008).[38]

NOTES

1. Historically, the majority of compatibilists have neglected the issue of consciousness, instead focusing on the correct semantic analysis of the expression 'could have done otherwise' or thought experiments designed to show that the ability to do otherwise is not required for free will and responsibility. In surveying a number of compatibilist articles that defend hypothetical or conditional analyses—i.e., G.E. Moore (1912), A.J. Ayer (1954), Bruce Aune (1967), David Lewis (1981), Michael Levin (2004, 2007), and several others—I found almost no mention of consciousness. Newer approaches to compatibilism, those that do not focus on hypothetical analyses, appear

to fare no better. Perhaps no two papers have been more influential in shaping modern compatibilism than Harry Frankfurt's "Alternative Possibilities and Moral Responsibility" (1969) and P.F. Strawson's "Freedom and Resentment" (1962), neither of which makes reference to consciousness. Other modern classics of the compatibilist cannon, such as Gary Watson's essay "Free Agency" (1975) and Susan Wolf's "Asymmetrical Freedom" (1980), also fail to mention or discuss consciousness. The same is true for a number of recent defenses of compatibilism (e.g., Perry 2010). There are of course exceptions. Frankfurt's "Freedom of the Will and the Concept of a Person" (1971) does touch on consciousness to some degree, but it makes no attempt to spell out in detail the relationship between consciousness and free will—ultimately leaving a number of important questions unresolved (see next paragraph). Further evidence of this neglect of consciousness can be found in the indexes of contemporary collections on free will. For example, Fischer's (1986) anthology on free will and moral responsibility—which includes a number of leading compatibilist essays—has no index entry for 'consciousness' or related concepts like 'awareness,' 'experience,' 'conscious will,' 'self-consciousness,' 'phenomenology,' 'first-person,' or 'conscious control.' *The Oxford Handbook of Free Will* (Kane 2002), one of the most comprehensive modern collections available in the literature, does have index entries for 'consciousness' and 'conscious will' but these almost universally refer to articles by determinists (G. Strawson 2002), libertarians appealing to quantum mechanical accounts of consciousness (Hodgson 2002), and Libet's (1999) article on the timing of brain processes. With the exception of one passing reference (Berofsky 2002, 192-193), there was no discussion of 'consciousness,' 'self-consciousness,' or 'conscious will' by any compatibilists. There have been some recent moves toward explicit consideration of consciousness (e.g., Mele 2009; Baumeister, Mele, and Vohs 2010), but the general neglect of consciousness by compatibilists is unfortunate since it leaves them unable to grapple with recent discoveries in the behavioral, cognitive, and neurosciences that raise important questions about the relationship between consciousness and free will.

2. In chapter 5 I will argue that we do not have direct, immediate, and infallible access to our own mental states. If correct, I believe this creates a potential problem for Frankfurt's conception of *identification*. If, for example, we are not always aware of our true motivational states—if, perhaps, we are even capable of confabulating reasons for why we act as we do—what does identification amount to? Is the split brain patient who confabulates reasons for action, or the person acting out a posthypnotic suggestion who rationalizes their behavior, "free" if they do not oppose acting on the unconscious functional states that move them? Is the online dater who says he's looking for a certain "type" of woman, but is always attracted to the opposite type, "free" when he acts on an unopposed desire to ask out a woman who is the exact opposite of what he *claims* he wants (even though he doesn't see this)? Furthermore, does having an unopposed second-order "volition" to act in accordance with a first-order desire require any kind of *active conscious control*, or are we to view "free agents" here as mere *passive* possessors of wants? In fact, a number of critics have criticized Frankfurt on exactly this point. These critics argue that Frankfurt's account treats both first-order and second-order desires as passive affairs and because of this fails to identify the functional role that the *will* plays in the process of a person's deliberation and evaluation of competing desires (see Watson 1987; Raz 2006; Vezér 2007). Because most compatibilists say very little (if anything) about consciousness, it's unclear what role it is meant to play in their accounts. As suggested in the previous note, compatibilists need to spell out in far more detail the role (if any) consciousness plays in identification, deliberation, evaluation, and control.

3. In one such case, the Steven Steinberg Case (Maricopa County Superior Court 1982), Steven Steinberg was accused of stabbing his wife 26 times. Steinberg claimed he did not remember the crime and pleaded not guilty. He was found innocent by the jury on the grounds that he was temporarily insane when he killed his wife. In another recent case, the Kenneth Parks Case (Ontario, Canada 1987), Kenneth Parks—an individual with a history of insomnia and somnambulism—reportedly got in his car one

night, drove 23 kilometers to his in-laws' home, and stabbed to death his mother-in-law and assaulted his father-in-law (who survived). During the trial, defense experts—including psychiatrists, a psychologist, a neurologist, and a sleep specialist—concluded Ken Parks was asleep when he committed the crime and was therefore unaware of his actions. He too was found not guilty.

4. I do not mean to suggest that intentional, purposeful, goal-directed behavior cannot be performed unconsciously. In fact, the rest of this chapter will be dedicated to making the case that this commonsense, intuitive assumption is false. The point I wish to make here is that this *assumption* is an essential part of our folk-psychological theory and is especially important to our understanding of willfulness.

5. Such automatisms not only involve a "lack of the feeling of doing an action but may even go beyond this to include a distinct feeling that we are *not* doing" (Wegner 2002, 99). Common examples include automatic writing, Ouija board spelling, the Chevreul pendulum, dowsing, and the phenomenon of ideomotor action (Wegner 2002, ch.4). The absence of an experience of conscious will in such cases is profound. According to Wegner, "The loss of perceived voluntariness is so remarkable during an automatism that the person may vehemently resist describing the action as consciously or personally caused. It seems to come from somewhere else or at least not from oneself" (2002, 99).

6. For the details of Wegner and Wheatley's (1999) *I-spy* experiment and a discussion of the relationship between conscious intention and the initiation of action, see chapter 6.

7. I will also argue in chapter 7 that consciousness of self (or *self*-consciousness) plays an important role in generating our sense of agency. Disorders that involve breakdowns in self-consciousness, like alien hand syndrome and schizophrenic thought insertion, result in profound disturbances of the sense of agency. See ch.7 for details.

8. Searle writes, "I want to situate an account of the consciousness of free action, a form of consciousness I will call 'volitional consciousness', within an account of consciousness generally" (2000, 3; see also 2001a, 2001b).

9. For Hodgson: "[I]f the choice between doing or refraining from doing an action is to be considered an exercise of free will, the subject must to some minimum extent grasp the possibility of either doing an action or not doing it, and must know-how to do the action and also know-how to refrain from doing it. This again is intelligible and plausible" (2005, 5-6).

10. Both Searle and Hodgson advocate *indeterminist* accounts of free will while at the same time rejecting the metaphysical commitments of libertarian agent-causation. They both maintain that consciousness is physically realized at the neurobiological level and advocate naturalist accounts of the mind. Yet they also maintain that there is true (not just psychological) indeterminism involved in cases of rational, conscious decision-making. Searle attempts to round this square by arguing that "consciousness is a system feature" (see 2000, 2001a) and that the whole system moves at once, but not on the basis of causally sufficient conditions. He writes: "What we have to suppose, if we believe that our conscious experience of freedom is not a complete illusion, is that the whole system moves forward toward the decision making, and toward the implementing of the decision in actual actions; that the conscious rationality at the top level is realized all the way down, and that means that the whole system moves in a way that is causal, but not based on causally sufficient conditions" (2000, 16). According to Searle, this account is only intelligible "if we postulate a conscious rational agent, capable of reflecting on its own reasons and then acting on the basis of those reasons (2000, 16). That is, this "postulation amounts to a postulation of a self. So we can make sense of rational, free conscious action, only if we postulate a conscious self" (2000, 16). For Searle, this means that you cannot account for the rational self just in terms of a Humean bundle of perceptions. For Searle, the *self* is a primitive feature of the system that cannot be reduced to independent components of the system or explained in different terms. I believe this account fails for two reasons: (1) Searle's postulate of a

non-Humean self is hard to defend. I argue in chapter 7 that the *experience* of a non-Humean self can be explained away (see ch.7 for more). (2) Secondly, Searle's claim that the *system itself* is indeterminist makes sense only if you think a quantum mechanical account of consciousness (or the system as a whole) can be given. He writes, "the lack of causally sufficient conditions at the psychological level goes all the way down. That will seem less puzzling to us if we reflect that our urge to stop at the level of the neurons is simply a matter of prejudice. If we keep on going down to the quantum mechanical level, then it may seem less surprising that we have an absence of causally sufficient conditions" (2000, 17). This appeal to quantum mechanics to account for conscious, rational behavior is, I maintain, empirically unfounded and theoretically flawed. I have already argued in chapter 2 that such an account must fail. This move, especially in the way that Searle attempts to motivate it, comes off as an act of desperation. In fact, when Searle asks himself, "How could the behavior of the conscious brain be indeterminist? How exactly would the neurobiology work on such an hypothesis?" He candidly answers, "I do not know the answer to that question" (2000, 17). I believe Hodgson's account fails for similar reasons. He too appeals to quantum mechanics to account for the indeterminacy and adopts a conception of the *self* similar to Searle's.

11.   For similar compatibilist claims, see the "valuation" or "reasons" theories of Gary Watson (1975, 1987), Susan Wolf (1990), and Joseph Raz (2006).

12.   Sean Spence has also argued that "a conscious free will (in the sense of consciousness initiating action) is incompatible with the evidence of neuroscience, and the phenomenology described in the literature of normal creativity, psychotic passivity, and the neurological syndrome of the alien limb or hand" (1996, 75). I will discuss the neuroscientific threat to free will in chapter 6, and I will discuss the phenomenon of alien hand syndrome in chapter 7.

13.   For a comprehensive introduction into this research, see Wilson (2002), Bargh and Chartrand (1999), Bargh and Ferguson (2000), and Bargh (1997). For a popular treatment of some of this research, see Malcolm Gladwell (2005).

14.   It is important to note, as Wilson points out, that "Several other terms were invented to describe mental processes that occur outside of conscious awareness, such as 'automatic,' 'implicit,' 'pre-attentive,' and 'procedural.' Sometimes these terms do a better job of describing a specific type of mental process than the general term 'nonconscious.' The study of automatic processing has flourished, for example, and a lack of awareness of these processes is only one of its defining features" (2002, 5).

15.   According Sie and Wouters, new compatibilism entails a shift away from what I previously labeled *classical compatibilism*. "Contrary to views that connect personal responsibility with the ability to do otherwise, new compatibilism does not need to assume the existence of a metaphysical obscure *counterfactual* freedom, i.e., 'that we could have done otherwise than we actually did.' They just point out that we are the kind of beings who regularly act for reasons and that it is our ability to do so that determines our status as responsible agents"(2010, 125).

16.   For more on the differences between the Freudian unconscious and the adaptive unconscious, see Wilson (2002, ch.1).

17.   See Wilson (2002), Bargh and Ferguson (2000), Bargh and Chartrand (1999), Bargh (1990, 1994, 1996, 1997), Bargh et al. (2001), Chartrand and Bargh (1996), Bechara et al. (1997), Dijksterhuis (2004), Dijksterhuis, van Knippenber, Spears, et al. (1998), Aarts and Dijksterhuis (2000, 2003), Dijksterhuis and van Knippenberg (1998), Steele and Aronson (1995), and Libet (1985, 1987, 1993, 1999).

18.   Timothy Wilson makes it clear that the adaptive unconscious is not a single entity with a mind and will of its own. He points out that: "[H]umans possess a collection of modules that have evolved over time and operate outside of consciousness. Though I will often refer to the adaptive unconscious as a convenient shorthand, I do not mean to characterize it as a single entity, as the Freudian unconscious typically is. For example, we have a nonconscious language processor that enables us to learn and use language with ease, but this mental module is relatively independent of our ability to recognize faces quickly and efficiently and our ability to form quick evalua-

tions of whether environmental events are good or bad. It is thus best to think of the adaptive unconscious as a collection of city-states of the human mind and not as a single homunculus like the Wizard of Oz, pulling strings behind the curtain of conscious awareness" (2002, 7). I will follow Wilson in referring to the adaptive unconscious as convenient shorthand for the multitude of seemingly independent sub-mental cognitive modules, as well as for higher-level nonconscious mental processes.

19. Baumeister uses the terms "self-control" and "self-regulatory" interchangeably.

20. Baumeister has speculated that perhaps ego-depletion has something to do with blood-glucose levels: "Gailliot et al. (2007) began studying blood-glucose dynamics. Glucose is a chemical in the bloodstream that is the fuel for the brain (and other) activities. Although all brain processes use glucose, some use much more than others, and self-control is a likely candidate to be one of these more expensive processes. Gailliot et al. (2007) found that acts of self-control caused reductions in the levels of glucose in the bloodstream, and that low levels of blood glucose after initial acts of self-control were strongly correlated with poor self-control on subsequent tasks. Moreover, experimental administrations of glucose counteracted some of the ego-depletion effects. That is, drinking a glass of lemonade with sugar enabled people to perform well at self-control even if they had recently gone through a depleting exercise of self-control. Lemonade made with a sugar substitute (thus not furnishing glucose) had no effect. . . . These findings suggest that human evolution developed a second, new, and expensive way of controlling action. It involved using relatively large quantities of the body's caloric energy to fuel complex psychological processes" (2008, 17).

21. In chapter 6 I will actually argue that our sense of *conscious will*, understood as consciously initiated action, is not only severely limited but wholly illusory—cf. Libet et al. (1983), Libet (1985), Haggard and Eimer (1999), Haggard, Newman, and Magno (1999), Sirigu et al. (2004), Wegner (2002), Jeannerod (1997, 2006), Pockett (2006).

22. Bargh and colleagues placed a 10-minute limit on how long the participant would have to wait.

23. . Bargh and colleagues write: "The crucial factor in concluding that these results show automatic affects on behavior derives from the perceiver's lack of awareness of the influence of the words. Previous research (see review in Bargh, 1992) has indicated that it is not whether the primes are presented supraliminally or subliminally, but whether the individual is aware of the potential influence of the prime that is critical" (1996, 237).

24. Similar findings were found in experiments designed to test the tendency to be helpful. Macrae and Johnston (1998), for example, found that when they primed participants with words about helpfulness, the participants were more likely to pick up dropped objects for the experimenter. Like in this experiment, these participants were unaware of the significance of the scrambled-sentence word prime and unaware of its effect on their behavior.

25. Right after this experiment, Bargh and his colleagues actually conducted a subsequence study to explicitly test whether the participants were aware of the potential influence of the scrambled-sentence task. Using a version of the contingency awareness funnel debriefing, modeled after Page (1969), they found that only one participant showed any awareness of a relationship between the stimulus words and the elderly stereotype. "However, even this participant could not predict in what form or direction their behavior might have been influenced had such an influence occurred. Thus, it appears safe to conclude that the effect of the elderly priming manipulation on walking speed occurred nonconsciously" (Bargh, Chen, and Burrows 1996, 237).

26. Again, this occurs in a two-stage process. With regard to the first stage, researchers have found that stereotypes of social groups become activated automatically upon the mere perception of the distinguishing features of a group member (e.g., Devine 1989; Brewer 1988; Bargh 1994, 1999). In this experiment, of course, priming manipulations were used to activate the stereotype instead of actually presenting the participants with a member of the stereotyped group. In principle, though, the envi-

ronment could automatically and unconsciously guide people's actions and behaviors through the automatic activation of these stereotypes and trait constructs (see Bargh and Chartrand 1999; Bargh, Chen, and Burrows 1996; Dijksterhuis and van Knippenberg 1998).

27. In fact, it has even been shown that reinforcing a negative stereotype about oneself can cause one to live up to (or, more accurately, live down to) the negative stereotype. Experiments conducted by Steele and Aronson (1995; see also Steele 1997) have shown that when African American males are primed with negative stereotypes about themselves, they performed worse on a standardized test than those who were not primed with the negative stereotype.

28. In terms of method, participants were instructed to work on a computerized visual task that pretesting had shown was considered to be very boring and tedious. Immediately before each trial, the computer flashed a subliminal picture of a young African American male face or a picture of a young Caucasian male face. On the 130th trial, the computer alerted the participant of an ostensible data-saving failure and also informed the participant that he or she would have to do the entire computer task again. For details, see Bargh, Chen, and Burrows (1996).

29. The fact that participants were unaware of any change in their subjective emotion even after they were asked to introspect—despite the fact that the experiment subsequently demonstrated behavioral and judgmental consequences of such change—indicates that these emotional and affective reactions truly occur unconsciously. The fact that participants were asked to rate their subjective emotion *immediately* after they were exposed to the subliminal faces should rule out deficits of attention, motivation, or memory as potential causes for the lack of awareness. As Berridge and Winkielman conclude: "we consider this pattern of findings a demonstration of *unconscious affective reaction*. It meets the criteria for a strong sense of truly implicit emotion. That is, a behaviorally demonstrable affective reaction of which the person is simply not aware, even when that person deliberately introspects and reports in detail on his/her own conscious emotional state. Our thirsty participants were unaware not only of the subliminal facial stimuli, but also of their own emotional reaction to those stimuli. Further, our results demonstrate that both positive affect as well as negative affect can be unconscious, as revealed in bivalent shift from a neutral baseline" (2003, 190). For more on why these findings should be interpreted as a genuine case of unconscious emotion see Berridge and Winkielman (2003).

30. In their second experiment, Winkielman and his colleagues presented participants with the same series of subliminal happy or angry faces. After the primes, some participants were asked to report their subjective emotion on an expanded 20-question mood rating scale, while others were given a taste of the fruit beverage and asked to rate how much they liked it, how much they wanted to consume, and how much they would be willing to pay for a hypothetical can of the beverage. Thirsty participants who were subliminally primed with happy faces liked the beverage more, desired more of it, and were willing to pay nearly double what the angry-primed participants were willing to pay. Again, no change in subjective emotion was produced in these participants.

31. Participants were told that they could receive a gift certificate for either themselves or for a friend. Those who held the hot pack proved to be more likely to ask for the gift certificate for a friend, while those who held the frozen pack tended to keep the gift.

32. Experiments conducted by White, Fishbein, and Rutstein (1981) further confirm these findings.

33. Who we find attractive will also be affected by other automatic processes like the so-called similarity-liking effect. As John Bargh writes, "Here is another example that most people find surprising, again because it involves important life decisions. It has long been know what we have a strong preference and liking for people who are similar to ourselves in appearance, attitude, and beliefs, and this plays a significant role in interpersonal attraction (Byrne, 1971). Recent research has shown that this

similarity-liking effect extends to new people who resemble significant others such as our parents (Andersen & Chen, 2002), although people are not aware of and do not report any such resemblance as a factor in their liking. The similarity effect is so strong, in fact, that it extends even to preferences for places to live and occupational choices that are similar to ourselves in merely superficial ways" (2008, 138-39).

34.   A good example of how automatic goal pursuit can be activated directly by an environmental stimulus or situation can be found in Moskowitz et al. (1999). In an experiment on automatic stereotyping, Moskowitz et al. found that chronic, long-term egalitarian goals (e.g., wanting to treat others fairly) can be activated automatically by a situational feature—i.e., the presence of an ethnic minority group member. That is, the environmental presence of minority-related stimuli automatically activates the associated goal to be fair in chronic egalitarians.

35.   In a series of experiments, Dijksterhuis (2004) presented participants with a number of complex decision problems in which they had to choose between various alternatives, each with multiple attributes. In one experiment, for example, subjects were provided with information about four different apartments. Each apartment was described by 12 attributes, for a total of 48 pieces of information. In another experiment, participants were provided information about potential roommates. In each experiment, there were three conditions (or groups). In the "immediate decision" condition, participants were provided with the relevant information and then had to immediately decide. In the "conscious thought" condition, participants could think about the decision for a few minutes and weigh the various information. In the "unconscious thought" condition, participants were distracted for a few minutes and then prompted to make a decision, thereby enabling them to think unconsciously while at the same time preventing conscious thought. Throughout the experiments, Dijksterhuis consistently found that unconscious thinkers made the best decisions. Experiments by Wilson and Schooler (1991) and Dijksterhuis et al. (2006) have also found that consciousness is a poor decision maker, largely because of its limited capacity (see Miller 1956). And experiments by Dijksterhuis and van Olden (2006) found that not only do people make better choices after engaging in unconscious thought (i.e., unconscious activity during periods of distraction), but weeks later unconscious thinkers tend to be more satisfied with their choice than conscious thinkers. Commenting on these findings, Bargh writes, "From the perspective of modern decision theory these are very surprising findings, but from the present perspective it makes sense that left to its own devices of integrating various disparate pieces of information and coming to the best answer—the task for which the unconscious mind evolved for eons prior to the late add-on of conscious processing—the unconscious route worked best" (2008, 146).

36.   I do not want to suggest here that consciously controlled actions should, on the other hand, be considered free. I believe conscious processes are as causally determined as unconscious processes and hence should be considered "unfree" on the proper incompatibilist understanding of free will. See the next chapter for more on this issue.

37.   I should address a few potential compatibilist replies here before moving on to my last point. Some compatibilists will argue that there *is* an important difference between actions that are supraliminally and subliminally determined—i.e., in the latter case there is an external agent (or agents) trying to manipulate our desires, whereas in the former the external causes are nonagential. Is this distinction, however, as clear as the compatibilist would like to make it? For one, if compatibilists want to argue that desires and actions caused by subliminal images are unfree because they involve agents trying to influence them, what will they say about movies, books, political speeches, TV advertisements, children's cartoons, and educational programs? Isn't *all* advertising, after all, an attempt to manipulate our desires? Aren't external agents involved in making commercials and billboards? What about the millions of dollars corporations spend on creating logos, packaging, and store layouts that are designed to increase desire and sales? Secondly, I do not find the agential/nonagential distinc-

tion all that relevant to the issue at hand—i.e., *the issue of conscious will and control.* Levin, for example, has argued that this distinction is important since in cases where external agents are involved, the way to reform a subject's desires is to reform the external agent's desires; whereas this makes no sense in the case of external causes that are nonagential (2004, and in correspondence). Although this may be true, Levin's point seems more relevant to the issue of reconditioning than the issue I am concerned with here. It says nothing about the growing realization that much of what we think, feel, and do is "driven by current features of the environment (i.e., people, objects, behaviors of others, settings, roles, norms, etc.) as mediated by automatic cognitive processes of those features, without any mediation by conscious choice or reflection" (Bargh 1997, 2). It is *this* type of determinism that I maintain is threatening to free will, regardless of the agential/nonagential distinction, since it threatens the kind of conscious executive control we associate with willfulness.

38. See Wegner (2008) for speculation on some of the evolutionary advantages this illusion may serve.

FIVE

Consciousness and Free Will (II): Transparency, Infallibility, and the Higher-Order Thought Theory

Despite the arguments in the previous chapter there are still many who believe consciousness not only provides us with evidence that we are free but that consciousness itself is the vehicle by which freedom is secured. We typically feel that our conscious selves are in the driver's seat and that we're able to exercise agent-causal control over our actions through our conscious intentions, decisions, and volitions. Upon introspection, we also feel as though we are not causally determined to act as we do. Whereas compatibilists often avoid discussions of consciousness, libertarians generally rest their entire case on the phenomenology of conscious agency and our feeling of freedom. It is not uncommon to appeal to conscious experience, especially the supposed consciousness we have of our own freedom, as evidence for the reality of free will. As Simon Blackburn points out, "Consciousness of freedom seems closely allied to any kind of consciousness at all" (1999, 82). We all seem to be aware of our own freedom in the very act of deliberation, choice, and action. This, I take it, is what gives strength to the libertarian argument and what makes it difficult, perhaps impossible, for us to admit we are not free. The way we experience our own minds, and the fact that we do not experience the multitude of unconscious determinants acting on us, gives us the false sense that the conscious self is in control.

Since our sense of free will is primarily a libertarian one, I would here like to explore the libertarian approach to consciousness and mentality as an entry point into my account of the illusion of free will. I will lay the groundwork for my account of the illusion in this chapter and then build on it in subsequent chapters. In this chapter, I attempt to explain one feature of consciousness—the apparent transparency and infallibility of consciousness—that contributes to the cognitive illusion of free will. In chapters 6 and 7, I will explore additional aspects of consciousness that further contribute to the illusion—e.g., the apparent spontaneity of intentional states, the feeling that we consciously cause and initiate behavior, and the nature of self-consciousness. Although the scientific data reveals a pervasive adaptive unconscious that controls a good deal of our day-to-day lives, our own experience supports a different view of the mind. Phenomenologically we feel as though we, our conscious selves, are in complete control of our intentional/voluntary behavior and that we are in the best position to judge why we act as we do. I will argue that this is due, in part, to a belief in the transparency and infallibility of consciousness. I argue that our belief in the introspective transparency and infallibility of consciousness (which is supported by phenomenology and the way we experience our own mental states), coupled with a failure to introspect any deterministic processes underlying our own decision making, leads us to (wrongly) infer that we are free and causally undetermined.

In this chapter, I also examine two different approaches to consciousness. I first examine theories of consciousness that deny the existence of unconscious mental states. Although these theories are empirically unwarranted given the psychological data presented in the last chapter, they are worth analyzing because they are supported by phenomenology and are more accommodating to free will. Analyzing this approach to consciousness can help us understand why the belief in free will is so powerful. As an alternative, I introduce and defend the *higher-order thought* (or HOT) theory of consciousness as developed by David Rosenthal (2005a). I argue that this theory has several virtues, not the least of which is that it can explain why certain mental states are conscious and not others. I will use the HOT theory in this chapter to explain away the *apparent* transparency and infallibility of consciousness, and I will use it in subsequent chapters to analyze additional aspects of the illusion of free will. The HOT theory is one of the few authentic theories of consciousness available in the literature. Although consciousness has become a hot topic over the last few decades, there are surprisingly few theories out there that venture to formulate necessary and sufficient conditions for consciousness. The HOT theory is one of those theories and it is the one I wish to defend here.

In addition to presenting and defending the HOT theory, I will also consider a larger question: namely, what causal powers does consciousness actually add? Since I have already argued that higher mental processes are largely controlled and determined by unconscious and automatic processes, this will be an important question. I will argue that although conscious mental states do possess distinctive causal powers, these powers are more limited than we typically think and are no different in *type*. I maintain that although consciousness brings with it a *feeling of freedom* it does not bring with it actual freedom. And I conclude that our *subjective feeling of freedom* is nothing but a conscious illusion.

5.1 CONSCIOUSNESS AND FREEDOM: THE INTROSPECTIVE ARGUMENT FOR FREE WILL

In the free will debate, libertarians put a great deal of emphasis on our *conscious feeling of freedom* and our introspective abilities. In fact, many libertarians have suggested that our introspection of the decision-making process, along with our strong feeling of freedom, provides some kind of *evidence* for the existence of free will. As Ledger Wood describes the libertarian argument: "Most advocates of the free will doctrine believe that the mind is directly aware of its freedom in the very act of making a decision, and thus that freedom is an immediate datum of our introspective awareness. 'I feel myself free, *therefore*, I am free,' runs the simplest and perhaps the most compelling of the arguments for freedom" (1941, 387). We can call this the *introspective argument* for free will. The introspective argument essentially maintains that, upon introspection, we do not *seem* to be causally determined—instead, we *feel* that our actions and decisions are freely decided by us—hence, we *must* be free. Libertarians, especially agent-causal theorists, take this introspective datum as their main evidence in support of free will. Timothy O'Connor, for example, writes:

> [T]he agency theory is appealing because it captures the way we experience our own activity. It does not seem to me (at least ordinarily) that I am caused to act by the reasons which favor doing so; it seems to be the case, rather, that I produce my decision *in view of* those reasons, and could have, in an unconditional sense, decided differently . . . Just as the non-Humean is apt to maintain that we not only perceive, e.g., the movement of the axe along with the separation of the wood, but the axe *splitting* the wood . . . , so I have the apparent perception of my actively and freely deciding to take Seneca Street to my destination and not Buffalo instead. (1995b, 196)

Richard Taylor, another leading agent-causal theorist, maintains that there are two introspective items of data: (1) That I *feel* that my behavior is sometimes the outcome of my deliberations, and (2) that in these and other cases, I *feel* that it is sometimes up to me what I do (1992, ch.5). He then concludes: "The only conception of action that accords with our data is one according to which people—and perhaps some other things too— are sometimes, but of course not always, self-determining beings; that is, beings that are sometimes the cause of their own behavior" (1992, 51). C.A. Campbell makes a similar point with regard to moral deliberation:

> The appeal is throughout *to one's own experience* in the actual taking of
> the moral decision as a *creative* activity in the situation of moral tempta-
> tion. "Is it possible," we must ask, "for anyone so circumstanced to
> *dis*believe that he could be deciding otherwise?" The answer is surely
> not in doubt. When we decide to exert moral effort to resist temptation,
> we feel quite certain that we *could* withhold the effort; just as, if we
> decided to withhold the effort and yield to our desires, we feel quite
> certain that we *could* exert it—otherwise we should not blame ourselves
> afterwards for having succumbed. (1957, 169)

The *introspective argument* is therefore important because "all libertarians
assign introspective evidence some role, for it is our feeling of metaphysically open branching paths that is the raison d'être of libertarian freedom" (Ross 2006, 135).[1]

This kind of argument only works, however, if we assume the data is
veridical. But how do we know that our feeling of freedom isn't an illusion? How do we know that what we introspect is accurate? Such arguments, I maintain, fail to *prove* that our phenomenological appearances
accurately represent reality. For one, it is a mistake to think that one
could establish a metaphysical conclusion from phenomenology alone.
More than an appeal to our introspective experience is needed to prove
that we actually *enjoy* agent-causation. Secondly, and perhaps more importantly, I will now argue that there is reason to doubt the reliability of
such introspective evidence. Despite such concerns, however, libertarians
seldom question the "I feel myself free, therefore, I am free" argument. In
fact, the introspective argument can be found throughout the literature.
Although such arguments may not prove we are actually free, they do
reveal that the libertarian conception of agency—a conception I have
argued is shared by common sense—is deeply rooted in our conscious
feeling of freedom and a belief in the accuracy of introspection. Given
this, it is important that we investigate both the role of consciousness and
the accuracy of introspection. I will argue that a closer examination of
these issues will reveal that the nature of consciousness, rather than sup-
porting free will, further impugns it.[2]

Libertarianism and Consciousness

Although libertarians put a great deal of emphasis on consciousness
when it comes to introspecting our own freedom, they ironically overlook the importance of consciousness when it comes to explaining its role
in *producing* free actions. O'Connor, for example, seems to be aware of
this shortcoming when he writes:

> Something the philosopher ought to be able to provide some general
> light on is how consciousness figures into the equation. It is a remark-
> able feature of most accounts of free will that they give no essential role
> to conscious awareness. One has the impression that an intelligent

automata could conceivably satisfy the conditions set by these accounts—something that is very counterintuitive. (2000, 122)

I share O'Connor's surprise at the fact that consciousness has not played
a larger role in accounts of free will, especially given the obvious importance of conscious awareness. It truly is counterintuitive to think that one
could exercise free will unconsciously. As I argued in the previous chapter, any successful account of free will must explain the role consciousness plays in the exercise of free agency and account for the prominence
we give to *conscious will*. According to folk psychology (as well as many
philosophers and psychologists) it is logically inconceivable to imagine
an *automaton*—a creature that lacks all conscious awareness—that has
freedom. An intelligent automaton *cannot* and *should not* be the paradigm
of a free agent, for the picture one gets of an automaton is that of an
intelligent robot; a robot that perhaps can learn to adapt to its environment, a robot that may even have a certain amount of flexibility, but one
that completely lacks freedom. When we say that an action is free, we
typically mean (among other things) that it was the result of a voluntarily
choice, *consciously willed*. Conscious will is believed to be an essential
aspect of free will.

Given that consciousness seems to be a necessary condition for freedom, why have so many accounts of free will overlooked it? O'Connor
speculates at an answer: "That accounts of free will fail to provide an
essential role for consciousness is nonetheless not surprising, given that
its basic biological functions are presently quite mysterious to most theorists" (2000, 122). Although I agree that not *all* of the biological functions
of consciousness are presently known, it is a mistake to think that none of
them are. Consciousness research has a long way to go, but at a minimum
we know that consciousness plays an important role in monitoring our
internal and external environments, contemplating long-range action
plans, and in facilitating memory formation and reasoning.[3] In addition,
libertarians and compatibilists cannot simply neglect the importance of
consciousness because the whole story is not yet in. Libertarians especially have to take the active role of showing that consciousness somehow
imparts to agents a power not possessed by automata or unconscious
creatures.

Immediately after the previous quote, O'Connor continues: "Another
aspect of the puzzle is that whereas various suggestions have been put
forth concerning what specific function or functions consciousness
serves, it is readily imaginable that many of these functions can be carried
out by automata" (2000, 122). If libertarian accounts of freedom are to be
successful, they *must* show that this is not the case. That is, they need to
show that *one* of the functions of consciousness is that it somehow exercises or facilitates free will. To his credit, O'Connor recognizes this point.
He states:

It is highly plausible that this self-determining capacity strictly requires conscious awareness. This appears to follow from the very way in which active power has been characterized as structured by motivating reasons and as allowing the free formation of executive states of intention in accordance with one of the possible courses of action represented to oneself. (I am tempted to think that one should be able to explicitly demonstrate the absurdity of supposing an agent-causal capacity as being exercised entirely unconsciously). (2000, 122)

Given the requirement of conscious awareness, then, it is a sad state of affairs when libertarians, like O'Connor and others, dedicate no more than a few lines to the issue. O'Connor himself only presents one, very vague proposal. He claims, "The agency theorist can conjecture that *a function of biological consciousness, in its specifically human (and probably certain other mammalian) manifestations, is to subserve the very agent-causal capacity I sketched in previous chapters*" (2000, 122). Beyond this, O'Connor does not explain *how* or *in what way* consciousness 'subserves' these presumed agent-causal powers. And this general failure can be found throughout the libertarian literature. Essentially libertarians give us a mere promissory note for the key component of their theory. They fail to provide us with any substantial account of how consciousness carries out this key biological function—i.e., the agent-causal exercise of libertarian freedom.

It seems then that libertarians lack a complete story. On the one hand they appeal to our conscious feeling of freedom as evidence of free will, while on the other hand they neglect to explain the role and importance of consciousness. O'Connor's comments simply amount to the following two claims: (1) That the "self-determining capacity [required for libertarian freedom] strictly requires conscious awareness"; and (2) *somehow* consciousness aids in this capacity. This exposes, I believe, another major problem with libertarianism (and, in general, most defenses of free will)—they typically fail to explain the role of consciousness in the exercise of free will. (In some ways compatibilists are even worse since they usually avoid discussions of consciousness altogether.) Since it is not my job to speculate on how consciousness can aid in self-determination—in fact, I will explicitly attempt to show that it cannot—I will instead focus on the nature of conscious awareness to see what else it can tell us about free will. I will attempt to show that certain features of consciousness lead us to impute more control to the conscious self, and put more faith in the introspective argument, than we should.

Let us return to the introspective argument for a moment. As I have already stressed, from the fact that I *feel* free, it does not necessarily follow that I *am* free. The feeling could be an illusion. What this argument does show, however, is that people often infer their own freedom from their introspective phenomenology of freedom. Why is this so? I propose that people implicitly believe that they have access to all the causal factors and processes underlying their own decision-making. If people were to believe in such introspective transparency, then it would be appropriate, given the above phenomenology, for them to infer that they are undetermined. For if one introspects no deterministic processes underlying one's decision making, and one also thinks that if there *were* a deterministic process one *would* introspect it, one would infer that there is no deterministic process.[4] I therefore argue that a standing phenomenological belief in the introspective transparency and infallibility of consciousness, coupled with a failure to introspect any deterministic processes underlying our own decision making, helps contribute to our sense of free will.[5] From the first-person point of view, we feel as though consciousness is immediate, direct, transparent, and infallible. The *apparent* immediacy, transparency, and infallibility of consciousness leads us to assume a kind of first-person authority where we believe that there can be no mental causes for our actions other than the ones we are aware of. Because we do not experience the multitude of unconscious determinants at work, and because we (wrongly) believe that we *would* be aware of such determinants if they were present, we conclude that no such determinants exist. The phenomenology tricks us here into thinking that it is our conscious will alone that is in control.[6]

This proposal assumes, of course, that consciousness is *not* transparent and does *not* provide us with infallible knowledge of our own mental processes. Am I right to assume this? Clearly, from a first-person point of view, we *feel* as though we are immediately and infallibly connected to our own minds. Can we be wrong about this? Many find it difficult, even impossible, to question our introspective authority. This, of course, is not surprising given the nature of conscious experience. It is important, however, to further examine the nature of consciousness and mentality to see whether we really are transparently and infallibly aware of the inner workings of our mind; for it is our belief in the transparency and infallibility of consciousness that gives the introspective argument whatever power it possesses and contributes to our sense of freedom.

5.2 TWO CONCEPTS OF CONSCIOUSNESS

I would now like to examine two different approaches to consciousness; one that supports the reasoning behind the introspective argument, and one that questions its core assumptions.[7] Given that the majority of support for free will comes from our introspective awareness of the decision-making process, and consciousness appears to be a necessary condition for free will, it would seem that an account of the mind which claims that all mental states are conscious states would be more accommodating to defenders of free will. Such an account of the mind can be traced back to

René Descartes. One can find at the heart of Descartes' philosophy of mind three main theses:

1. That the mind and body are two mutually exclusive, interacting substances—the mind being completely nonphysical.
2. That there is nothing in our mind of which we are not conscious; i.e., all mental states are conscious states; and
3. Our knowledge of our own mental states is certain and infallible; our judgments about them cannot be erroneous.

These three theses comprise the core of Descartes' philosophy of mind. I have already presented an argument against the first of these theses. I have argued, following Kim and Papineau, that worries over mental causation show that interactive substance dualism is an indefensible position. In fact, such worries have caused most to give up the thesis—Antonio Damasio has even dubbed it "Descartes' error" (1994). I would now like to focus on the latter two theses.

Despite a retreat from the metaphysics of substance dualism, the rest of the Cartesian concept of mind remains largely intact when it comes to theorizing about consciousness and free will. Theses (2) and (3) combined amount to the claim that all mental states are conscious and that such consciousness is infallible. Essentially this is the belief in the *transparency* and *infallibility* of consciousness.[8] From a first person point of view these two theses seem compelling. We are conscious of our mental states in a way that seems, at least subjectively, to be direct, immediate, and infallible.

What we need to investigate is whether our phenomenology, which seems to support these two theses, is accurate. I will argue that it is not. From a first-person point of view, it may *seem* as though we are aware of all our mental states and processes—including reasoning and decision making—in an immediate, direct, and infallible way, but from a third-person point of view we can often see that this is not the case. I believe that it is partly because consciousness appears transparent from the first-person point of view that we impart so much power to the conscious will. The fact that, subjectively, mental functioning *appears* transparent to consciousness leads us to attribute more power to consciousness than it actually has. The way we are connected to our own minds produces a misleading feeling of confidence. If consciousness is *not* transparent, then the introspective argument for free will lose its force.

In this section, I will argue that a Cartesian conception of consciousness is neither theoretically desirable nor empirically supported. I will then turn, in the following section, to an alternative conception of consciousness: the *higher-order thought theory* of consciousness. I will argue that consciousness is best viewed as extrinsic to mental states, and that what makes a mental state conscious is one's being *conscious of* that state in some suitable way. I will end the chapter with a look at what this alternative conception of consciousness tells us about free will and some speculation on the function of consciousness.

Let us begin with the claim that all mental states are conscious states. This belief is a main tenet of the Cartesian concept of mind. Descartes famously writes that:

> [T]here can be nothing in the mind, in so far as it is a thinking thing, of which it is not aware, this seems to me to be self-evident. For there is nothing that we can understand to be in the mind, regarded in this way, that is not a thought or dependent on a thought. If it were not a thought or dependent on a thought it would not belong to the mind *qua* thinking thing; and we cannot have any thought of which we are not aware at the very moment when it is in us. (CSM, II:171)[9]

And in the *Second Set of Replies*, Descartes defines "thought" as follows: "I use this term to include everything that is within us in such a way that we are immediately aware of it" (CSM, II:113; AT, VII:160).[10] Since the reference here to thoughts was meant to cover all mental states of whatever kind, including intentional states and sensory states, these remarks are representative of the Cartesian idea that all mental states must be conscious states.[11]

This conception of mentality and consciousness has influenced many philosophers. As Rosenthal points out, "This view is epitomized in the dictum, put forth by theorists as otherwise divergent as Thomas Nagel (1974: 174) and Daniel Dennett (1991: 132), that the appearance and reality of mental states coincide" (2004b, 17; see also Caruso 2005). Not only does it claim that consciousness is an essential property of mental states, but also that consciousness is the mark of the mental. For on the Cartesian concept of mind, what makes a state a mental state is its being a conscious state. States that are not conscious are also not mental. This, however, has significant theoretical drawbacks. If consciousness is what makes a state a mental state, consciousness will not only be an intrinsic, nonrelational property of all mental states, it will also be unanalyzable. Rosenthal, for example, has argued that if being mental means being conscious, we can invoke no mental phenomenon whatever to explain what it is for a state to be a conscious state. And "Since no nonmental phenomenon can help, it seems plain that, on the Cartesian concept of mentality, no informative explanation is possible of what it is for a mental state to be conscious" (1986, 31). Since the Cartesian concept of mind tacitly conflates mentality and consciousness—thereby making consciousness essential to all mental states—no reductive explanation of consciousness can be given in terms of other higher-level cognitive or mental processes. And this precludes giving any informative, nontrivial account of what such consciousness consists in (see Rosenthal 1986, 2002c).

The main difficulty with equating mind and consciousness has to do with understanding the nature of consciousness. If mental states are all conscious, argues Rosenthal, we will simply be unable to understand the very nature of consciousness itself. The problem is the following:

> Suppose mental states are all conscious. How could we then explain what it is for a mental state to be conscious? There are two ways we might proceed. One of these appeals to something mental; we explain what it is for one mental state to be conscious in terms of other mental states or processes. This will not do. If all mental states are conscious states, then the other mental phenomena to which our explanation appeals will themselves be conscious. So this kind of explanation results in a vicious regress. We cannot explain what it is for any mental state to be conscious except in terms of another mental state, whose being conscious itself requires explanation. (2002c, 235)

Since this is unacceptable, the only alternative is to explain what it is for a mental state to be conscious without appealing to any other mental phenomena. The problem with this, however, is that it is highly unlikely that we can understand what it is for a mental state to be conscious appealing only to things that are themselves not even mental. As Rosenthal argues:

> Consciousness is the most sophisticated mental phenomenon there is and the most difficult to understand; nothing in nonmental reality seems to be at all suited to help us grasp its nature. If we are to have any informative explanation of what it is for a mental state to be conscious, it is all but certain that it will have to make reference to mental phenomena of some sort or other. (2002c, 236)

It is important to realize that what we are after here is not a scientific explanation. What we want, instead, is "to understand just what the phenomenon is that a scientific theory might then explain" (Rosenthal 2002c, 235). Since we are looking for a theoretical account of what makes a mental state a conscious state, and not a scientific account, I agree with Rosenthal that an appeal to other mental phenomenon is necessary. [12]

It would seem then that if all mental states are conscious, we can give no informative account of what such consciousness consists in—i.e., we would be unable to explain what makes a mental state conscious. This, I maintain, is a serious problem for any theory of consciousness that equates mind and consciousness. But what is equally troubling, or perhaps even more troubling, is what accepting this equivalence means for understanding the mind itself, not only consciousness. If we were to equate mind and consciousness, we would then have to understand mental processes in terms of consciousness. But doing so would also prevent us from ever developing an informative account of mind (see Rosenthal 2002c, 237). We would be unable to investigate mental processes without at the same time investigating conscious processes. This, I believe, is not only theoretically unacceptable, but given everything I argued in the previous chapter, it is also empirically unjustifiable.

There is more than ample reason, as we've seen, to believe that not *all* mental states are conscious states. Many types of mental states—such as thoughts, desires, beliefs, judgments, goals, and intentions—often occur without being conscious. Both common sense and cognitive science typically posits mental states that are not conscious to explain certain behaviors and cognitive capacities. The most widely accepted of these unconscious mental states are intentional states. There are not only experimental results which provide good reason to hold that beliefs and desires exist that are not conscious, but everyday folk psychology makes much use of intentional states that are not conscious to explain the actions of others. In fact, the majority of philosophers, *pace* John Searle (1990, 1992), now agree that there are nonconscious intentional states. One could even argue that the majority of our intentional states are probably nonconscious.

As I noted earlier, the work of Timothy Wilson, John Bargh, Benjamin Libet, and others have shown that the higher mental processes that have traditionally served as quintessential examples of choice and free will—such as goal pursuits, judgment, interpersonal behavior, and action initiation—can and often do occur in the absence of conscious choice or guidance. It is no longer believed that *only* lower-level processing—or what we can call sub-mental processing (such as perceptual processing)—can occur outside the reach of consciousness. There is now growing evidence that a great deal of higher-level mental functioning is also nonconscious. Psychologists and cognitive (and social-cognitive) scientists have accumulated a great deal of evidence for determinism by demonstrating that high-level mental and behavioral processes can proceed without the intervention of conscious deliberation and choice. All of this mounting research, I believe, proves that high level unconscious cognitive states— states that are best described as *mental*—actively and frequently play a role in human behavior. Some of this research was discussed in chapter 3.

I should point out that when talking about nonconscious mental states, I do not mean simply to be talking about dispositional states; states that are disposed to be occurrent conscious states. I mean to be making the stronger claim that these are occurrent nonconscious states—states that influence behavior and interact with other mental states, both conscious and nonconscious. I also believe discussion of unconscious mental states should not be limited simply to intentional states. Although nonconscious intentional states are more widely acknowledged, there is, indeed, good reason to believe that unconscious sensory states also exist (see Rosenthal 1986, 1991a, 1997; Grahek 2007; Caruso 2005). Following Rosenthal, I believe:

[T]here is reason to hold that the sensory qualities characteristic of our conscious sensations occur even when sensations of the relevant types fail to be conscious, as in peripheral vision and subliminal perceptions and in laboratory contexts such as experiments involving masked priming. When sensations occur without being conscious, they often still affect our behavior and mental processes in ways that parallel the effects of conscious sensations. (2002c, 242)[13]

We have already seen, for example, how unconscious perception can affect behavior in subliminal perception and masked priming experiments. These would be examples of unconscious sensory states. Many theorists also posit nonconscious sensory states—states with sensory qualities—to explain cases of so-called "blindsight" (see Weiskrantz 1986, 1997; Caruso 2005).

The Cartesian thesis, then, that all mental states are conscious states— though perhaps supported by phenomenology—is simply false. Timothy Wilson has even compared it to "Descartes' error" of Cartesian dualism. He writes:

Descartes made a related error that is less well known but no less egregious. Not only did he endow the mind with a special status that was unrelated to physical laws; he also restricted the mind to consciousness. The mind consists of all that people consciously think, he argued, and nothing else. This equation of thinking and consciousness eliminates, with one swift stroke, any possibility of nonconscious thought—a move that was called the "Cartesian catastrophe" by Arthur Koestler and "one of the fundamental blunders made by the human mind" by Lancelot Whyte. Koestler rightly notes that this idea led to "an impoverishment of psychology which it took three centuries to remedy." (2002, 9-10)

Theories of consciousness which still maintain that all mental states are conscious—like those of Searle (1990, 1992), Dretske (1995), and Tye (1995)—therefore remain a stumbling block in the way of progress. What we need is a theory of consciousness that is able to explain why certain mental states are conscious and not others. As Rocco Gennaro puts it, "One question that should be answered by any viable theory of consciousness is: What makes a mental state into a conscious one?" (2004, 1). Any theory that is unable to answer this fundamental question leaves, what Rosenthal has called, *state* consciousness completely unexplained.[14]

Knowing Thy Self: Consciousness and Self-Reports

In addition to the assumption that all mental states are conscious, libertarian and folk-psychological accounts of consciousness usually make the related assumption that consciousness provides us with infallible knowledge of our own minds. The claim of infallibility is another part of the traditional Cartesian concept of mind.[15] From a first-person point of view, this assumption seems to makes sense. Who else, we feel, is in a better position to know which mental states we are in than ourselves? It is often assumed, almost at a definitional level, that we are immediately, directly, and infallibly connected to the content of our own minds. From a first-person point of view, it never seems as though consciousness and mentality come apart. Subjectively, it never seems to us that consciousness mischaracterizes or misidentifies the mental states we are in. It is hard for us to believe that our consciousness can mislead us about the nature of our own minds or that we can be in mental states that we are unaware of.

Although this is undoubtedly how things seem from a first-person point of view, I do not think we can rely on phenomenology alone to the exclusion of all other information. There is a great deal of research suggesting that we are not always the best judges of what's going on in our own minds. As Rosenthal points out:

> [C]onsciousness does not always represent our mental states accurately. Consciousness seems infallible because it never shows itself to be mistaken and it's tempting to think that there's no other way to know what mental states one is in. But consciousness is not the only way to determine what mental state one is in, and there is sometimes compelling independent evidence that goes against what consciousness tell us. (2004b, 27)

Researchers, for example, are increasingly realizing that the mental states and processes that they are interested in measuring are not always consciously accessible to their participants, forcing them to rely on alternative methods (see Wilson 2003). The introspective method—i.e., the method of relying on the introspective reports of subjects—has, in fact, come under attack numerous times throughout the history of psychology (e.g., Nisbett and Wilson 1977; Lieberman 1979; Jack and Roepstorff 2002). In attitudes research, for example, a number of researchers now argue that people can simultaneously possess different implicit and explicit attitudes toward the same object, with self-reports measuring only the explicit attitude (e.g., Wilson, Lindsey, and Schooler 2000). This has led some to develop implicit measures to explore the nature of these attitudes and people's awareness of them (Greenwald, McGhee, and Schwartz 1998).[16]

Our ability to know our own mental states is limited and fallible. People have access to many of their mental states, no doubt, but there is also a pervasive adaptive unconscious that is often inaccessible via introspection. In addition, consciousness, which is accessible to introspective reports, does not always represent our mental states and processes accurately. Individuals often confabulate stories for why they do certain things. When this happens, one's first-person reports fail to match the actual causes for their action. This has been shown to happen, for example, in hypnotized subjects. After being hypnotized, subjects can enact a posthypnotic suggestion—e.g., "when you awake you will immediately crawl around on your hands and knees." When asked what they are doing, subjects almost immediately generate a rationale—"I think I lost an earring down here" (Gazzaniga 1985; Hilgard 1965; Estabrooks 1943). From a first-person point of view, these individuals are conscious of a particular reason for why they are doing what they are doing, but from a third-person point of view we can see that this is not the real cause of their action. Similar examples of confabulation have also been found in "split brain" patients (Gazzaniga and LeDoux 1978) and patients with Korsakoff's syndrome—a form of organic amnesia where people lose their ability to form memories of new experiences (Sacks 1987). [17]

Although it may be tempting to think such confabulation is limited to these rare occasions, some theorists have suggested that similar confabulation occurs throughout everyday life (see Nisbett and Wilson 1977; Gazzaniga and LeDoux 1978; Wilson 2002). These theorists argue that our conscious selves often do not fully know why we do what we do and thus have to confabulate stories and create explanations. In one of the most famous papers on the subject, Nisbett and Wilson (1977) placed subjects in identical situations save for the fact that one or two key features were varied. They observed that although these key features influenced people's judgments or behavior, when asked to explain why they responded the way they did, subjects remained unaware of the varied features and instead confabulated different explanations for their behavior.

In one study, for example, Nisbett and Wilson attempted to see if people could express accurately all the reasons why they preferred one pair of panty hose to another. In the study, conducted in a commercial establishment under the guise of a consumer survey, passersby were invited to evaluate four identical pairs of nylon stockings. The panty hose were arranged neatly on a table labeled A, B, C, and D, from left to right. Nisbett and Wilson found a pronounced left-to-right position effect, such that the right-most object in the array was heavily over-chosen by a factor of almost four to one. They knew that this was a position effect and not that pair D had superior characteristics because all the pairs of panty hose were identical—a fact that went unnoticed by almost all the participants. When asked about the reasons for their choice, no subject ever mentioned spontaneously the position of the article in the array. And, when asked directly about a possible effect of the position of the article, virtually all subjects denied it. Instead of accurately reporting why they chose their preferred pair, people confabulated reasons having to do with superior knit, sheerness, or elasticity. Studies like this seriously question the accuracy of consciousness awareness, because they reveal that consciousness does not provide us with transparent and infallible knowledge of our own minds. We may consciously think we are doing something because of reason X, when in reality we are doing it because of reason Y.[18]

What does this mean for the introspective argument for free will? I believe it shows that we cannot rely on our conscious experience *alone* to determine the causes of our actions. We are often unaware of important causal determinants. The fact that we do not *feel* causally determined, or that we are not consciously aware of the various internal and external influences on our behavior, does not mean such determinants do not exist. Worse still, if consciousness can confabulate and/or misrepresent the causes for our choices and/or actions, then to rely on such conscious data to infer our own freedom would be a mistake. Whatever persuasiveness the introspective argument originally had depended on the assumption that we had direct, infallible access to our own decision-making process. The argument assumes that consciousness reveals everything about our mental functioning, or at least everything relevant to the issue at hand. This, however, is not the case. What we are conscious of, and hence what we can report on, is not always in line with what is otherwise going on mentally.

We have now seen that identifying mind and consciousness not only makes it impossible to give an informative account of what consciousness consists in, it is also incompatible with everything we know about mental processes. Recent research into automaticity and the adaptive unconscious has revealed that sophisticated, higher mental processes can occur without conscious awareness, control, or intervention. We have also seen that consciousness can at times confabulate stories and misidentify the states we are in. What we need, then, is a conception of consciousness that does justice to these two insights. We need an account of consciousness which explains why consciousness *appears* transparent from a first-person point of view, yet also explains why it is not. As Rosenthal puts it, "Consciousness does reveal the phenomenological data that a theory of consciousness must do justice to. But to save these phenomena, we need only explain why things appear to consciousness as they do; we need not also suppose that these appearances are always accurate" (2004b, 31). I will now introduce a theory of consciousness which explains state consciousness in terms of higher-order awareness. I will argue that consciousness is best viewed as extrinsic to mental states, and that what makes a mental state conscious is one's being conscious of that state in some suitable way. This account of consciousness, while accurately capturing the phenomenology, will explain how there can be unconscious mental states. It will also explain how we can misrepresent or even on occasion confabulate the mental states we are conscious of.

5.3 THE HIGHER-ORDER THOUGHT (HOT) THEORY OF CONSCIOUSNESS

Let me begin by sketching in its most basic outline the *Higher-Order Thought* (HOT) theory of consciousness. David Rosenthal has made the clearest and best case for the HOT hypothesis in a series of cogent and convincing papers (1986, 1991a, 1993a, 1993c, 1993d, 1997, 2002c, 2002d, 2003, 2004b). Accordingly, I will concentrate on Rosenthal's version of the theory, focusing specifically on how it deals with the research on automaticity and the adaptive unconscious. I will argue that the HOT theory is particularly well suited to account for how there can be unconscious mental states, as well as to accommodate disparities between our higher-level mental processes and our first-person reports of those processes.

The HOT theory belongs to a larger class of theories known as *higher-order* (or HO) theories of consciousness. Such theories can be traced as far back as John Locke (1689). Recently, HO theories have been presented by a number of philosophers. Besides Rosenthal, HO theories have been advanced by Armstrong (1968, 1981), Lycan (1996), Carruthers (1996, 2000), and Gennaro (1996, 2005). Gennaro describes the basic idea behind HO theories as follows: "In general, the idea is that what makes a mental state conscious is that it is the object of some kind of higher-order representation (HOR). A mental state M becomes conscious when there is a HOR of M. A HOR is a 'meta-psychological' state, i.e., a mental state directed at another mental state" (2004, 1). According to HO theories, then, my desire to get this chapter done becomes conscious when I somehow become *aware* of that desire; i.e., when I have a HOR of that desire. HO theories have intuitive appeal since a state of which one is in no way aware does not intuitively count as conscious. As Rosenthal writes:

> If an individual is in a mental state but is in no way whatever conscious of that state, we would not intuitively count it as a conscious state. So a state's being conscious consists of one's being conscious of it in some suitable way.... It is this equivalence of a state's being conscious with one's being conscious of it in some suitable way that points toward a higher-order theory of what it is for a mental state to be conscious. (2004b, 17)

According to HO theories, we can explain a state's being conscious in terms of a higher-order state's being directed on that state. This hierarchical or iterative structure is what distinguishes HO theories from other theories of consciousness—especially first-order representational (FOR) theories, like those of Tye (1995) and Dretske (1995).[19]

There are essentially two types of higher-order theories, differing on how they understand the HOR. There are higher-order *thought* (HOT) theories—like those of Rosenthal (2005a), Carruthers (1996, 2000), and Gennaro (1996)—and there are higher-order *perception* (HOP) or higher-order *sensory* theories—like those of Lycan (1996) and Armstrong (1968, 1981). These two HO theories differ over the nature of the higher-order representation. HOT theorists, like Rosenthal, argue that the higher-order state should be viewed as a thought. HOP theorists, on the other hand, argue that the HOR is closer to a *perceptual* or *experiential* state of some kind. The central difference between these two views is over the need for conceptual content. More specifically, HOT theorists maintain that the HOR is a *cognitive* state involving some kind of conceptual component, whereas higher-order perception or sensory theories argue that the HOR is closer to a *perceptual* or *experiential* state of some kind which does not require the kind of conceptual content invoked by HOT theorists. Because of this difference, and largely due to Kant (1781), the latter are sometimes referred to as "inner sense" theories as a way of emphasizing this sensory or perceptual aspect. So whereas the HOT theory contends that a mental state is conscious just in case it is the object of a higher-order thought (i.e., a cognitive state with conceptual content), the HOP (or "inner sense") theory holds that the HOR is a kind of internal scanning or monitoring by a quasi-perceptual faculty.

Some philosophers have argued that the difference between these theories is perhaps not as important or as clear as some think it is (Gennaro 1996; Van Gulick 2000). Others, like Guzeldere (1995), have argued that the HOP theory ultimately reduced to the HOT theory. I, myself, believe that the HOT theory, as developed by Rosenthal, has distinct advantages over the HOP theory. I also maintain that Rosenthal's version of the HOT theory is superior to those of Carruthers and Gennaro. Some of my reasons for believing this will come out below, but for the most part I will not discuss these other HO theories. I will instead focus on Rosenthal's version of the HOT theory, pointing out, where possible, how it differs from these other theories. For a more detailed account of why Rosenthal's version of the HOT theory is superior to these other HO accounts, see Rosenthal's "Varieties of Higher-Order Theory" (2004b).

Although there are significant differences between these accounts, all HO theories agree that what makes a mental state conscious is its relation to another, higher-order, mental state. Because of their hierarchical nature, "HO theories are also attractive to some philosophically inclined psychologists and neuroscientists partly because they suggest a very natural realization in the brain structure of humans and other animals" (Gennaro 2004, 2). See, for example, Rolls (1999), Weiskrantz (1997), and Lau (2007, 2010). Gennaro describes the basic appeal of HO theories as follows: "At the risk of oversimplification, if we think of the brain as developing layers upon layers corresponding to increasing sophistication in mental ability, then the idea is that mental states corresponding to various 'higher' areas of the brain (e.g., cortex) are directed at various 'lower' states rendering them conscious" (2004, 2). In fact, a number of HO theorists have maintained that first-order perceptual representations, for example, depend on neural activity in early sensory regions, whereas higher-order representations depend on neural activity mainly in prefrontal (and parietal) cortex (e.g., Lau and Rosenthal 2011; Lau 2010; Kriegel 2009). And although not a necessary condition of such theories, this empirical interpretation of HO theories has recently received support from emerging findings in cognitive neuroscience, giving the view substantial empirical credibility and an advantage over its competitors (see Lau and Rosenthal 2011). It's important to point out, however, that HO theories themselves do not, in general terms, attempt to reduce consciousness *directly* to neurophysiological states. As Gennaro describes:

> Unlike some other theories of consciousness (Crick & Koch, 1990; Crick, 1994), they are not reductionist in the sense that they attempt to explain consciousness directly in physicalistic (e.g., neurophysiological) terms. Instead, HO theories attempt to explain consciousness in *mentalistic* terms, that is, by reference to such notions as 'thoughts' and 'awareness.' . . . HO theorists are normally of the belief that such mental states are identical with brain states, but they tend to treat this matter as a further second step reduction for empirical science. (2004, 2)

HO theories, then, provide a mentalistic reduction of consciousness. Although this is different from a physicalistic reduction, HO theories are more accommodating to materialist accounts of the mind than are Cartesian accounts.

A mentalistic reduction of consciousness would be the first step in reducing consciousness to brain states. Armstrong, for example, endorses a HO theory of consciousness for the mentalistic reduction, and then famously proposes a *causal-functionalist* theory (1966, 1968, 1977, 1981) — like that of David Lewis (1966, 1972, 1980) — for the reduction of mental states to brain states. The neurophysiological *realizers* for these causal-functional states would be a matter for empirical science to discover, but by combining these two theories one could see how a completely materialistic account of the mind is possible. Although one need not be a materialist to accept a HO explanation of consciousness, HO theories (as I see them) provide a nice accompaniment to the kind of mind-brain materialism I argued for in chapter 2. Given that we have some intuitive understanding of mental states (like thoughts) independent of the problem of consciousness, HO theories promise a mentalistic reduction of consciousness. Once we have reduced consciousness to more tractable mental states, one could then, in turn, adopt whichever mind-brain account of mental states they see fit to round out the picture.

Let me now turn to the HOT theory itself. The leading principle behind the HOT theory, like all other HO theories, is that a mental state is conscious only if one is, in some suitable way, conscious of that state. This is what we can call the *transitivity principle*. According to this principle, to be *conscious of* something, or *transitively conscious of* something is to be "in a mental state whose content pertains to that thing" (Rosenthal 1997, 737). For Rosenthal, it is to have a *higher-order thought* of that state. Conscious states themselves, according to this theory, are always *intransitively conscious*. This is what Rosenthal calls *state consciousness* and it is what we seek to explain. State consciousness is a property only of mental states. It is the property of being conscious that some mental states have and others lack. Rosenthal distinguishes state consciousness from both *transitive* consciousness and *creature* consciousness (see 1993c). What we want, Rosenthal argues, is "an account of what it is for mental states to be intransitively conscious on which that property is relational and not all mental states are conscious" (1997, 737). Rosenthal's way of doing this is to explain intransitive or state consciousness in terms of transitive consciousness. And he does this by giving a HOT, as opposed to a HOP, account of transitive consciousness.[20]

A higher-order thought, or HOT, is a thought about some mental state. The core idea of the HOT model is that a mental state is a conscious state when, and only when, it is accompanied by a suitable HOT. And a *thought*, according to Rosenthal, is "any episodic intentional state with an assertoric mental attitude" (1993b, 913 fn.2). Roughly, then, the HOT hypothesis states that a mental state is conscious "just in case one has a roughly contemporaneous thought to the effect that one is in that very mental state" (1993d, 199). This statement of the hypothesis, however, still needs some further restrictions. According to the HOT theory, we must also specify that our transitive consciousness of our mental state "relies on neither inference nor observation . . . of which we are transitively conscious" (1997, 738). One's HOT, that is, must be *noninferential*. This restriction is needed to exclude cases in which one has a thought that one is in a mental state because of the testimony of others, or because one has observed one's own behavior.

We are now in a better position to state the core idea behind the HOT theory of consciousness. We can say that the HOT must be an *assertoric, noninferential, occurrent propositional state*. And we can explain state consciousness as follows: a mental state is a conscious state when, and only when, we have an *assertoric, noninferential, occurrent thought* to the effect that one is in that very mental state.

The HOT theory says that what makes a mental state conscious is the presence of a suitable HOT directed at it. The fact that when we are in conscious states we are typically unaware of having any such HOTs is no objection, for the theory actually predicts that we would not be. Since a mental state is conscious only if it is accompanied by an assertoric, noninferential, occurrent HOT, that HOT will not itself be a conscious thought unless one has a third-order thought about the second-order thought; and Rosenthal points out that this rarely happens. We are conscious of our HOTs only when those thoughts themselves are conscious, and it is rare that they are. In the rare cases in which this does happen, we would be *introspectively* conscious of being conscious of one's mental states. Hence:

> Most of the time, our mental states are conscious in an unreflective, relatively inattentive way. But sometimes we deliberately focus on a mental state, making it the object of introspective scrutiny. The HOT model readily explains such introspective consciousness as occurring when we have a HOT about a mental state and that HOT is itself a conscious thought. (Rosenthal 2002c, 242)

Introspective consciousness, according to the HOT theory, is the special case of conscious states in which the accompanying HOT is itself a conscious thought because it is the object of a yet higher-order (or third-order) thought.

It is important to note, however, that the HOT theory is *not just* an account of introspective consciousness. Some theorists, I believe, have made this mistake (e.g., Papineau 2002, ch.7).[21] At bottom, the HOT theory explains state consciousness in terms of transitive consciousness or HOTs. But our HOTs, in normal non-introspective conscious experience, are usually nonconscious. As Rosenthal (1986, 1997) and others have pointed out, one can be aware of an experience (via a nonconscious HOT) without introspectively thinking about that experience (see also Gennaro 1996, 16-21; 2003). When one introspects, on the other hand, one's conscious focus is directed back into one's mind, and this will involve a third-order thought (which itself is nonconscious) directed at the HOT. When one is *introspectively aware*, one is conscious of being conscious. The HOT theory has the resources to easily account for this, but one should not confuse the theory with a theory simply of introspective consciousness.

On Rosenthal's account, then, state consciousness turns out to be non-intrinsic and relational. Since a mental state is a conscious state when, and only when, it is accompanied by a suitable HOT, no mental state is essentially conscious. In fact, one of the merits of the HOT model is that it requires that no mental state is essentially conscious. Rosenthal's theory requires that consciousness is a contingent property of mental states, for any mental state that is the object of a HOT presumably need not have been. A mental state is a conscious state only when it is accompanied by a HOT, and is unconscious otherwise. This account fits very nicely with what I have been arguing here. In particular, the HOT model recognizes the existence of unconscious mental states, something Cartesian theories fail to do. This allows us a way of understanding all the interesting research on the automaticity of higher mental processes and the adaptive unconscious discussed in the previous chapter. Reference to noncon-scious mental states can be made, according to the theory, on the basis of the causal role those states play with regard to behavior, shifts in attention, interaction with other mental states, and the like.

Before moving on, there are a few additional aspects of the theory that are worth pointing out. For one, on Rosenthal's account our HOTs should be understood as *extrinsic* to (i.e., entirely distinct from) its target mental state. This differs from Gennaro (1996), for example, who argues that, when one has a first-order conscious state, the HOT is better viewed as *intrinsic* to the target state, so that we have a complex conscious state with parts. He calls this the "wide intrinsicality view" (WIV). I believe Rosenthal's extrinsic account is preferable. For one, it allows a more plausible explanation of cases of misrepresentation and confabulation. If one were to view the HOT as intrinsic to the target states, then it would be hard to explain cases where there is a divergence between the mental states we are in and our awareness of those states. As I argued before, consciousness does not provide us with infallible knowledge of our mental states. [22]

Rosenthal's theory should also be viewed as an *actualist* HOT theory. That is, what makes a mental state conscious, according to Rosenthal, is that it is the object of an *actual* HOT directed at the mental state. This differs, for example, from Carruthers's (1996, 2000) *dispositional* HOT theory, which holds that the HOT need not be actual, but can instead be a dispositional state of some kind. Against the dispositional view, Rosenthal writes, "Simply being disposed to have a thought about something does not result in my being conscious of that thing. For a state to be conscious, my HOT must actually occur" (2002c, 243; also see 2004b). I agree here with Rosenthal, and hence will be appealing to the *extrinsic-actualist* version of the HOT theory in what's to follow.

Furthermore, according to Rosenthal's version of the theory, one should not view the first-order (or target) state as the *only* or *primary* cause of its accompanying HOT (see 1993a). Our HOTs, according to Rosenthal, are sometimes caused by their target states, but there can be other factors that figure in causing it as well. Given that mental states often occur without any accompanying HOT, it cannot be that the states are, by themselves, causally sufficient to produce HOTs; instead "other mental occurrences must enter into the aetiology" (2002c, 245). These other mental occurrences could include our expectations, focus and attention, unconscious monitoring of the environment, and connection to other mental states (both conscious and unconscious). According to the HOT theory, then, which states become conscious is a complex matter determined by a number of different factors. Sometimes the target state will be implicated in causing the accompanying HOT, other times the HOT will be caused by its relation to states other than the target state (both conscious and unconscious).

5.4 MISREPRESENTATION AND CONFABULATION

Since HOTs are extrinsic to lower-order mental states, we can now better understand how misrepresentation and confabulation can occur. HOTs can sometimes represent mental states fully and accurately, but they can also *under-represent, misrepresent,* or even *confabulate* those states. As Rosenthal writes: "Typically we see things accurately, and it's also likely that consciousness ordinarily represents correctly what mental states we are in. But misrepresentation of such states can happen (see, e.g., Nisbett & Wilson 1977), and it is an advantage of a higher-order theory that it accommodates such occurrences" (2004b, 35). The HOT theory, I believe, is particularly well suited to explain cases in which the way a conscious state appears differs from the way it actually is. According to the theory, whatever the actual character of a mental state, that state, if conscious, is conscious in respect of whatever mental properties one's HOT represents the state as having. So if our HOT represented us as being in a sensory state with such-and-such a sensory quality, for example, then we would be conscious of that state as having that quality. But since we are dealing with a representational relation between two states, the possibility of misrepresentation always exists. Our HOTs, that is, can fail to represent their targets accurately or fully.

Perhaps the most common form of misrepresentation happens when our HOTs under-represent their target states. As Rosenthal likes to point out, a particular mental state need not be conscious in respect of all of its mental properties. One may be aware, for example, of a throbbing pain only as painful, and not also in respect of its throbbing qualities. Or one may be aware of a sensation of red not in respect of its particular shade, say magenta, but simply as red. According to Rosenthal:

> When one consciously sees something red, one has a conscious sensa-
> tion of red. The sensation, moreover, will be of a particular shade of
> red, depending on what shade of red one sees. But, unless one focuses
> on that shade, one typically isn't conscious of the red in respect of its
> specific shade; the sensation is conscious only as red of some indeter-
> minate shade. (2002c, 245)

In cases like this, we can say that our HOTs misrepresent the target states they are about since what we are subjectively conscious of does not cap-ture the full nature of those states. Sometimes our HOTs will represent their targets in coarse-grained ways (i.e., *red of some indeterminate shade*), other times—as when one focuses on the experience—the content of our HOTs will be more fine-grained (i.e., *magenta*).

This kind of misrepresentation is probably common with mental states that monitor the environment. Take, for example, the cocktail party effect. When we are at a cocktail party engrossed in a conversation, the other conversations going on around us typically turn into background noise. In a case like this, we can say that our HOTs represent those other conversations as indistinguishable chatter. This does not mean, however, that our auditory states possess only those properties we are aware of. In fact, our auditory states continue to monitor the environment looking for relevant information. If, for example, our name were to come up in one of those other conversations our attention would quickly shift to that conversation. This suggests that our auditory states have properties and represent the environment in ways that our HOTs do not make us aware of. Because our focal attention is not on those other conversations but is on the conversation we are in, our HOTs do not fully represent those auditory states. This, then, would be another example where our HOTs misrepresent (in the sense of under-represent) our mental states. When our attention is focused on only one part of our conscious experience, the rest of the environment is being under-represented.[23]

If our HOTs can misrepresent the mental states they are about, might it happen that HOTs sometimes occur in the absence of the relevant target state altogether? I believe that if we allow for the misrepresentation of mental states, we need to also allow for the possibility of confabulation—for it is very difficult, perhaps impossible, to distinguish between a case where one drastically misrepresents the mental state they are having, and where one confabulates the state. How much misrepresentation, for example, should we allow before we say it is a different state? Rosenthal, in fact, argues that the distinction between an absent target and a misrepresented target is in an important way arbitrary:

> Suppose my higher-order awareness is of state with property P, but the target isn't P, but rather Q. We could say that the higher-order awareness misrepresents the target, but we could equally well say that it's an awareness of a state that doesn't exist. The more dramatic the misrepresentation, the greater the temptation to say the target is absent; but it's plainly open in any such case to say either. (2004b, 32)

In addition, Rosenthal argues that from a first-person point of view it would be indistinguishable when we are having a HOT together with a target state and when we are having a HOT without a target. If I am conscious of myself as being in a P state, he maintains, "it's phenomenologically as though I'm in such a state whether or not I am" (2004b, 35). This aspect of the HOT theory, then, allows us to explain how cases of confabulation could occur, while at the same time preserving the phenomenological appearance.

With these details in place, we can now explain the kind of confabulation discussed earlier by saying that our HOTs represent us as being in states that we are not actually in (or, if you prefer, that our HOTs drastically misrepresent their target states). When this happens, what we are experiencing from a first-person point of view is not the same as what is otherwise going on mentally. We can consciously report being in a P state when, in fact, we are not in any such state. This allows for the possibility of our lower-order mental states causing our behavior in one way, while our HOTs make us aware of a different causal story. Since it is our HOTs which determine *what it's like for us*, and since our HOTs are extrinsic to their target states, Rosenthal's version of the HOT theory is particularly well suited to explain how this can happen. If, for example, we were to confabulate a want or desire, *P*, to explain a particular action *X* —when in reality the true cause for *X* was *Q*—according to the HOT theory, we would subjectively feel as if we are doing *X* because of *P*. Although our HOTs will usually represent their targets accurately, I think it is a virtue of the theory that it allows for the possibility of misrepresentation and confabulation.

Confabulation (or, if you prefer, drastic misrepresentation) is not limited to intentional states either. I have previously argued that we can even confabulate being in pain (Caruso 2005). Children, for example, dislike going to the dentist because it hurts. Researchers have found, however, that there are two components to children's dental pain, painful sensations and anxiety (see Chapman 1980). And researchers have found that anxiety is often confounded with pain (Schacham and Daut 1981) and accounts for about a third of the variance in assessment of pain (Melzack and Torgerson 1971). In fact, this has led researchers to try to devise treatments for dental pain by treating anxiety. These treatments work by changing the patient's attention and imagery (Shapiro 1982) and by heightening the patient's perceptions of self-control (Chapman 1980; Baron, Logan, and Hoppe 1993; Baron and Logan 1993). Giving patients instructions, for example, to focus on sensory (vs. emotional) stimuli during a root canal procedure was found to significantly reduce self-reported pain among patients who were classified as having strong desire for control and low felt control in dental situations (Baron, Logan, and Hoppe 1993).

These findings support the HOT model's claim that one's expectations and interests can help determine what HOTs one will have. We can hypothesize that these patients experience anxiety or fear, along with the lack of control, and consciously react as though in pain, even when local anesthetic makes it unlikely that such pain could be occurring. In these cases the patient can be said to be misidentifying one state, anxiety or fear, for another, pain. And as it turns out, giving the patients back some sense of control (e.g., providing information and stress inoculation training) actually reduces self-reported pain in many of the patients (Baron and Logan 1993). Similar findings have been found in areas other than dental pain. Peter Staats and colleagues (1998), for example, report findings in which rehearsed positive and negative thoughts—whose content is independent of pain—modify the effects of painful stimuli, both as subjectively reported and by standard physiological measures. He found that self-suggestion and the placebo effect, in which genuine assertoric

HOTs presumably occur, significantly altered participants' pain threshold, pain tolerance, and pain endurance.

We can say then that according to the HOT theory: (a) it is the HOT that determines *what it's like* for us; (b) the content of our HOTs can be influenced by factors other than the target state (e.g., the need for control, anxiety, expectations, social preconceptions, idiosyncratic beliefs, conceptual resources, etc.); and (c) our HOTs can misrepresent or confabulate the mental states we are in.

Thus far I have only discussed the possibility of error occurring between our HOTs and their targets, but presumably error can also occur at the level of introspection. Since introspective consciousness, according to the HOT theory, is also the product of a representational relation between two mental states—i.e., when we are introspectively conscious, our HOT is itself the target of a yet higher-order (or third-order) thought—error can happen here too. Some may even find error at this level easier to accept than at the earlier level (e.g., Schooler and Schreiber 2004). At least three independent sets of investigators have recently offered compelling arguments for how discrepancies can occur between our conscious states and our introspective awareness of those states (Schooler 2000, 2001, 2002a, 2002b; Lambie and Marcel 2002; Jack and Shallice 2001; Jack and Roepstorff 2002; for a review, see Schooler and Schreiber 2004).

The approach taken by Jonathan Schooler, for example, focuses on dissociations between consciousness and what he calls *meta-consciousness* (what I am calling introspective consciousness). Schooler and Schreiber describe such dissociations as follows:

> The basic idea underlying the distinction between consciousness and meta-consciousness is simply that individuals often have experiences without necessarily explicitly introspecting about them. As a consequence introspection can fail for two very general reasons. First, introspection may not be invoked. Such introspective failures are what Schooler (2002b) refers to as 'temporal dissociations' in which experience occurs in the absence of meta-awareness. . . . Second, introspection can fail because, in their attempt to characterize an experience, individuals may distort it. [These introspective difficulties] can be characterized as 'translation dissociations' between consciousness and meta-consciousness. Some of the sources of these translation dissociations may result from processes associated with *detection, transformation*, and *substitution*. (2004, 31)

So just as our HOTs can distort or misrepresent their target states, our third-order thoughts can likewise distort our conscious mental states. According to Schooler, substitutions, transformations, and difficulties in detection can occur when we attempt to introspect. Anthony Marcel has likewise found that, "Attending to one's experience, introspecting, changes the content, nature and form of the experience" (2003, 179). And

Lambie and Marcel (2002) have argued that introspection can *influence its object*, *create its object*, and *distort its object*.

In terms of the HOT theory, when we introspect and attend to our own conscious experience—whether to examine it, remember it, or report it—our third-order representational states can be influenced by expectations and motivations (just like our second-order HOTs can) thereby distorting the original experience. As Schooler and Schreiber argue, "Introspections may sometimes go awry because the information accessed is not the record of actual experience" (2004, 33). It's possible that instead of retrieving the memory of conscious experience, "people may instead bring beliefs to meta-awareness without realizing that the contents of meta-consciousness may diverge substantially from what was experienced in consciousness" (2004, 33). Expectations, motivations, and idiosyncratic beliefs are among the forces involved in this type of error. Introspection, especially when dealing with introspective reports on behavior, is often more a matter of retro-diction or inference than direct introspection. In fact, many cases of confabulation are probably the result of attempts to introspect mental causes that are no longer occurrent or were unconscious in the first place. When we turn inward in an attempt to introspect why we just behaved as we did, or why we just made the evaluation or judgment we just made, we do not introspect the original mental causes, we introspect a conscious memory. Such introspection is susceptible to influence by internal and external pressures. The content of our third-order state can be influenced, that is, by social expectations and personal idiosyncratic theories.

Some forms of confabulation may therefore be better explained as errors occurring at the level of introspection. I need not make any principled claims, however, about which kinds of errors occur at the level of consciousness and which occur at the level of introspection. Discerning at which level an error occurs might be extremely difficult to do. My interest here is simply to establish that consciousness is neither transparent nor infallible.

5.5 WHAT THE HOT THEORY TELLS US ABOUT FREE WILL

What does the HOT theory tell us about free will? For one, it tells us that Cartesian and libertarian accounts of consciousness, accounts which fit more comfortably with our folk-psychological beliefs about free will, are ill conceived. What the growing research on automaticity and the adaptive unconscious shows us, and what the HOT theory is able to explain, is that: (1) not all mental states are conscious states; and (2) we do not have infallible knowledge of all our higher-level mental states and processes. The HOT theory provides an account of consciousness that complements the research on automaticity and the adaptive unconscious. It explains why certain mental states are conscious and not others. It also explains, by revealing the relational nature of consciousness, how we can misrepresent or confabulate the mental states we are in.

As we witnessed in chapter 4, higher-level processes (such as goal directed behavior) can occur completely without conscious involvement, and thus automatically. Bargh's (1990) *auto-motive model* of environmentally driven, goal directed behavior, explains how this can happen. The auto-motive model assumes that external events can trigger goals directly, without an explicit conscious choice, and that they then operate without the person knowing it. This fits with the findings of Aarts and Dijksterhuis (2000), who conjecture that habitual behaviors are automatically linked not to relevant environmental events per se but rather to the mental representations of the goal pursuits they serve. Hence, when a goal is unconsciously activated, the habitual plan for carrying out that goal can automatically be activated as well; without need of conscious planning or selection. This can happen when environmental features become automatically associated with the top level or trigger of the goal structure—the same internal representation that is presumably activated by conscious will (see Bargh 1990; Chartrand and Bargh 1996; Bargh and Ferguson 2000).

On the HOT model, such cases of automatic goal-directed behavior would be explained in terms of unconscious first-order mental states. The environment unconsciously and automatically causes in us a first-order mental state—in this case, a mentally represented goal—which carries out its action plan without conscious processing or selection. These first-order mental states remain unconscious since they are not accompanied by HOTs. As Bargh and Ferguson argue:

> Theoretically, this is possible if one assumes that goal representations behave by the same rules as do other mental representations and develop automatic associations to other representations that are frequently and consistently active at the same time (i.e., Hebb's, 1949, principle of contiguous activation; see Shiffrin & Dumais, 1981; Shiffrin & Schneider, 1977). Thus, if a person consistently chooses to pursue the same goal within a given situation, over time that goal structure becomes strongly paired with the internal representation of that situation (i.e., the situational features). Eventually, the goal structure itself becomes active on the perception of the features of that situation. (2000, 934)

Thus, the environment itself could directly activate a first-order unconscious goal as part of the preconscious analysis of the situation. The goal would then operate in the same manner—without the individual knowing it—as when put into play consciously.

Bargh asserts that this can happen not only with habitual behaviors, but also with novel and nonhabitual behaviors (see Bargh 1990; Chartrand and Bargh 1996; Bargh and Ferguson 2000). And the work of Gollwitzer (1993, 1999; Gollwitzer and Brandstätter 1997) seems to support this claim. All of this research is threatening to free will as normally conceived, for actions that are performed automatically and unconsciously cannot occur freely.

Since the HOT theory is compatible with the automaticity of higher mental processes—especially Bargh's auto-motive model—it too is threatening to free will. Nonconscious mental states have causal roles that are not controlled by our conscious will and these causal roles can be triggered by the environment via a mentally represented goal. Such automatic behavior has traditionally been the paradigm of unfree behavior—for it is commonly defined as unwilled, unintentional, and unaware. According to this traditional perspective, then, "the complexity and the abstract, protracted nature of the kinds of mental processes and social behavior that social-cognition research has recently discovered to operate and occur without conscious, aware guidance have bestowed an unprecedented legitimacy to the traditional conception of determinism" (Bargh and Ferguson 2000, 926). Hence, unlike Cartesian accounts which wrongly deny the existence of unconscious mental states, the HOT theory is compatible with the determination of human behavior by unconscious, automatic processes.

Bargh and Ferguson (2000) point out, however, that the traditional conception of determinism in cognitive and social-cognitive science is inappropriately constrained by the equation of determination with the lack of conscious awareness, choice, and guidance of the process. This constraint gives the impression that consciously mediated acts might be freely willed (i.e., nondetermined). But as Bargh and Ferguson point out:

> [A]lthough the growing social-cognitive evidence of the degree to which higher mental processes can proceed nonconsciously is consistent with the traditional determinist position, by showing that these processes do not require an intervening act of conscious will to occur, it should not be concluded from this that those processes that require conscious or controlled processes (such as those involving temporary and flexible use of working memory; see E.E. Smith & Jonides, 1998) are any less determined. (2000, 926)

Bargh and Ferguson maintain, as I do, that those processes and behaviors that do entail an act of conscious choice are *equally* determined. They write:

> As scientists studying human behavior and the higher mental processes, we reject the thesis of free will as an account of the processes that require conscious control (see also Prinz, 1997). Instead, we embrace the thesis that behavior and other responses are caused, including a person's choices regarding those responses; every deliberation, thought, feeling, motivation, and impulse, conscious or nonconscious, is (often multiply) caused. (2000, 926)

Hence, the presence of conscious control may be a *necessary* condition for free will—as witnessed by our earlier examination of the libertarian position—but it is by no means a *sufficient* condition. Both conscious and nonconscious processes are causally determined according to my account. There is absolutely no reason, then, "to invoke the idea of free will or a nondetermined version of consciousness as a causal explanatory mechanism in accounting for higher mental processes in humans" (Bargh and Ferguson 2000, 939).

There are essentially three reasons for rejecting a nondetermined account of consciousness. For one, as we've already seen, there are insurmountable problems facing libertarian accounts of freedom. Those problems extend to libertarian accounts of consciousness (i.e., nondetermined versions of consciousness). The brain functions according to the principles of classical physics, not quantum physics. Secondly, psychology, cognitive science, and the social-cognitive approach to higher mental processes adopt a deterministic stance toward psychological phenomena (see Bargh and Ferguson 2000; Amsel 1989; Bargh 1997; Barsalou 1992; Zuriff 1985). If one wishes to understand these processes, one should give appropriate due to the deterministic presumptions that underlie such investigation.[24] Thirdly, according to the HOT theory, conscious processes are no different in kind from unconscious processes. Consciousness, according to the HOT theory, is a matter of two mental states being in a certain relation. Although this requires more cognitive energy and resources, one should not think that consciousness operates according to some ontologically distinct set of laws. I therefore second Bargh and Ferguson when they say, "It seems undeniable that conscious processes are themselves causal agents within the same deterministic framework as nonconscious processes" (2000, 939). Conscious and nonconscious processes presumably act in concert with one another and with stimuli outside of our bodies according to the laws of classical physics.

The HOT theory, then, allows us to see that the introspective phenomenology of freedom (at least to the extent that we have examined it here) is misleading. One of the reasons why we impart so much power to the *conscious will*, I maintain, is that we mistakenly believe that we are transparently aware, in an infallible way, of the workings of the mind—particularly the higher-level workings of the mind. It would stand to reason that if one believed that they were infallibly aware of all their mental states, *and one also remained unaware of all the unconscious mental processes that go into guiding judgment, choice, and behavior,* that they would believe the conscious will had far more power than it actually does. But now that we see that a great deal of mental activity is controlled by unconscious mental states, and that we can also misrepresent and confabulate the states we are in, the libertarian argument from introspections loses its force. One may begin to wonder at this point: What function, or functions, does consciousness actually have? If unconscious processes can control sophisticated behavior, perhaps the causal efficacy of consciousness is itself an illusion (just like our subjective feeling of freedom is an illusion)? To that question I now turn.

5.6 ON THE FUNCTION OF CONSCIOUSNESS

There are many divergent theories on the function, or functions, of consciousness (cf. Baars 1988; Blakemore and Greenfield 1987; Marcel and Bisiach 1988; Velmans 1991; Dehaene and Naccache 2001: Rosenthal 2008). Some of these theories impart a major causal role to consciousness while others argue that consciousness plays little or no role in information processing and higher-level functioning. Over the last two chapters a picture has emerged of a set of pervasive, adaptive, and sophisticated mental processes that occur largely outside conscious awareness. Some theorists have even taken this growing research to the extreme, claiming that the unconscious mind does virtually all the work and that the causal efficacy of consciousness may be an illusion (Huxley 1898; Velmans 1991; Wegner and Wheatley, 1999; Wegner 2002). Although I think there is a danger of going too far here, the role that consciousness plays in causing behavior is probably much smaller than previously believed.

Libet, for example, has shown that the initiation of a spontaneous voluntary act appears to begin in the brain unconsciously, well before one is even aware of the intention to act (Libet et al. 1983).[25] He found that spontaneous voluntary acts are preceded by a specific electrical charge in the brain, a "readiness potential" (RP), that begins 550 msec. before the act. Human subjects, however, only became aware of the intention to act 350-400 msec. after RP starts. It would seem, then, that the voluntary process is therefore initiated unconsciously. Libet argues, however, that even though the conscious awareness of an intention to act comes only after RP, it can still play a role in the final outcome. Since it comes 350-400 msec. after RP, but 200 msec. before the muscle is activated, it can still exercise a "veto" function. Hence, for Libet, "Potentially available to the conscious function is the possibility of stopping or vetoing the final progress of the volitional process, so that no actual muscle action ensues" (1999, 556). On this proposal, conscious will could thus affect the outcome of the volitional process even though the latter was initiated by unconscious cerebral processes. If Libet is correct, and there is much dispute about this, one function of consciousness, at least in spontaneous voluntary action, is its veto power.[26] This, of course, imparts to consciousness a causal function, thereby avoiding epiphenomenalism, but the picture that emerges is a relatively limited one.

This limited role also seems to fit with what we know about the adaptive unconscious. The adaptive unconscious plays a major executive role in our mental lives. It gathers information, interprets and evaluates it, and sets goals in motion, quickly and efficiently (Wilson 2002). For example, in the Bechara et al. (1997) card game study, we saw that people can figure out which decks had the best payoffs quickly and nonconsciously, without being able to verbalize why they preferred decks C and D. Such ability affords us an invaluable advantage in everyday life. It appears "Our conscious mind is often too slow to figure out what the best course of action is, so our nonconscious mind does the job for us" (Wilson 2002, 36). What was once thought of as the "proper work" of consciousness (e.g., reasoning, evaluation, judgment) can be, and often is, performed nonconsciously. But once we acknowledge that people can think unconsciously in quite sophisticated ways, questions arise about the relation between conscious and nonconscious processing. If we can reason, evaluate, and make judgments without consciousness, what function, if any, does consciousness have?

Theorists have suggested a number of possibilities. Consciousness has been thought to be necessary for the analysis of novel stimuli or novel stimulus arrangements (e.g., Posner and Snyder 1975; Bjork 1975). Some theorists, like Mandler (1975, 1985), have argued that consciousness allows us to choose amongst competing input stimuli. Other theorists have assumed that conscious processing is necessary for a stimulus to be remembered (James 1890; Underwood 1979; Waugh and Norman 1965) and for the production of anything other than an automatic, well-learnt response—e.g., for a voluntary response that is flexible or novel, or for a response that requires monitoring or planning (Romanes 1895; Mandler 1975, 1985; Shiffrin and Schneider 1977; Underwood 1982). Although consciousness may play a role in these functions, one should be careful not to overstate the case. One should not, for example, claim that consciousness is necessary or essential for these functions. Recent research on automaticity has shown that many of these functions can be performed nonconsciously.

Proving that consciousness is necessary for a particular function is extremely hard to do (see Rosenthal 2008; Flanagan and Polger 1995, 1998). Owen Flanagan, for example, has introduced something he calls the thesis of conscious inessentialism. This is the thesis that for any intelligent activity, i, performed in any cognitive domain d, even if we do i with conscious accompaniments, i can in principle be done without these conscious accompaniments (1992, 5). Although some have objected to this thesis (Dennett 1995), it is important to point out that conscious inessentialism is a very weak claim. As Polger and Flanagan describe the thesis:

> It is a claim about the mere possibility of some creature that can behave as we conscious beings do, but without consciousness. One way this might be true, of course, is if consciousness is an epiphenomena. But that is not the only way. It may be the case that consciousness is causal-

ly efficacious, but that the functions that it performs can be accomplished—at least in principle—by non-conscious mechanisms. So conscious inessentialism is compatible with a thorough-going naturalism about the mechanisms and subvenient basis of consciousness, and with a variety of claims about the causal efficacy of consciousness for us. According to this view, consciousness is a mechanism by which some important cognitive functions are performed in human beings. But the fact that we perform these functions consciously is contingent. (1999, 2)

Conscious inessentialism, then, is consistent with consciousness being causally efficacious. It only creates a challenge for those who wish to maintain that a particular function of consciousness is necessary or essential. For that reason, I think it is best to avoid claims of necessity altogether. It may well be that the conscious cognitive functions in human beings, whatever those may be, are contingent.[27] For my purposes, I need not take a stand on this.

All I wish to argue here is that consciousness is not epiphenomenal. I have all along maintained three main theses: (1) that our mental states (both conscious and unconscious) do, at least sometime, play a causal role in our choices and actions; (2) that these causal roles are completely determined by conditions we, ourselves, have no ultimate control over; and (3) although consciousness is not epiphenomenal, our conscious feeling of freedom is deeply deceptive.

Hence, the thesis of conscious inessentialism does not create a problem for what I wish to argue. It does, on the other hand, create a problem for libertarians like O'Connor who wish to argue that a necessary function of consciousness is its agent-causal capacity. As we witnessed in the first section of this chapter, libertarians *must* argue that one essential function of consciousness is that it somehow exercises an agent-causal power. If—even if only theoretically—all mental functions can be performed nonconsciously, the need for an agent-causal function to explain human behavior would vanish. If high-level voluntary action can be performed without conscious control and guidance, it is unnecessary to posit an agent-causal function for such behaviors. Hence, one of the biggest challenges for the libertarian—a challenge I do not believe they can meet given everything we know about human cognition—is to prove that agent-causation is an essential function of consciousness.

I believe the most appropriate view of the role of consciousness is somewhere between the extremes. Although consciousness lacks the kind of libertarian control we traditionally assume it has, it is also far from epiphenomenal. Following Timothy Wilson, I reject both the analogy of consciousness-as-chief-executive of the mind and the view that consciousness is epiphenomenal (2002, 46-47). I agree with Wilson that "we know less than we think we do about our own minds, and exert less control over our own minds than we think. And yet we retain some ability to influence how our minds work" (2002, 48). My position is that consciousness performs a number of important functions—functions that unconscious and automatic processes are not as good at (e.g., dealing with variable and novel stimuli, making long-range action plans)—but that these functions are more limited than we typically think. I maintain that conscious mental states are causally efficacious, just as nonconscious mental states are, but that the cognitive energy and resources required to generate HOTs means that conscious processes are often slower than nonconscious processes and often follow such processes.

As Wilson points out, the adaptive unconscious is extremely good at detecting patterns in the environment and evaluating them. Such a system has obvious advantages, but it also comes with a cost: "the quicker the analysis, the more error-prone it is likely to be" (2002, 50). Wilson speculates, "It would be advantageous to have another, slower system that can provide a more detailed analysis of the environment, catching errors made by the initial, quicker analysis" (2002, 50). This, he argues, is the job of conscious processing. If this is correct, consciousness acts more like an after-the-fact checker and balancer than as an executive controller of everything mental. This fits in with Libet's suggestion that consciousness has a veto function over spontaneous voluntary action but is not itself the initiator of the action. It also fits with Joseph LeDoux's (1996) suggestion that humans have a nonconscious "danger detector" that sizes up incoming information before it reaches conscious awareness. As Wilson describes this nonconscious danger detector:

> If it determines that the information is threatening, it triggers a response. Because this nonconscious analysis is very fast it is fairly crude and will sometimes make mistakes. Thus it is good to have a secondary, detailed processing system that can correct these mistakes. Suppose that you are on a hike and suddenly see a long, skinny, brown object in the middle of the path. Your first thought is "snake!" and you stop quickly with a sharp intake of breath. Upon closer analysis, however, you realize that the object is a branch from a small tree, and you go on your way. (2002, 5)

According to Wilson and LeDoux, we first perform an initial, crude analysis of the stick nonconsciously, followed by a more detailed conscious analysis. In terms of the HOT theory we can say that unconscious mental states are continually processing and analyzing information about the environment, but when something is deemed important additional cognitive resources are brought to bear causing a HOT of that state.

I do not mean to suggest, however, that consciousness is simply a back-up system for the adaptive unconscious, or that its only function is to veto what unconscious processes have already set in motion. Consciousness, I maintain, also helps facilitate long-term memory formation, plays an important role in non-spontaneous decision-making, provides focal-attention to help prioritize and recruit subgoals and functions, and serves a metacognitive or self-monitoring function (see Baars 1988). Take the encoding of long-term memory for example. On intuitive grounds, as Max Velmans writes, "it is difficult to envisage how, without consciousness, one could update long-term memory, for if one has never experienced an event, how could one remember it? How could an event which is not part of one's psychological present become part of one's psychological past?" (1991, sec. 4.2). I think it would be relatively uncontroversial to claim that one important function of consciousness is the role it plays in encoding long-term memory.[28] Although preconscious (or nonconscious) contents may influence the way the contents of consciousness are interpreted and consequently remembered (see Lackner and Garrett 1972; MacKay 1973), preconscious contents themselves do not usually enter into long-term memory.[29] Hence, as Velmans points out, "It is the accepted wisdom (backed by numerous experiments) that unless preconscious contents are selected for focal-attentive processing and enter consciousness, they are quickly lost from the system (within 30 seconds)" (1991, sec. 4.2). One should be very careful, however, not to confuse the contents of consciousness and long-term memory with the processes which encode information, transfer it to long-term memory, and search and retrieve it. Such processes are not under our conscious control and are inaccessible to introspection.

In addition to the role consciousness plays in encoding long-term memory, it's also likely that it plays an important role in representing and adapting to novel and significant events. Whereas the adaptive unconscious is fast, automatic, and effortless, it is also rigid. Consciousness processes, on the other hand, though slower and effortful, are much more flexible. According to Bernard Baars, "the most fundamental function [of consciousness] is . . . the ability to optimize the trade-off between organization and flexibility." He argues that, "Organized responses are highly efficient in well-known situations, but in cases of novelty, flexibility is at a premium" (1988, 348). It's useful, then, that the adaptive unconscious make "canned" solutions available automatically in predictable situations, but that the cognitive system be capable of combining all possible knowledge sources in unpredictable circumstances. Although the adaptive unconscious allows us to perform many behaviors quickly, effortlessly, and automatically, consciousness allows for plasticity and flexibility when it comes to novel situations. As Baars points out, "as soon as we flag some novel mental event consciously, we may be able to recruit it for voluntary action" (1988, 352).

According to the HOT theory, consciousness adds a spotlight to mental processes making certain mental states "light up." In so doing, it brings focal-attention to those states and processes allowing the mind to use that information in novel ways. It is important to note, however, that the kind of conscious control one has in such situations is nothing like the kind of conscious control assumed by libertarians. Baars argues, for example, that conscious goals can help recruit novel subgoals and motor systems to organize and carry out mental and physical actions, but that such recruitment is not itself a matter of conscious control—since "conscious goal-images themselves are under the control of unconscious goal contexts, which serve to generate a goal-image in the first place" (1988, 352). Baars further argues, when automatic systems cannot routinely resolve some choice-point "making it conscious helps recruit unconscious knowledge sources to make the proper decision" (1988, 349). Hence, in the case of indecision, we can make a goal conscious to "allow widespread recruitment of conscious and unconscious 'votes' for and against it" (1988, 349). Although consciousness may not control which choice we make, making the indecision or deliberation conscious allows unconscious knowledge and subgoals to work more effectively on the problem. Making a choice-point conscious allows the answer to be searched for unconsciously. In turn, "candidate answers are returned to consciousness, where they can be checked by multiple unconscious knowledge sources" (1988, 352).

If this is correct, although consciousness does not exercise executive control, it can still play a causal role in setting goals and making decisions. Consciousness can serve, that is, as "the domain of competition between different goals, as in indecisiveness and in conscious, deliberate decision" (Baars 1988, 353). When I become conscious of a choice—"Should I finish this chapter now, or should I stop for lunch?"—this allows a coalition of unconscious systems to build up in support of either alternative, as if they were voting one way or another. Once a decision is reached it can be "broadcast" to the rest of the system—i.e., the decision can be made conscious by having a HOT of it—and action can be taken. Although this is a very important function of consciousness, it is far from the kind of conscious control we often assume exists in libertarian and folk-psychological accounts of free will.

In this way consciousness can also act as the theatre of deliberation for long-range decision making and planning about the future. Hence, consciousness can play an active role in choosing a career path, deciding on what classes to take next semester, and whom to marry.[30] As Wilson points out, unconscious processes are more concerned with the here-and-now whereas conscious processes are better suited for the long view (2002, 50-52). Although the adaptive unconscious reacts quickly to our current environment, skillfully detects patterns, alerts us to any dangers, and sets in motion goal-directed behaviors, it cannot anticipate what will happen tomorrow, next week, or next year, and plan accordingly. "Nor can the adaptive unconscious muse about the past and integrate it into a coherent self-narrative" (Wilson 2002, 51). Consciousness, on the other hand, affords us the ability to reflect on the past and to contemplate the future. Having a flexible mental system that can muse, reflect, ponder, and contemplate alternative futures and connect those scenarios to the past is therefore a great advantage.

I have here only speculated on a few functions consciousness may perform. This is not meant to be an exhaustive list. Baars (1988), for example, lists no less than eighteen different functions. Whatever the final story turns out to be with regard to the functions of consciousness, I believe we will find that consciousness is not epiphenomenal, as some have assumed, but that it is also not the chief executive of the mind either. Current research, I argue, points to something in between. Whereas the adaptive unconscious appears to be a parallel processing system with multiple modules all functioning and working away at the same time, consciousness is more than likely a serial, limited capacity system. It allows us to perform a number of important tasks, no doubt, and it imparts to us advantages that an unconscious system would lack, but it is not the vehicle of libertarian freedom.

NOTES

1. For additional examples of libertarians appealing to introspective evidence as support for their position, see C.A. Campbell (1957, 176-178), O'Connor (2000, 124), and Kane (1996, 147). Thomas Reid goes even further in claiming that the conception of a cause is itself dependent on our introspective consciousness of self-agency. He writes: "It is very probable, that the very conception or idea of active power, and efficient causes, is derived from our voluntary exertions in producing effects; and that, if we were not conscious of such exertions, we should have no conception at all of a cause, or of active power" (Reid 1895, 2:604).

2. Given the libertarian reliance on introspection, Peter Ross has recently argued that "psychological research into the accuracy of introspection is the source of the most powerful empirical constraint for the problem of free will" (2006,134). According to Ross, "The Libertarian claims that the best explanation of our feeling that there are metaphysically open branching paths is that we become aware of an absence of sufficient mental causes. A specific question for research is whether this is the best explanation. If psychologists were to provide an alternative explanation which not only indicates that there are sufficient mental causes even in ordinary cases where our introspection indicates otherwise, but also offers a model explaining the illusion of their absence, this would undermine any . . . libertarianism" (2006, 139).

3. See section 5.6 of this chapter for more on the possible functions of consciousness.

4. Shaun Nichols (2004, 2006a, 2006b) offers this analysis up as one possible psychological explanation of where the belief in libertarian freedom comes from. Nichols ultimately rejects it in favor of another alternative—one based on the notion of moral obligation. I, on the other hand, believe the hypothesis should be given more weight than Nichols. It is my contention that phenomenology plays a much larger role in producing the illusion of libertarian freedom than Nichols acknowledges.

5. To be clear, I am not arguing that this fully explains the illusion of free will. My position is that the *apparent* transparency and infallibility of consciousness contributes to the illusion but is only one component of the overall story. I do not think it is the *whole* story because it does not explain why we also feel the positive power of active freedom and self-determination. Not being aware of deterministic causes may explain why we believe no such causes exist, but it does not fully explain the phenomenology

of agent-causation. To fully explain why we feel free, I believe we will also have to examine the phenomenology surrounding our feeling of "self-causation" and our feeling of "intentional control" over our actions. I will attempt to explain these features of the illusion in the following chapters.

6. Evidence for my proposal can be found in the fact that when the *feeling* of transparency and infallibility is thrown into question for various reasons, we tend to experience a loss or reduction in the feeling of will. When, for example, we become aware of reasons for acting that are different than the ones that appear directly in consciousness, as when we come to infer (e.g., through some kind of causal reasoning) that the best explanation for our action is something other than the one we were consciously aware of at the time (e.g., habit, emotion, addiction, or other unconscious action tendencies), we often experience a diminished sense of freedom. See Wegner (2002) for documented examples of this.

7. The arguments in this section will mirror the reasoning and structure found in Rosenthal (1986, 1997, and 2002c). I do not claim originality here. These arguments are meant to show that the HOT theory is preferable—empirically and explanatorily— over a Cartesian alternative.

8. I have elsewhere called this the "Cartesian assumption" and have presented arguments against it. See Caruso (2005).

9. All Descartes references will be to either, *The Philosophical Writings of Descartes Vols. 1-3,* translated by John Cottingham, Robert Stoothoff, and Dugald Murdoch (hereafter referred to as CSM) or to *Oeuvres de Descartes,* eds. Charles Adam and Paul Tannery (hereafter AT). This quote, for example, can be found in CSM, volume II, page 171. References to AT will follow the same pagination.

10. In the *Principles* (I, 9) Descartes also defines "thought" in terms of consciousness or immediate consciousness (AT, VIII:7-8). And in the *First Set of Replies* Descartes says he can "affirm with certainty that there can be nothing within me of which I am not in some way aware" (CSM, II:77; AT, VII:107). He's even more forceful in a letter to Mersenne where he writes: "What I say later, 'nothing can be in me, that is to say, in my mind, of which I am not aware', is something which I proved in my *Meditations"* (CSM, III:165; AT, III:273).

11. For Descartes, sensations, as far as they are mental states, are just a special kind of thought. He believed that sensations were either a special kind of thought and therefore conscious, or bodily states and hence never conscious. So for something to be considered a mental state, for Descartes, it had to be a thought. And since all thoughts are conscious, all mental states must be as well.

12. For more on this issue, see Rosenthal (1986, 2002c).

13. For a full account of how sensory qualities can exist independently of consciousness, see Rosenthal (1991a).

14. Rosenthal (1993c) has introduced a widely acknowledged distinction between *creature* consciousness and *state* consciousness. *Creature* consciousness recognizes that we often speak of whole organisms as conscious or aware. *State* consciousness, on the other hand, recognizes that we also speak of individual mental states as conscious. Explaining state consciousness is the primary focus for most researchers, and it is what I am here seeking to explain.

15. Although Descartes famously entertained the possibility that the content of my mental states may not match reality, he never entertained the possibility that my own mental states may diverge from my conscious awareness of them. Descartes claims in numerous places that one cannot be mistaken about how things *seem* to them to be in consciousness (e.g., CSM, II:19; AT, VII:29). For Descartes, our judgments about our mental states are certain and infallible.

16. See Wilson (2003) for more on the limits of introspective reports.

17. For a review of confabulation, which includes examples from split-brain patients, people suffering from organic amnesia, and people acting out posthypnotic suggestion, see Wilson (2002, ch.5).

18. In their original paper, Nisbett and Wilson (1977) argued that people often make inaccurate reports about the causes of their responses because there is little or no introspective access to higher order cognitive processes. They theorized that when people try to give introspective reports on the causes of their behavior, what they are really doing is making reasonable inferences about what the causes must have been, not giving direct introspective reports of the actual causes. A number of critics accurately pointed out that this thesis was far too extreme (Smith and Miller 1978; Ericsson and Simon 1980; Gavanski and Hoffman 1987), and Wilson has since modified his views (see Wilson and Stone 1985; Wilson 2002). My position is that we often do have direct access to our own mental states (i.e., our higher cognitive processes), but that the way we are aware of such states allows for the possibility of misrepresentation and confabulation. I further maintain that we need to distinguish between ordinary consciousness and introspective consciousness. I believe that error can occur at both levels and that people often conflate the two types of mistakes. My position is more fully spelled out in section 5.4.

19. Because of its hierarchical or iterative nature, Guzeldere (1995) has called such theories "double-tiered" theories.

20. It is important to point out that there is no circularity here, since the transitively conscious state (or HOT) is not normally itself intransitively conscious.

21. For an analysis of this mistake, see Gennaro (2003).

22. See Rosenthal (2004b) for more on why the extrinsic version of the HOT theory is preferable. And see section 5.4 below for an account of how Rosenthal's extrinsic HOT theory explains cases of misrepresentation and confabulation.

23. Rosenthal suggests that our HOTs can also misrepresent our mental states in the opposite direction; they can fill in information. See, for example, Rosenthal (2004b, 35).

24. The field of psychology presupposes determinism. As three leading psychologists have recently put it: "For psychology to make any sense, the universe must be, to some degree at least, predictable. A psychology that doesn't accept causes of behavior or the possibility of prediction is no psychology at all" (Baer, Kaufman, and Baumeister 2008, 4).

25. There are, however, critics of Libet's findings but I will address these in the following chapter. In chapter 6, I will discuss Libet's methodology along with alternative interpretations and criticisms. I will also offer my HOT interpretation of the findings and differentiate it from similar accounts given by Rosenthal (2002a) and Wegner (2002).

26. Although Libet's "veto power" represents a *potential* function of consciousness, it's important to keep in mind that Libet's proposal is much disputed. The best Libet himself can say for it is that it is not absolutely ruled out by the evidence. In fact, there have been a number of criticisms of Libet's claim (see Velmans 2003) and recent empirical findings by Simone Kühn and Marcel Brass (2009) appear to suggest that the decision to "veto" an action is itself determined unconsciously, just as the initiation of spontaneous voluntary actions appears to be.

27. Rosenthal, for example, claims: "Indeed, it is in any case puzzling what evolutionary pressure there could have been for mental states to be conscious, whatever the explanation of their being conscious. Evolutionary pressure on mental functioning operates only by way of interactions that such functioning has with behavior. And mental functioning interacts with behavior solely in virtue of its intentional and qualitative properties. If a mental state's being conscious does consist in its being accompanied by a higher-order state, that higher-order state would contribute to the overall causal role, but this contribution would very likely be minimal in comparison with that of the first-order state. So there could be little adaptive advantage in states' becoming conscious" (2004b, 27; see also 2008). For a different view of the adaptive value of higher-order thoughts, see Rolls (2004).

28. As I said earlier, though, it is important to steer clear of claims of necessity. Although a strong case could be made for the thesis that consciousness is necessary for

the encoding of long-term memory, Velmans (1991) has argued that some studies on hypnosis indicate that information may be able to enter long-term memory and be recalled without first entering consciousness.

29. Velmans (1991) points out, however, that preconscious processing can affect the memory trace of an input stimulus even if that stimulus cannot later be explicitly recognized or recalled. For an example, see Eich (1984).

30. It should be noted, however, that unconscious evaluations, judgments, and goals also factor heavily in such decisions. Although consciousness allows us to look into the future and try to set long-term goals, it cannot go completely against what the rest of the mental system wants. It is constrained, to a large degree, by our unconscious states and processes.

SIX

Consciousness and Free Will (III): Intentional States, Spontaneity, and Action Initiation

In the last chapter I introduced the HOT theory of consciousness, discussed some functions consciousness may serve, and began to develop my account of the cognitive illusion of free will by explaining away a misleading phenomenological datum of experience—the *apparent* transparency and infallibility of consciousness. I argued that a standing phenomenological belief in introspective transparency and infallibility, coupled with a failure to introspect any deterministic processes underlying our own decision making, helps contribute to our sense of free will. I used the HOT theory to account for the phenomenology while at the same time explain why it's misleading. Since we never phenomenally experience the relational nature of our HOTs, we feel, from the first-person point of view, as though consciousness is intrinsic to our mental states. We feel as though consciousness is immediate, direct, transparent, and infallible. The apparent immediacy, transparency, and infallibility of consciousness leads us to assume a kind of first-person authority where we believe that there can be no mental causes for our actions other than the ones we are aware of. Because we do not experience the multitude of unconscious determinants at work, and because we (wrongly) believe that we *would* be aware of such determinants if they were present, we conclude that no such determinants exist. The phenomenology tricks us here into thinking that it is our conscious will alone that is in control.

In this chapter I further develop my account of the cognitive illusion of free will by focusing on two additional phenomenological feature of consciousness. The first is the feeling that our intentional states arise spontaneously and are causally undetermined. The second, which lies at the heart of our sense of *conscious will*, is the feeling that we consciously cause or initiate behavior directly through our conscious intentions, decisions, and willings.

6.1 THE APPARENT SPONTANEITY OF INTENTIONAL STATES

From the first-person point of view, we often feel as though our wants, desires, beliefs, and intentions come to us spontaneously and are causally undetermined; in contrast (say) to our sensory states, which are experienced as caused by states of the world. My intention to turn on my desk lamp—which *experientially* precedes my action—appears to come to me spontaneously and in a way that feels undetermined by causal antecedents. I do not experience the intention as the necessary result of a deterministic chain of events, or as caused by impersonal forces over which I have no control, but rather as free and uncaused. It is not unusual for us to experience our intentional states in this way. In fact, even though there is no actual reason to think that our intentional states arise *ex nihilo* from a theoretical perspective, we cannot shake the subjective impression that "our conscious thoughts, desires, and intentions occur freely and that this apparent freedom enhances our ability to reason and make rational choices" (Rosenthal 2002d, 417). Given the *prima facie* importance of the *apparent* freedom of intentional states to our sense of free will, we have here another important aspect of our experience worth exploring.

The phenomenology surrounding our intentional states, I maintain, plays an important role in generating the illusion of free will—especially the feeling that our intentional *actions* are causally undetermined. The fact that we experience our desires and intentions as spontaneous and uncaused, imparts a sense of freedom to those intentional actions that appear to follow from them. To be clear, though, I am not saying that we experience our actions themselves as being completely uncaused. To the contrary, we often feel a sense of *self*-agency—that is, we often feel (as libertarians are quick to point out) that we, *ourselves*, cause or initiate our actions (more on this in ch.7). Furthermore, even when we experience our actions as free, we also experience them as resulting from conscious desires and intentions we have (see Rosenthal 2002b, 216). We feel as though our actions result from our own internal psychological states, not that they are capricious and uncaused. Nevertheless, even though we are conscious of desires and intentions that seem to cause our actions, *we typically are not also conscious of anything as causing those desires and intentions* (Rosenthal 2002b, 216). And, as Rosenthal argues, "Because we are typically conscious of our desires and intentions as being spontaneous and uncaused, we experience the resulting actions as also being free and uncaused" (2002b, 216).

Rosenthal's thesis is that: "Actions appear to be free when they appear to result from spontaneous, uncaused desires and intentions" (2005a, 361). Although I caution against attributing the phenomenology of free will to just *one* aspect of experience, I do agree with Rosenthal that, in part, we feel that our actions are free and causally undetermined, not because we experience the actions themselves as uncaused, but because we experience the antecedent thoughts, desires, and intentions as being spontaneous and uncaused.[1] The fact that we experience our intentional states as spontaneous and uncaused leads us to experience our actions as likewise free and causally undetermined. In fact, in those rare cases where we experience our intentional states *as* causally determined, or somehow outside our control, we typically experience an associated loss or reduction in our feeling of freedom.

Before going further, though, it's important to note that if we examine our phenomenology more carefully, we will also find that *not all* intentional states are experienced as spontaneous and uncaused. When we attend to our stream of consciousness, we often feel a kind of causal connectedness among our thoughts. That is, sometimes we are conscious of a desire or intention as resulting from other, earlier mental states; "when we consciously deliberate, for example, we are aware of our desires as being due to that process of deliberation" (Rosenthal 2002b, 216). These conscious chains of deliberation, however, do not continue indefinitely. "There is always an antecedent intentional state we are conscious of but for which we are not conscious of any cause, and we will accordingly be conscious of it as being spontaneous and uncaused" (Rosenthal 2002b, 216). The fact that these conscious chains *originate* from intentional states that *appear* to be spontaneous and uncaused is enough to generate the feeling of freedom. Of course:

> None of this shows that any of our desires and intentions are actually uncaused. We are conscious of only relatively few of our mental states; so there will always be some mental antecedent of which we fail to be conscious. Still, the result is that we are always conscious of our desires and intentions and, indeed, our intentional states generally as being up to us. If we experience them as being caused at all, we experience them as resulting from a causal sequence of intentional states whose initial member we are conscious of as being uncaused. (2002b, 216-217)

On this proposal, then, the sense we have of free agency results in part from the way we are conscious of our conscious wants, desires, beliefs, and intentions.

But *why* do we experience our intentional states as we do? What is it about the way we are conscious of our intentional states that explains *why* these states, at least the initial ones, appear to be spontaneous and uncaused? To answer this question we must once again consider the nature

of mentality and consciousness. Rosenthal offers up the following explanation:

> Because our mental states are not all conscious, we are seldom if ever
> conscious of the mental antecedents of our conscious states. And con-
> scious desires and intentions whose mental antecedents we are not
> conscious of seem to us to be spontaneous and uncaused. The sense we
> have of free agency results from our failure to be conscious of all our
> mental states. It does not point to an underlying metaphysical unity of
> the self. (2005a, 361-362)

According to Rosenthal, since we are not conscious of all our mental
states, and since we do not experience the unconscious mental antecedents of our conscious states, we experience our conscious intentions as
spontaneous and causally undetermined. According to the HOT theory,
when I have a conscious mental state I am usually unaware, generally
speaking, of the antecedent mental causes of that state—i.e., the unconscious mental states that trigger our HOTs. Our HOTs are caused in a
myriad of ways. Sometimes HOTs are caused by other conscious states,
but in many cases the antecedent mental states that cause our HOTs are
themselves unconscious. Since these antecedent states are unconscious,
we experience our conscious intentional states as spontaneous and uncaused. Hence, from a phenomenological point of view, we're not conscious of where our conscious beliefs, desires, and intentional states come
from, as well as how our conscious mental states become conscious,[2] and
because of this we incorrectly conclude that there are no causal antecedents.

I believe this account goes a long way in explaining why we experience intentional states as spontaneous and uncaused. I'm not convinced,
however, that this is the *whole* story. My main concern is that I do not see
how it explains an important asymmetry between intentional states and
sensory states. *Sensory states do not feel spontaneous and uncaused in the same
way that intentional states do.* Although we experience our intentional
states as being uncaused, we seldom feel the same way about bodily
sensations or visual perceptions. Why is this the case? Rosenthal's account does a good job explaining *one* important feature of consciousness—namely that conscious mental states often have unconscious mental antecedents—but this alone does not explain this asymmetry. Like
intentional states, sensory states are caused by antecedent nonconscious
mental states. If the simple fact that conscious mental states had unconscious mental antecedents were responsible for generating the feeling
that those states were uncaused, this would presumably hold true for
both intentional states *and* sensory states; yet it does not. I would like to
offer an explanation of this asymmetry—one that has to do with the way
our HOTs represent their target states, the different ways these states are
caused and acquired, and the different functions they serve. I do not take

my account of the asymmetry between intentional states and sensory states to be in any way inconsistent with the account given thus far; rather, it should be viewed as a supplement to this existing account.

6.2 THE ASYMMETRY BETWEEN INTENTIONAL STATES AND SENSORY STATES

According to Rosenthal, since we never experience the unconscious mental antecedents of our conscious mental states, we incorrectly infer that they are uncaused. The question, however, is why do we make this fallacious inference with intentional states and not also with sensory states? I believe the answer lies in the different way these states are connected to their external environment and the different representational properties these states, and the HOTs that make them conscious, typically possess. I maintain that for sensory states, our HOTs make us conscious not only of the sensory states themselves (i.e., conscious of being in a state with such-and-such sensory qualities), but also in many cases the *proximate environmental causes* of those states. This conjecture fits the way we typically experience sensory states. With sensory states, unlike intentional states, we are often conscious (or predisposed to be conscious) of the cause of the sensation along with the sensation. That is, with conscious sensory states we are not only conscious of the state itself (e.g., a throbbing pain in my foot), but we are also often conscious of the environmental cause of that sensation (e.g., the nail I just stepped on or my new pair of dress shoes). Typically, perceptual, auditory, tactile, olfactory, and other sensory states are experienced in this way, not as arising spontaneously.

John Searle provides the following description of this phenomenological asymmetry with regard to perceptual experiences.

> There is a striking and dramatic difference between the qualitative character of perceptual experiences, and the qualitative character of voluntary actions. In the case of perceptual experiences, I am a passive recipient of perceptions which are experienced as caused by the external environment. So if I hold up my hand in front of my face, for example, it is not up to me whether or not I see a hand. The perceptual apparatus and the external stimuli are sufficient by themselves to cause in me a visual experience of my hand in front of my face. I do not have a choice in the matter; the causes are sufficient to produce the experience. But if we contrast the experience of seeing my hand in front of my face with, for example, raising my hand we notice that I experience the causal relations quite differently. In the case of raising the hand over my head, I experience my voluntary effort as causing the bodily movement, whereas in the case of seeing my hand I experience the hand as causing the conscious visual experience. (2000, 6)

The perceptual experience Searle describes is not experienced as free or within my control because the perceptual state itself is not experienced as spontaneous and uncaused, as intentional states are, but rather as causally determined by the external environment. The character of voluntary actions, on the other hand, are different because they seem to stem from intentional causes that themselves are experienced as uncaused. I feel as though I freely control my hand movement in part because the psychological states (i.e., the intentional states) that precede the behavior are experienced in a dramatically different way than are sensory states.[3] We do not experience the intentional states as causally determined by the external environment in the same way. (This of course does not mean they are not causally determined, only that we do not *experience* them as such!) This, I maintain, is why the experiential asymmetry between sensory states and intentional states is important to the phenomenology of "free" agency.

Luckily, the HOT theory can explain this asymmetry. According to the theory, what we are conscious of, and hence what we can report on, is a matter of how our HOTs represent their target states (or cluster of states). It's conceivable, then, that our HOTs represent sensory states *along with their causes*, at least some of the time, making us aware, not only (say) that I have a particular pain, but what the cause of that pain is. A sensory state is conscious in virtue of the representational content of the HOT. How a HOT represents its target determines *what-it-is-like* for us to be in that state. Sensory states, however, not only possess qualitative properties, they also possess their own representational properties. Among the potential properties a HOT can represent a sensory state as having are certain representational properties that themselves point outward to the cause of those states. Our sensory states are therefore tied to their environmental causes in a different way than intentional states. Since sensory states are monitoring states, these states typically represent local features of the environment. It's not unusual, therefore, to become conscious not only of the qualitative properties of a sensory state but also the environmental cause(s) of those properties. This is perhaps easiest to see with visual perceptions.

When I consciously perceive the tree outside the window of my study, I am not only aware of the color, shape, and texture of the tree (i.e., aware of certain qualitative properties), I am also conscious of the tree as the cause of my visual perception. I *feel* as though the visual perception is caused by the tree. I may be wrong about this, I may be hallucinating or dreaming a tree, but I nonetheless *experience* things in this way. I feel, for example, as though I have no control over whether or not I perceive the tree. This is because the conscious visual perception is directed outward toward its (perceived) physical cause. The perceptual state represents features of the environment spatially and otherwise, and these environmental features are experienced as the cause of the sensation. We feel as though the physical object(s) represented by the perceptual state are sufficient to cause in me the experience.

The same is true with other types of sensory states. It's quite common, for example, to be conscious of *pain in my foot* not only in terms of its qualitative properties (say, as a *throbbing pain*) but also, at the same time, as a pain caused by the new pair of shoes I'm wearing today. In fact, throughout the day I may simply become aware in an apparently direct and non-inferential way of the feeling "*Ouch, these shoes are killing me.*" Similarly, sometimes we are conscious of a *mild stinging pain* not only in terms of its qualitative properties but also, at the same time, *as a mosquito bite*. The fact that we are aware of the pain *as a mosquito bite* picks out or identifies a likely cause. Assuming we are familiar with what a mosquito bite feels like and have the conceptual resources available to represent the pain state in this way (via the HOT that makes the state conscious), it's possible for us to *experience* the pain as one *caused by a mosquito bite*. Our HOTs can represent their target states in various ways making us conscious of different features of those states.[4] In this case, for example, the pain state can be represented as having certain qualitative properties (e.g., *mild* and *stinging*), being spatially located (e.g., occurring on the back of my neck), *and* as caused in a certain way (e.g., by a mosquito bite). As long as we have the conceptual resources to represent the pain state as a *mosquito bite*, there is nothing preventing us from becoming conscious of it as such. Here we are not only conscious of the qualitative nature of the pain (mild and stinging) but we are conscious of it in a direct and non-inferential way *as* a mosquito bite.

In this way, our HOTs can make us aware not only of the qualitative properties of our sensory states but of the causes of those properties; and this in turn explains why we experience sensory states as we do. If the way our HOTs represent their target states determines *what-it's-like* for us to be in those states, and our HOTs represent sensory states (at least most of the time) as arising from certain environmental causes, then we would experience these states as caused and outside our control; not as arising spontaneously. Since we typically experience sensations as caused by local features of the environment, we have no illusions of free will here. Again, as Searle points out, "In the case of perceptual experiences, I am a passive recipient of perceptions which are experienced as caused by the external environment." This differs from the way we experience intentional states and the intentional acts that appear to follow from them.

Of course we are not *always* conscious of the causes of our sensory states, but the fact that we often are conditions us to believe, when unaware of the causal origin of a particular sensation, *that there still must be one*. If I have a headache that *appears to have come out of nowhere*, I do not assume that it was uncaused. Nor do I believe that *I* freely brought it about. I may not be sure what caused it but I assume there must be some cause. The constant conjunction we experience between sensory states and their environmental causes leads us to believe that all such states have causal antecedents. Since external stimuli are generally sufficient for causing in me various sensations and perceptions, we build up an expectation that those states have those causes. Since we associate sensory states with environmental causes, we experience sensory states as causally determined. No such expectation or association takes place with intentional states since our HOTs rarely make us aware of how we acquired such states—for reasons I will explain in a moment. Since our HOTs fail to represent the original causes of our beliefs, desires, and other intentional state, we remain unaware of these causes and hence do not build up the same sort of expectations or association as we do with sensory states.[5]

There are several reasons why our intentional states do not represent their environmental causes in the same way as sensory states. Many of our beliefs and desires are caused by environmental factors—experiences, societal influence, upbringing, education, etc.—but we are seldom conscious of these environmental causes while consciously entertaining a belief or desire token. This is probably because (1) we typically acquire (and build up) our beliefs and desires over time. That is, our intentional states usually have multiple causes and are seldom caused by one singular event. With sensory states, on the other hand, the presence of a single cause is often sufficient to generate a sensation. A hand plus having eyes is sufficient to cause in me a visual experience of a hand. (2) Secondly, the original cause(s) of intentional states are not usually spatio-temporally present beyond their initial acquisition. I may have acquired a particular belief from my father when I was a child, but now my father need not be, and usually *is not*, present whenever I am conscious of a token of that belief. This differs for sensory states. When we are conscious of seeing something red (or being appeared to redly), it is usually because a red object is present in the external environment.[6] This is not true of most intentional states. I can be conscious of my desire for Barack Obama to be reelected without being aware of how I acquired that desire and with no immediate environmental, spatio-temporal cause(s) for the content of that desire being present. In fact, the ability to have intentional states removed from the environmental causes of the content of those states represents an important cognitive development; not all animals have this ability. Our imaginative and creative abilities may in large part depend upon our ability to have thoughts about things that are not present and may not even be possible. (3) Thirdly, even in conditions of initial acquisition we often remain unaware of the environmental causes of our beliefs and desires. That is, we remain unaware of the impact certain environmental triggers have on our belief/desire formation. I may find a particular woman attractive (or not) and be wholly unaware that this is because I am standing on a suspension bridge and not sitting on a park bench. I may believe that a particular individual would make a better employee than another candidate but not be aware that this has to do with his/her height. I may desire a particular soft drink and not realize it's because of packaging. I may prefer to buy one pair of socks instead of another simply because of where they are positioned on the display table, etc.

From an evolutionary standpoint the asymmetry between sensory and intentional states makes sense. The primary function of sensory states is to monitor our internal and external environment, to make us aware of what's going on in our local environment and at the interface between our bodies and the world. It is not surprising then that the representational properties associated with these two different types of states would have evolved to represent the external environment differently. It is far more advantageous for us to be aware of the causes of our sensory states, and to know that these states are caused by external stimuli, than it is to represent the causal origin of our intentional states. It is important for an organism to know that the pain they are experiencing, or the auditory or perceptual sensation they are having, is being caused by something in their immediate environment. This information is crucial to survival. There is no equivalent advantage in knowing the origin of a particular belief or desire. In fact, from a design perspective it would be virtually impossible and a waste of cognitive energy for the organism to store all the causal information necessary for each intentional state.

To recap the argument thus far: (1) We often experience our intentional states as spontaneous and uncaused; (2) An intentional state experienced *as* caused is experienced as the result of a sequence of intentional states whose first member is experienced as uncaused; (3) Actions appear free when they appear to result from spontaneous, uncaused intentions; (4) The sense we have of free agency results, in part, from the way we experience conscious desires and intentions; (5) Since we do not experience the unconscious antecedents of conscious states, our conscious intentions are experienced as spontaneous and undetermined; (6) Sensory states, however, are experienced as caused because (a) their representational properties point outward to environmental causes, (b) they occur in the presences of their environmental causes, and (c) this regular conjunction between cause and effect leads us to experience them as causally determined and outside our control.

This account helps us understand why our *intentional actions* feel free and causally undetermined; they inherit this feeling from the intentional states that precede action. We typically feel as though our actions are the result of our choices, and our choices are the result of our intentional states. We feel as though we control our behavior via our intentional states—my intention to turn on my reading lamp is what causes me to behave as I do. In a moment I will question whether our conscious intentions actually cause behavior, but the fact that we *feel* as though they do helps explain why we experience our actions as causally undetermined.

Since our intentional states appear to be spontaneous and uncaused (unlike sensory states), a feeling of control and *up-to-me-ness* is extended to the actions that *appear* to result from them. On the current analysis, then, when one acts on the basis of conscious wants, beliefs, and other intentional states, one is unaware of the unconscious mental antecedents of those states. Additionally, when our HOTs make a particular want conscious they do not make conscious the causal origin of that want—largely because the environmental causes are diverse, often unconscious even initially, and usually no longer present. This being the case, I hypothesize that *from a very early age we begin to equate the fulfilling of a conscious want (which appears spontaneous and uncaused) with the exercise of a positive power over our actions.* Since the want appears to us to be spontaneous and undetermined, we come to equate over time the fulfillment of that want with the exercise of a positive power of self-determination. Of course, if we were to become aware, not in a theoretical way but in a phenomenologically immediate way, of the myriad causes behind these intentional states, we would cease to feel free. If our intentional states *felt* caused in the same way that our sensory state do—if, for example, our beliefs and desires *felt* tied to causal determinants just as our sensations and perceptions do—then I predict the subjective feeling of freedom would fade.

Thus far then we have discussed two phenomenological features of consciousness that are involved in the feeling of free will: (1) the *apparent* transparency and infallibility of conscious; and (2) the *feeling* that our intentional states arise spontaneously and are uncaused. I will now discuss a third phenomenological feature: the *feeling* that we consciously cause or initiate behavior directly through our conscious intentions, decisions, and willings; or, put more simply, the feeling of *conscious will.* It's important to note that this feeling differs from the previous two, for even if our intentional states do not arise spontaneously and without causal antecedents as we believe, it is still an open question whether they cause behavior. Even if our intentional states are causally determined, contrary to the way we experience things, it still may be the case that the feeling of conscious will (i.e., the feeling that our conscious intentions cause and initiate behavior) is veridical. It is important, therefore, to investigate to what extent, if at all, we actually exercise conscious will. For even if our sense of libertarian freedom is an illusion, perhaps *some* sense of freedom is still salvageable according to which our conscious intentions—although part of a deterministic chain—nonetheless cause behavior. If, however, this turns out to be an illusion too, any remaining hope we had of preserving even a small portion of our intuitive sense of free will would be lost.

6.3 DO OUR CONSCIOUS INTENTIONS CAUSE OUR ACTIONS?

A major part of the folk psychology of free will is the belief that *our conscious intentions cause action*. As Patrick Haggard and Benjamin Libet write, "Most of us navigate through our daily lives with the belief that we have conscious free will: that is, we have conscious intentions to perform specific acts, and those intentions can drive our bodily actions, thus producing a desired change in the external world" (2001, 47). This commonsense intuition plays a major role in our sense of free agency and is essential to the *up-to-me-ness* that we associate with free will. It is also well supported by phenomenology. In normal cases of voluntary behavior, we experience a conscious intention before the onset of action and naturally take the former to be the cause of the latter. When I switch on my reading lamp, for example, I feel as though it is *I*, my conscious self, that controls the movements of my arms and hands through the conscious formation of goals, intentions, and decisions. Whether or not this phenomenology corresponds to reality is one thing, but there should be little doubt that the *order* in which *we experience* such events helps create our subjective experience of control. As Obhi and Haggard write, "We seem aware of a certain temporal order of events that contributes to our perception of the direction of causation that flows from within our minds (such as formulating an intention) to external space (such as turning on a light switch to light up a room)" (2004, 358). The fact that we experience conscious intentions as occurring prior to movement causes us to believe that these intentions *cause* behavior. Although this experiential order of events plays a major role in generating our feeling of freedom, does our sense of conscious will match the underlying pattern of neural events? Do our conscious intentions *actually* cause actions?

Although phenomenology supports this commonsense belief, empirical evidence in neuroscience now seriously questions it. In fact, a growing number of theorists now conclude that *conscious will*—in the sense of consciously initiated action—is incompatible with the evidence of neuroscience (Libet et al. 1983; Libet 1985; Wegner 2002; Spence 1996; Castiello, Paulignan, and Jeannerod 1991; Haggard and Eimer 1999; Pockett 2006; Jeannerod 2006). Much of the contemporary case for this conclusion is derived from the experimental work of Benjamin Libet and his colleagues. I will therefore discuss Libet's work at length along with some objections to it. I will also discuss some additional work in neuroscience that further suggests that conscious will is an illusion. My thesis will be that the empirical results from neuroscience do in fact reveal that conscious will is an illusion—at least in the cases we can currently study empirically.

Perhaps no empirical investigation into the nature of conscious will has had a greater impact on our ordinary conception of free will than that conducted by Benjamin Libet and his colleagues. In their groundbreaking experiment, Libet et al. (1983) investigated the timing of brain processes and compared them to the timing of conscious will in relation to self-initiated voluntary acts and found some startling results. They found that volitional acts were preceded by a readiness potential (RP) which arose in the brain some 350-400 milliseconds before the conscious decision to act was experienced. In the experiment, they had subjects rest a finger on a button as they stared at a specially designed clock. The clock had only one hand which swept through a revolution once every 2.5 seconds. Libet et al. asked subjects to push the button at a time of their own choosing. Participants were instructed to wait for one complete revolution of the clock and then, at any time thereafter when he/she felt like doing so, to abruptly flex the fingers and/or wrist of the right hand. In some runs, participants were asked to report the position of the clock hand at the time when he/she first became aware of the "urge, desire or intention" to move. Libet and his colleagues called this subjective judgment W, for "will." In other parts of the experiment, participants judged when they actually moved, and Libet called this judgment M, for "movement." The timing of these W and M judgments told Libet and his team when—subjectively speaking—a participant formulated a will to move and actually moved.[7]

Timing these subjective judgments was important for the experiment, and Libet and his team came up with an ingenious method that proved to be quite reliable (to within 50 ms). The key was the specially designed clock they used for the experiment, which had a "hand" that moved across the clock face at a speed that allowed subjects to precisely judge the time of occurrence of their intentions. Since the clock had to be much faster than a usual clock, in order to accommodate time differences in the hundreds of milliseconds, Libet et al. had a spot of light of a cathode ray oscilloscope revolve around the face of the scope like the sweep-second hand of an ordinary clock, but at a speed approximately 25 times as fast. This meant that each of the marked off "seconds" around the periphery was thus equivalent to about 40 ms. The timing of W and M was then determined by having subjects report back the location of the revolving spot of light on the oscilloscope "clock." As a control for the ability to successfully time events in this way, Libet et al. conducted a pilot study where subjects were stimulated at random times with a mild shock and were asked to time this event (called S) by reporting the clock-time at which he/she felt each such stimulus. At the same time, EEG were recorded and movement-related cortical potentials (MRCPs) were assessed to determine the timing of brain activity. Libet and his team found that subjects were reasonably accurate in determining the timing of S (within

50 ms) indicating that their method of timing subjective experience was acceptable.[8]

In addition to measuring the subjective timing of W and M, Libet and his colleagues also measured two objective parameters. Using an electro-encephalogram (EEG), they measured the electrical activity over the motor areas of the brain; and using an electromyograph (EMG), they measured the activity of the muscles involved in the hand/wrist movement. Over the motor areas, Libet recorded a well-known psychophysiological correlate of movement preparation called the *readiness potential* (RP). This readiness potential had been detected much earlier by Kornhuber and Deecke (1965). The RP is measured using electroencephalographic recoding electrodes placed on the scalp overlying the motor areas of the frontal lobe, and appears as a steady buildup of electric activity that precedes actual movement by up to 1 sec or more. The obvious question then becomes, *when* does the *conscious* intention to perform the act first appear? As Libet writes, "In the traditional view of conscious will and free will, one would expect conscious will to appear before, or at the onset, of the RP, and thus command the brain to perform the intended act" (1999, 49). What Libet and his team found, however, went contrary to this traditional view.

With both the subjective and objective parameters in hand, Libet and his colleagues could now examine the temporal order of conscious experience and neural activity by comparing the subjective W and M judgments with the objective RP and muscular activity. First, they found that W came before M. This is unsurprising and is what one would expect— i.e., the subjects consciously perceived the intention to move as occurring before a conscious experience of actually moving. But when Libet and his team compared the temporal relation between subjective experience and individual neural events—i.e., when they matched the subjective reports up with the objectively measured readiness potential (RP) that preceded the movement—they found that participants became aware of the "urge, intention or decision" to move 200 ms before the motor act, *but* 350-400 ms *after* RP! That is, the actual neural preparation to move (RP) preceded conscious awareness of the intention to move (W) by 350-400 milliseconds.[9] These experimental findings are shocking because they reveal that spontaneous voluntary acts are preceded by a specific electrical change in the brain (RP) that begins (on average) -550 ms before the act, but individuals become aware of the intention to act only -200 or so milliseconds before movement. Put simply, "the brain is preparing the purportedly 'free' action significantly before the subject himself is aware that he intends to move" (Haggard and Libet 2001, 49). This temporal gap poses a difficulty for the traditional concept of free will. It tells us that, contrary to our sense of conscious will, the volitional process (at least in these cases) is *initiated* unconsciously.

Although there have been several critics of Libet's experiment, these results have been reproduced by others (see Haggard and Eimer 1999; Haggard, Newman, and Magno 1999; Sirigu et al. 2004; Fried, Mukamel, and Kreiman 2011) and the basic findings are now widely accepted. Most of the criticism surrounding Libet's work has to do with interpreting these findings, not with the findings themselves.[10] Even one of Libet's most vocal critics, Susan Pockett, considers the basic finding that RP precedes W to be unassailable (2004, 2006). One methodological criticism that is often made, however, is based on the possibility of timing errors caused by attentional biases. Some studies have shown that subjects are generally poor at judging the synchrony of two events occurring in different perceptual modalities or perceptual streams (Sternberg and Knoll 1973). In particular, events in an attended stream appear to occur earlier than simultaneous events in an unattended stream—the so-called Prior Entry phenomenon (see Haggard and Libet 2001, 49). Some critics worry that since Libet's subjects presumably divided their attention in varying proportions between the external clock and their own internal states in order to make the W judgment, the precise numerical value of 200 ms must be treated with caution. One should be careful, however, not to overstate this concern. Although the *prior entry effect* could make it hard to precisely pinpoint the timing of W, it does not seem large enough to affect Libet's central discovery that RP preceded W. As Haggard and Libet points out, "Estimates of the prior entry effect run from 70 ms (Sternberg & Knoll, 1973) down to 12 ms (Shore, Spence, and Klein 2001; Haggard and Johnson 2001). Even the largest of these values is an order of magnitude smaller than Libet's gap between readiness potential and W judgment" (2001, 49). It would seem then that even calculating in time for the prior entry effect, unconscious processes have begun the ball rolling on action-initiation before a person even experiences the conscious intention to move.[11]

Additional research has further confirmed Libet's main discovery, while raising some doubts about particular aspects of Libet's own interpretation (e.g., Haggard and Eimer 1999). In the original paper Libet et al. suggested that the readiness potential (RP) was the *cause* of subsequent conscious awareness (W)—i.e., that a person's feeling of intention was an effect of motor preparatory activity in the brain rather than a cause. Since RP onset preceded W judgments by several hundred milliseconds, Libet and his colleagues suggested that the initiation of action involves an unconscious neural process, which eventually produces the conscious experience of intention. The logic of this causal argument is based on the temporal precedence of RP onset over conscious intention. Patrick Haggard, however, has pointed out that temporal precedence is a necessary rather than a sufficient condition for a causal relation, and he has instead argued that there are other neural premotor events that are more plausible than the RP as causes of conscious intention (see Haggard and Eimer 1999; Haggard and Libet 2001; Haggard 2005).[12] Experiments conducted by Haggard and Eimer (1999) suggest that W relates more closely to the onset of a later component of the RP that is known as the *Lateralized Readiness Potential* (LRP).[13] According to Haggard and Eimer, the RP isolated by Libet corresponds to a *generalized* preparation to act, and a subsequent LRP initiates *specific* motor behavior. The early portions of the RP are symmetrical over both hemispheres, but Haggard and Eimer found that the later portions of the RP show an increasing shift toward the hemisphere contralateral to the hand that will make the forthcoming action. This lateralized readiness potential (LRP) typically begins some 500 ms prior to movement onset. Haggard writes:

> The LRP has a particular psychological significance in situations where the subject must choose between a left- and a right-handed action: once the LRP has begun, the selection of which action to make must be complete. That is, by LRP onset the intention has progressed from abstract stage ('Do something or other!') to drive a specific movement ('Do precisely this!'). (Haggard and Libet 2001, 50)

Haggard and Eimer found that W covaried with the LRP rather than the RP, suggesting that W correlates with the choice of *which* movement will be made, rather than simply *a* movement (of a generally type) will be made.

Haggard and Eimer therefore conclude that the RP could not be the cause of conscious intention, but the LRP could be. Conscious intention, they suggest, arises after the selection process, through development of a specific command for the selected action. They hypothesize that the "processes underlying the LRP may cause our awareness of movement initiation"—i.e., that conscious intention is caused by the brain processes which prepare and monitor *specific* actions. Haggard suggests that conscious intention is a consequence of the preparation for action in the frontal and parietal areas of the brain (Haggard 2005). The frontal and parietal lobes, he maintains, jointly form a circuit which elaborates and monitors motor plans in advance of action, producing a conscious experience of intention as part of this simulation. On this hypothesis, "Preparatory activity in the motor areas of the brain initiates action, and produces a conscious sensation of intention as a correlate" (2005, 291). Regardless of who is correct here, the central point about conscious will nonetheless remain unchanged. Libet's basic discovery about the temporal order of events remains intact. Though the LRP occurs after RP, it also occurs prior to W—hence, *motion is still initiated before there is a conscious intention to move.* I need not speculate on who (if either) is correct about the underlying neural causes of W. What is important here, as Haggard himself writes, is that "However a scientist looks at all of these data, the brain is going full speed ahead well before a person experiences the conscious intention of moving" (Obhi and Haggard 2004, 360).

Implications for Free Will

What do these findings mean for free will? Well, I maintain that if our conscious intentions do not actually cause or initiate action then we can conclude that, at least in cases of spontaneous voluntary behavior like those studied by Libet, conscious will is an illusion. Our conscious selves are not in the driver's seat as we typically believe. This is a devastating blow to our everyday understanding of free will. Libet's discovery undermines the strongly held belief, which is supported by phenomenology and the way we experience our own voluntary acts, that we consciously cause or initiate action directly through our conscious intentions, decisions, and willings. As Obhi and Haggard write, "These experiments reveal that the chain of causation going from our intentions to our actions is not in the intuitive direction" (2004, 361). In a very important sense these neuroscientific finds put the cart before the horse. Since a fundamental, perhaps nonnegotiable, part of our folk-psychological theory of agency is the belief that we consciously control our movements and actions, one would expect to find that the conscious intention to move one's hand would come slightly before, or at least at the same time, as the readiness potential (or LRP). This, however, is not what we find. The fact that there is a temporal gap between RP and W (or LRP and W) means the brain initiates action before consciousness even enters the picture. This shows that conscious will is an illusion, at least for one large class of actions, since "conscious intention cannot cause an action if a neural event that precedes and correlates with the action comes before conscious intention" (Roediger, Goode, and Zaromb 2008, 208). Since we become aware of an intention or desire to act only after the onset of preparatory brain activity, the conscious intention cannot be the true cause of the action.

I therefore take Libet's findings to be a serious threat to our intuitive sense of free will. I should note, however, that not everyone shares this interpretation. Less threatening interpretations have been proposed by David Rosenthal (2002a) and Alfred Mele (2009). Let me focus for the moment on Mele's criticism of Libet—I'll postpone a discussion of Rosenthal's interpretation until the following section.[14] In his recent book, *Effective Intentions* (2009), Mele argues that the RP that precedes action by a half-second or more need not be construed as the *cause* of the action. Instead, it may simply mark the beginning of forming an *intention* to act. According to Mele, "it is much more likely that what emerges around -550 ms is a *potential cause* of a proximal intention or decision than a proximal intention or decision itself" (2009, 51). Hence, the RP for Mele is more accurately characterized as an "urge" to act or a preparation to act—that is, it is more accurately characterized as the advent of items in what Mele calls the PPG (the preproximal-intention group). This interpretation allows Mele to maintain that conscious intentions can still be causes and that "Libet's striking claims about decisions and intentions are not justified by his results" (2009, 64).

Mele's interpretation, however, suffers from a number of problems. The first is that it does not amount to a proof that conscious intentions are causally effective in producing action. All it establishes, if it establishes anything, is a relatively weak *consistency* claim—i.e., that Libet's findings are consistent with the *possibility* of causally effective conscious intentions. Furthermore, it does not rule out Haggard's claim that conscious intention itself is a consequence of the preparation for action in the frontal and parietal areas of the brain. In fact, Haggard and Eimer's findings do seem to indicate that pre-conscious brain activity "initiates action, and produces a conscious sensation of intention as a correlate" (Haggard 2005, 291). Their findings also indicate that by the time the LRP has begun, not only has a *general* action plan been initiated, but the decision of which *specific* action to perform has already been made.

Secondly, Mele himself admits that our conscious intentions are causally embedded in a process that originates somewhere beyond the realm of consciousness. In discussing the causal sequence of action, Mele write:

> Processes have parts, and the various parts of a process may have more and less proximal initiators. A process that is initiated by an item in the PPG may have a subsequent part that is directly initiated by a consciously made decision. The conscious self—which need not be understood as something mysterious—might more proximally initiate a voluntary act that is less proximally initiated by an item in the PPG. (2009, 69)

Some commentators, however, have rightly pointed out that by acknowledging that voluntary actions are "less proximally initiated" by pre-conscious brain activity, Mele is "essentially conceding the point that the causal buck *doesn't* stop with the agent" (Vargas 2009). Manuel Vargas, for example, writes:

> I am not convinced [that the above passage from Mele] answers the core of the threat. . . . Indeed, it might seem to merely constitute part of a fuller statement of the worry. I say this because the willusionists seem to be implicitly working with something like the following picture: When we hold ourselves or others responsible, when we treat people as free, we think we are justified in doing so precisely because we believe that the causal buck stops, in the relevant sense, with the agent. Mele could (and does, I think) agree with this much. What Libet and like-minded folks seem to have in mind, though, is the thought that Libet's results show that *in the relevant sense* the causal buck doesn't stop with the agent. (2009)

The fact that Mele acknowledges that our actions have causal roots in pre-conscious brain activity ends up simply highlighting the problem, not solving it. Mele's interpretation "does nothing to block the basic worry of how we could be the kinds of beings that stop the buck enough to count as free, or as deserving of moral praise and blame" (Vargas 2009). Mele's interpretation is therefore unsatisfying since it does very little to assuage the traditional concerns raised by Libet's discovery. What Libet's findings show, and what Mele does not deny, is that the *ultimate source* of voluntary action is *not* the conscious self but unconscious brain activity. Hence, even on Mele's interpretation, the causal process that ultimately results in spontaneous voluntary action is unconsciously *initiated*.

Does this mean that consciousness is epiphenomenal? While many philosophers and neuroscientists are now going in this direction, Libet could not bring himself to accept such a conclusion. To preserve some causal role for consciousness, Libet proposed that consciousness could still exercise a kind of *veto* power in the time between W and muscle contraction. Since consciousness arises slightly in advance of movement, it could still play a role in deciding whether or not to let the action (which has already been initiated) go forward. For Libet, although consciousness does not actually initiate the voluntary movement in these cases, it could still act as a *veto* or *control* agent by allowing the unconsciously initiated process to go to completion or veto it and prevent the actual act from occurring. Whether or not consciousness actually has this veto power, however, is still uncertain since Libet's proposal remains largely theoretical and no complete account has been given of how it would be accomplished. In a very important sense, though, it doesn't matter! For one thing, there is nothing ruling out the possibility that this conscious "veto" is itself initiated unconsciously (see Velmans 2003). In fact, recent findings by Kühn and Brass (2009) appear to suggest that it is. Secondly, as some commentators have pointed out, this is more a case of *free won't* than free will (Obhi and Haggard 2004). Thirdly, and more pertinent to our current discussion, even if consciousness has this type of veto power, our sense of *conscious will* would still be an illusion. The feeling we have that our *conscious intentions ultimately cause our actions*—i.e., that we consciously *initiate* behavior—would remain illusory. Libet's proposed veto power, though preserving some role for consciousness, does not preserve the kind of causal role we typically assume. The main point therefore remains: "these elegant experiments do show quite clearly that at least some simple, but definitely self-initiated and voluntary, movements are triggered not by consciousness, but by the subconscious workings of the brain" (Pockett, Banks, and Gallagher 2006, 2).

Can we expand this conclusion beyond the kind of spontaneous voluntary acts studied by Libet? In the original experiment, Libet et al. studied a relatively simple form of spontaneous voluntary behavior, button-pressing. What about more complicated voluntary movements? As the neuroscientist Susan Pockett writes, "The next step in extending this sort of work to movements that are of more everyday utility is to investigate the situation when the subjects are asked to make a relatively realistic decision before deciding to press the button" (2006, 19). This is exactly what Haggard and Eimer (1999) attempted to study in their experimental paradigm when they asked subjects to choose between moving *either* their right or left hand. For this task, using the method of Libet, Haggard and Eimer looked carefully at the timing of W compared to RP onset (and LRP onset). Significantly, Haggard and Eimer found no difference in the reported time of intention to move between this "free movement condition" and the usual Libet paradigm. Like Libet, they also found that RP (and LRP) preceded W. This experiment suggests that movement *selection* also precedes awareness. Findings by Soon et al. (2008) also expand Libet's findings in important ways. Using functional magnetic resonance imaging (fMRI) and a different experimental paradigm than Libet, Soon et al. were able to predict with 60% accuracy whether subjects would press a button with either their right or left hand up to 10 seconds before the subject became aware of having made that choice. These findings further indicate that consciousness of a decision may be a mere afterthought and not the true cause of the action.

Moving away from action initiation for a moment, what about the control of ongoing movements? As Pockett notes, "After an action has been intended, planned, and initiated . . . the action must be seen through to its conclusion. There must be ongoing *control and correction* of the movements involved, using feedback from proprioception and from the effects of the action on the external world, as received by various sensory systems" (2006, 12). Even if we do not consciously cause or initiate spontaneous voluntary behavior, one might think that some form of conscious control can still be exercised in seeing the unconsciously selected and initiated action through to completion. Although this would be one way to preserve our folk-psychological intuition that we consciously control our movements, it seems even *less* likely that conscious control is involved here. It is now pretty clear that basic motor responses and control of ongoing movements are primarily carried out unconsciously (see Jeannerod 2006; Castiello, Paulignan, and Jeannerod 1991; Pockett 2006).

Although the average person normally thinks of involuntary reflexes and tics when they think about unconscious movements, it's actually the case that any voluntary act of any complexity — "be it as simple as picking up a coffee cup or as complicated as walking down to the beach for a swim or sight-reading a piece of Chopin — is *performed* largely unconsciously" (Pockett 2006, 19). Take the rather simple act of picking up a coffee mug. Although we are (probably) aware of a general intent to perform the act, and may (or may not) be aware of a specific decision to initiate the act, we are, as Pockett argues, "certainly quite unaware of the complex calculations of coordinates and joint angles and forces and the sequential action of muscles that are required to move the arm to the right place, curve the hand in anticipation of the shape of the mug, grasp the mug and lift it to the lips without spilling coffee" (2006, 20). Furthermore, we remain completely unaware of the comparisons of performance with intention, the ongoing readjustments to cope with changing environmental circumstances, and the automatic activation of various motor programs. The control and correction of ongoing movements requires constant feedback from the somatosensory system—for example, the visuomotor system—generated during their execution. We may be aware of a general intent to act (e.g., the decision to pick up the coffee mug), but the somatosensory/visuomotor system selects in the goal a small number of parameters that will be transformed into motor commands that will ensure compliance of the effector (e.g., the hand) with the object (Jeannerod 1997, 2006). The nature of these actions and the relatively rapid speed at which they are performed generally precludes conscious involvement (see Castiello, Paulignan, and Jeannerod 1991; Jeannerod 1997, 2006)—and this is, generally speaking, a good thing. As I argued in chapter 4, the adaptive unconscious is undoubtedly a great biological boon. In fact, when we perform the sort of novel or difficult acts that do involve the constant presence of consciousness, "(a) our movements tend to lack smoothness and precision and (b) the allocation of attention to the ongoing movement means that we are unable to be aware of much else" (Pockett 2006, 20). It's a good thing then that most motor responses are carried out automatically and unconsciously, since actions that do require the constant presence of consciousness (e.g., actions performed during the first attempts at learning a new skill) are usually slow and inaccurate.

The fact that we *feel* as though we consciously control our everyday bodily movements probably has more to do with us identifying ourselves with the behavior than with any actual conscious control over it. If we are aware of a general intent to act, and the sensory experiences generated during the performance of the movement are in accordance with the overall goal, we will more than likely experience the movement as willed and owned. There are occasions, though, where this feeling of conscious control can break down. In everyday life, for example, there are situations where actions in response to visual events are clearly dissociated from the conscious experience of the same event—i.e., cases where we "respond first and become aware later" (Jeannerod 2006, 27). Quickly moving out of the way of a flying object, or swerving one's car to avoid a sudden obstacle, are good examples. In such cases, we experience a disconnect between our awareness of the action and our motor responses: "we consciously see the obstacle after we have avoided it" (2006, 27). Although these types of experiences are relatively rare, which is lucky for our sense of conscious will, the dissociation between motor responses and subjective experience is important because it reveals something about the dual processing of sensory information.

The sensorimotor system processes information quickly and unconsciously, hence is able to respond quickly to changes in the environment.

The conscious processing of the same sensory information, if it occurs at all, happens more slowly—sometimes even *after* we have already acted. The fact that we seldom experience a disconnect is due to the fact that these parallel processing streams, though working at different rates, generally function at a speed that allows us to maintain a sense of unity. The conscious processing of sensory information generally occurs within the window of time it takes to carry out a normal motor response, hence we do not experience any temporal gap. On the other hand, when we have to act quickly (e.g., when a time constraint is placed on the motor response), it's not uncommon for us to experience a temporal dissociation.

Castiello, Paulignan, and Jeannerod (1991) designed a series of experiments to measure this temporal dissociation. In one experiment, participants were instructed to reach by hand and grasp an object (a vertical dowel) placed in front of them, as soon as it became illuminated. They were also instructed to signal, by vocal utterance (Tah!), the time at which they became aware of the illumination of the object. The team found that the hand movement aimed at the object began about 50 milliseconds *before* the vocal response signaling the subject's awareness of its change in visual appearance. This difference, however, was not noticed by the subjects; participants experienced their hand movements as occurring at the same time as their perception of the illumination of the object. In a second experiment, though, Castiello and his colleagues had the illuminated object jumped by 10° on either side at the time when the reaching movement started. The onset of the motor adjustment was measured using kinematic landmarks obtained from the hand trajectory. The first sign of correction of the hand trajectory appeared shortly (about 100 ms) after the shift in target position. By contrast, the vocal utterance corresponding to this same event occurred 420 ms following object displacement, some 300 ms after the beginning of the change in movement trajectory. In this trial, the subjects' reports were in accordance with this temporal dissociation between the two responses: "they reported that they saw the object jumping to its new position near the end of their movement, just at the time they were about to take the object (sometimes even after they took it)" (Jeannerod 2006, 28).

Marc Jeannerod (2006), a member of the team conducting the experiment, takes these results to show that under normal circumstances, when the target object remains stationary and no time pressure is imposed on performing the task, the time to awareness of a visual event is roughly compatible with the duration of motor reaction times: "when we make a movement toward an object, we become aware of this object near the time when the movement starts, or shortly after it has started, hence the apparent consistency between our actions and the flow of our subjective experience" (2006, 28). Yet when motor reaction times are shortened under conditions of time pressure, consistency breaks down and conscious awareness becomes dissociated from the movement. This naturally leads Jeannerod to suggest that perhaps the normally long reaction time (ca. 300 ms) of reaching movements have the function of keeping our subjective experience in register with our actions. "Imagine what life would be like," Jeannerod writes, "if the above temporal dissociation were the usual case, and if our awareness of the external events were systematically delayed from our actions in response to these events!" (2006, 28).

According to Castiello, Paulignan, and Jeannerod, assuming that the vocal responses in this experiment did signal the subject's awareness, the observed delay between motor corrections and these responses suggest that neural activity must be processed during a significant and quantifiable amount of time before it can give rise to conscious experience.

> The dissociation between motor responses and subjective experience, when it happens, as well as the more usual synchrony between the two, reflects the constraints imposed by brain circuitry during the processing of neural information. Different aspects of the same event are processed at different rates, and the global outcome is constrained by the slowness of the process that builds up awareness. Consciousness of the goal of an action is not immediate, it takes time to appear (the Time-On Theory; see Libet 1992). Adequate timing of neuronal activity in different brain areas is a critical condition for achieving subjective temporal consistency between external events. (Jeannerod 2006, 28)

This experiment helps show that fast accurate movements can only be executed automatically. One of Libet's (1979) first important findings was that the brain needs at least a 500 ms cascade of electrical stimulation to trigger a conscious experience.[15] It's not surprising that there should be some delay between an event and our becoming aware of it, but what is surprising is the length of that delay. Half a second is a noticeable period of time and it is evident that we often respond to events more quickly than that. The only way this could occur is if our unconscious sensorimotor system is able to respond in a time interval quicker than it takes to produce conscious awareness. Hence, consciousness is a relatively slow process and takes time to appear, in some cases appearing after a bodily movement has already occurred. In normal cases this temporal gap is not large enough for us to experience any dissociation, but in situations where motor reaction time shortens under conditions of time pressure it is possible for us to experience this temporal dissociation.

At this point I think we can make some general conclusions. How, then, does one answer the central question: *Does consciousness cause behavior?* I maintain that given the neuroscientific findings discussed above, we have to answer this question in the negative—at least for those actions and movements that can currently be studied empirically. As Pockett writes:

In the case of very simple voluntary acts such as pressing a button whenever one feels like it, good experimental evidence shows that the consciousness of being about to move arises before the movement occurs, but after the neural events leading up to the movement have begun. It is a reasonable conclusion that consciousness is not the immediate cause of this simple kind of behavior . . . In the case of the correction of ongoing actions, consciousness of having moved more often than not arises *after* the correcting movement has been completed (and sometimes does not arise at all). Clearly, consciousness does not cause this extremely complex kind of behavior, either. (2006, 21)

Although these conclusions do not bode well for our intuitive sense of conscious will, one should always keep in mind that neuroscience still has a long way to go. Pockett has argued, for example, that in the case of the initiation of actions based on complex decisions or long-term intentions, "our question has not yet been answered one way or the other" (2006, 21). This is because, neurophysiologically speaking, nobody has yet been able to design experiments that would unequivocally nail down the temporal relationship between the appearance of this consciousness and the onset of whatever neural events underpin the intentions and movement-initiations (see Pockett 2006).

Given what we *do* currently know, however, and what we are now capable of testing empirically, I believe it is fair to conclude that consciousness does *not* play a role in causing spontaneous voluntary acts or in controlling ongoing movements. It is quite possible, and I believe likely, that consciousness plays an important role in *formulating* long-term actions plans and intentions, but whether or not consciousness actually *initiates* these action plans when it comes time is an open question. I think it's more likely that a prior intention or action plan is set consciously, then at the moment of action the movement is initiated unconsciously (cf. Gollwitzer 1993). But even if consciousness does not actually cause action I believe it can still play a causal role. For one, it's quite possible that consciousness performs the veto-function that Libet suggests; the jury is still out on this. In addition, consciousness can have an impact on behavior via the role it plays in complex decision making and long-range planning. Even if it does not initiate action in these cases, I think it would be unfair to say it plays *no* role in such behavior. As I argued in the previous chapter, consciousness can play an important role in non-spontaneous decision making by providing focal-attention to help prioritize and recruit subgoals and functions. In this way it can have an effect on the final outcome even if it does not cause the action per se.

6.4 LIBET'S FINDINGS AND THE HOT THEORY

How can the HOT theory explain Libet's findings? I would like to offer the following interpretation. The HOT theory posits and makes sense of unconscious mental states. Since on the HOT theory, what makes a mental state a conscious state is its being the target of a suitable HOT, mentality and consciousness are separable; unlike the Cartesian model which conflates the two. This being the case, we can hypothesize that certain first-order mental states (i.e., nonconscious mental states) initiate action before conscious awareness is present. Since our first-order mental states have their causal powers independent of consciousness, they can—and probably do—initiate our actions prior to conscious awareness. We can theorize that our HOTs make us aware of our first-order mental states—thereby making us aware of an intention to act—but that the first-order mental state actually initiates the action before the HOT is generated, if it is generated at all. The time lag that Libet found between RP and W can then be explained in terms of the time necessary for the appropriate HOT to be caused.

There are perhaps good evolutionary reasons for this time lag. The cognitive energy and resources required to make a state conscious means that conscious processes are often slower than nonconscious processes and often follow such processes. In the case of spontaneous voluntary action, it's not surprising then that the conscious awareness of intention comes only after the fact. Unconscious processes are far better suited to initiate such actions. The same is true with the control of ongoing movements, where unconscious sensory states are causally involved prior to conscious awareness. On Haggard's theory, for example, W comes only after a *specific* action (which corresponds with the LRP) has been selected. According to Haggard, this makes good evolutionary sense:

> Logical considerations . . . suggest that conscious intention should arise *after* selection. Consciousness presumably evolved because it is an efficient and functional way of using limited neural resources to optimize behavior. This precious resource would be most effectively used in representing the selected, to-be-performed action, and should not be wasted in representing alternative possible actions that are not selected. (2005, 292)

If Haggard is correct, one could speculate that the evolutionary function of coming-to-consciousness is to broadcast the selected action to the global workspace, thereby making all subsystems aware of the action to be performed. This broadcast could help with reafference, whereby other mental modules set up expectations about the feedback they should be receiving, so are prepared to take corrective action if they don't receive it. This can also help preserve our sense of unity and ownership over the action. Choudhury and Blakemore argue, for example, that "the *conscious awareness of unconsciously monitored actions* is the means by which our actions are experienced as subjectively real, willed, and owned" (2006, 49). Even if we do not consciously initiate voluntary actions, or consciously control them once they are being carried out, it is still important for our sense of self to associate and identify ourselves with those actions (see ch.7).

On my interpretation, then, first-order nonconscious mental states initiate action prior to the awareness of conscious intent. This is consistent with the neuroscientific data. Before going further, though, I would like to consider one possible way of reconciling Libet's discovery with the existence of free will. As I stated earlier, I take Libet's discovery to be a strong argument against our ordinary conception of free will (at least for spontaneous voluntary acts). There are, however, others who though they accept, or at least do not challenge, Libet's findings, do not consider them as threatening. Although my account of the cognitive illusion of free will is built on Rosenthal's HOT theory, Rosenthal himself ironically accepts a compatibilist conception of free will and interprets Libet's findings differently than I do (2002a). I reject the idea that free will can be exercised unconsciously—as does Libet (2006) himself—but there are some who believe that conscious intentions and volitions are not necessary for free will (e.g., Rosenthal 2002a; Mele 2009). The question, then, is whether or not conscious executive control is required for free will. Does it make sense to speak of unconsciously exercised free will? I believe it does not, for the notion of unconscious volition is quite far removed from a straightforward conception of free will. Rosenthal, on the other hand, though acknowledging the conflict between common sense and Libet's results (2002a, 219), nonetheless believes free will can be preserved by giving up the requirement that *conscious* intentions cause actions.

Rosenthal's solution is to argue that Libet's results do not show that "no volitions occur until after neural initiation, but at best only that no *conscious* volitions do" (2002a, 216). He argues that there can be unconscious volitions and that Libet's findings are consistent with these unconscious volitions initiating action. According to Rosenthal:

> [A]n individual's mental state might well be conscious at one moment but not another; states might start nonconsciously and only subsequently become conscious. And then the volitions whose occurrence Libet fixes by way of subjects' reports might well have started prior to those reports, though without having been conscious before those reports. Those reports indicate when subjects become conscious of those volitions, that is, when the volitions come to be conscious. . . . If the volitions whose conscious occurrence Libet detects might have occurred earlier, but without yet being conscious, those volitions might have begun simultaneously. (2002a, 218)

In general terms, I agree with Rosenthal—although I would not use the term "volitions" here for reasons to be explained in a moment. Given the HOT theory of consciousness and with it the existence of unconscious mental states, including intentions, it is plausible, indeed likely, that unconscious intentions are causally involved prior to W. The difficulty I have with Rosenthal's position is that he goes on to argue that *actions that stem from unconscious volitions are (or can be) nonetheless free.* Rosenthal maintains:

> [I]t is plain that there is no difference in respect of freedom between conscious and nonconscious volitions. In both cases volitions result from various antecedent mental occurrences of which we are largely unaware. Conscious volitions differ from those which are not conscious only in that we are conscious of them. Acting freely consists not in our volitions being uncaused, but in those volitions fitting comfortably within a conscious picture we have of ourselves and of the kinds of things we characteristically want to do. (2002a, 219)

Although this is an intriguing proposal in that it preserves a causal role for intentions (albeit unconscious ones), Rosenthal does not defend the claim that "free actions" can be caused by unconscious intentions and volitions beyond the above quote. Rosenthal may think it "plain" that "there is no difference in respect of freedom between conscious and nonconscious volitions," but this claim clearly needs an argument; and I do not think an argument can be given that does justice to our common sense picture of free will.

I argued in chapter 4 that we cannot understand free will without consciousness. Let me summarize my main points again. For one, recent studies have shown that conscious deliberation and guidance are an integral part of our folk-psychological understanding of free will (Stillman et al. 2006; Baumeister 2008). The *up-to-me-ness* that we associate with "free will" is understood by ordinary folk in terms of *conscious intentional agency.* If compatibilists want to reconcile free will with our folk-psychological intuitions they have to give appropriate due to the importance of conscious willing. To redefine "free action" in such a way that conscious guidance and control is no longer required is to deviate too dramatically from our ordinary understanding of "free action." It also seems ad hoc. To simply state that unconscious intentions are enough to preserve freedom seems too quick and easy; a way to make the scientific data fit a philosophical position, namely compatibilism, instead of the other way around.[16]

Secondly, it's questionable that we can even make sense of the idea of *willing* or *the exercise of volition* being carried out unconsciously. As Bargh and Ferguson point out, "Willfulness is assumed to reside in consciousness, and, therefore, a lack of conscious involvement in a process implies it was not willed" (2000, 925-926). Rosenthal and others may disagree,

but it's incumbent on them to explain what an unconscious volition ultimately amounts to. Normally volitions are understood to be more than
mere causes—i.e., they are taken to involve *conscious* choices and decisions, which is part of what distinguishes them from other causal antecedents to behavior. If we allow unconscious willing, however, it's hard to
see any philosophically relevant difference between volitions and other
unconscious causes. There are plenty of unconscious states and processes
that result in movements and actions that we would not consider volitional or, for that matter, freedom-conferring—e.g., those that result in
"slips of the tongue," involuntary movements, and, more rarely, behavior
associated with "alien hand" syndrome and certain forms of schizophrenia (see ch.7). To be charitable, then, perhaps we should limit volitions to
those unconscious causes of behavior that later become conscious and we
do not disapprove of (and whatever additional compatibilist conditions
one wishes to add). This remains unsatisfying, however, since regardless
of the importance we place on identification, hierarchical integration, and
the like, we are still left with a queer notion of volitions—i.e., *"volitions"
without (conscious) willing.*

In fact, some compatibilists have gone so far as to argue that not only
is consciousness not necessary for volition, but *no* act of will or choice is
even needed for free will. Levin, for example, has argued that "Compatibilists should not say 'choice' causes action." This is because, "choices as
traditionally conceived—spurts of pure will—are strangely elusive"
(2007, 435 fn.8). Levin instead argues that we should view the *onset of a
want/desire/intention* as the cause of action. As I understand his position,
the raising of my arm is not caused by a choice or an act of will, but rather
an event involving me—i.e., the onset of a want/desire/preference for my
arm being up.[17] The problem with this proposal, I maintain, is that it
leaves out completely the *active* role of the agent—something most of us
assume is required for free will. This is also the problem with Rosenthal's
conception of unconscious volitions. Contra the compatibilist, we do not
see ourselves as mere possessors of wants, passively becoming aware of a
want/desire/intention to act *only after the act has been initiated.* This is true
even if the want/desire/intention that initiates action is the same one that
later becomes conscious. For there to be free will, there must be a difference between what happens to an individual and an individual's *active
participation* in the process of deliberation, choice, and action initiation.
This distinction is important not only to our self-conception but to most
theoretical and folk-psychological accounts of free will. Free agents, as
ordinarily conceived, must be capable of willful authorship—"as opposed to merely holding a drove of desires like a container which *passively* waits for the most pressing desire to spring into action" (Vezér 2007, 9).
To label, then, the unconscious states that cause or initiate action "volitions" (regardless of whether or not these states later become conscious)

is, I maintain, to provide an account of "free will" that leaves out the functional role of the *will* and the active role of the conscious agent.

The fact that we demand more than "unconscious volitions" for free will is further revealed by my third point: we generally do not hold people responsible for acts performed without conscious intent—e.g., involuntary actions or actions performed while sleepwalking. This is why Leonard Kaplan (2006) concludes that the Western legal system, which has always relied on the demonstration of conscious intent for an act to be considered punishable, would be seriously compromised if Libet was correct and consciousness does *not* cause behavior. As the study conducted by Monterosso and his colleagues (2005) showed, individuals mitigate blame based on the perceived *automaticity* of an action. There seems to be an inverse correlation between ascriptions of moral responsibility and the perception that a behavior is "automatic" (i.e., outside the conscious control of the agent). The more one views a behavior as outside the conscious control of the agent, the less likely one is to ascribe moral responsibility. In fact, when a behavior was characterized as "automatic," willpower and character were less likely to be cited as relevant to the behavior. Hence, Rosenthal's move also fails to preserve our ordinary conception of moral responsibility—another stated goal of compatibilists.

Lastly, if one cares about phenomenology it's important to acknowledge the role conscious intentions play in generating our *feeling* of free will. Appealing to the work of Daniel Wegner, I will now argue that conscious intentions play an essential role in agentive experience (see 2002, 2003; Wegner and Wheatley 1999). Hence, to claim that "there is no difference in respect of freedom between conscious and nonconscious volitions," is to overlook the importance conscious intentions and volitions play in generating our feeling of freedom. Rosenthal may want to defend a philosophical account of free will by giving up the requirement of conscious will, but to do so would disregard phenomenology and our folk-psychological intuitions. Phenomenology is important here because our *beliefs* and our *pretheoretical intuitions* regarding free will are entwined with the way we *experience* our actions. As Spence says, "Consciousness provides the medium for the experience of free will, and beliefs pertaining to the latter" (1996, 78).

6.5 EXPLAINING THE PHENOMENOLOGICAL ILLUSION

If consciousness (in the form of conscious intentions and volitions) is necessary for free will, and in cases of spontaneous voluntary behavior conscious intentions (or, at least, the conscious properties of intentions) arise only *after* such actions have been initiated, then free will (at least in these cases) is an illusion. If so, if we do *not* consciously cause or initiate behavior directly through our conscious intentions, decisions, and will-

ings, why do we *believe* in conscious will? I believe the answer once again
has to do with phenomenology. The fact that we *experience* a certain temporal order of events, even if that temporal order is inaccurate, helps
generate the cognitive illusion of free will. The fact that we experience the
conscious intention to act prior to acting, yet remain unaware of the
neurological antecedents of the conscious intention, leads us to mistakenly conclude that the conscious intention is the cause of the action. The
illusion of conscious free will is to be explained in part by this *experiential*
order of events. In fact, recent work by Daniel Wegner (2002; see also
Wegner and Wheatley 1999) has shown just how important the presence
of a conscious intention prior to action is for experiencing conscious will.
According to Wegner (2002), the experience of conscious will is due to the
priority, consistency, and *exclusivity* of the thought about the action. That
is, for one to feel a sense of conscious will, the thought (or intention)
should: (a) precede the action; (b) be consistent with the action; and (c)
not be accompanied by other potential causes.[18]

It's important to point out, however, that people *experience* conscious
will quite independently of any *actual* causal connection between their
thoughts and their actions—all that needs to be preserved is the *appearance* of priority, consistency, and exclusivity. According to Wegner, "The
intentions we have to act may or may not *be* causes, but this doesn't
matter, as it is only critical that we *perceive* them as causes if we are to
experience conscious will" (2002, 65). The importance of Wegner's work
comes in his discovery that the feeling of self-control of behavior can be
dissociated from actual causes of behavior—e.g., people may cause an
action but not be aware of it, or they may think they caused an action that
was actually triggered by external forces. In one experiment, known as
the *I-spy* experiment, Wegner and Wheatley (1999) discovered that when
the thought of an event immediately precedes its actual occurrence, people believe they have caused it, even if in reality they have not. The study
focused on the *priority principle* and was inspired by the ordinary house-
hold Ouija board. The question was whether people would feel they had
moved a Ouija-like pointer if they simply thought about where it would
go just in advance of its movement, even though the movement was in
fact produced by another person.

In the experiment, two participants worked together to move a cursor
over objects on a computer screen—akin to having four hands on the
pointer of a Ouija board. One of the participants served as a confederate
of the experimenter, but the test subject never knew this. The subject
heard words over headphones that related to particular objects on the
screen. For example, a subject might hear the word "swan" while moving
the cursor over a picture of a swan. Unbeknownst to the subject, all of the
movement of the cursor came from the confederate. The results showed
that, when the relevant word was presented 1 to 5 seconds prior to the
action, subjects reported feeling that they had acted intentionally to make

the movement. In other words, they had experienced will. When the word was presented 30 seconds prior to the action or 1 second after it, however, there was no false feeling of willing the action. It would appear that the priority of a thought related to and consistent with an action is sufficient to generate a feeling of conscious will, but that thought cannot precede the action in time beyond a certain threshold. The thoughts must appear within a particular window of time for the experience of will to develop—if it occurs too far in advance of the action there will be no sense of conscious will, and if it occurs after the action there will likewise be no sense of will.[19]

Wegner's *I-spy* experiment shows just how important the phenomenological order of events is to our sense of causal agency. The experiment also shows that the experience of will can be created by the manipulation of thought and action in accord with the principle of priority, and "this experience can occur even when the person's thought cannot have created the action" (Wegner 2002, 78).[20] Hence, if a thought or intention precedes a related movement within a certain window of time, even if that thought or intention is not the *actual* cause of the movement, one will still feel a sense of causal agency (assuming, of course, the conditions of consistency and exclusivity are also met). This, I believe, can help explain the illusion of *conscious will*. I maintain that the *apparent* priority of a conscious intention before the onset of action, as long as it is consistent with the action and not undercut by other potential causes available to the agent, is enough for one to feel that their conscious will is the cause of the action.

Returning to Libet's findings, we can now say that the experience of W (conscious will) preceding M (awareness of movement) is absolutely critical for people to *believe* that a movement is a result of their own free will. The fact the W precedes M satisfies the priority principle and therefore contributes to the sense of agency. The problem for conscious will, however, comes in the fact that W is *itself* preceded by RP (and LRP). As Libet himself indicates, this runs directly contrary to the classical conception of free will. The *apparent* priority of a conscious volition before the onset of action, though phenomenologically accurate, appears to be neurophysiologically undermined by the causal priority of RP! The temporal sequence that Libet discovered explains why the phenomenology appears as it does, while at the same time explaining why it is misleading. Since we are unaware of the electric shift in the brain that initiates action and precedes our awareness of conscious intent, yet conscious intent still precedes movement (and our awareness of movement), the experiential order necessary for the *feeling* of agency is preserved.

The conclusion of this section, then, is that the empirical results from neuroscience reveal that conscious will is an illusion—at least for those cases that can currently be studied empirically—while the presence of a conscious intention prior to movement, whether or not the intention is causally involved in initiating the movement, is enough to generate the feeling of conscious will. Wegner's work reveals just how important the perceived causal link is between our conscious intentions and actions. On the one hand, there are numerous cases where a reduction or break in the perceived link between thought and action results in a sense of involuntariness even for actions that are voluntary (see Wegner 2002). On the other hand, inflated perceptions of this link, like those studied by Wegner and Wheatley, explain why people experience conscious will at all. Even though our conscious intentions do not causally initiate voluntary behavior, the fact that we perceive them as doing so leads us to experience conscious will.

6.6 WEGNER'S THEORY OF APPARENT MENTAL CAUSATION

I will conclude this chapter by commenting on Wegner's *theory of apparent mental causation* (see 2002, 2003, 2004) and explain some of the differences between our two accounts. According to Wegner, the experience of conscious will is a result of an interpretation of the apparent link between the conscious thoughts that appear in association with action and the nature of the observed action. As Wegner describes it, "The theory of apparent mental causation . . . is this: *People experience conscious will when they interpret their own thought as the cause of their action.* This means that people experience conscious will quite independently of any actual causal connection between their thoughts and their action" (2002, 64). One can identify at least two main components of this theory. I will briefly outline them below and argue that one need not accept both; in fact, I advocate rejecting one of the central theses of the theory. The first component of Wegner's theory, the one I agree with, maintains that the conscious intentions we have may or may not be causes but this doesn't matter as it is only critical that we *perceive* them as causes if we are to experience conscious will. Conscious will is experienced as a function of the *priority, consistency,* and *exclusivity* of the thought about the action. Although I focused on the *priority principle* above, I generally agree with Wegner that all three conditions are important and I find this portion of Wegner's theory useful (see ch.7). It does an excellent job explaining why we experience conscious will even when it appears as though our conscious intentions do not initiate or cause voluntary behavior. It is also supported by Wegner's experimental findings.

A second component of the theory of apparent mental causation—at least as far as I interpret it—maintains that there is *no genuine mental causation involved in voluntary action.* According to Wegner, unconscious mental processes give rise to conscious thought about the action (e.g., intention, belief), and *other* unconscious mental processes give rise to the voluntary action. The guiding idea here is that there may be one set of neural mechanisms that allow us to perform voluntary actions, and a different set of mechanisms that leads to conscious thought and the experience of conscious will. For Wegner, there may or may not be links between these underlying unconscious systems. As Wegner and Wheatley (1999) describe their thinking here:

> [T]he degree of conscious will that is experienced for an action is not a direct indication of any causal link between mind and action. Rather, our analysis suggests that conscious will results from a causal illusion that is the psychological equivalent of the third-variable problem in causal analysis. We can never be sure that A causes B, as there could always be a third variable, C, that causes both of them. In the same sense, we can never be sure that our thoughts cause our actions, as there could always be unconscious causes that have produced them both. (1999, 482)

According to Wegner, then, the experience of conscious will arises when a person infers an apparent causal path from thought to action. The actual causal path is not present in the person's consciousness since they do not have access to it. On this model, "The thought is caused by unconscious mental events, and the action is caused by unconscious mental events" (2002, 68). And according to Wegner, the causal pathways leading to each are distinct. Hence, "The will is experienced as a result of what is apparent, though, not what is real" (2002, 68).

I find this aspect of Wegner's theory confused and ambiguous for several reasons. For one, it's unclear what Wegner means by "mental causation" and why it would be an illusion if actions are caused by "unconscious mental events." If, as the name of his theory suggests, we are to interpret him as claiming that in all cases of voluntary action, mental causation is an illusion (only *apparent*, not real), then I must disagree with him. The account of consciousness and mentality I have been defending allows for the separation of the two. I therefore believe there can be *real* mental causation occurring at the level of unconscious mental states. That is, at the lower-level, unconscious mental states can cause and initiate behavior thereby preserving mental causation, though not conscious will. I believe we are justified in taxonomizing mental states in this way; it makes perfect sense to talk about unconscious mental states here—particularly unconscious intentional states. Wegner appears to be holding onto an outdated Cartesian theory of mind whereby only conscious mental causation counts as real mental causation. This is evidenced by the fact that he believes our *thoughts never cause our actions because our actions are caused by unconscious events.* There seems to be several assumptions being made here. Why can't these unconscious events be construed as mental? And if we do construe them as mental, why isn't this mental causation? The only thing precluding us from viewing things in this way is the Cartesian assumption that all mental states must be conscious states.

Some critics have argued that Wegner makes some additional Cartesian assumptions here (see Andersen 2006). Wegner interprets Libet's experiment as showing that *thoughts and intentions cannot cause action* because of the neurological activity (RP) that ramps-up and initiates action prior to W. This interpretation assumes, however, that *thoughts are not the same as neurological activity*! This assumption implies a Cartesian dualism of sorts. Van Duijn and Bem (2005) have argued, for example, that Wegner is guilty of making a category mistake here: Intentions don't *cause* neural processes, they *are* neural processes. Holly Andersen has likewise argued, "There is something dubiously Cartesian about treating mental intentions as separate from and able to stand in certain causal relations to neural processes: what might such incorporeal intentions be, if they do not involve neural processes?" (2006, 8). At times Wegner speaks of intentions as distinct from neural processes, and of the mind as distinct from the brain (e.g., 2004, 665). As Andersen writes, "Wegner's picture is one where intentions either cause the neural processes that lead to action, or else are causally disconnected from these processes. In light of Libet's results, Wegner thinks the latter is the only scientifically respectable answer" (2006, 8). Wegner's mistake appears to be that he conceives of intentions and neural processes as distinct entities and therefore believes, either the intentions come first or the neural processes come first. He then takes Libet's results to show that intentions cannot come first, here assuming something like all intentions must be conscious. Both of these assumptions are flawed and part of an outdated model of the mind.

I agree that our feeling of conscious will is an illusion. I also agree that the experience of conscious will arises when we infer that our conscious intention was the cause of our voluntary action, although the brain initiated the action prior to us consciously deciding to act and both intention and action were themselves caused by mental processes that do not feel willed. I disagree with Wegner, however, on a number of other important points. For one, I do not think there are two different causal pathways here, one that leads to conscious thought and a separate one that actually generates action.[21] Secondly, Wegner seems to think that mental causation, in general, is an illusion (at least this is what he seems to be saying). I disagree with this. Wegner believes the feeling of conscious will arises from processes that are psychologically and anatomically distinct from the processes whereby "mind" creates action. I don't know if he views the latter as a form of mental causation or not (he seems not to), but he clearly views these as two separate causal pathways. I, on the other hand, believe that if we allow for the possibility of unconscious mental states, and view mental states as identical to neurological states, there is nothing barring mental causation (understood as mentally initiated action) from occurring. Contra Wegner, my proposal is that we view the unconscious processes that initiate action as mental, not only as neurological. To view the mental and the neurological as mutually exclusive is to buy into a kind of dualism. I therefore think Wegner is over-looking a fundamental distinction that I view as central; not all mental states are conscious. Wegner seems (at least at times) to conflate mentality with consciousness, which is why he thinks unconscious mental causation is only apparent causation.

Now, some commentators might think my interpretation of Libet preserves free will because it preserves mental causation (e.g., Rosenthal 2002a; Van Duijn and Bem 2005; Andersen 2006; Mele 2009). This, however, would be mistaken. Van Duijn and Bem (2005) and Andersen (2006), for example, view their criticism of Wegner as a defense of free will—arguing that "once we remind ourselves that intentions are physically instantiated, that they are constituted by neural processes, then Libet's results are innocuous" (Andersen 2006, 8). I, on the other hand, do *not* believe that allowing for the unconscious (mental cum neurological) initiation of action preserves any intuitive sense of free will. Libet's results unequivocally show that *conscious will* is an illusion—our conscious intentions and decisions do not initiate action as we believe. This discovery remains disturbing whether or not you interpret the neurological precursors to the conscious intention (desire or decision) to act as mental. Our folk-psychological theory requires not only mental causation but conscious will! A central component of my argument has been that we should take the phenomenology of agency and our folk-psychological intuitions regarding free will at face value. We should then compare our scientific findings to this ordinary conception of free will. I believe the neuroscientific findings discussed in this chapter, and the psychological findings discussed in chapter 3, reveal that the up-to-me-ness we feel, our sense of conscious will, and the belief that our conscious selves are in the driver's seat are largely an illusion.

NOTES

1. I say "in part" because I believe there are additional phenomenological features of consciousness (like the one discussed in the previous chapter and the two to be discussed shortly) that are also responsible for creating the illusion of free will.

2. According to the HOT theory, when I have a conscious mental state I am usually unaware of two important aspects of that state: (1) I am unaware, from the first person point of view, of the relational and non-intrinsic nature of consciousness. This, as I explained in the previous chapter, helps account for the seeming immediacy, transparency, and infallibility of conscious experience. (2) I am also unaware (generally speaking) of the antecedent mental causes of that state—i.e., the unconscious mental states that trigger our HOTs.

3. In point of fact, this is only a partial explanation but one which will suffice for now. In chapter 7, I will provide a more detailed account of our sense of agency for action. In addition to the asymmetry being discussed here, I argue that the nature of *self*-consciousness and Wegner's (2002) priority, consistency, and exclusivity conditions are also important. See chapter 7 for details. For the moment, though, I will focus on the asymmetry between intentional states and sensory states.

4. Our HOTs can represent our sensory states in more or less fine grained ways. In some cases we might be conscious of a pain only as *throbbing* or *stinging*, in other cases we might represent the state in a way that makes us conscious of a *stinging mosquito bite* or *throbbing tooth ache*. Of course (as I stressed in the last chapter) our HOTs can also misrepresent their target states, so it's quite possible for us to be conscious of a particular sensation—be it a visual, auditory, olfactory, or tactile sensation—as caused in a way other than how it is *actually* caused. I might be conscious of a *cutting pain*, for example, when during a fraternity initiation one blindfolds me and runs an ice cube across my neck (Shoemaker's example). If I'm told that as part of the initiation I will be cut with a knife, the fear and anxiety leading up to the experience can cause my HOT to misrepresent the target state, thereby affecting the way I experience the sensation (the *what-it's-like* for me to be in that state).

5. In the rare case when I *am* aware of the causal origin of an intentional state, as when I am introspectively conscious of the fact that *I have a particular belief, x, because of Y*, I nonetheless remain unaware of *that* belief. That belief (i.e., the *belief that I hold a particular belief, x, because of Y*) is still experienced as uncaused and arising spontaneously. This is because that (second-order) belief arises from mental antecedents we are unaware of, and the second-order state (or the third-order HOT that makes us aware of it) makes no reference to *its* own causal origin.

6. Of course we can always close our eyes and imagine something red. But as David Hume pointed out, using the language of his time, there is a major difference between *ideas* and *impressions*. Conjuring up an image of red, or recalling a past experience of seeing something red, is qualitatively different than having a red sensation caused by an occurrent red object. Keeping this distinction in mind, the majority of occurrent sensory states are had in the presence of the environmental causes of those states.

7. See Obhi and Haggard (2004, 358).

8. This 50 ms is far within the margin of error and a significant magnitude shorter than the temporal gap that Libet and his colleagues found between W (the conscious "urge, desire or intention" to move) and RP (a specific electrical shift in the brain that precedes movement) .

9. As Libet describes the results: "For groups in which all the voluntary acts were freely spontaneous, with no reports of rough preplanning of when to act, the onset of RP averaged -550 msec. (before the muscle was activated). The W times for first awareness of wish to act averaged about -200 msec., for all groups. This value was the same even when subjects reported having preplanned roughly when to act! If we correct W for the -50 msec. error in the subjects' reports of timings of the skin stimuli, we have an average corrected W of about -150 msec. Clearly, the brain process (RP) to prepare for this voluntary act began about 400 msec. before the appearance of the conscious will to act (W). This relationship was true for every group of 40 trials and in every one of the nine subjects studied. It should also be noted that the actual difference in times is probably greater than the 400 msec; the actual initiating process in the brain probably starts before our recorded RP, in an unknown area that then activates the supplementary motor area in the cerebral cortex" (1999, 50-51).

10. See, for example, the essays in *The Volitional Brain: Towards a Neuroscience of Free Will*, edited by Libet, Freeman and Sutherland (1999); and *Does Consciousness Cause Behavior?* edited by Pockett, Banks, and Gallagher (2006).

11. Furthermore, a recent experiment conducted by Matsuhashi and Hallett (2008) appears to have replicated Libet's findings without relying on subjective reports or clock memorization on the part of participants.

12. For Libet's reply, see Haggard and Libet (2001).

13. Haggard and Eimer investigated the relation between neural events and the perceived time of voluntary actions or the perceived time of initiating those actions using the method of Libet. They found no difference in either movement-related potentials or perceived time of motor events for both a fixed movement condition, where subjects made voluntary movements of a single finger, and a free movement condi-

tion, in which subjects chose whether to respond with the left or right index finger on each trial. They next calculated both the readiness potential (RP) and lateralized readiness potential (LRP) for trials with early and late times of awareness. They found RP tended to occur later on trials with early awareness of movement initiation than on trials with late awareness, which they interpreted as "ruling out the RP as a cause of our awareness of movement initiation" (1999, 128).

14. Rosenthal argues that Libet's findings do not threaten free will since one might have unconscious intentions and these unconscious intentions might play a role in the production of action. I will address this attempt to reconcile Libet's findings with free will in the following section when I spell out in more detail my interpretation of the data based on the HOT theory. Although there are aspects of Rosenthal's interpretation I agree with (i.e., the role that unconscious intentions play in the production of action), I do not think it is capable of preserving free will.

15. According to Libet's "time-on" theory (see 1989, 1992; Libet et al. 1991) the subjective experiences elicited by sensory signals are delayed by substantial times since they require periods of neuronal activities of up to about 0.5 sec before cerebral "adequacy" is achieved for producing a conscious experience. However, the actual delays are subjectively "corrected" for by subjectively antedating the experience back in time (with small delays of 20 msec). The *content* of the sensory experience is thus normally altered, in relation to the fast initial timing signal, in a way that makes the actually delayed experience appear to occur without significant delay. Simply put, it takes about half a second for us to become consciously aware of something but the 'conscious mind' dates it back and we think we experience the event in the temporally right moment.

16. One even wonders whether the compatibilist would allow for *any* conditions of falsification. For example, would a compatibilist allow for the possibility of a "free" automaton—a creature that lacked *all* consciousness but was nonetheless free because it acted in accordance with its nonconscious "wants" and "desires"?

17. Levin informs me (in correspondence) that in his view events within the self that affect other parts of the self, such as the onset of a desire, are neither done by the self nor happen to the self. What the self *does* is its effects on the world outside the self. What happens to the self are effects on the self of the world outside. When different parts of the self interact so that a desire forms and then innervates the efferent nervous system, the self is neither doing nor undergoing.

18. According to Wegner, *"People experience conscious will when they interpret their own thought as the cause of their action"* (2002, 64). On his account, this means "For the perception of apparent mental causation, the thought should occur before the action, be consistent with the action, and not be accompanied by other potential causes" (2002, 69). And according to Wegner, *thought* should here be read as "intention, but belief and desire are also important" (2002, 66).

19. The precise window of time is still unknown since researchers have not yet tested the precise bounds for the perception of consecutiveness of thought and action. Wegner, however, suggests the following: "One indication of the lower bounds for willful experience is Libet's (1985) observation that in the course of a willed finger movement, conscious intention precedes action by about 200 milliseconds. Perhaps if conscious thought of an act occurs past this time, it is perceived as following the act, or at least as being too late, and so is less likely to be seen as causal" (Wegner and Wheatley 1999, 484).

20. Mark Hallett (2007) and Matsuhashi and Hallett (2006) have also found that movement initiation and the perception of willing the movement can be separately manipulated.

21. There are essentially two different ways to interpret Libet's findings (see Haggard 2005). You can interpret them, as Wegner does, as showing that conscious intention is part of an illusion of mental causation, retrospectively inferred to explain behavior. On this view, conscious intentions are the result of a different causal pathway than action. On the other hand, one could interpret Libet as I do, that conscious

intention is the *consequence* of the brain processes (which can be construed as unconscious mental processes) that prepare action. Here conscious intentions are *not* the result of an altogether separate pathway, but rather the latter correlate of preparatory neural activity. There are several recent studies that support my interpretation over Wegner's (see Haggard 2005). These studies suggest "Preparatory activity in the motor areas of the brain initiate action, and produces a conscious sensation of intention as a correlate" (Haggard 2005, 291). Contrary to Wegner's claim that our conscious thoughts are produced by a completely separate causal pathway than the one that causes action, there seems to be evidence that conscious intention arise as a direct consequence of pre-movement brain activity in the frontal and parietal motor areas (Haggard 2005).

SEVEN

Consciousness and Free Will (IV): Self-Consciousness and Our Sense of Agency

In the previous two chapters I have identified and explained away a number of key contributing factors to the phenomenology surrounding our subjective feeling of freedom—including (1) the feeling that we have immediate, direct, and infallible access to our own mental states and processes; (2) the feeling that our intentional states arise spontaneously and are causally undetermined; and (3) the feeling that we consciously cause or initiate behavior directly through our conscious intentions, decisions, and willings. I have argued that each of these phenomenological components of experience play an important role in generating our sense of free will but that by combining the theoretical framework of the HOT theory with empirical findings in the behavioral, cognitive, and neurosciences we can come to see that each is an illusion. In this final chapter I will conclude my account of the cognitive illusion of free will by examining the nature of self-consciousness and our sense of agency.

The first-person, subjective experience of "freely willing" an action requires that the actor feel a *sense of agency*. By *sense of agency* I mean the reflexive feeling that 'I' control my actions. When I reach out to pick up my cup of coffee, I feel as though it is *I* (my-*self*) who does so. I am conscious both of the action and myself as the cause of the action. The phenomenology of agency therefore includes an experience of *self-as-cause* or *self-as-initiator* (see Horgan, Tienson, and Graham 2003; Bayne 2008). It also includes a sense of ownership. That is, such actions normally come "bearing [one's] signature" (Pettit 2001); what some theorists refer to as the "myness" of the experience (Zahavi and Parnas 1998; Kircher and Leube 2003; Stephens and Graham 2000). We can define our

217

sense of agency, then, in terms of these two subjective components: *ownership* and *authorship*. Phenomenologically, we feel both a sense of *self-generation* or *authorship* (i.e., being the willful initiator of an action) and a sense of *ownership* (a sense that it is *I* who am experiencing the movement or thought) (see Gallagher 2004, 2000; Choudhury and Blakemore 2006).

Where, however, do our senses of authorship and ownership come from and do they point to a unified self who is the willful initiator of our voluntary acts? As Nietzsche asks, "What gives me the right to speak of an 'I,' and indeed of an 'I' as a cause . . . ?" (1914, I:16; as quoted by Choudhury and Blakemore 2006, 39). No doubt, from the first-person perspective, the phenomenology of agency presents in experience "a self that is an apparently embodied, apparently voluntarily behaving, agent" (Horgan, Tienson, and Graham 2003, 323). Horgan and colleagues have argued, for example, that "your phenomenology presents your own behavior to you as having *yourself as its source*, rather than (say) presenting your own behavior to you as having your own occurrent mental events as its source" (2003, 325). I agree that the phenomenology of agency largely reflects a libertarian agent-causal belief system. Not only do we experience ourselves as agent-causes, a number of philosophers and psychologists have suggested that in acting we experience ourselves as *homunculi*—i.e., as "ghosts in the machine" or "uncontrolled controllers" (Preston and Wegner 2005; Wegner 2005). Others, such as Tim Bayne, hedge slightly over the homunculus nature of our phenomenal selves, but nonetheless agree that we experience ourselves as things or substances:

> I am not at all convinced that we ever experience ourselves as homunculi, strictly speaking, but I do think there is something to the idea that in acting we experience ourselves as things—as substances rather than bundles. Bundle theories of the self might be correct as accounts of the self's ultimate nature, but they do not seem to have much going for them as accounts of how the self is represented in agentive experience. It's not just that the experience of the self is neutral on the question of whether or not the self is a bundle—instead, it seems to be flatly inconsistent with such a view. (2008, 194)

Given our experience, then, it's not hard to understand "the impulse we have to think of the mind as a place or subject" (Honderich 2002a, 23). In fact, in the attempt to account for the apparent unity of experience and our sense of agency, many philosophers have found it natural to posit a robust, unified *Self* as the willful author of behavior. Is it necessary, however, to posit an *indivisible Cartesian soul* (as Descartes did) or a *transcendental unity of self-consciousness* (as Kant did) to explain our intuitions about self and agency?

I maintain that although libertarians are essentially correct in describing the phenomenology, no such "indivisible" or "transcendental" self exists. The arguments against this conception of the self are well known and I will not rehearse them here (see Ryle 1949; Dennett 1991). I will simply assume that there is no Cartesian or libertarian *Self* (with a capital 'S')—i.e., a Self which is a thing or substance and stands separate from our individual thoughts and perceptions. The more interesting question, I believe, is why do we believe in such a Self? The goal is to provide a philosophically respectable account of self-consciousness that is true to the phenomenology of agency, while, at the same time, revealing why this sense of Self is an illusion. Here, I believe, the HOT theory can once again help.[1]

In section 7.1, I begin by motivating the need for a theory of self-consciousness by examining cases where self-consciousness breaks down. By examining self-conscious experience under conditions of stress and disturbance, it can help us understand the importance of self-consciousness in generating our sense of agency and our feeling of free will (see Stephens and Graham 2000). In section 7.2, I then propose an account of self-consciousness based on the HOT theory. The HOT theory of self-consciousness will not only provide a basic understanding of our sense of ownership, it will also provide a way of understanding our sense of unity without positing a Cartesian or libertarian Self. Since our sense of self, according to the theory, arises from the indexical nature of individual HOTs, the theory can explain the phenomenology of ownership and unity without positing a Self separate from our individual thoughts, perceptions, and sensations. In section 7.3, I turn to a discussion of Sydney Shoemaker's (1968) *immunity to error through misidentification* thesis and argue that, *pace* Shoemaker, genuine cases of misidentification can and do happen. I conclude in section 7.4 by sketching an account of the first-person phenomenology of agency which builds on the HOT model of self-consciousness and hence is consistent with the denial of a libertarian Self. This account attempts not only to explain our normal sense of agency but also how various breakdowns in the sense of agency can and do occur.

7.1 WHEN SELF-CONSCIOUSNESS BREAKS DOWN

Self-consciousness is crucial to our sense of agency for one of the classical features of self-consciousness is the feeling of ownership, which can include the feeling of ownership over one's body, thoughts, and/or movements. Such ownership is important to our sense of agency since the ability to attribute one's own thoughts and actions to the self is crucial to feeling that the experience is "mine" (Choudhury and Blakemore 2006, 39). Self-consciousness, however, is also important to our sense of authorship, since it is through self-consciousness that people discern their own willed actions from those of others. The experience of agency requires a recognition that one's thoughts and body are indeed one's own, that one's actions are actually initiated by the self, rather than by any other person, and that the actions we initiate belong to us. The importance of self-consciousness to the phenomenology of agency can easily be seen when one considers the various ways it can break down. In fact, there are a number of cases where people deny a sense of agency for their own actions or thoughts, which range from cases of action under hypnosis to far more exotic phenomenon (see Wegner 2002; Stephens and Graham 2000). For example, in certain forms of dissociative disorders such as alien-hand syndrome, schizophrenic thought-insertion, auditory hallucination, and movement disorders, we experience little in the way of willfulness.

Take, for example, *alien hand syndrome*, a neuropsychological disorder where individuals experience one hand as "operating with a *mind of its own*" (Wegner 2002, 4). Patients with this disorder often report feeling no sense of authorship over their *anarchic* or way-ward hand (see Della Sala, Marchetti, and Spinnler 1991; Goldberg, Mayer, and Toglia 1981; Goldberg and Bloom 1990; Geschwind et al. 1995). The syndrome is often characterized by unwanted movements that arise without any sense of their being willed. As Obhi and Haggard describe:

> For patients with alien hand syndrome . . . one hand evades voluntary control. That is, one hand performs meaningful but often inappropriate actions that the person did not intend. In fact, patients report not being able to control the affected limb and often have to physically stop the alien hand from performing inappropriate actions. In one often-cited example, a lady with the condition was given a cup of tea and immediately commented that it was too hot to drink, so she would let it cool first. As soon as she stated the intention, however, her alien hand grabbed the cup of tea in an effort to drink it, and she had to restrain it with her other hand. In one case, a woman's alien hand tried to throttle her by grabbing her neck, leaving the good hand to physically pull off the alien one. The same patient also experienced her alien hand involuntarily tearing off the bedcovers. The patient remarked that the hand was 'a law unto itself' and didn't act according to will. On occasion, while she was drinking from the glass, the alien hand grabbed it—fighting with the good hand until the drink spilled. (2004, 364)

What is remarkable about such cases is that sophisticated movements that are clearly generated by the patient can be experienced as involuntary and alien. For these patients, there is a kind of disconnect between their bodily movements and their sense of self. Although, from a third-person point of view, we would clearly ascribe these actions to the agent, from the first-person point of view, alien hand patients experience no sense of agency or authority over their anarchic hand. The phenomenology of the anarchic hand is therefore one of "alienation authorship"—the anarchic hand patient fails to experience their actions as their own (Bayne and Levy 2006, 57).

Additional examples of involuntariness and lack of control are experienced by schizophrenic patients. It is well known that schizophrenic patients can suffer from hallucinatory and delusional experiences, such as hearing "voices," as well as a variety of movement disorders (Frith 1992; Owens, Johnstone, and Frith 1982; Manschreck 1986; Daprati et al. 1997; Stephens and Graham 2000). As with alien hand syndrome, it is not unusual for schizophrenic patients to report feelings of alien control. Many schizophrenic patients describe an external agent as causing their actions, thoughts, speech, or emotions.[2] For this reason, Sass and Parnas (2003) has argued that schizophrenia is fundamentally a *self-disorder* or *ipseity* disturbance (*ipse* is Latin for "self"), and Jaspers (1913, 1963) has referred to these delusions of control as *Ego-disturbances*. Schizophrenic patients, for example, often make mistakes about the agency of various bodily movements. And, as Shaun Gallagher describes, "Not only do they fail to recognize their own agency in such cases, but schizophrenics suffering from delusions of control misattribute agency for their movements to someone or something else" (2004, 10). In such cases, although the action or thought belongs to the individual, patients suffering from such Ego-disturbances experience no sense of agency. "Their movements typically look normal, are goal directed, and are clearly generated by the patient's brain, but do not get associated with a sense that the patient him or herself has willed the movement" (Hallett 2007, sec. 4.0).

According to one of the leading accounts of schizophrenia, Christopher Frith's (1987, 1992) *neurocognitive model,* such experiences are due to a breakdown or disruption in basic *self-monitoring* processes.[3] Self-monitoring systems enable one to distinguish the products of self-generated actions or thoughts from those of other-generated actions or thoughts. Firth sees the failure of self-monitoring processes as a likely explanation of how self-ascriptions of thoughts and actions may be subject to errors of identification in regard to agency. This is perhaps easiest to see with the phenomenon of *thought insertion,* where schizophrenic patients report that someone/thing has inserted thoughts into their mind. As Frith describes it:

> Thought insertion, in particular, is a phenomenon that is difficult to understand. Patients say that thoughts that are not their own are coming into their head. This experience implies that we have some way of recognizing our own thoughts. It is as if each thought has a label on it saying 'mine.' If this labeling process goes wrong, then the thought would be perceived as alien. (1992, 80; as quoted by Gallagher 2000, 207)

C.S. Mellor provides the following example:

A 29 year old housewife said, "I look out of the window and I think the garden looks nice and the grass looks cool, but the thoughts of Eamonn Andrews come into my mind. There are no other thoughts there, only his . . . He treats my mind like a screen and flashes his thoughts on to it like you flash a picture." (1970, 17)

Although somewhat controversial, I will argue later that the phenomenon of thought insertion involves an error of self-identification which affects both the sense of agency and the sense ownership for thought (cf. Gallagher 2000). As John Campbell writes:

What is so striking about the phenomenon of thought insertion as described by schizophrenic patients is that it seems to involve an error of identification . . . A patient who supposes that someone else has inserted thoughts into his mind is right about which thoughts they are, but wrong about whose thoughts they are. So thought insertion seems to be a counterexample to the thesis that present-tense introspectively based reports of psychological states cannot involve errors of identification. (1999a, 609-610)

Whether or not this is a correct interpretation of thought insertion, it does seem that our normal sense of agency requires that we experience a sense of ownership for our actions and thoughts. If we do not self-ascribe our actions and thoughts—if we do not experience actions and thoughts as owned by a seemingly unified self—we will not experience a sense of agency over them.

Clearly, then, self-consciousness is important for agentive experience. In normal cases of agentive experience, we feel ownership over our thoughts, feelings, and movements. As William James says in the *Principles of Psychology*, "The universal conscious fact is not, 'Feelings exist,' or 'Thoughts exist,' but 'I think' and 'I feel'" (1918, 226; as quoted by Stephens and Graham 2000, 1). It is self-consciousness that allows us to be aware of thoughts and feelings *as* one's own—i.e., as things that I myself think or feel. This self-consciousness, however, can break down: "Thinking, like all conscious activities, is experienced as an activity which is being carried out by the subject . . . There is a quality of 'my-ness' connected with thought. In schizophrenia this sense of the possession of one's thought may be impaired and the patient may suffer from alienation of thought" (Fish 1962, 48). The phenomenon of schizophrenic "thought insertion" therefore demonstrates that disturbances of the self can happen even at the seemingly direct and unmediated level of thought. These breakdowns or disturbances in self-consciousness are examples of what Stephens and Graham (2000) call *alienated self-consciousness*—i.e., experiences in which the subject is directly or introspectively aware of some episode in his/her mental life, but experiences the episode as alien (i.e., as somehow attributable to another person rather than to the subject).[4]

It is important, then, in attempting to understand our sense of agency that we ask ourselves: What features of self-consciousness make alienated experience possible? And what, if anything, do cases of alienated self-consciousness reveal about our sense of agency and free will generally? I believe cases like these reveal just how fragile our sense of self really is. They also indicate that our experience of *self-as-cause*, though perhaps important to the illusion of free will, may not be so important to the actual causal mechanisms that lead to action. As Frith writes, "Most of us share in common the useful delusion that we have free will. Schizophrenic patients have lost this experience. As a consequence they develop idiosyncratic, and in many cases harmful, delusions instead" (Frith 1987; as quoted by Spence 1996, 85). If schizophrenics can engage in seemingly "purposeful" actions without experiencing a sense of authorship or self-determination, then perhaps our normal sense of agency, and the seemingly unified *self* we take to be causally involved in such agency, is really an illusion. In fact, if self-ascriptions of thoughts and actions may be subject to errors of identification, as I will argue they can, then it's possible to draw a distinction between an individual's thoughts and actions, on the one hand, and the feeling of agency, on the other. These neuropsychological disorders show that it is possible for thought and action to be isolated from the senses of authorship and ownership normally associated with them — and this suggests that the causal processes that lead to each may be distinct (see Spence 1996; Wegner 2002). [5]

The thesis I wish to defend in this chapter is that our normal sense of agency, rather than indicating the presence of a libertarian Self who is the willful initiator of our thoughts and actions, is actually the result of how we go about self-ascribing thoughts and actions to a seemingly unified self; which, I will argue, is really a matter of self-interpretation. I maintain that the feeling of ownership results from the particular way HOTs represent their target states. The feeling of authorship, on the other hand, occurs when the intentions and thoughts that precede action are experienced as owned and there is thought/action consistency. My account will draw heavily on Wegner's claim that "a person infers that an event is due to the self as a result of perceiving a causal link between own thoughts and that event" (2008, 228), but I will supplement Wegner's proposal with a detailed account of self-consciousness based on the HOT theory. The HOT theory will provide us with an understanding of how the self-construct is created. We can then use that account of self-consciousness to explain why certain actions and thoughts are self-ascribed to a seemingly unified self and others are not. I maintain that if the relevant intentions and thoughts that precede an action are tagged with a sense of *self* (i.e., if they are experienced as owned by a seemingly unified self), and (a) the subsequent action is perceived as consistent with those thoughts, and (b) there are no other competing causes available for the action, then an individual will likely experience a sense of agency over the associated action. On this account, one experiences a sense of *self*-generation or authorship when they draw causal inferences relating prior self-ascribed thoughts with consistent and self-ascribed actions.

In the following section, I will offer an account of self-consciousness based on the HOT theory. The account will help explain the nature of self-consciousness and the apparent unity of consciousness. It will also help explain how errors of self-identification can happen (cf. Shoemaker 1968). Since our sense of self is extremely important to the first-person phenomenology of agency, an investigation into the nature of self-consciousness can help explain not only our sense of *ownership* but our sense of *authorship*.

7.2 SELF-CONSCIOUSNESS AND HIGHER-ORDER THOUGHTS

Let us begin, then, by examining where our sense of self, including our senses of ownership and unity, come from. Why do I experience my conscious thoughts, perceptions, and feelings as belonging to a unified self? As Kircher and Leube write:

> Experiences are always and only experiences of an "I" . . . The "I" in every primary experience is implicitly and pre-reflectively present in the field of awareness and is crucial to the whole structure. The "I" is not a 'pole' but more a field, through which all experiences pass . . . This basic self does not [appear to] arise from any inferential reflection or introspections, because it is not [experienced as] a relation, but an intrinsic property of primary experiences. When I have a perception of pain, this perception is simultaneously a tacit self-awareness, because my act of perception is given to me in the first-person-perspective, from my point of view and only in my field of awareness. . . . It is this feeling of 'myness,' that makes our experiences feel as a united, single being. (2003, 659)

According to the HOT theory, to understand where our sense of self comes from we need to look to the content of our higher-order thoughts. Recall that on the HOT theory, a mental state becomes a conscious state in virtue of being the target of a HOT. To understand self-consciousness, then, we need to take a closer look at how a HOT represents its target, since it is this representational relationship that makes us aware of our conscious mental states and determines what-it-is-like for us to be in those states.

According to Rosenthal's account of self-consciousness (2001, 2002b, 2003, 2004a, 2005b), a HOT represents its target state to the effect that "I am in such-and-such a state." That is, our HOTs employ the indexical concept 'I' in representing their target states, and in this way make one conscious not only of the target state, but also of a self to which the HOT represents the target state as belonging. Since our HOTs represent their target states in this way, each HOT characterizes the self to which it assigns its target solely as the bearer of that target state and, by implication, as the individual that thinks that HOT itself (Rosenthal 2003, 343). According to Rosenthal, "Just as we understand the word 'I' as referring to whatever individual performs a speech act in which the word occurs, so we understand the mental analogue of 'I' as referring to whatever individual thinks a thought in which the mental analogue occurs" (2003, 343). On this account, every HOT tacitly represents its target state as belonging to the individual that thinks that very HOT. Our sense of self therefore arises because of the indexical nature of the 'I' contained in the content of individual HOTs. Because a mental state's being conscious consists in it being accompanied by a HOT that one is, oneself, in that state, the conscious state is represented as belonging to an 'I' or self that is the bearer of that state. In this way, the HOT model is able to explain "not only how we are conscious of our conscious mental states, but how we are conscious of ourselves as well" (2004a, 161).

Of course, much more needs to be said. Any account of self-consciousness should be able to explain three essential features of our awareness of ourselves: (1) our sense of ownership; (2) our sense of unity; and (3) our sense (whether accurate or not) that we are conscious of ourselves in a way that affords a certain immunity from error. To understand how the HOT theory explains these phenomenological features of self-consciousness, we need to better understand the nature of the *essential indexical* (Perry 1979) that makes us conscious of ourselves. Perhaps the best way to approach this is to first consider a potential problem confronting the theory. As Rosenthal describes it: "The way we are conscious of ourselves seems, intuitively, to be special in a way that simply having a thought about something cannot capture. For one thing, there is a difference between having a thought about somebody that happens to be oneself and having a thought about oneself, as such; HOTs presumably must be about oneself, as such" (2004a, 161). The problem is that, if a HOT makes one conscious of oneself as being in a particular mental state because it has the content that one is, oneself, in that state, how does the HOT refer to oneself, as such, without some special awareness of the self that is antecedent to and independent of the thought? It may seem that to have a thought about oneself, as such, requires some special awareness of an antecedent self. This apparent problem, however, can be easily dealt with once we understand the nature of essential indexical self-reference.

According to the HOT theory, an essentially indexical thought about myself will have the content that I am *F*, where the word or mental analogue of 'I' functions in the same way as our speech acts. So just as the word 'I' plainly refers to the individual who performs a speech act in which that word occurs, similarly, "the mental analogue of that word refers to the thinker of the containing thought, the individual that holds a mental attitude toward the relevant intentional content" (2004a, 166). Of course, as Rosenthal notes, "The word 'I' does not have as its meaning *the individual performing this speech act*; nor does the mental analogue of 'I' express the concept *the individual holding a mental attitude toward this content*" (2004a, 166). Hence, since what the mental analogue of 'I' refers to is determined by which individual thinks the thought, one can refer to oneself using 'I' or its mental analogue without explicitly referring to an antecedent self independent of the thought.

Just as the reference of 'I' in speech acts is determined by a function from the context of utterance to the individual that produced that utterance (see Kaplan 1989), the mental analogue of 'I' refers to whatever individual holds a mental attitude toward a content in which that mental analogue figures (see Rosenthal 2003, 2004a). As Josh Weisberg writes:

> It is important to note the indexical features of the concept "I." "I" serves a function much like that of the term "here," which automatically refers to the location of the utterance, and gets its more specific content on the particular occasion [of] its use from the location that it occurs in. "I" works in a similar way. When "I" occurs in a HOT, it refers back to the thinker that tokens the thought. It is the function of a HOT to pick out various states that the organism is in, and by employing the indexical "I" there is a thin sort of immunity to error present in the self-ascription by the HOT, reminiscent of the way that uses of "here" are immune to error by automatically referring to the location of utterance. Our conscious states are owned by us because in becoming conscious of them, we represent the states in conjunction with "I," which automatically refers back to the producer of the thought (cf. Shoemaker, 1968). (2001, 1119-1120)

Since HOTs are simply first-person thoughts, and function semantically just as other first-person thoughts do, the HOT hypothesis explains why, when a mental state is conscious, one is conscious of oneself in an essentially indexical way as being in that state. Hence, when I have the essential indexical thought that "I am in such-and-such a state," my thought in effect describes as being in that state the individual that thinks that very thought.[6]

It would seem, then, that the HOT theory is capable of explaining our sense of ownership. But is it also capable of explaining our sense of unity? Well, first we need to get clear on what we mean by unity. Weisberg points out that:

> Researchers often have several distinct phenomena in mind when they discuss the unity of consciousness. One issue, which occupies a large part of the neuroscientific focus on unity, is the "binding problem." How are features processed in disparate anatomical and functional locations in the brain brought together into one coherent experience? Closely related is the problem of accounting for apparent "spatial" relations that hold between our sensations, relations that allow us to view one feature as next to another in the same experience. A third

phenomenon associated with unity is the apparent clear and seamless nature of our conscious experience. (2001, 1117)

Although I am primarily concerned with this last phenomenon, the feeling of a unified self enduring over time, I would briefly like to say something about the binding problem. Cognitive science tells us that the brain processes that underwrite perception are widely distributed. This raises the question of how the disparate elements of perception are combined into a single coherent experience—i.e., how does the brain bring it all together? Although I do not wish to speculate on the underlying neurological mechanisms that carry out such binding (cf. Crick and Koch 1990; Llinas and Ribary 1993; Edelman and Tononi 2000), I maintain that the "layered explanatory model" of the HOT theory allows for this issue to be dealt with largely at the level of nonconscious processes (Weisberg 2001). I do not think the HOT theory (or, for that matter, any theory of consciousness) needs to explain how binding occurs, since binding does not appear to involve any conscious processes at all. In fact, there is good reason to think binding occurs prior to consciousness since unconscious perceptions, like those registered in priming, subliminal perception, and blindsight, influence behavior in virtue of their perceptible properties— which presumably need to be bound. Since it appears perceptions are bound whether they are conscious or not, "this aspect of unity is not one that a theory of consciousness has to explicate" (Weisberg 2001, 1118).

The same is not true, however, for the kind of unity relevant to our sense of agency—i.e., the feeling of a unified self enduring over time. Any theory of self-consciousness needs to explicate this sense of unity. It is important to the success of my account, then, that the HOT theory be capable of explaining such unity.

Unity of Consciousness

One obvious advantage of the HOT theory's account of self-consciousness is that it's consistent with a Humean *bundle theory* and therefore can help explain where our sense of *self* comes from without positing a Cartesian or libertarian *Self*. In *The Treatise of Human Nature*, David Hume famously wrote, "For my part, when I enter most intimately into what I call *myself*, I always stumble on some particular perception or other, of heat or cold, light or shade, love or hatred, pain or pleasure. I never can catch myself at any time without a perception, and never can observe anything but the perception" (1739, 252). This led Hume to conclude that the *self* is "no more than a bundle or collection of different perceptions." Because of this famous passage, views that deny the existence of a Cartesian Self and instead focus on individual experiences or other mental particulars are often referred to as *bundle theories*. The HOT theory too denies the existence of an indivisible Cartesian soul or libertarian Self and instead appeals only to mental particulars (e.g., individual HOTs) to account for our sense of self. This, however, may lead one to wonder: If there is no metaphysical unity of self, why do we experience a *sense of unity*? Where does our pervasive feeling of *selfhood* come from? Clearly, as Rosenthal acknowledges, "People have a compelling experience of many of their actions as being free, and that experience of seeming freedom encourages the idea of a unified, conscious self as the source of such action." Luckily, the HOT model provides "a natural explanation of these [libertarian] ideas about freedom that doesn't posit any underlying unity of self" (2003, 361).

I maintain that our sense of unity is largely a construct, an illusion of sorts. Although we feel in direct contact with our*selves*, we do not realize that it is just a construct that can be easily overthrown, for example in cases of depersonalization or delusions of alien control (Kircher and Leube 2003, 660). Phenomenon like alien hand syndrome, schizophrenic thought insertion, and other delusions of control, reveal just how fragile our sense of self really is. I believe cases like these, as well as split-brain cases and Dissociative Identity Disorder (previously known as Multiple Personality Disorder), require us to reject the very notion of a unified *Self*. There is no Cartesian or libertarian Self; no "inner puppeteer who pulls the body's strings" (Dennett 2008) or who stands separate from our individual thoughts and perceptions.[7] Although this conception of Self is an illusion, the HOT theory, I maintain, can explain the *subjective appearance of unity* while respecting the actual and potential disunity witnessed in these neuropsychological cases.

The interesting question, then, is why do we believe in a single, unified Self? Why do we believe in what Wegner calls the "magic self" (2008) and Dennett calls "some concentrated internal lump of specialness" (2008)? My answer to this question is once again based on the HOT theory (see Rosenthal 2001, 2002b, 2003, 2004a). Thus far we have seen that, according to Rosenthal's version of the HOT theory, each HOT characterizes the self it refers to solely as the bearer of target states and, in effect, as the thinker of the HOT itself. Although nothing in that characterization implies that this bearer is the same from one HOT to the next, "there is also nothing to distinguish one such bearer from any other." And, according to Rosenthal, our seeming to be aware in a direct and unmediated way of the self each HOT refers to "tilts things towards apparent unity." Since we seem to be directly aware of the self in each case, "it seems subjectively as though there is a single self to which all one's HOTs refer, a single bearer for all our conscious states" (2003, 344).

Note, however, that this sense of unity is relatively weak since it's the kind of intrinsic unity we experience in all primary or nonreflective experiences. In such primary experiences, the self that is referred to as the bearer of target states is not picked out or characterized in any kind of detailed way—we are simply aware, in an apparently direct and unmediated way, of an experiencing self (i.e., a self that is the bearer of a state).

Since we seem to be directly aware of this experiencing self, it appears prereflectively and subjectively as though there is a single bearer for all our conscious states. "And the sparse way HOTs characterize that bearer bolsters that sense of unity" (2003, 345). But, as Rosenthal points out, "this sparse characterization is not enough to identify ourselves; we do not, *pace* Descartes, identify ourselves simply as bearers of mental states" (2003, 345). For us to experience a more robust sense of unity, the kind of unity of self that comes in thinking that the present 'I' of experience is the same 'I' that fancies himself a philosopher, has a beautiful daughter named Maya, and comes from a large Italian family, we need to become introspectively conscious of our own consciousness. It is at the level of introspection where self-identification really takes place, since introspection is often, if not always, "a process of conscious self-interpretation" (2005b, 126).

When I discussed introspective consciousness in chapter 5, I pointed out that HOTs are not typically conscious thoughts. For a HOT to be conscious it has to be the target of a third-order thought about it. Although this rarely happens, when it does we become introspectively conscious of being conscious. That is, introspective consciousness occurs when we are not only conscious of our mental states, but also conscious that we are. With regard to unity, then, when HOTs become conscious— i.e., when we become introspectively aware of our conscious mental states (or cluster of mental states)—this results in a conscious sense of unity among those states even when the states are conscious by way of distinct HOTs. As Rosenthal writes:

> Introspective consciousness is . . . pivotal for our conscious sense of mental unity. . . . Each HOT represents its target state as belonging to some individual. One secures reference to that individual by way of other first-person thoughts, each of which contributes to the heterogeneous collection of contingent properties by way of which we identify ourselves. We thereby identify the individual to which each HOT assigns its target as being the same from one HOT to the next. Since introspecting consists in being conscious of our HOTs, it results in our being conscious of those HOTs *as* seeming to all assign their targets to some single individual. One becomes conscious of oneself as a center of consciousness. (2003, 347)

According to the HOT model, we identify ourselves as individuals in a variety of ways that have little systematic connection, relying on considerations that range from personal history, bodily features, and psychological characteristics to current location and situation. There is no "magic bullet" by which we identify ourselves, "only a vast and loose collection of considerations, each of which is by itself relatively unimpressive, but whose combination is enough for us to identify ourselves whenever the question arises" (2003, 346). Introspective consciousness therefore re-

sults in a sense of one's conscious states as all unified in a single conscious subject, even though we identify that conscious subject in heterogeneous ways.

So even though we have a sense of self when we are not introspecting,
the sparse way HOTs characterize their bearer is not enough to identify a
single, unified subject. For all we know, the self to which each HOT refers
might be different from one HOT to the next. For one to become conscious of a seemingly unified self, an introspective act of construction
needs to take place. Here we appeal to a broad, heterogeneous collection
of contingent properties to specify the individual each HOT represents its
target as belonging to, and we take that battery of descriptions to pick out
a single individual. Rosenthal refers to this as the *battery model* (2003).

> In the first person, the essential indexical in effect identifies the self it
> refers to as the individual who thinks a thought or performs a speech
> act. This thin way of identifying oneself provides almost no informa-
> tion. But, by the same token, there is no conflict between our referring
> to ourselves in this way and the battery model of how we identify
> ourselves. The essential indexical picks something out as the individual
> that thinks a particular thought; the battery model provides an infor-
> mative way of saying just which individual that is. This is why we
> seem unable ever to pin down in any informative way what the essen-
> tial indexical refers to. The essential indexical refers to the thinker of a
> thought; an informative characterization of the self depends on one's
> applying some battery of descriptions to oneself in an essentially index-
> ical way. (2003, 350)

Since HOTs are first-person thoughts, when a HOT becomes conscious
(via a third-order thought), this enriches our description of the self to
which our HOTs assign their target states, and in so doing reinforces and
consolidates the subjective sense each of us has that our conscious states
all belong to a single individual (2003, 346-347). On this model, the way
we are conscious of ourselves relies on a subset of the essentially indexical first-person thoughts we have about ourselves—namely, our HOTs.
Although there is no single way we identify ourselves, the battery of
descriptions we draw on include all the properties we believe ourselves
to have. "Each of these factors reflects some belief we have about ourselves, such as what one's name is, where one lives, what one's physical
dimensions and location are, and what the current contents are of one's
consciousness" (2004a, 177). Since all these beliefs self-ascribe properties
by making essentially indexical self-reference, they provide us with a
broad, heterogeneous collection of contingent descriptions by which we
can identify ourselves.

If we identify ourselves, however, through a battery of descriptions,
then this is consistent with there being no underlying metaphysical unity
of self; only an *appearance of unity* created by a relatively unsystematic
subset of essentially indexical first-person thoughts. Although this goes

contrary to the picture conjured up by libertarians and, in fact, our own phenomenology, it fits with the kind of disunity witnessed in certain neuropsychological phenomenon (e.g., schizophrenic thought insertion, Dissociative Identity Disorder, and certain phenomenon associated with split-brain patients). In fact, Rosenthal has argued that the HOT model's approach to unity suggests natural ways to explain various failures of unity, such as the puzzling phenomenon of Dissociative Identity Disorder. According to Rosenthal:

> The compelling appearance of distinct selves presumably results in part from there being disjoint sets of beliefs, emotions, and other intentional states specific to the apparent selves, though many general desires and background beliefs will be shared. But it's also very likely due to there being distinct sets of HOTs each operating on a distinct group of intentional states. And, because each disjoint group of HOTs operates on a distinct set of first-person thoughts, that group of HOTs will assign its target to an apparent self characterized by the battery that derives from that set of first-person thoughts. Such an individual will accordingly be conscious of itself in dramatically different terms, depending on which alter is active. (2003, 361 fn.42)

Not only does this approach to unity explain various failures of unity, it also avoids positing the philosophically and theoretically troublesome idea of a homunculus who stands separate from our individual thoughts and perceptions. Since our sense of self, according to the theory, arises from the indexical nature of individual HOTs, the theory remains consistent with a Humean bundle theory while, at the same time, accounting for the subjective appearance of unity.[8] If the HOT model of self-consciousness is correct, there is no mysterious unified *Self* that takes in perceptions, has infallible access to thoughts, and initiates actions. Instead, our vivid sense of a unified self is really a construct, a process of conscious self-interpretation. Although many will find this threatening to free will, to account for our libertarian phenomenology one need only preserve appearances—and for this task "it is arguable that the appearance of conscious unity is, itself, all the reality that matters" (Rosenthal 2003, 341).

7.3 ERRORS OF IDENTIFICATION, THOUGHT INSERTION, AND THE HOT THEORY

Now that we've seen how the HOT theory can account for the appearance of unity and our sense of ownership, I would like to examine whether it can account for break downs in self-consciousness and errors of identification. I have already argued in chapter 5 that one can be mistaken about what mental states one is in, even when those states are conscious. But can one be right that someone is in a particular mental state, but wrong about *whose* mental state it is? For example, if an individual says "I am thinking about apples," can he or she be right that someone is thinking about apples, but wrong about who it is that is doing the thinking? Sydney Shoemaker has argued that this cannot happen. According to Shoemaker (1968), the special introspective access we have to our own conscious states is, in his now famous phrase, *immune to error through misidentification*. Shoemaker's immunity principle is based on what Wittgenstein (1958) called the "subject" use of the first-person pronoun 'I.' In all first-person statements, the word 'I' serves the function of identifying the subject to which the predicate of the statements must apply. Wittgenstein, however, distinguished two different uses of the word 'I' — "the use as object" and "the use as subject" (1958, 66-67). According to Shoemaker, the "object" use of the first-person pronoun is open to possible error, like when I identify myself through observation or inference. I might think, for example, "I am bleeding" but be mistaken because my body is tangled up with that of someone else (e.g., we are wrestling) or because I am seeing my identical twin or double in a mirror (1968, 556). The "subject" use of the first-person pronoun, however, is "immune to error through misidentification" (1968, 556).

According to Shoemaker, if a person says that he/she has a certain experience, it would be nonsensical to ask, "Are you sure that it is *you* who are having the experience?" If , for example, you claim to be in pain, it makes no sense to ask, "Are you sure that it is *you* who is in pain?" As Shoemaker puts it: "The statement 'I feel pain' is not subject to error through misidentification relative to 'I': it cannot happen that I am mistaken in saying 'I feel pain' because, although I do know of someone that feels pain, I am mistaken in thinking that person to be myself" (1968, 557). Shoemaker maintains that this is also true of other first-person statements like "I see a canary." Although I can be mistaken in saying "I see a canary" because what I actually see is a goldfinch, "it cannot happen," according to Shoemaker, "that I am mistaken in saying this because I have misidentified as myself the person I know to see a canary" (1968, 557). For Shoemaker, if I consciously feel pain or see a canary, it may be that I can be wrong about whether the state I am in is one of feeling pain or seeing a canary, but it *cannot* be that I am right that somebody feels pain or sees a canary but wrong that it is *I* who does so. Hence, according to the immunity principle, first-person statements in which 'I' is used "as subject," have "absolute immunity" to error through misidentification (1968, 557).

Although many interpretations of the immunity principle focus on grammatical structure and the function of the first-person pronoun, Shoemaker's thesis pertains to more than grammatical form. As Shaun Gallagher writes:

[Shoemaker's] immunity principle is based on what Wittgenstein (1958) called the use of the first-person pronoun *"as subject"* . . . [Although] there are grammatical interpretations of this principle . . . Wittgenstein's characterization points to a more experiential sense of immunity to error through misidentification. His examples are cognitive or experiential ones: "I see so-and-so," "I try to lift my arm," "I have a toothache," and "I think it will rain." It would be nonsensical to ask, "Are you sure that it is *you* who thinks it will rain?" This is nonsensical, not because it concerns an issue pertaining to grammatical structure, but because it concerns the proximity of experience, the surety of access to one's own experience, or more precisely, to one's own *ipseity*, an access that Shoemaker calls "non-observational." (2000, 204-205)

Shoemaker's thesis is that present-tense, introspectively based reports of first-person mental states cannot involve errors of identification. Shoemaker's immunity principle is significant not because of what it says about grammatical structure but because of what it purports to say about the nature of introspection. Shoemaker (1986), in fact, argues that the "perceptual model" of introspection (e.g., Armstrong 1968, 1981) is the wrong model of self-awareness because perception allows for the possible of misidentification, while introspection is immune from errors of misidentification.[9]

Is Shoemaker correct, however, in claiming that such first-person psychological judgments are not subject to error through misidentification? I do not believe he is—at least not in any meaningful way. Perhaps it's tempting to think that the character of the seemingly spontaneous, unmediated access we have to mental states guarantees that those states cannot belong to anybody other than oneself. But, as Rosenthal has argued, "since we have no reason to think that this access is actually spontaneous and immediate, as against merely apparent, no such guarantee holds" (2003, 356). According to the battery model of self-identification, immunity to error from misidentification does not obtain. On the battery model, we identify the individual each first-person thought refers to by appeal to a heterogeneous collection of contingent properties. But it could turn out that any or, indeed, all of the properties in such a battery do not actually belong to me. So, if we do identify ourselves in that way, then "whatever state I think I am in and whatever my basis for thinking that, I could be right that somebody is in that state but wrong that I am the person who's in that state" (Rosenthal 2003, 355). Although Shoemaker's immunity to error through misidentification may seem intuitive to many, there is good reason to think authentic cases of misidentification can and do happen. Sometimes, when self-consciousness breaks down or becomes disturbed, like in cases of *alienated self-consciousness* (Stephens and Graham 2000), it appears to the self-conscious person as if *other* selves or agents are involved in his/her stream of consciousness. I maintain that cases of alienated self-consciousness like schizophrenic thought insertion provide good counterexamples to Shoemakers thesis.

John Campbell (1999a), for example, has recently argued that the phenomenon of thought insertion should be described as a case in which the subject is introspectively aware of a certain thought and yet is wrong in identifying *whose* thought it is (cf. Coliva 2002; Gallagher 2000). As Campbell writes:

> What is so striking about the phenomenon of thought insertion as described by schizophrenic patients is that it seems to involve an error of identification. The patient might say, "Thoughts come into my head like 'Kill God.' It's just like my mind working, but it isn't. They come from this chap, Chris. They're his thoughts." (Frith 1992, 66). A patient who supposes that someone else has inserted thoughts into his mind is right about which thoughts they are, but wrong about whose thoughts they are. So thought insertion seems to be a counterexample to the thesis that present-tense introspectively based reports of psychological states cannot involve errors of identification. (1999a, 609-610)

Frith, himself, seems to agree:

> Thought insertion, in particular, is a phenomenon that is difficult to understand. Patients say that thoughts that are not their own are coming into their head. This experience implies that we have some way of recognizing our own thoughts. It is as if each thought has a label on it saying 'mine.' If this labeling process goes wrong, then the thought would be perceived as alien. (1992, 80)

The view that there is here a labeling process that can go wrong, according to Campbell, is exactly the idea that self-ascriptions of thoughts are subject to mistakes about *whose* thoughts they are; i.e., that errors of identification are possible (1999a, 610).

However counterintuitive this may seem, this interpretation is indeed supported by the way schizophrenic patients describe their experiences. Patients suffering from this phenomenon report feeling these "inserted thoughts" as not actually their own. It's not just that they experience them as thoughts or ideas communicated to them, but rather it is as if *another's thoughts* have been engendered or inserted into them. Cahill and Frith, for example, provide the following vivid example: "One of our patients reported physically feeling the alien thoughts as they entered his head and claimed that he could pin-point the point of entry!" (1992, 278). Paradoxically, the thought "inserted" into the subject's mind is in some sense his, since it exists in his stream of consciousness; that is, he has, for example, "some especially direct knowledge of it" (Campbell 1999a, 610). On the other hand, there is, the patient insists, another sense in which the thought is not his, a sense in which the thought is someone else's, "and not just in that someone else originated the thought and communicated it to the subject; there is a sense in which the thought, as it were, remains the property of someone else" (Campbell 1999a, 610). Since the schizophrenic patient is aware, through introspection, of a thought of which he does not recognize himself to be the agent, it is hard *not* to interpret these cases as errors of identification. As Campbell points out, "The schizophrenic seems to find himself with first-person knowledge of a token thought which was formed by someone else" (1999a, 620).

If this interpretation of thought insertion is correct, then Shoemaker is mistaken in thinking that introspectively based reports of first-person mental states cannot involve errors of identification. Although there might be what Rosenthal calls *thin immunity* to error (see 2003, 2004a), strong immunity to error through misidentification does not obtain. According to Rosenthal, the temptation to think that there is an actual guarantee of some strong immunity to error rests "on the assumption that being conscious of a mental state in the relevant subjective way ensures that I'm not wrong about whether I'm the individual I'm conscious of as being in that state." But this assumption, he maintains, suggests a weaker form of immunity that does hold, despite cases of actual and potential first-person errors of identification. Rosenthal describes this weaker form of immunity as follows:

> I may think in that seemingly immediate way that I am in pain and be right that somebody is in pain, and yet be wrong that I'm the one who's in pain. But I cannot in such a case be wrong about whether it is I who I think is in pain. Similarly, if I think in that seemingly immediate way that I believe or desire something, I cannot be mistaken about whether it is I who I think has that belief or desire. Because this constraint is weaker than the immunity to error Shoemaker describes, I'll refer to it as *thin* immunity to error through misidentification. (2003, 356)

It's important to recognize, however, that even if we grant Rosenthal's sense of thin immunity, this thin immunity is "no more than an echo of the immunity Shoemaker describes, and the error against which it protects is not substantive" (2003, 357). According to Rosenthal, such thin immunity does not protect against substantive errors of misidentification, hence there is no conflict with the battery model. Thin immunity to error only guarantees that the individual one is noninferentially conscious of as being in pain is the individual that's conscious of the pain. The battery of contingent properties, by contrast, enables us to distinguish that individual from others, described in terms of various distinguishing properties—hence, thin immunity still allows for the possibility of error in respect of the contingent properties in such a battery (2003, 357). The battery model is therefore consistent with thin immunity to error but not the kind of immunity to error through misidentification Shoemaker has in mind.

Although I believe Rosenthal's thin immunity is all that can be preserved, some, like Shaun Gallagher (2000, 2004), have defended Shoemaker's stronger immunity principle by distinguishing between the *sense of ownership* and the *sense of authorship* (or what he calls the "sense of agency"). In the normal phenomenology of voluntary or willed action, the senses of agency and ownership coincide and are indistinguishable. In the case of involuntary action, however, it is quite possible to distinguish between the two. As Gallagher writes, "I may acknowledge ownership of a movement—for example, I have a sense that I am the one who is moving or is being moved—and I can self-ascribe it as *my* movement, but I may not have a sense of causing or controlling the movement, that is, no sense of agency" (2000, 204). He maintains that this is also true in the case of involuntary *cognitive* processes—I may acknowledge that I am the one who is thinking, but claim that the thoughts are not willfully generated by me. He provides as an example unbidden thoughts or memories that impinge on consciousness even if we do not intend for them to do so, or even resist them (see also Frankfurt 1976). In such cases, he maintains, "my claim of ownership (my self-ascription that I am the one who is undergoing such experiences) may be consistent with my lack of a sense of agency" (2000, 204).

Although I agree with Gallagher that the senses of ownership and authorship are distinct and can come apart in involuntary action, he goes on to argue that immunity to error through misidentification *remains intact for both senses*. He starts out by arguing:

> The application of the immunity principle does not depend on there being intact for action both a sense of ownership and a sense of agency. In the case of involuntary action, where I lack a sense of agency, there is still a sense of ownership, so I cannot deny that I experience my arm as moving, or that it is my tooth that is aching, or that I am the one who is thinking. (2000, 206)

According to Gallagher, in such cases the immunity to error through misidentification which is linked to the sense of ownership therefore remains intact. He admits, however, that things are not as clear cut when it comes to our sense of agency.

> If, on the other side of this distinction, we consider cases in which the sense of agency remains intact, but there is no sense of ownership, it may be tempting to argue that the sense of agency is not as robust as the sense of ownership in regard to the immunity principle, that is, that we can find cases in which the sense of agency is not immune to error. Consider a case of delusion. A delusional subject may report that he is causing other people to act or to think in a certain way: "It is not my action—she is the one acting—but I am causing the action, I am the one willing her to do it." In this case, where there is a sense of agency but not a sense of ownership for action (I do not self-ascribe the action), the immunity principle does not hold for the sense of agency, that is to say, I am not immune from error in such cases—after all, we call this a delusion, and it turns out that it is a delusion that involves misidentifi-

cation. It would make perfect sense to ask: "are you sure that it is *you* who are causing the action?" (2000, 206)

Gallagher goes on to argue, however, that the sense of agency at stake in the delusion example does not involve the subject's own motor action and in that regard is more remote and conceptual than the sense of agency a normal subject might have in reaching to pick up a glass. He further argues that the example of delusion and, more generally, first-person judgments pertaining to remote agency, involve what Wittgenstein calls the *object* use of the first-person pronoun, and no claim is made that the immunity principle holds in such cases. In contrast, he maintains, where the sense of agency is immediately linked to motor action, or to the subject's own stream of consciousness, and is expressed by the first-person pronoun used *as subject*, the sense of agency does in fact remain immune to error through misidentification (see 2000, 207).

According to Gallagher, then, the phenomenon of thought insertion and other delusions of control do *not* represent a failure of the immunity principle. Gallagher maintains that our sense of ownership remains immune to error through misidentification because even in cases of involuntary action, where I lack a sense of agency, there is still a sense of ownership. This holds true, he argues, even in cases of thought insertion (see 2000, 231). Our sense of agency, on the other hand, remains immune to error, he argues, when it's immediately linked to motor action or to the subject's own stream of consciousness. I disagree with both of these claims, but let me consider each in turn starting with the latter. I find the claim that the immunity principle remains intact for our sense of agency odd, even when restricted in the way Gallagher describes. For one, patients suffering from delusions of control often report that their movements are made or caused by someone or something else (see Frith 1992, 66; Mellor 1970, 17; Spence 1996). This happens in alien hand syndrome and numerous phenomena associated with schizophrenia. Gallagher himself admits that many of the symptoms associated with schizophrenia involve such errors of identification (2000, 208). Here is just one example provided by Mellor (which Gallagher, himself, cites): "A 29 year old shorthand typist described her actions as follows: 'When I reach my hand for the comb it is my hand and arm which moves, and my finger pick up the pen, but I don't control them'" (1970, 17). If such claims about agency can involve errors of identification, which Gallagher admits they do, then what more restricted realm of first-person statements about agency does he have in mind? According to Gallagher, "expressions that use the first-person pronoun to express the sense of (immediate) agency are immune to error thought misidentification" (2000, 236 fn.28). But what does Gallagher mean here by "immediate" agency? He does not spell this concept out. In fact, Gallagher admits that errors of identification with regard to agency can happen even for thought—and it's hard to imagine a situation where our sense of agency can be any more "immediately linked" than this.[10]

For example, in describing the phenomenon of thought insertion, Gallagher describes the subject's experience as follows:

> [H]e has a sense of ownership for the stream of conscious which is impossible to misidentify (and is, in fact, in no need of identification, since it is his own), but into which are inserted thoughts for which he has no sense of agency. His judgment that it is he who is being subject to these thoughts is immune to error through misidentification, *even if he is completely wrong about who is causing his thoughts.* In the latter case, with respect to agency, he is in a position to make only statements in which he uses the first person pronoun as object—and in such cases the immunity principle is not at stake, and therefore cannot be violated. (2000, 231; italics added)

If this case is excluded because it employs the "object use" of the first-person pronoun, it's unclear whether *any* cases remain where first-person statements about agency remain immune to error through misidentification. In fact, Gallagher admits in a footnote that he can think of *no class of actions* that involve an immediate sense of agency that can be expressed in statements which are immune to errors through misidentification, but that involve no sense of ownership. He therefore speculates, "This raises the possibility, which I shall not explore here, that a sense of agency depends on some form of a sense of ownership for its immunity to error through misidentification" (2000, 232 fn.4).

I therefore find claims of immunity to error through misidentification more plausible when applied to our sense of ownership. In many experiences of involuntariness, it is often the case that I maintain a sense of ownership (i.e., I have a sense that I am the one who is moving or thinking) even though I lack a sense of agency. Does this mean, however, that our sense of ownership has "absolute immunity" to error through misidentification? I do not believe it does. Although I agree that we need to make a distinction between our senses of ownership and authorship, I propose that a further distinction needs to be introduced; one that *does* allow for errors of identification to take place at the level of ownership. According to the HOT theory, we can distinguish between two senses of ownership. When one's HOT make one conscious of being in a particular mental state, the essential indexical in effect identifies the self it refers to as the individual who is the bearer of that state. This thin way of identifying oneself, however, provides almost no information. The battery model, on the other hand, provides an informative way of saying just which individual that is—i.e., we identify the individual each first-person thought refers to by appeal to a heterogeneous collection of contingent properties. It is this latter sense of self-identification, the one that is responsible for our conscious sense of unity, the unity important for *self-identity*, that allows for errors of identification.

According to the HOT theory, one picks out the individual referred to in first-person thoughts by reference to a diverse collection of contingent properties. This means that for any new first-person thought, the reference that thought makes to oneself is secured by appeal to what many other, prior first-person thoughts have referred to, and "this process gradually enlarges the stock of self-identifying thoughts available to secure such reference" (Rosenthal 2003, 346). Although it's not easy to override the default assumption that all tokens of the mental analogue of 'I' in one's first-person thoughts refer to the same individual, it does on very rare occasion happen. Since we come to have HOTs in a variety of ways, the process by which HOTs arise can, like any other process, go wrong. So, although it is unlikely that one is ever right in thinking that somebody is in a particular mental state but wrong that the individual in that state is oneself, such error is not impossible. "One might, perhaps, have such strong empathetic access to another's state that one becomes confused and thinks that it is oneself that is in that state" (Rosenthal 2004a, 170-171). Likewise, one might find a particular thought or action so inconsistent with their battery of descriptions, ongoing action plans, and/or prior train of thought, that they do not experience it as their own (see section 7.4). Wegner, for example, appeals to such inconsistency to explain the phenomenon of thought insertion and the schizophrenic experience of "hearing voices." Referencing Ralph Hoffman's theory of verbal hallucinations, Wegner writes:

> Hoffman (1986) has proposed that this experience occurs when people find that their thoughts do not match their current conscious goals for thinking. The thoughts come to mind without a clear preview, and in fact may be highly discordant with the person's thoughts of what to think or say next. In the context of a conversation about the weather, for example, the person might experience the thought "Eat the wax fruit." The inconsistency produces such a strong sense that the self did not will the thought that the thought is judged to be the action of an outside agent. (Wegner and Wheatley 1999, 485-486; see also Wegner 2002)

In terms of the HOT theory, we can say that the first-person conscious thought "Eat the wax fruit" (or, more accurately, the HOT that makes that thought conscious) tokens the essential indexical 'I' which refers to the individual who is the bearer of the state, yet the thought is nonetheless experienced as "alien" since it is not incorporated into the heterogeneous collection of contingent properties used to identify the individual. In this way, the individual will acknowledge that the thought exists in their stream of consciousness (i.e., that they are the bearer of the state), yet they will not experience the thought as belonging to *themselves* (i.e., the seemingly unified self they identify through the battery of descriptions).

Gallagher, of course, is right that these subjects will not experience a sense of agency over the so-called "alien" thoughts or voices, but I believe he is wrong in assuming that a *normal* sense of ownership is experienced in such cases. Of course subjects will experience some sense of ownership since they are the bearer of the state. Nonetheless, there remains a disturbance of ownership since the thought is not experienced as *belonging to the unified self* identified through the heterogeneous collection of contingent properties. In fact, subjects report experiencing these thoughts or voices as *belonging to someone else* — "and not just in that someone else originated the thought and communicated it to the subject; there is a sense in which the thought, as it were, remains the property of someone else" (Campbell 1999a, 610). By making the distinction between essential indexical self-reference and the battery model of self-identification, the HOT theory is not only capable of explaining how errors of identification can happen, it is better able to capture the way schizophrenic patients actually report their experiences. Contra Gallagher, subjects do *not* experience a normal sense of ownership in cases of thought insertion and hearing voices. Hence, immunity to error through misidentification does not obtain.

7.4 ACCOUNTING FOR OUR SENSE OF AGENCY

If what I have just argued is correct, what makes my occurrent thoughts *mine* is not just that they show up in my stream of consciousness. What makes them "mine" is also the fact that they appear part of a seemingly unified self. According to the HOT theory, each HOT represents its target state as belonging to the bearer of the state. This sparse characterization, however, is not enough to identify ourselves. An informative characterization of the self depends on one's applying some battery of descriptions to oneself in an essentially indexical way. Although we typically identify the individual to which each HOT assigns its target as being the same from one HOT to the next, the phenomenon of thought insertion reveals that it *is* possible for one to jettison a particular thought or set of thoughts and identify them as coming from someone else. *Why* such errors of identification occur, and what is required for one to experience a normal sense of agency/ownership for actions and thoughts, is what I would now like to explore. For the most part I will shift to discussing the sense of agency for action but will, along the way, comment on the sense of agency for thought as well. My aim in this concluding section is to present an account of the first-person phenomenology of agency which explains our sense of authorship and self-determination but which is also consistent with the HOT theory's denial of a libertarian or Cartesian Self.

The challenge, then, is to answer the following question: If there is no libertarian Self, no indivisible "ghost in the machine" that willfully initiates action, then what accounts for our sense of agency, particularly our sense of authorship? Where does the experience of *self-as-cause* or *self-as-initiator* come from? In attempting to understand our sense of agency, I would like to take as my starting point Daniel Wegner's account of the illusion of conscious will (2002, 2008). According to Wegner, "a person infers that an event is due to the self as a result of perceiving a causal link between own thoughts and that event" (2008, 228). Following an earlier proposal by Theodor Ziehen (1899), Wegner suggests that thinking of self before action helps yield the sense of agency. As Ziehen originally proposed, "We finally come to regard the ego-idea as the cause of our actions because of its very frequent appearance in the series of ideas preceding each action. It is almost always represented several times among the ideas preceding the final movement" (1899, 296; as quoted by Wegner 2002, 65). Wegner views this proposal as a "global version of the more specific process that appears to underlie apparent mental causation" (2002, 65). Wegner's overall account of the illusion of conscious will is a causal one based on Humean reasoning. Since we experience certain events (i.e., thoughts) as occurring prior to other events that are regularly conjoined with them (i.e., actions), we infer that the one is the cause of the other. For Wegner, we tend to see ourselves as the authors of an act when we have experienced relevant thoughts about the act at an appropriate interval in advance and so can infer that our own mental processes have set the act in motion (2002, 65). Putting aside those aspects of Wegner's theory that I have already criticized, the general suggestion that we experience a sense of agency because the "ego-idea" appears in the sequence of thoughts preceding action makes a lot of sense. If the intentions and thoughts that precede an action are tagged with a sense of *self*, and the action is perceived as consistent with those thoughts, it's likely that we will experience ownership and agency over the associated action.

Normal voluntary actions, for example, are typically preceded by a sequence of relevant conscious thoughts that one self-identifies with—i.e., thoughts that the actor experiences as owned. This, however, is not always the case with experiences of involuntariness, where there is no sense of agency. Experiences of involuntariness can occur for a number of reasons. The more common cases are when a bodily movement or reaction is not preceded by relevant conscious thoughts about the movement—for example, with sneezes, twitches, and basic stimulus-response reactions. In such cases, there is no antecedent action plan one is aware of. We feel no sense of agency here because we have no conscious intention, thought, desire, or urge to act prior to acting. Hoffman, for example, notes that "a nervous tic feels involuntary because it does not reflect a motor plan consonant with accessible goals/beliefs. Similarly, a slip of the tongue feels involuntary because it is not consonant with the current speech goal, that is, to articulate a particular 'message'" (1986, 506). Other cases of involuntariness arise when there *are* prior thoughts, but they are either experienced as inconsistent with the action or undermined by other causal explanations (see Wegner 2002). Wegner, for example, appeals to thought/action inconsistency to explain the involuntariness experienced by schizophrenic patients. He notes that in some 65 percent of people with this disorder, "the symptoms include unusual experiences that seem to emerge from inconsistency of thought and action" (2002, 84-85; see also Frith and Fletcher 1995). He writes, "Certain of the person's thoughts or action do not seem to issue voluntarily from the self, perhaps because they do not arise in the context of consistent prior thoughts" (2002, 85). I will return to schizophrenia and the possible causes of this inconsistency in a moment, but I do agree with Wegner that thought/ action consistency is essential for the sense of agency and that breakdowns in such consistency are likely responsible for schizophrenic experiences of involuntariness and alien control (see Frith 1992; Frith and Done 1989; Malenka et al. 1982; Campbell 1999a).

Wegner's basic Humean suggestion, therefore, is a good starting point, but I do not believe it provide us with a full account of self-agency. Wegner focuses exclusively on the priority, consistency, and exclusivity of the thought about the action. These, of course, are all important. To feel a sense of authorship over an action, thoughts pertaining to that action should come before the action, be consistent with the action, and not be in competition with other potential causes. *What Wegner's proposal does not explain, however, is how the "I" gets represented in the series of thoughts preceding action.* Where does the "ego-idea" come from and how does it get attached to our thoughts and intentions? The phenomenon of thought insertion shows us that impairments of the self can take place at this level; here schizophrenic patients report feeling no *ownership* over their thoughts. When schizophrenic patients report that their thoughts are being controlled by someone/thing else, there seems to be, as Firth says, an error in the labeling processes; the thoughts are not experienced as "mine." This is where one needs a theory of *self-consciousness*—i.e., a theory that explains how the *self* gets represented in consciousness and how errors of self-reference and/or identification can happen. Wegner does not provide us with such a theory; and I believe one is critical for understanding the feeling of self-agency. Wegner's theory also fails to explain, at least in specific terms, how the self-construct is created. Why is it that we experience a *unified Self* that stands behind our actions and thoughts and remains the same over time? The simple priority of thought before action cannot explain this. Nor can thought/action consistency.

Since Wegner's theory is not based on any particular theory of consciousness, it does not have the resources to explain self-consciousness in any detailed way. If, however, we combine Wegner's Humean conditions with the HOT theory's account of self-consciousness, I believe we can gain a fuller understanding of our sense of agency. According to Wegner, we tend to see ourselves as the authors of an act when we have experienced relevant thoughts about the act at an appropriate interval in advance and so can infer that our own mental processes have set the act in motion. Consider, for example, the act of turning on the light. Wegner writes:

> This is something that sometimes can feel quite willful, and at other times can feel absentmindedly automatic. If you have just thought about turning on the light and then do so, it may feel more willful—whereas if you have been thinking about having a cookie and then suddenly find yourself turning on a light instead, it is likely to feel less willed and more like some sort of alien control. To support a feeling of will, the thought of turning on the light must occur just prior to the action to maximize the experience of will, as thoughts that occur far beforehand (and that then are forgotten until the action) or thoughts of flipping that switch that only appear after the light is on do not seem to promote a sense of willed action. And if someone else presses your hand to the lamp, you must discount entirely the causal role of your prior thought and feel the act is unwilled. These observations point to three key sources of the experience of conscious will—the *consistency*, *priority*, and *exclusivity* of the thought about the action. (2008, 228-229)

In line with Wegner's proposal, I maintain that if the relevant intentions and thoughts that precede an action are tagged with a sense of *self* (i.e., if they are experienced as owned by a seemingly unified self), and (a) the subsequent action is perceived as consistent with those thoughts, and (b) there are no other competing causes available for the action, then an individual will likely experience a sense of agency over the associated action. On this account, one experiences a sense of *self*-generation or authorship when they draw causal inferences relating prior self-ascribed thoughts with consistent and self-ascribed actions.

Let's discuss this proposal in more detail starting with the importance of self-consciousness. I agree with Ziehen that we come to regard the "ego-idea" as the cause of our actions because of its very frequent appearance in the series of ideas preceding each action. As Sean Spence writes, "'I' have the impression that my conscious 'I' generates acts. This illusion is fostered by the chronology of my awareness (both of 'intent' and 'resulting' act)" (1996, 87). Even though our conscious intentions may not cause or initiate our actions, the fact that we are aware of a certain order of events is all that matters. Since the conscious thoughts that precede an action all appear to belong to a seemingly unified self, at least in normal cases, we naturally infer (assuming other conditions are also met) that the seemingly unified self is the cause of the action. When Nietzsche asks, "What gives me the right to speak of an 'I,' and indeed of an 'I' as a cause?" We can answer this question by appealing to the nature of self-consciousness itself. Self-consciousness provides the sense of which actions are to have their causes and effects characterized using 'I.' As Campbell writes, "we should think of self-consciousness as a matter of having the programme of characterizing what it is that stands in causal relations to one's surroundings. It is this kind of explicit understanding that allows one to form ideas like: 'I am the one who broke the vase,' or 'I am the one they are all looking at'"(2004, 478). According to the HOT theory, we come to have this concept of an 'I' or *self* because of the way individual HOTs token the essential indexical and the way we engage in introspective acts of self-interpretation. The 'I' that is referred to in such statements need not, of course, be anything like the libertarian or Cartesian Self we take ourselves to be. In fact, if what I have argued thus far is correct, we can say that the illusion of a unified *Self* as the willful initiator of our voluntary acts is a result of an introspective act of interpretation. This illusion can be broken in cases of depersonalization or delusions of alien control. In normal cases, though, the fact that we perceive our conscious thoughts as belonging to a seemingly unified self, and we take the related actions as belonging to the same unified self, leads us to draw a causal inference between the two. *It is a combination of the way we come to perceive ourselves as unified individuals, and the way we draw causal inferences between self-ascribed thoughts, intentions, and actions, that creates the illusion of a mysterious agent-causal Self.*

The importance of self-consciousness to the experience of agency, and, hence, the feeling of will, is therefore crucial. It not only provides us with a sense of ownership over our thoughts and actions, it also accounts for self-ascriptions of agency. It is through self-consciousness that we take *ourselves* to be agent causes of actions and thoughts. Of course, experiencing a sense of agency only means that we have interpreted things in a certain way, not that actual agency has been exercised. As Wegner and Wheatley's (1999) *I-spy* experiment reveals, it is possible for people to feel that they willfully performed an action that was actually performed by someone else when conditions suggest their own thought may have caused the action. That experiment focused on the priority condition, but other experiments have suggested that *self-attention* is also associated with perceived causation of action. Wegner, for example, describes an experiment conducted by Duval and Wicklund (1973) in which people were asked to make attributions for hypothetical events (see 2002, 65). Duval and Wicklund found that when participants were asked to decide who was responsible for such events, "they assigned more causality to themselves if they were making the judgments while they were self-conscious." And in this study, self-consciousness was manipulated by having the participants sit facing a mirror, "but other contrivances, such as showing people their own video image or having them hear their tape-recorded voice, also enhanced causal attributions to self (Gibbons 1990)" (Wegner 2002, 65). A heightened sense of self, it seems, can lead to an enhanced sense of agency. Spence, for example, notes that: "When anxious an individual may become acutely aware of his own actions, interrupting the flow of normally fluent activities e.g., walking and speech. In such a condition the experience (perception) of voluntary activity is heightened . . . " (1996, 78). Some clinicians have even proposed that certain positive symptoms of schizophrenia may be due to a kind of *hyperreflexivity* or hyperreflexive awareness of self (see Sass 1992, 1998; Perez-Alvarez 2008).[11]

On the other end of the scale, there are many voluntary acts we perform throughout the day where we experience little or no agency. Our sense of self-generation or authorship ebbs and flows throughout the day and even changes by the moment. As Wegner writes:

> We feel ourselves willing our actions almost the way we use the accelerator pedal in an automobile: Once in a while we floor it; more normally we give it a little punch from time to time; but for long periods we just have a foot on it and maintain speed, experiencing little sense at all that we are pushing on the pedal. Either because we are very good at what we are doing, because we have simply lost interest, or for yet other reasons, there are intervals when we lose the experience of agency even while we are performing voluntary actions. (2002, 99)

There are various reasons why we might experience a loss or reduction in our sense of agency for action, but clearly focal attention and what we're consciously thinking just prior to and during the act will make a difference. In terms of Wegner's priority condition, we can say that when one discovers having done an act that was not consciously considered in advance, one feels little in the way of conscious will. Actions that are not preceded by relevant conscious intentions and thoughts typically feel more automatic and less willed. On the other hand, when I have relevant conscious thoughts about an act at an appropriate interval in advance, I feel as though I am the author of the act; that the act is under my control and that I consciously willed it. We can say, then, "that conscious thoughts of an action appearing just before an act yield a greater sense of will than conscious thoughts of an action that appear at some other time—long beforehand or, particularly, afterwards" (Wegner 2002, 70). This, of course, does not mean that prior conscious intentions are necessary or required for one to *believe* they have exercised free will. There is, I maintain, an important difference between *beliefs about free will*, on the one hand, and occurrent, first-person *experiences of agency* on the other. One may *believe* they are the author of an action even if they feel no sense of agency at the time. For example, if I am able to understand an action in light of my self-identified beliefs, desires, and interests, I will *believe* I am the voluntary author of the action even if I experienced no sense of conscious will at the time—this is common in mindless routine action (e.g., making a cup of coffee in the morning without thinking about it) and

highly advanced skilled movements (e.g., playing an instrument or returning a volley).[12]

The consistency and exclusivity of the thought about the action is also
relevant to the amount of agency we will experience. The exclusivity
requirement is relatively straight forward. It is well known that people
discount the causal influence of one potential cause if there are others
available (Wegner 2002, 90; Kelley 1972; McClure 1998). With regard to
action, we can say that for one to feel a sense of agency for a particular
action—i.e., for one to feel that their own conscious thoughts and intentions are the cause of the action—the action should not be accompanied
by other potential causes. Wegner's exclusivity principle therefore suggests that "people will be particularly sensitive to the possibility that
there are other causes of an action besides their own thoughts." That is,
"When their own thoughts do not appear to be the exclusive cause of
their action, they experience less conscious will. And when other plausible causes are less salient, in turn, they experience more conscious will"
(2002, 90).

According to Wegner, the causes that compete with thoughts and
intentions are two kinds: internal and external. The plausible internal
causes for an action might include "one's emotions, habits, reflexes, traits,
or other unconscious action tendencies—psychological causes other than
thoughts" (2002, 90). A person who washes their hands up to a hundred
times a day, for example, may feel no sense of agency if they suffer from
Obsessive-Compulsive Disorder and believe the action is attributable to
their internal compulsion. This may be true even if they have prior, consistent thought about the action. "People seem to know their own
psychology well enough to grasp several possible alternatives to
thoughts as causes of their actions. In particular, they may discount
thoughts and so bypass the experience of will when they find their behavior attributable to *emotions, impulse, disposition,* or *habit*" (2002, 91). It is
quite common, for example, for one to experience little in the way of
voluntariness when acting out of blind rage or other strong emotions, or
when one thinks their behavior is primarily due to habit or impulse.
Whether one interprets their actions as attributable to the conscious self
or, instead, to some alternative internal cause of which they were, perhaps, previously unconscious, will therefore affect one's sense of agency.
Awareness of plausible internal alternative causes can threaten one's belief that one's conscious self is the exclusive cause of the action.

On the other hand, the plausible external causes for an action might
include "real external agents, such as people or groups, or imagined outside agents in the form of spirits, voices, angels, ghosts, or other disem-
bodied entities" (2002, 90). In many cases of involuntary action, like when
a doctor hits my knee with a mallet and my leg moves, I feel no sense of
agency because I attribute the action to other people or external forces
that impinge on me. This can happen even when we are thinking of the

action in advance. Wegner gives the example of starting to open a door only to find that someone else is simultaneously opening it from the other side (2002, 93). What might initially feel like a willed action immediately becomes the action of someone else. Hence, the exclusivity of thought as a cause of action can be challenged by external causes. This is relatively easy to see in cases of co-action where two people are jointly involved—e.g., walking hand-in-hand, kissing, dancing, wrestling, having sex, and the like. In such cases "the proper attribution of causality to self and other can be a major puzzle" (2002, 93). Although this type of confusion about agency is more common when there are real external agents involved, the perceived causation of one's actions by an outside agent is not necessarily limited to real agents or forces.

According to Wegner, once the possibility of outside agency is allowed, it becomes clear that people can imagine or invent outside agents to account for actions of themselves or others (see also Gilbert et al. 2001). The belief that one's actions or thoughts are being caused by outside agents is, as we've already seen, common in schizophrenia. It is not, however, limited to schizophrenia.

> [T]he appeal to hypothetical outside agents is far too common an experience in human life to be attributed to schizophrenia alone. The occurrence of spirit possession or channeling, for example, is so widespread across cultures and so highly prevalent in some cultures—affecting as much as half of the population (Bourguignon 1976)—that it has become a major focus of the field of anthropology. Attribution of behavior to angels, spirits, entities, and the like is sufficiently common throughout the world that it is a mistake to assume it is limited to traditional cultures. Industrialized cultures have their share of channels, trance dancers, and people who "speak in tongues" or otherwise attribute their action to divine intervention as part of religious ceremonies. (2002, 94-95)

It is not uncommon for people to project agency away from themselves and attribute it to spirits, ghosts, or angels even in cases where they are responsible for the action. This can happen when there are no real external agents involved or when one misattributes a co-action to an imagined third part. In fact, the puzzle of co-action mentioned above turns out to be the basis of a number of common automatisms, including table turning and Ouija board spelling (see Wegner 2002). The common denominator, however, for all these phenomena is the attribution of what otherwise appears to be voluntary behavior to an imagined outside agency.

The perceived exclusivity of one's conscious thought as the cause of an action can therefore be threatened by both internal and external alternatives. Whether one experiences a sense of agency, then, depends on how one interprets events; and this is really a matter of self-consciousness since it is through distinguishing *self* from *other* and attributing cause and effect that we come to have a sense of self in the first place. "In the extensive field of possible causes of a person's behavior, there exists only one self, an author that has thoughts and does actions. This self competes with internal causes and with an array of external causes of action in the individual's assessment of what he or she has willed" (Wegner 2002, 95). It is in the process of identifying causes of action, therefore, that we develop our sense of self and experience a sense of agency. And it is here that the experience of personal identity really takes shape. On the account of self-consciousness I've been defending, we identify ourselves through a heterogeneous collection of contingent properties. Available for inclusion in that heterogeneous collection of properties will be those actions we exclusively attribute to the seemingly unified self. Those actions, on the other hand, that are not attributed to the self but to alternative causes like outside agents or forces, will not play the same role in the formation of the individual's own identity. But which actions are attributed to the self is a matter of self-interpretation. It is through self-consciousness that people discern their own willed actions from those of others, and they do this by employing *a priori* causal theories designed to account for the relation between thought and action. It is in these introspective acts of self-interpretation that the priority, consistency, and exclusivity of thought and action are important.

Turning to the last of Wegner's conditions, then, consistency of thought and action, we can say that when people do what they think they are going to do, there exists consistency between thought and action, and the experience of will is typically enhanced. On the other hand, "When they think of one thing and do another—and this inconsistency is observable to them—their action does not feel as willful" (Wegner 2002, 79). According to Wegner, consistency of thought and action depends on a cognitive process whereby the thoughts occurring prior to the act are compared to the act as subsequently perceived. This proposal is consistent with several leading theories of schizophrenia (Frith 1987, 1992; Frith and Done 1989; Malenka et al. 1982; Frith, Blakemore, and Wolpert 2000; Blakemore 2000; Blakemore and Frith 2003). According to, perhaps, the most widely cited and influential of these theories, Christopher Frith's (1987, 1992) neurocognitive model, such experiences are due to a breakdown or disruption in basic *self-monitoring* processes. Self-monitoring systems enable one to distinguish the products of self-generated actions or thoughts from those of other-generated actions or thoughts. Firth sees the failure of self-monitoring processes as a likely explanation of how self-ascriptions of thoughts and actions may be subject to errors of identification in regard to agency. According to Frith, self-monitoring consists of a central monitoring process that determines deviations between the predicted and observed consequences of physical or mental actions. When predicted and observed consequences match, the observed consequences are experienced as self-generated. Schizophrenics with hallucinatory and delusion experiences, however, appear to suffer from a disruption of monitoring of self-generated acts—i.e., they cannot correctly compare the expected and observed consequences of an action and therefore have problems with identifying their actions and thoughts as the cause for events they perceive (see also Kircher and Leube 2003, 664).

In terms of the mechanism(s) involved in such self-monitoring, Frith and colleagues maintain that the future consequences of actions are predicted on the basis of an efference copy of each motor program that is issued (see Frith 1992; Blakemore and Frith 2003; Frith, Blakemore, and Wolpert 2000; Campbell 1999a). On this model, there is a mechanism called the *comparator* which monitors efferent copies of motor instructions. In terms of motor control theory, the comparator model states that when a motor instruction to move is sent to a set of muscles, a copy of that instruction, the *efferent copy*, is also sent to a comparator or self-monitoring system. Held (1961) suggested that the efferent copy sent to the comparator is stored there, and then compared to the proprioceptive or visual "reafferent" information about the movement that is actually made. Others have further suggested that the comparator is part of a nonconscious, pre-motor system responsible for the control of movement, operating prior to the actual execution of movement and prior to sensory feedback. On this "forward model," motor control does not depend on perceptual feedback (see Jeannerod 1994; Georgieff and Jeannerod 1988).

There are many different uses this efference copy may serve with regard to motor control, but in terms of our present discussion it is match at the comparator that presumably bestows a sense of agency for the action. As John Campbell describes it, "in the case in which we do have a sense of agency, in which the movement performed is felt to be your own, what grounds that sense of agency is match at the relevant comparator between the efferent copy and the sensory feedback you have about the movement" (1999a, 612). The feeling that it is *I* who just moved my arm would therefore be explained by saying that at the comparator, an efferent copy was received of the instruction to move my arm which matches the movement perceived. On the other hand, a breakdown in the mechanism of efferent copy and comparator would result in the breakdown in the sense of agency that is characteristic of schizophrenia. Although Frith and Campbell's account of self-monitoring makes use of a subpersonal comparator, others have postulated that self-monitoring is normally based on a more direct comparison between the intention underlying an action and its observed outcome (Jeannerod 1999; Jeannerod et al. 2003).

Regardless of whether or not one accepts Frith and Campbell's particular account of self-monitoring, there does seem to be sufficient empirical evidence to support the claim that self-monitoring is impaired in schizophrenic patients with Ego-disturbances. For example, some studies have shown that patients with formal thought disorder were more severely impaired in detecting a mismatch between self-generated movements and their visual consequences (see Knoblich, Stottmeister, and Kircher 2004). Several other studies have shown that schizophrenics suffering from hallucinatory and delusional experiences have difficulties correcting movement errors in the absence of visual feedback, although there were no clinical indications of a disorder of the motor system (Frith and Done 1989; Malenka et al. 1982; Mlakar, Jensterle, and Frith 1994; Stirling, Hellewell, and Quraishi 1998).[13] Although schizophrenic patients, like normal subjects, correct their errors when visual feedback is provided, they often fail to correct their mistakes when deprived of visual feedback. Other studies further suggest an impaired working memory/executive function deficit in schizophrenia as one of the contributing factors of an action monitoring deficit (Posada et al. 2003). All of these findings seem to support Frith's conclusion that there is in schizophrenia an impairment of self-monitoring (see also Blakemore et al. 2000; Franck et al. 2001; Kircher and Leube 2003).

Several theorists have further proposed that a failure to properly monitor or (better) experience one's own causal role in thinking also helps to explain the bizarre experiences reported in thought insertion and auditory hallucination (see Feinberg 1978; Frith 1992; Campbell 1999a, 2004; Hoffman 1986; Wegner 2002). How is it, one may wonder, that the schizophrenic patient develops the sense that an episode occurring in the mind is attributable to someone else rather than to the self? Wegner offers up the following proposal:

> This seems to occur primarily because the episode is inconsistent with prior thought. Thoughts that come to mind in a willful way typically do so in a format that make sense. They follow. A person thinking this way can say, "I have a sense of deliberately directing my thinking toward a certain project or theme, such as crafting an apology, finding a solution to a problem, recollecting my trip to Berlin or Tenerife, without having some specific sequence of thoughts in mind at the outset" (Graham and Stephens 1994, 98-99). It is not that we need to know everything in advance of thinking it, but that we need to know something about where our thoughts may be going that then is consistent with what we think when we get there. Usually, we have a general idea of what we will think or do next. When inconsistent thoughts or actions appear, we lose our sense that we are the ones in charge. (2002, 86-87)

Wegner's proposal is consistent with the idea that the schizophrenic symptoms of thought insertion and auditory hallucination represent failures to self-monitor one's own thinking or conscious mental activity. There are differences, however, in the manner in which various theorists describe the relevant monitoring failure and its explanatory role (cf. Campbell 1999a, 2002, 2004; Stephens and Graham 2000; Frith 1992). Campbell, for example, appeals to the comparator model and claims that something akin to motor instructions accompanies thinking—and that part of what is monitored by a person, or in a person, is whether his/her thoughts reflect those instructions. Absent proper monitoring, thinking which otherwise meets instructions may be experienced as alien or as the mental activity of another person. Others find the notion of instructions to think unhelpful and have instead proposed alternative accounts of self-monitoring that do not appeal to these analogues of motor commands (see Stephens and Graham 2000; Gallagher 2000, 2004).

Although the comparator model was first developed in the context of motor-control theory (Held 1961), where it remains ubiquitous, it was later extended to the realm of cognition by people like Feinberg (1978), Frith (1992), and Campbell (1999a). According to Campbell, the mechanism functions "to keep your thoughts on track, to check that the thoughts you actually execute form coherent trains of thought" (1999a, 616). Frith postulates a similar mechanism for cognition and proposes the following explanation of thought insertion:

> Thinking, like all our actions, is normally accompanied by a sense of effort and deliberate choice as we move from one thought to the next. If we found ourselves thinking without any awareness of the sense of effort that reflects central monitoring, we might well experience these thoughts as alien and, thus, being inserted into our minds. (1992, 81)

On this account, an efferent copy of the intentional generation of thought (or instruction to think) is sent to a comparator or central monitor, which also registers the occurrence of the actual thought, thus matching up intention and thought. The proper function of this mechanism, according to this theory, is the element that bestows a sense of agency for thought; it is what distinguishes the thinking of an ordinary subject from the formal thought disorder of the schizophrenic. If, however, the efference copy is blocked or not properly generated, thinking still occurs, but it is not experienced as under my control—it appears to be an alien or inserted thought. Campbell goes even further and maintains that the proper function of this mechanism is also responsible for the sense of ownership with regard to thought. For Campbell, "it is the match between the thought detected by introspection, and the content of the efferent copy picked up by the comparator, that is responsible for the sense of ownership of the thought." Hence, "when things go wrong, as with the schizophrenic, with central monitoring, the sense of ownership of the occurrent thought will be disturbed too" (1999a, 617). Although there are several different versions of the comparator model, and many involve substantive disagreements on the nature of self-monitoring, they all share the basic idea that consistency among thought is important in generating our sense of agency/ownership. When something occurs that is completely unexpected (i.e., when an occurrent thought fails to match our cognitive expectations) the subject finds himself lacking in any sense of being the agent of a thought of which he has immediate introspective knowledge.[14]

Regardless of whether or not one accepts Campbell's particular account of self-monitoring with regard to cognition, it does seem that Wegner's condition of consistency is important for the sense of agency. Even those theorists that reject the comparator model with regard to thought insertion agree that our sense of agency for thought requires that our occurrent thoughts match our cognitive expectations (e.g., Gallagher 2000, 2004). Gallagher, for example, rejects the comparator model and offers an alternative model inspired by the phenomenological analysis of time-consciousness. On his view, part of the explanation for the senses of ownership and agency for thought, and the loss of the sense of agency in schizophrenic thought insertion, can be found in Edmund Husserl's model of the retentional-protentional structure of time-consciousness (2000). According to Gallagher, what Husserl called 'retentions' and 'protentions' may be regarded as subpersonal operations that generate the flow-structure of consciousness. My conscious experience includes a sense of what I have just been thinking (perceiving, remembering, etc.) and a sense that this thinking will continue in a particular way. On Gallagher's model, "This phenomenological temporal sense is based on retentional and protentional dynamics that ultimately need to be cashed out in terms of neurological processes" (2000, 222). In an enduring act of consciousness, *retention* "retains previous phases of consciousness and their intentional content," whereas *protention* "anticipates experience which is just about to happen" (2000, 223).

To help understand these concepts, Gallagher provides the example of speaking or listening to a sentence. Consider the beginning of the following sentence: "I often think that Julia." According to Gallagher:

> When in uttering this sentence I reach the word 'Julia' I am no longer saying the previous words, but I still retain a sense of what I have just said. For a sentence to be meaningful, the sense of the earlier words must be kept in mind in some fashion when I am uttering the later words. *Retention*, or what cognitive scientists call working memory, keeps the intentional sense of the words available even after the words are no longer sounded. Built into this retentional function is the sense that *I* am the one who has just said these words. The words do not become part of a free-floating anonymity, they remain part of the sentence that *I* am in the process of uttering. Also, at the moment that I am uttering 'Julia', I have some anticipatory sense of where the sentence is going, or at the very least, that the sentence is heading to some kind of ending. This sense of knowing where the sentence (the thought) is heading, even if not completely definite, seems essential to the experience I have of speaking in a meaningful way. It helps to provide a sense that I am speaking in a sentential fashion, and not speaking a disconnected or meaningless set of phrases. (2000, 224)

Protention therefore provides consciousness with an intentional direction toward the future. It also provides, according to Gallagher, a sense of agency for thought: "I want to suggest that the dynamics of *protention* underlie the sense of agency for thought, or more precisely, that the protentional registration is necessary but not a sufficient condition for the sense of agency" (2000, 225). According to this model, when something goes wrong with the protentional mechanism, when something goes wrong with the normal anticipatory sense of what my own thinking will be, this will result in a sense that the thought is not being generated by me. Without protention, Gallagher maintains, thought continues, but it "appears already made, not generated in my own stream of conscious-ness, but appearing suddenly, already formulated as it enters into reten-tion" (2000, 227). In such cases, the thought will feel neither intended nor anticipated. And, Gallagher further suggests, when the protentional mechanism breaks down in this way, a metarepresentational process might be initiated in the patient which results in a "reflective introspec-tion that is likely to become the hyperreflection characteristic of schizo-phrenic experience" (2000, 228). That is, motivated by something gone wrong with the flow of consciousness, in metarepresentation the patient may start to ascribe the thought to some particular force or individual and report that it is inserted.[15]

Although there are important and significant differences between these various accounts of self-monitoring, they all share the basic belief that the sense of agency for thought requires consistency of thought and expectation. For my present purposes, I simply maintain that there is an important relationship between the sense of coherency in thought and the sense of agency. When individual first-person thoughts flow along consistently, one after the other, creating a coherent train of thought, we automatically take the bearer of those states to be the same unique indi-vidual. We also feel a sense of agency over those thoughts. When, howev-er, something goes wrong with the mechanisms which monitor our thinking and anticipate what's to come, a disruption in the sense of agen-cy will occur. Regardless of which model is correct about how we antici-pate and monitor our thinking, I propose that if an occurrent thought fails to match our cognitive expectations, the individual will experience no sense of agency over the thought.

Let me conclude this section by suggesting one additional sense of consistency that I believe is important for the sense of agency—i.e., *consis-tency between our long-standing propositional states and our occurrent thoughts/actions*. I maintain that this type of consistency is not only funda-mental to our sense of agency it is also fundamental to our ordinary psychological lives. For as Campbell writes:

> Our commonsense picture of the causation of conscious thought is that it depends on a background of beliefs, desires and interests, most of which are not themselves conscious at any one time. For example, if you are idly looking out the window, your idle thoughts will be about

people you know or plans you have. Of course, seeing something unexpected, as you look out the window, can be the cause which opens up new trains of thought. But which trains of thought are opened up will depend on your particular background of beliefs, desires, and interests. Different people could see the same thing yet have quite different thoughts in consequence. This dependence of which thoughts you have on your underlying psychology has to do with our sense of ownership of thoughts. (1999a, 616-617)

Stephens and Graham (2000) take this point further and argue:

We propose that a person's sense that he is a thinker or agent of his *mental* activity—of his conscious thoughts and feelings—likewise depends on his conviction that his occurrent mental episodes express his intentional states. That is, whether a person regards a thought (subjectively) in him as something that he *thinks*, rather than a mere episode in his psychological history, depends upon whether he finds it explicable in terms of his conception of what he believes and desires. (2000, 165)

According to Stephens and Graham, then, for one to experience an agentive sense for thought or action, a higher-order act of self-interpretation is required. On this top-down approach, we reflectively make sense of our actions and thoughts in terms of our beliefs and desires. Hence, "whether I take myself to be the agent of a mental episode [or action] depends upon whether I take the occurrence of this episode [or action] to be explicable in terms of my underlying intentional states" (Graham and Stephens 1994, 93). That is, whether something is to count for me as my action depends upon whether I take myself to have beliefs and desires of the sort that would rationalize its occurrence in me. "If my theory of myself ascribes to me the relevant intentional states, I unproblematically regard this episode as my action. If not, then I must either revise my picture of my intentional states or refuse to acknowledge the episode as my doing" (Graham and Stephens 1994, 102). This top-down or interpretative approach, I maintain, fits nicely with the HOT model of self-consciousness.

According to the HOT model, the reference that any new first-person thought makes to oneself is secured by appeal to what many other, prior first-person thoughts have referred to, and this process gradually enlarges the stock of self-identifying thoughts available to secure such reference (Rosenthal 2003, 346). Hence, when a question arises as to the author/owner of a thought or action, an introspective act takes place which constructs one's self-image or theory of self. It is through introspection that one picks out, through a battery of descriptions, a unique individual. And available for use in this battery of descriptions are the stock of first-person thoughts that comprise one's beliefs, desires, and interests. If one finds an occurrent mental episode or action so inexplicable that they are unable to rationalize or explain its occurrence in terms of their theory of self, they will feel no sense of agency over that mental episode or action. On the other hand, if one does find the mental episode or action explicable in terms of their self-conception (i.e., if one is able to explain it in terms of the beliefs, desires, and interests one is predisposed to identify themselves with), then they will experience it as *their own* action or thought. Rosenthal has written that, "part of what it is to be a person is having the kind of reflective consciousness that gives one a sense of oneself as a being with a reasonably coherent, unified mental life. Seeing one's mental life as coherent and unified is a crucial necessary condition for a creature to be a person" (2001, 128). I would further maintain that it is a necessary condition for experiencing a sense of agency.

7.5 CONCLUSION

I have here presented an account of the sense of agency for thought and action which explains the first-person phenomenology of authorship and ownership but without accepting a libertarian or Cartesian Self. According to the HOT theory, we "need not posit an indivisible Cartesian soul or any special kind of consciousness to explain traditional intuitions about self-consciousness and our sense of the unity of consciousness" (Rosenthal 2002b, 213). Since the HOT model appeals only to the existence of mental particulars, it rejects the metaphysical commitments of libertarianism and with it libertarian freedom. The fact that our phenomenology presents our behavior to us as having a unified Self as its source, is, I have argued, misleading. There is no "magic self," no "inner puppeteer who pulls the body's strings." I have instead argued that it is a combination of the way we come to perceive ourselves as unified individuals, and the way we draw causal inferences between self-ascribed thoughts, intentions, and actions, that creates the illusion of a mysterious agent-causal Self. On this proposal, which actions are attributed to the seemingly unified self, and which actions one feels a sense of agency for, is a matter of self-interpretation. One can, for example, experience a sense of agency for actions they did not cause just as one can perform "purposeful" actions without experiencing a sense of agency. It is through self-consciousness that people discern their own willed actions from those of others, and they do this by employing *a priori* causal theories designed to account for the relation between thought and action.

This proposal is threatening to our ordinary conception of free will since it claims that the apparently unified *Self* we take to be the willful author of behavior—though important to our subjective feeling of freedom and our sense of agency—can be accounted for and explained away. The HOT model of self-consciousness can explain the apparent unity of self without positing an actual metaphysical unity, and this threatens our folk-psychological conception of free will since it undermines and explains away one of its necessary conditions—a Self as thing or substance. As we've seen in previous chapters, our folk-psychological intuitions are largely agent-causal in nature, and such intuitions require more than simple event causation. The HOT model of self-consciousness can help account for such intuitions by explaining away the phenomenology that appears to support them. So, although people "have a compelling experience of many of their actions as being free, and that experience of seeming freedom encourages the idea of a unified, conscious self as the source of such action," the HOT model "provides a natural explanation of these [libertarian] ideas about freedom that doesn't posit any underlying unity of self" (Rosenthal 2003, 361). According to the HOT model, our folk-psychological conception of self is misleading since it goes beyond what is really there in our minds. Although we need not reject completely the notion of self (with a small 's')—for the HOT model does not deny the phenomenological unity of consciousness or the autobiographical continuity we typically experience—this account does imply that the self is not what we ordinarily take it to be. Hence, despite our phenomenology and our folk-psychological beliefs, there is no agent-causal Self, no mysterious homunculus who takes in perceptions, has infallible access to thoughts, and initiates actions.

In this book I have argued two main things. The first is that there is no such thing as free will—at least not in the sense most ordinary folk take to be central or fundamental. The second is that the strong and pervasive *belief* in free will can be accounted for through a careful analysis of our phenomenology and a proper theoretical understanding of consciousness. I have focused on the phenomenology of free will, especially in the last few chapters, because it is our experience of freedom that keeps the belief in free will alive. As Samuel Johnson long ago said, "All theory is against freedom of the will; all experience for it." Since our experience of freedom "is something real, complex, and extremely important, even if free will itself is not real" (Strawson 2010, vi), it is something that should be accounted for regardless of one's position. Some philosophers, however, have gone to extreme measures to do so. As Tamler Sommers correctly notes, "Philosophical theories of free will have understandably tried to save this phenomena, or phenomenology, but at the expense of either dodging the central objections raised by anti-free will arguments or by lapsing into a stubborn mysterianism" (2007, 62-63). This book has offered a third option—one that remains naturalistic but faces the problem squarely. I have argued that instead of trying to justify our belief in free will, especially in light of strong theoretical and empirical arguments against it, we should explain it away (see also Sommers 2007; Strawson 2010).

One of the primary goals of this book has therefore been to argue that our undeniable feeling of freedom, as reflected in the first-person phenomenology of agentive experience, is an illusion created by certain aspects of our consciousness. In particular, I have argued that by combining the theoretical framework of the HOT theory with empirical findings in the behavioral, cognitive, and neurosciences, it can be shown that the illusion of free will is created by the particular way our higher-order thoughts make us conscious of our mental states and how our sense of self is constructed within consciousness. Although many will still find it difficult to accept the idea that "the experience of freedom is really all there is, so far as free will is concerned" (Strawson 2010, vi), my hope is that I have at least made it easier to accept. By accounting for the phenomenology of freedom in the way that I have, it is now possible for one to take seriously *both* our belief in free will *and* our best scientific theories (including those related to consciousness) without "dodging" the latter or "lapsing into a stubborn mysterianism" to save the former.

NOTES

1. To be clear, the datum in need of explanation is our first-person experience of a robust, unified *Self* who is the willful author of behavior. What we're looking for, then, is an account of self-consciousness that, among other things, explains "the impulse we have to think of the mind as a place or subject" (Honderich 2002a, 23). We cannot simply say, for example, that the *self* is the body/brain or the physical individual that walks, talks, and eats, since this does not even respect or attempt to explain our mental sense of unity. What contributes to our feeling of freedom, and hence what I am interested in explaining, is the phenomenal "I" (the robust, unified Self) we take to be the cause of behavior. It is this "I" that Nietzsche has in mind when he asks, "What gives me the right to speak of an 'I,' and indeed of an 'I' as cause . . . ?"

2. Jaspers provides the following example: "A patient said: 'I never shouted, it was the vocal cords that shouted out of me...The hands turn this way and that, I do not guide them nor can I stop them'" (1963, 23; as quoted by Spence 1996, 82). Another vivid example is provided by Mellor: "A 29 year old shorthand typist described her actions as follows: 'When I reach my hand for the comb it is my hand and arm which moves, and my fingers pick up the pen, but I don't control them . . . I sit there watching them move, and they are quite independent, what they do is nothing to do with me . . . I am just a puppet who is manipulated by cosmic strings. When the strings are pulled my body moves and I cannot prevent it'" (1970, 17-18; as quoted by Spence 1996, 82).

3. Frith's neurocognitive model is perhaps the most cited and discussed account of schizophrenia in the literature. According to Frith, Schneiderian "first rank" symptoms of schizophrenia are due to a disruption of metarepresentational self-monitoring. Others that similarly propose that the positive symptoms of schizophrenia are due to deficits in self-monitoring include Feinberg (1978), Malenka et al. (1982), Kircher and Leube (2003), Campbell (1999a, 2004), Blakemore and Frith (2003), Blakemore (2000), and Choudhury and Blakemore (2006). For findings that appear to support this proposal, see Frith and Done (1989). I will discuss Frith's account in more detail in section 7.4.

4. In schizophrenic experiences of alien control, it is likely that two things are occurring: "firstly an alienation from their own volitional processes, e.g. movement, or thought; and secondly, a delusional elaboration of an often bizarre quality which 'seeks' to explain the former" (Spence 1996, 81).

5. Spence, for example, writes: "What does the alien hand tell us of free will? It suggests that the sense of free will accruing to action may have a neurological component which is discrete from (but related to) the neurological correlates of action itself; in other words that the initiation of action and the 'labeling' of that action as 'intentional' ('willed' or 'belonging to the subject') are potentially separate" (1996, 81).

6. According to Rosenthal, this claim should be understood as follows: "Suppose, then that I have the essential indexical thought that I am *F*. My thought in effect describes as being *F* the individual that thinks that very thought, 'in effect' because, although the thought does not describe the individual in that way, it still does pick out just that individual. It does not pick out that individual because the intentional content of my thought so describes the individual. But whenever I do have a first-person thought that I am *F*, my having that thought disposes me to have another thought that identifies the individual that thought is about as the thinker of that thought. In that way, every first-person thought thus tacitly or dispositionally characterizes the self it is about as the thinker of that thought. Nothing more is needed for essential indexical self-reference" (2004a, 167).

7. Appealing to Dennett here may seem strange since Dennett, himself, is a compatibilist. There is no inconsistency, however, in endorsing Dennett's argument against the existence of an "inner puppeteer" or libertarian Self while at the same time rejecting his compatibilism. The fact that Dennett defends a conception of free will that runs counter to our phenomenology and our folk-psychological beliefs, does not affect the strength of his other arguments—including his views on the self. Dennett, in fact, does not shy away from the fact that he's working with a revisionist (or, what I would call, deviant) definition of freedom: "I can't deny that tradition assigns properties to free will that my variety lacks. So much the worse for tradition, I say" (Dennett 2003, 225).

8. Although the HOT model is consistent with a Humean bundle theory, I believe it has certain advantages over Hume's own *perceptual* model of introspection. According to Hume, when we introspect all we find is a "mere heap or collection of different perceptions" (1739, 207). Rosenthal, however, writes: "It's worth noting in this connection that Hume's famous problem about the self results from his tacit adoption of a specifically perceptual model of introspecting; one cannot find a self when one seeks it perceptually. The HOT model, by contrast, provides an informative explanation of the way we do seem to be introspectively conscious of the self" (2003, 344-345). According to the HOT theory, "Constructing introspective awareness in terms of conscious HOTs explains how awareness of oneself occurs" (2003, 358).

9. In "Introspection and the Self" (1986), Shoemaker criticizes the perceptual model of introspection as an "inner sense" that would take primary consciousness as an object, or that would involve an identification of self. Shoemaker does not regard introspection as a separate act of reflective consciousness. Shoemaker's notion of introspection is clearly stated by Cassam: "introspective awareness, properly so called, is a form of awareness that serves as the basis for making first-person statements in which the first-person pronoun is used as subject. First-person statements in which 'I' is used in this way are those that, in Shoemaker's terminology, are immune to error through misidentification relative to the first-person pronoun" (1995, 315).

10. Gallagher (2000) admits that thinking is a kind of action and is therefore subject to a sense of agency. He writes: "Problem solving, thinking through a set of instructions, and narrating a story are good examples. I may intend to solve a problem and to do so by following precise steps in a known procedure. I have a sense of where I am going in the procedure, and I push the thinking process along from one step to another in a controlled manner. When I follow a set of instructions, or when I tell a story (perhaps just to myself), I have the same sense that I am promoting my thinking along a path that is, or is becoming, relatively well-defined...[In such cases, I have] a sense that the thinking process is being generated in my own stream of consciousness and, to some degree, under my control" (2000, 225-226).

11. Although some symptoms of schizophrenia may be due to Frithian break-downs in metarepresentational self-monitoring (see Frith 1987, 1992), it also seems possible that there can be too much metarepresentation. Sass (1992, 1998), for example, suggests "metarepresentation can be generated in a hyperreflexive attitude, and as a result, the schizophrenic can overmonitor aspects of his own experience" (Gallagher 2004, 14). According to Sass, hyperreflexivity is an intensified form of self-conscious-ness in which the subject disengages from normal forms of involvement with nature and society, often taking itself, or its own experiences, as its own object (1992, 37).

12. Ironically, as Wegner points out, "many of the most skilled acts we can do, the actions that others enjoy or find simply marvelous because of their high level of skill, and that others may therefore ascribe uniquely to us, may not be things we experience willing" (2002, 84). In fact, "the loss of a sense of authorship is even sought-after as a badge of skilled performance. Going 'unconscious' is a good thing when you're play-ing basketball . . ." (2002, 84).

13. In one such experiment, Frith and Done (1989) found that schizophrenic pa-tients suffering from delusions of control, as compared with those without such expe-riences, were less able to correct their movement errors on a video game task which required using a joystick to move an arrow on a computer screen in the absence of visual feedback.

14. I do not mean to gloss over the differences between these various accounts. There are, for example, significant differences between Frith's theory of self-monitor-ing and Campbell's—at least as it applies to the sense of agency for thought. As Gallagher describes: "[Frith] speaks of a *conscious* feeling of effort for a willed inten-tion to think, and he equates this with a *conscious* monitoring of an efference copy. Frith's analysis relies, not just on an intention to act (to move or to think), but on an *awareness* of the intention to act, and he defines this awareness as a case of 'metarepre-sentation.' Metarepresentation is a second-order reflective consciousness, 'the ability to reflect upon how we represent the world and our thoughts.' This is part of what it means to monitor our actions and, he claims, it is precisely what is missing or dis-rupted in the schizophrenic's experience. In schizophrenic delusions of control and inserted thought, there is a failure of metarepresentation; the metarepresentational monitoring of movement or thought breaks down" (2004, 11). Although I agree that delusions of control and the phenomenon of inserted thought are due to a failure of self-monitoring, I believe Frith's characterization of what the agent is aware of, and hence what is being monitored, is inconsistent with the phenomenology of agentive thought (see Gallagher 2004). Gallagher, for example, has criticized Frith along the following lines: "most cases of normal thinking are neither prefaced by conscious intentions to think, nor followed by an introspective awareness of that intention. In the normal phenomenology, at least in the large majority of cases, there is not first an intention and then a thinking, nor thinking plus a concurrent but separate awareness of intention to think" (2004, 12). Campbell (1999a), however, has offered some impor-tant modifications to Frith's model that I believe can help avoid some of these difficul-ties. On Campbell's account, the efferent copy (and thus the intention to think that it represents) is not itself available to consciousness. He instead maintains that the effer-ent copy is part of a *subpersonal* and nonconscious process that generates an awareness of effort as thought itself is generated. That is, he moves the intention to think under-ground to a subpersonal mechanism. This corrective to Frith's model is an important improvement since, as Campbell notes, "Conscious thoughts are obviously not, in general, the upshot of conscious intentions to think those very thoughts" (1999a, 616). What Frith calls "intentions to think" are, on Campbell's account, part of a subperson-al, nonconscious process. So instead of positing a conscious intention to think, noncon-scious processes generate both the occurrent thought and the efferent copy, which then allows for self-monitoring to occur. For Campbell: "You have knowledge of the content of the thought only through introspection. The content of the efferent copy is not itself conscious. But it is match at the monitoring between the thought of which you have introspective knowledge and the efferent copy that is responsible for the

sense of being the agent of that thought. It is a disturbance in that mechanism that is responsible for the schizophrenic finding that he is introspectively aware of a thought without having the sense of being the agent of that thought" (1999a, 618). Of course applying the comparator model to the cognitive level assumes, even on Campbell's account, that when I think a thought, some cognitive equivalent of a motor instruction to think that thought has to be issued, and a copy of that instruction sent to the comparator, so that when the thought is available to introspection it can be experienced as a thought that one produced oneself. One might seriously question whether it is even coherent to think of mental activity in this way. For criticisms of this approach, see Gallagher (2000, 2004) and Stephens and Graham (2000). For a reply, see Campbell (2004). As Campbell, himself, asks, "what is the source of the motor instruction to think a particular thought?" Campbell's solution is to identify instructions to think not with instructions per se but with instruction analogues in the long-standing attitudes (such as beliefs) of a person. For an alternative that does not involve long-standing attitudes and beliefs functioning, in any robust sense, as instructions, see Stephens and Graham (2000).

15. Hoffman (1986) suggests something similar with regard to the schizophrenic phenomenon of "hearing voices," or what is sometimes referred to as *auditory hallucination*. Although neuropsychological evidence indicates that the voices are self-generated (e.g., Gould 1948; Inouye and Shimizu 1970; McGuire, Shah, and Murray 1993; Green and Kinsbourne 1989), schizophrenic patients with this symptom describe the voices as coming from someone other than themselves (see Wegner 2002 for a review). Hoffman (1986) has argued that these alien voices may occur when people find that their thoughts are radically mismatched with their current conscious goals for thinking. As Wegner describes: "Hoffman proposed that a speaker normally generates an abstract cognitive plan that reflects the gist or intention of what he or she will say and that is sensitive to the goals and beliefs of the speaker. This plan is then transformed into actual words and syntax" (Wegner 2002, 87). But, as Wegner (2002) notes, this discourse planning activity breaks down in schizophrenia and thus can lead to unexpected utterances and thoughts (Deese 1978; Hoffman 1986). Schizophrenic subjects often experience their manifest speech as being poorly matched to what they had in mind to say (see J.P. Chapman 1966). When this discourse planning activity breaks down, "Ideas appear that don't fit the prior plan, and when this happens, perhaps it begins to seem reasonable to attribute the thoughts to a 'voice'" (Wegner 2002, 87).

Works Cited

Aarts, Henk, and Ap Dijksterhuis. 2000. Habits as knowledge structures: Automaticity in goal-directed behavior. *Journal of Personality and Social Psychology* 78 (1): 53-63.

———. 2003. The silence of the library: Environment, situational norm, and social behavior. *Journal of Personality and Social Psychology* 84 (1): 18-28.

Albert, David. 1994. Bohm's alternative to quantum mechanics. *Scientific American* 270:58-67.

Amsel, Abram. 1989. *Behaviorism, neobehaviorism, and cognitivism in learning theory: Historical and contemporary perspectives.* Hillsdale, NJ: Erlbaum.

Andersen, Holly. 2006. Two causal mistakes in Wegner's *Illusion of conscious will. Philosophy of Science Association: 20th Biennial Mtg (Vancouver): PSA 2006 Contributed Papers.* http://philsci-archive.pitt.edu/archive/00003008/

Andersen, Susan M., and Serena Chen. 2002. The relational self: An interpersonal social-cognitive theory. *Psychological Review* 109:619-45.

Anscombe, G.E.M. 1971. *Causality and determinism.* Cambridge: Cambridge University Press. Reprinted in *Metaphysics and the philosophy of mind: The collected philosophical papers of G.E. Anscombe, Vol. 2,* ed. G.E.M. Anscombe, 139-63. Minneapolis: University of Minnesota Press.

Armstrong, David M. 1966. The nature of mind. *Arts* (Proceedings of The Sydney University Arts Association) 3:37-48. Reprinted in *Mind/Brain identity,* ed. C.V. Borst, 67-79. London: Macmilliam, 1970.

———. 1968. *A materialist theory of mind.* New York: Routledge & Kegan Paul.

———. 1977. The causal theory of mind. *Neue Heft fur Philosophie* 11:82-95. Reprinted in *The nature of mind,* ed. David M. Rosenthal, 181-88. New York: Oxford University Press, 1991.

———. 1981. *The nature of mind.* Ithaca: Cornell University Press.

Audi, Robert. 1974. Moral responsibility, freedom and compulsion. *American Philosophical Quarterly* 19:25-39.

———. 1991. Responsible action and virtuous character. *Ethics* 101:304-21.

———. 1993. *Action, intention and reason.* Ithaca: Cornell University Press.

Aune, Bruce. 1967. Hypotheticals and 'can': Another look. *Analysis* 27 (6): 191-95.

Austin, J.L. 1956. Ifs and cans. *Proceedings of the British Academy* 42:107-32. Reprinted in *Philosophical papers,* J.L. Austin, 153-80. Oxford: Clarendon Press, 1961.

———. 1966. Three ways of spilling ink. *Philosophical Review* 75 (4): 427-40.

Ayer, A.J. 1954. Freedom and necessity. In *Philosophical essays,* A.J. Ayer, 271-84. London: Macmillan. Reprinted in *Free will,* ed. Derk Pereboom, 110-18. Cambridge: Hackett Publishing Company, 1997.

———. 1969. *Metaphysics and common sense.* London: Macmillan.

Baars, Bernard. 1988. *A cognitive theory of consciousness.* Cambridge: Cambridge University Press.

Baer, John, James Kaufman, and Roy Baumeister, eds. 2008. *Are we free? Psychology and free will.* New York: Oxford University Press.

Bandura, Albert. 1977. Self-efficacy: Toward a unifying theory of behavioral change. *Psychological Review* 84:191-215.

———. 1986. *Social foundations of thought and action: A social-cognitive theory.* Englewood Cliffs, NJ: Prentice-Hall.

———. 1997. *Self-efficacy.* New York: Freeman.

Barbosa, G.D., and Nelson Pinto-Neto. 2004. Noncommutative quantum mechanics and Bohm's ontological interpretation. *Physical Review* 69 (6): 065014.

Bargh, John A. 1989. Conditional automaticity: Varieties of automatic influences in social perception and cognition. In *Unintended Thought*, ed. James Uleman and John A. Bargh, 3-51. New York: Guilford Press.

———. 1990. Auto-motives: Preconscious determinants of social interaction. In *Handbook of motivation and cognition, Vol. 2*, ed. E. Tory Higgins and Richard M. Sorrentino, 93-130. New York: Guilford Press.

———. 1992. Why subliminality does not matter to social psychology: Awareness of the stimulus versus awareness of its influence. In *Perception without awareness*, ed. Robert F. Bornstein and Thane S. Pittman, 236-55. New York: Guilford Press.

———. 1994. The four horsemen of automaticity: Awareness, efficiency, intention, and control in social cognition. In *Handbook of social cognition*, 2nd ed., ed. Robert S. Wyer, Jr. and Thomas K. Srull, 1-40. Hillsdale, NJ: Lawrence Erlbaum Associates.

———. 1996. Automaticity in social psychology. In *Social psychology: Handbook of basic principles*, ed. E. Tory Higgins and Arie W. Kruglanski, 169-83. New York: Guilford Press.

———. 1997. The automaticity of everyday life. In *The automaticity of everyday life: Advances in social cognition, Vol. 10*, ed. Robert S. Wyer, Jr., 1-61. Mahwah, NJ: Lawrence Erlbaum Associates.

———. 1999. The cognitive monster: The case against controllability of automatic stereotype effects. In *Dual process theories in social psychology*, ed. Shelly Chaiken and Yaacov Trope, 361-82. New York: Guilford Press.

———. 2002. Losing consciousness: Automatic influences on consumer judgment, behavior, and motivation. *Journal of Consumer Research* 29:280-85.

———. 2008. Free will is un-natural. In *Are we free? Psychology and free will*, ed. John Baer, James Kaufman, and Roy Baumeister, 128-54. New York: Oxford University Press.

Bargh, John A., Shelly Chaiken, Rajen Govender, and Felicia Pratto. 1992. The generality of the automatic attitude activation effect. *Journal of Personality and Social Psychology* 62:893-912.

Bargh, John A., and Tanya L. Chartrand. 1999. The unbearable automaticity of being. *American Psychologist* 54 (7): 462-79.

Bargh, John A., Mark Chen, and Lara Burrows. 1996. Automaticity of social behavior: Direct effects of trait construct and stereotype activation on action. *Journal of Personality and Social Psychology* 71:230-44.

Bargh, John A., and Melissa J. Ferguson. 2000. Beyond behaviorism: On the automaticity of higher mental processes. *Psychological Bulletin* 126 (6): 925-45.

Bargh, John A., and Peter M. Gollwitzer. 1994. Environmental control of goal-directed action: Automatic and strategic contingencies between situations and behavior. *Nebraska Symposium on Motivation* 41:71-124.

Bargh, John A., Peter M. Gollwitzer, Annette Lee-Chai, Kimberly Barndollar, and Roman Trotschel. 2001. The automated will: Nonconscious activation and pursuit of behavioral goals. *Journal of Personality and Social Psychology* 81:1014-27.

Bargh, John A., and Ezequiel Morsella. 2008. The primacy of the unconscious. *Perspectives on Psychological Science* 3:73-79.

Bargh, John A., and Erin L. Williams. 2006. The automaticity of social life. *Current Directions in Psychological Science* 15 (1): 1-4.

Baron, Robert S., and Henrietta Logan. 1993. Desired control, felt control, and dental pain: Recent findings and remaining issues. *Motivation and Emotion* 17 (3): 181-204.

Baron, Robert S., Henrietta Logan, and Sieg Hoppe. 1993. Emotional and sensory focus as mediators of dental pain among patients differing in desired and felt dental control. *Health and Psychology* 12 (5): 381-89.

Barsalou, Lawrence W. 1992. *Cognitive psychology: An overview for cognitive scientists*. Hillsdale, NJ: Lawrence Erlbaum Associates.

Baumeister, Roy F. 2002. Yielding to temptation: Self-control failure, impulsive purchasing and consumer behavior. *Journal of Consumer Research* 28:670-76.

———. 2005. *The cultural animal: Human nature, meaning, and social life.* New York: Oxford University Press.

———. 2008. Free will in scientific psychology. *Perspectives of Psychological Science* 3 (1): 14-19.

Baumeister, Roy F., Ellen Bratslavsky, Mark Muraven, and Dianne M. Tice. 1998. Ego depletion: Is the active self a limited resource? *Journal of Personality and Social Psychology* 74 (5): 1252-65.

Baumeister, Roy F., and Brad J. Bushman. 2008. *Social psychology and human nature.* Belmont, CA: Thomson Wadsworth.

Baumeister, Roy F., Todd F. Heatherton, and Dianne M. Tice. 1994. *Losing control: How and why people fail at self-regulation.* San Diego, CA: Academic Press.

Baumeister, Roy F., E.J. Masicampo, and C. Nathan DeWall. 2009. Prosocial benefits of feeling free: Disbelief in free will increases aggression and reduces helpfulness. *Personality and Social Psychology Bulletin* 35:260-68.

Baumeister, Roy F., Alfred R. Mele, and Kathleen D. Vohs, eds. 2010. *Free will and consciousness: How might they work?* New York: Oxford University Press.

Baumeister, Roy F., Erin A. Sparks, Tyler F. Stillman, and Kathleen D. Vohs. 2008. Free will in consumer behavior: Self-control, ego depletion, and choice. *Journal of Consumer Psychology* 18:4-13.

Bayne, Tim. 2008. The phenomenology of agency. *Philosophical Compass* 3 (1): 182-202.

Bayne, Tim, and Neil Levy. 2006. The feeling of doing: Deconstructing the phenomenology of agency. In *Disorders of volition*, ed. Natalie Sebanz and Wolfgang Prinz, 49-68. Cambridge, MA: MIT Press.

Bechara, Antoine, Hanna Damasio, Daniel Tranel, and Antonio R. Damasio. 1997. Deciding advantageously before knowing advantageous strategy. *Science* 275:1293-95.

Beck, Friedrich, and John C. Eccles. 1992. Quantum aspects of brain activity and the role of consciousness. *Proceedings of the National Academy of Sciences US* 89:11357-61.

Bem, Daryl J. 1967. Self-perception: An alternative interpretation of cognitive dissonance phenomena. *Psychological Review* 74:183-200.

———. 1972. Self-perception theory. In *Advances in experimental social psychology, Vol. 6*, ed. Leonard Berkowitz, 2-62. New York: Academic Press.

Berofsky, Bernard. 1966. *Free will and determinism.* New York: Harper & Row.

———. 1971. *Determinism.* Princeton: Princeton University Press.

———. 1987. *Freedom from necessity: The metaphysical basis of responsibility.* London: Routledge & Kegan Paul.

———. 1995. *Liberation from self.* Cambridge: Cambridge University Press.

———. 2002. Ifs, cans, and free will: The issues. In *The Oxford handbook of free will*, ed. Robert Kane, 181-201. Oxford: Oxford University Press.

Berridge, Kent, and Piotr Winkielman. 2003. What is an unconscious emotion? (The case for unconscious 'liking'). *Cognition and Emotion* 17:181-211.

Bjork, Robert A. 1975. Short-term storage: The ordered output of a central processor. In *Cognitive theory, Vol. 1*, ed. Frank Restle, Richard M. Shiffrin, N. John Castellan, Harold R. Lindman, and David B. Pisoni, 151-71. Hillsdale, NJ: Lawrence Erlbaum Associates.

Blackburn, Simon. 1999. *Think.* Oxford: Oxford University Press.

Blakemore, Colin, and Susan Greenfield, eds. 1987. *Mindwaves: Thoughts on intelligence, identity and consciousness.* Oxford: Blackwell.

Blakemore, Sarah-Jayne. 2000. Monitoring the self in schizophrenia: The role of internal models. In *Exploring the self: Philosophical and psychopathological perspectives in self-experiences*, ed. Dan Zahavi, 185-202. Amsterdam: Benjamins.

Blakemore, Sarah-Jayne, and Christopher D. Frith. 2003. Disorders of self-monitoring and the symptoms of schizophrenia. In *The self in neuroscience and psychiatry*, ed. Tilo Kircher and Anthony David. Cambridge, UK: Cambridge University Press.

Blakemore, Sarah-Jayne, J. Smith, R. Steel, E.C. Johnstone, and Christopher D. Frith. 2000. The perception of self-produced sensory stimuli in patients with auditory hallucinations and passivity experiences: Evidence for a breakdown in self-monitoring. *Psychological Medicine* 30:1131-39.

Blanshard, Brand. 1958. The case for determinism. In *Determinism and freedom in the age of modern science*, ed. Sidney Hook, 19-31. New York: Collier-Macmillan.

Bloom, Paul. 2004. *Descartes' baby*. New York: Basic Books.

Bloom, Paul, and Deena Skolnick Weisberg. 2007. Childhood origins of adult resistance to science. *Science* 316 (May 18): 996-97.

Bohm, David. 1952a. A suggested interpretation of the quantum theory in terms of 'hidden variables' I. *Physical Review* 85:166-79.

———. 1952b. A suggested interpretation of the quantum theory in terms of 'hidden variables' II. *Physical Review* 85:180-93.

———. 1984. *Causality and chance in modern physics*. London: Routledge.

———. 1986. The implicate order. In *Beyond mechanism*, ed. David Schindler, 67-95. New York: University Press of America.

Bohm, David, and Basil J. Hiley. 1993. *The undivided universe: An ontological interpretation of quantum mechanics*. London: Routledge.

Bok, Hilary. 1998. *Freedom and responsibility*. Princeton: Princeton University Press.

Bourguignon, Erika. 1976. Introduction: A framework for the comparative study of altered states of consciousness. In *Religion, altered states of consciousness, and social change*, ed. E. Bourguignon, 3-35. Columbus: Ohio University Press.

Braddon-Mitchell, David, and Frank Jackson. 1996. *Philosophy of mind and cognition*. Malden, MA: Blackwell.

Brewer, Marilynn B. 1988. A dual process model of impression formation. In *Advances in social cognition, Vol.1*, ed. Thomas K. Srull and Robert S. Wyer, Jr., 1-36. Hillsdale, NJ: Lawrence Erlbaum Associates.

Broad, C.D. 1952. Determinism, indeterminism and libertarianism. In *Ethics and the history of philosophy*, C.D. Broad, 195-217. London: Routledge & Kegan Paul.

Brown, Jason W. 1996. *Time, will, and mental process*. New York: Plenum Press.

Bunge, Mario. 1980. *The mind-body problem: A psychobiological approach*. Oxford: Pergamon Press.

Byrne, Donn Erwin. 1971. *The attraction paradigm*. New York: Academic Press.

Cahill, Connie, and Christopher D. Frith. 1996. False perceptions or false beliefs? Hallucinations and delusions in schizophrenia. In *Methods in madness*, ed. P.W. Halligan and J.C. Marchell, 267-92. Hove: Psychology Press.

Campbell, C.A. 1951. Is 'free will' a pseudo-problem? *Mind* 60:446-65.

———. 1957. *Of selfhood and godhood*. London: Allen & Unwin.

———. 1967. *In defense of free will*. London: Allen & Unwin.

Campbell, John. 1999a. Schizophrenia, the space of reason, and thinking as a motor process. *Monist* 82 (4): 609-25.

———. 1999b. Immunity to error through misidentification and the meaning of a referring term. *Philosophical Topics* 26 (1-2): 89-104.

———. 2002. Ownership of thoughts. *Philosophy, Psychiatry and Psychology* 9:35-39.

———. 2004. The first person embodiment, and the certainty that one exists. *Monist* 87 (4): 475-88.

Cantor, Nancy, and John F. Kihlstrom. 1987. *Personality and social intelligence*. Englewood Cliffs, NJ: Prentice-Hall.

Cantor, Joanne R., Dolf Zillmann, and Jennings Bryant. 1975. Enhancement of experienced sexual arousal in response to erotic stimuli through misattribution of unrelated residual excitation. *Journal of Personality and Social Psychology* 32 (1): 69-75.

Carruthers, Peter. 1989. Brute experience. *Journal of Philosophy* 86 (5): 435-51.

———. 1996. *Language, thought and consciousness*. Cambridge: Cambridge University Press.

———. 2000. *Phenomenal consciousness*. Cambridge: Cambridge University Press.

———. 2005. *Consciousness: Essays from a higher-order perspective.* New York: Oxford University Press.

———. 2007. The illusion of conscious will. *Synthese* 159:197-213.

Caruso, Gregg. 2005. Sensory states, consciousness, and the cartesian assumption. In *Descartes and cartesianism,* ed. Nathan Smith and Jason Taylor, 177-99. Newcastle, UK: Cambridge Scholars Press.

Carver, Charles S., and Michael F. Scheier. 1981. *Attention and self-regulation: A control theory approach to human behavior.* New York: Springer.

———. 1998. *On the self-regulation of behavior.* New York: Cambridge University Press.

Cassam, Quassim. 1995. Introspection and bodily self-ascription. In *The body and the self,* ed. Jose Luis Bermudez, Anthony Marcel, and Naomi Eilan, 311-36. Cambridge, MA: MIT Press.

Castiello, U., Y. Paulignan, and Marc Jeannerod. 1991. Temporal dissociation of motor responses and subjective awareness: A study in normal subjects. *Brain* 114:2639-55.

Chaiken, Shelly, and Yaacov Trope, eds. 1999. *Dual-process theories in social psychology.* New York: Guilford Press.

Chapman, C. Richard. 1980. The role of anxiety in acute pain. In *Pain overview,* ed. John J. Bonica, 6-13. New York: Harper.

Chapman, James P. 1966. The early symptoms of schizophrenia. *British Journal of Psychiatry* 12:221-51.

Chartrand, Tanya L., and John A. Bargh. 1996. Automatic activation of impression formation and memorization goals: Nonconscious goal priming reproduces effects of explicit task instructions. *Journal of Personality and Social Psychology* 71:464-78.

———. 1999a. The chameleon effect: The perception-behavior link and social interaction. *Journal of Personality and Social Psychology* 76:893-910.

———. 1999b. *Consequences of automatic evaluation for current mood.* Manuscript in preparation, New York University.

———. 2002. Nonconscious motivations: Their activation, operation, and consequences. In *Self and motivation: Emerging psychological perspectives,* ed. Abraham Tesser, D.A. Stapel, and J.V. Wood, 13-41. Washington, DC: American Psychological Association.

Chen, Mark, and John A. Bargh. 1997. Nonconscious behavioral confirmation processes: The self-fulfilling consequences of automatic stereotype activation. *Journal of Experimental Social Psychology* 33:541-60.

———. 1999. Nonconscious approach and avoidance behavioral consequences of the automatic evaluation effect. *Personality and Social Psychology Bulletin* 25:215-24.

Chisholm, Roderick. 1964a. *Human freedom and the self.* Lindley Lecture, University of Kansas. Reprinted in *Free will,* ed. Gary Watson, 24-35. New York: Oxford University Press, 1982.

———. 1964b. J.L. Austin's *Philosophical papers. Mind* 73:20-25.

———. 1966. Freedom and action. In *Freedom and determinism,* ed. Keith Lehrer, 11-44. New York: Random House.

———. 1971. Reflections on human agency. *Idealistic Studies* 1:33-46.

———. 1976a. *Person and object.* Lasalle, IL: Open Court.

———. 1976b. The agent as cause. In *Action theory,* ed. Myles Brand and Douglas Walton, 199-211. Dordrecht: D. Reidel.

———. 1995. Agents, causes and events. In *Agents, causes and events: Essays on free will and indeterminism,* ed. Timothy O'Connor, 95-100. Oxford: Oxford University Press.

Choudhury, Suparna, and Sarah-Jayne Blakemore. 2006. Intentions, actions, and the self. In *Does consciousness cause behavior?* ed. Susan Pockett, William P. Banks, and ShaunGallagher, 39-51. Cambridge, MA: MIT Press.

Christman, John. 1991. Autonomy and personal history. *Canadian Journal of Philosophy* 21:1-24.

Clarke, Randolph. 1993. Toward a credible agent-causal account of free will. *Nous* 27:191-203.

———. 1995a. Freedom and determinism: Recent work. *Philosophical Books* 36:9-18.

———. 1995b. Indeterminism and control. *American Philosophical Quarterly* 32:125-38.

———. 1996. Agent causation and event causation in the production of free action. *Philosophical Topics* 24:19-48.

———. 2002. Libertarian views: Critical survey of noncausal and event-causal accounts of free agency. In *The Oxford handbook of free will*, ed. Robert Kane, 356-405. New York: Oxford University Press.

———. 2003. *Libertarian accounts of free will*. New York: Oxford University Press.

Cohen, Jonathan D., Kevin Dunbar, and James L. McClelland. 1990. On the control of automatic processes: A parallel distribution processing account of the Stroop effect. *Psychological Review* 97:332-61.

Coliva, Annalisa. 2002. Thought insertion and immunity to error through misidentification. *Philosophy, Psychiatry, and Psychology* 9 (1): 27-34.

Copp, David. 1997. Defending the principle of alternative possibilities: Blameworthiness and moral responsibility. *Nous* 31:441-45.

Crick, Francis. 1994. *The astonishing hypothesis: The scientific search for the soul.* New York: Charles Scribner's Sons.

Crick, Francis and Christof Koch. 1990. Towards a neurobiological theory of consciousness. *Seminars in Neurosciences* 2:263-75.

Damasio, Antonio. 1994. *Descartes' error: Emotion, reason, and the human brain.* New York: Avon Books.

D'Angelo, Edward. 1968. *The problem of freedom and determinism.* Columbia: University of Missouri Press.

Daprati, E., Nicolas Franck, Nicolas Georgieff, J. Proust, E. Pacherie, J. Daléry, and Marc Jeannerod. 1997. Looking for the agent: An investigation into consciousness of action and self-consciousness in schizophrenic patients. *Cognition* 65:71-86.

Davidson, Donald. 1970. Mental events. In *Experience and theory*, ed. Lawrence Foster and J.W. Swanson, 79-102. London: Duckworth. Reprinted in *Essays on actions and events*, Donald Davidson. New York: Oxford University Press.

———. 1973. Freedom to act. In *Essays in freedom of action*, ed. Ted Honderich, 67-86. London: Routledge & Kegan Paul. Reprinted in *Essays on actions and events*, Donald Davidson. Oxford: Clarendon Press.

———. 1993. Thinking causes. In *Mental causation*, ed. John Heil and Alfred R. Mele, 3-18. Oxford: Clarendon.

Davies, Martin, and Glyn Humphreys, eds. 1993. *Consciousness.* Oxford: Blackwell.

Deci, Edward L., and Richard M. Ryan. 1985. *Intrinsic motivation and self-determination in human behavior.* New York: Plenum.

Deese, James. 1978. Thought into speech. *American Scientist* 66:314-21.

Dehaene, Stanislas, and Lionel Naccache. 2001. Towards a cognitive neuroscience of consciousness: Basic evidence and a workshop framework. *Cognition* 79 (1-2): 1-37.

Della Sala, Sergio, Clelia Marchetti, and Hans Spinnler. 1991. Right-sided anarchic (alien) hand: A longitudinal study. *Neuropsychologia* 29 (11): 1113-27.

Dennett, Daniel C. 1984. *Elbowroom.* Cambridge, MA: MIT Press.

———. 1991. *Consciousness explained.* Boston: Little, Brown.

———. 1995. The unimagined preposterousness of zombies. *Journal of Consciousness Studies* 2 (4): 322-26.

———. 2003. *Freedom evolves.* New York: Viking.

———. 2008. Some observations on the psychology of thinking. In *Are we free? Psychology and free will*, ed. John Baer, James Kaufman, and Roy Baumeister, 248-59. New York: Oxford University Press.

Descartes, René. 1964-75. *Oeuvres de Descartes.* Revised ed., ed. Charles Adam and Paul Tannery. Paris: Vrin/C.N.R.S.

———. 1984-85. *The philosophical writings of Descartes Vols. 1-3.* Trans. John Cottingham, Robert Stoothoff, and Dugald Murdoch. Cambridge: Cambridge University Press.

Devine, Patricia G. 1989. Stereotypes and prejudice: Their automatic and controlled components. *Journal of Personality and Social Psychology* 56:5-18.

d'Holbach, Baron Paul Henri. 1770. *The system of nature*. Amsterdam.

Dijksterhuis, Ap. 2004. Think different: The merits of unconscious thought in preference development and decision making. *Journal of Personality and Social Psychology* 87 (5): 586-98.

Dijksterhuis, Ap, John A. Bargh, and Joost Miedema. 2001. On men and mackerels: Attention and automatic social behavior. In *The message within: The role of subjective experience in social cognition and behavior*, ed. Herbert Bless and Joseph P. Forgas, 36-51. Philadelphia: Psychology Press.

Dijksterhuis, Ap, Maarten Bos, Loran F. Nordgren, and Rick B. van Baaren. 2006. On making the right choice: The deliberation-without-attention effect. *Science* 311:1005-7.

Dijksterhuis, Ap, Russell Spears, Tom Postmes, Diederik A. Stapel, Willem Koomen, Ad van Knippenberg, and Daan Scheepers. 1998. Seeing one thing and doing another: Contrast effects in automatic behavior. *Journal of Personality and Social Psychology* 75:862-71.

Dijksterhuis, Ap, and Ad van Knippenberg. 1998. The relation between perception and behavior, or how to win a game of trivial pursuit. *Journal of Personality and Social Psychology* 74 (4): 865-77.

Dijksterhuis, Ap, Ad van Knippenberg, Russell Spears, Tom Postmes, Diederik A. Stapel, Willem Koomen, and Daan Scheepers. 1998. Seeing one thing and doing another: Contrast effects in automatic behavior. *Journal of Personality and Social Psychology* 75 (4): 862-71.

Dijksterhuis, Ap, and Zeger van Olden. 2006. On the benefits of thinking unconsciously: Unconscious thought can increase post-choice satisfaction. *Journal of Experimental Social Psychololgy* 42 (5): 627-31.

Double, Richard. 1991. *The non-reality of free will*. Oxford: Oxford University Press.

Dretske, Fred. 1993. Conscious Experience. *Mind* 102 (406): 263-83. Reprinted in *The nature of consciousness: Philosophical debates*, ed. Ned Block, Owen Flanagan, and Guven Guzeldere, 773-88. Cambridge, MA: MIT Press.

———. 1995. *Naturalizing the mind*. Cambridge, MA: MIT Press.

Durr, Detlef, Sheldon Goldstein, Roderich Tumulka, and Nino Zanghi. 2004. Bohmian mechanics and quantum field theory. *Physical Review Letters* 93 (9): 090402.

Dutton, Donald G., and Arthur Aron. 1974. Some evidence for heightened sexual attraction under conditions of high anxiety. *Journal of Personality and Social Psychology* 30 (4): 510-17.

Duval, Shelley, and Robert A. Wicklund. 1973. Effects of objective self-awareness on attributes of causality. *Journal of Experimental Social Psychology* 9:17-31.

Dworkin, Gerald. 1970a. Acting freely. *Nous* 4:367-83.

———. 1970b. *Determinism, free will and moral responsibility*. Engelwood Cliffs, NJ: Prentice-Hall.

———. 1976. Autonomy and behavioral control. *Hastings Center Report* 6:23-28.

———. 1986. Review of Dennett's *Elbow room*. *Ethics* 96:423-25.

———. 1988. *The theory and practice of autonomy*. Cambridge: Cambridge University Press.

Eccles, John. 1970. *Facing reality*. New York: Springer-Verlag.

———. 1994. *How the self controls the brain*. Berlin: Springer.

Eccles, John, and Karl Popper. 1977. *The self and its brain*. New York: Springer-Verlag.

Edelman, Gerald M. 1992. *Bright air, brilliant fire*. New York: Basic Books.

Edelman, Gerald, and Giulio Tononi. 2000. *A universe of consciousness: How matter becomes imagination*. New York: Basic Books.

Edwards, Paul. 1958. Hard and soft determinism. In *Determinism and freedom in the age of modern science*, ed. Sidney Hook, 117-25. New York: Collier-Macmillan.

Eich, Eric. 1984. Memory for unattended events: Remembering with and without awareness. *Memory and Cognition* 12:105-11.

Einstein, Albert. 1929. What life means to Einstein: An interview by George Sylvester Viereck. *The Saturday Evening Post*, October 26, 17, 110, 113-17.

Ekstrom, Laura. 1998. Protecting incompatibilist freedom. *American Philosophical Quarterly* 35:281-91.

———. 2000. *Free will: A philosophical study*. Boulder, CO: Westview Press.

———. 2002. Libertarianism and Frankfurt-style cases. In *The Oxford handbook of free will*, ed. Robert Kane, 309-22. New York: Oxford University Press.

Ericsson, K. Anders, and Herbert A. Simon. 1980. Verbal reports as data. *Psychological Review* 87:215-51.

Estabrooks, G.H. 1943. *Hypnotism*. New York: E.P. Dutton.

Falk, Arthur. 1981. Some model confusions in compatibilism. *American Philosophical Quarterly* 18:141-48.

Farrer, Austin. 1967. *The freedom of the will*. New York: Scribner's.

Fazio, Russell H., David M. Sanbonmatsu, Martha C. Pwell, and Frank R. Kardes. 1986. On the automatic activation of attitudes. *Journal of Personality and Social Psychology* 50:229-38.

Feinberg, Irwin. 1978. Efference copy and corollary discharge: Implications for thinking and its disorders. *Schizophrenia Bulletin* 4:636-40.

Feldman, Fred. 1986. *Doing the best we can*. Dordrecht: D. Reidel.

Feltz, Adam, Edward T. Cokely, and Thomas Nadelhoffer. 2009. Natural compatibilism versus natural incompatibilism: Back to the drawing board. *Mind & Language* 24 (1): 1-23.

Ferguson, Melissa J. 2007. The automaticity of evaluation. In *Social psychology and the unconscious: The automaticity of higher mental processes*, ed. John A. Bargh, 219-64. Philadelphia: Psychology Press.

Fischer, John Martin, ed. 1986. *Moral responsibility*. Ithaca: Cornell University Press.

———. 1994. *The metaphysics of free will: A study of control*. Oxford: Blackwell.

———. 1999a. Responsibility and self-expression. *Journal of Ethics* 3:277-97.

———. 1999b. Recent work on moral responsibility. *Ethics* 110:91-139.

———. 2002a. Frankfurt-type compatibilism. In *Contours of agency: Essays on themes from Harry Frankfurt*, ed. Sarah Buss and Lee Overton, 1-26. Cambridge, MA: MIT Press.

———. 2002b. Frankfurt-type examples and semi-compatibilism. In *The Oxford handbook of free will*, ed. Robert Kane, 281-308. New York: Oxford University Press.

Fischer, John Martin, Robert Kane, Derk Pereboom, and Manuel Vargas. 2007. *Four views on free will*. Oxford: Blackwell.

Fischer, John Martin, and Mark Ravizza. 1998. *Responsibility and control: A theory of moral responsibility*. Cambridge: Cambridge University Press.

Fish, Frank J. 1962. *Fish's schizophrenia*, 3rd ed. Ed. Max Hamilton. Bristol: John Wright and Sons.

Flanagan, Owen. 1992. *Consciousness reconsidered*. Cambridge, MA: MIT Press/Bradford Book.

———. 2002. *The problem of the soul: Two visions of mind and how to reconcile them*. New York: Basic Books.

Flanagan, Owen, and Thomas Polger. 1995. Zombies and the function of consciousness. *Journal of Consciousness Studies* 2 (4): 313-21.

———. 1998. Consciousness, adaptation, and epiphenomenalism. In *Consciousness evolving*, ed. James Fetzer, 21-41. Amsterdam: John Benjamins.

Fodor, Jerry. 1990. Making mind matter more. In *A theory of content and other essays*, Jerry Fodor, 137-59. Cambridge, MA: MIT Press.

Foster, John. 1991. *The immaterial self: A defense of the Cartesian dualist conception of mind*. New York: Routledge.

Franck, Nicolas, Chloe Farrer, Nicolas Georgieff, Michel Marie Cardine, Jean Dalery, Thierry d'Amato, and Marc Jeannerod. 2001. Defective recognition of one's own actions in patients with schizophrenia. *American Journal of Psychiatry* 158:454-59.

Frankfurt, Harry. 1969. Alternative possibilities and moral responsibility. *Journal of Philosophy* 66 (23): 829-39.

———. 1971. Freedom of the will and the concept of a person. *Journal of Philosophy* 68 (1): 5-20.

———. 1976. Identification and externality. In *The identities of persons*, ed. Amélie Oksenberg Rorty, 239-51. Berkeley: University of California Press.

———. 1987. Identification and wholeheartedness. In *Responsibility, character and emotions*, ed. Ferdinand Schoeman, 27-45. Cambridge: Cambridge University Press.

———. 1988. *The importance of what we care about.* New York: Cambridge University Press.

———. 1992a. The faintest passion. *Proceedings of the American Philosophical Association* 66:5-16.

———. 1992b. On the usefulness of final ends. *Iyyun* 41:3-19.

———. 1993. On the necessity of ideals. In *The moral self*, ed. Gil G. Noam and Thomas Wren, 16-27. Cambridge, MA: MIT Press.

———. 1994a. An alleged asymmetry between actions and omissions. *Ethics* 104:620-23.

———. 1994b. Autonomy, necessity and love. In *Vernunftbegriffe in der Moderne*, ed. Hans Friedrich Fulda and Rolf-Peter Horstmann, 433-47. Horstmann, Stuttgart: Klett-Cotta.

———. 1999. *Necessity, volition and love.* Cambridge: Cambridge University Press.

Freeman, Anthony, ed. 2001. *The emergence of consciousness.* London: Imprint Academic.

Freud, Sigmund. 1901. *The psychopathology of everyday life.* Trans. A.A. Brill. London: Fisher Unwin.

Fried, Itzhak, Roy Mukamel, and Gabriel Kreiman. 2011. Internally generated preactivation of single neurons in human medial frontal cortex predicts volition. *Neuron* 69 (3): 548-62.

Friedman, Marilyn. 1986. Autonomy and the split-level self. *Southern Journal of Philosophy* 24:19-35.

Friedman, Ron, and Andrew Elliot. 2008. Exploring the influence of sports drink exposure on physical endurance. *Psychology of Sports and Exercise* 9 (6): 746-59.

Frith, Christopher D. 1987. The positive and negative symptoms of schizophrenia reflect impairment in the perception and initiation of action. *Psychological Medicine* 17:631- 48.

———. 1992. *The cognitive neuropsychology of schizophrenia.* Hillsdale, NJ: Lawrence Erlbaum Associates.

———. 2004. Comments on Shaun Gallagher. *Psychopathology* 37: 20-22.

Frith, Christopher D., Sarah-Jayne Blakemore, and Daniel M. Wolpert. 2000. Explaining the symptoms of schizophrenia: Abnormalities in the awareness of action. *Brain Research Reviews* 31 (2-3): 357-63.

Frith, Christopher D., and D. John Done. 1988. Towards a neuropsychology of schizophrenia. *British Journal of Psychiatry* 153:437-43.

———. 1989. Experiences of alien control in schizophrenia reflect impairment in the perception and initiation of action. *Psychological Medicine* 17:359-63.

Frith, Christopher D., and Paul Fletcher. 1995. Voices from nowhere. *Critical Quarterly* 37:71-83.

Gailliot, Matthew T., Roy F. Baumeister, C. Nathan DeWall, Jon K. Maner, E. Ashby Plant, Dianne M. Tice, Lauren E. Brewer, Brandon J. Schmeichel. 2007. Self-control relies on glucose as a limited energy source: Willpower is more than a metaphor. *Journal of Personality and Social Psychology* 92:325-36.

Gallagher, Shaun. 2000. Self-reference and schizophrenia: A cognitive model of immunity to error through misidentification. In *Exploring the self: Philosophical and psychopathological perspectives on self-experience*, ed. Dan Zahavi, 203-38. Philadelphia: John Benjamins.

———. 2004. Neurocognitive models of schizophrenia: A neurophenomenological critique. *Psychopathology* 37 (1): 8-19.

Gasquoine, Philip G. 1993. Alien hand sign. *Journal Of Clinical and Experimental Neuropsychology* 15:653-67.

Gavanski, Igor, and Curt Hoffman. 1987. Awareness of influences on one's own judgments: The role of covariation detection and attention to the judgment process. *Journal of Personality and Social Psychology* 52:453-63.

Gazzaniga, Michael S. 1985. *The social brain.* New York: Free Press.

———. 1998. *The mind's past.* Berkeley: University of California Press.

Gazzaniga, Michael S., and Joseph E. LeDoux. 1978. *The integrated mind.* New York: Plenum.

Gennaro, Rocco J. 1996. *Consciousness and self-consciousness: A defense of the higher-order thought theory of consciousness.* Amsterdam: John Benjamins.

———. 2002. Jean Paul Sartre and the HOT theory of consciousness. *Canadian Journal of Philosophy* 32:293-330.

———. 2003. Papineau on the actualist HOT theory of consciousness. *Australian Journal of Philosophy* 81 (December): 581-86.

———. ed. 2004. *Higher-order theories of consciousness.* Amsterdam: John Benjamins.

———. 2005. The HOT theory of consciousness: Between a rock and a hard place? *Journal of Consciousness Studies* 12 (2): 3-21.

Georgieff, Nicolas, and Marc Jeannerod. 1998. Beyond consciousness of external reality: A 'who' system for consciousness of action and self-consciousness. *Consciousness and Cognition* 7 (3): 465-77.

German, Tim P., and Shaun Nichols. 2003. Children's counterfactual inferences about long and short causal chains. *Developmental Studies* 6:514-23.

Geschwind, Daniel H., M.S. Iacoboni, D.M. Mega, W. Zaidel, T. Cloughesy, and E. Zaidel. 1995. Alien hand syndrome: Interhemispheric motor disconnection due to a lesion in the midbody of the corpus callosum. *Neurology* 45:802-8.

Gibbons, Frederick X. 1990. Self-attention and behavior: A review and theoretical update. In *Advances in experimental social psychology, Vol. 23,* ed. Mark P. Zanna, 249-303. San Diego, CA: Academic Press.

Gilbert, Daniel T., Ryan P. Brown, Elizabeth C. Pinel, and Timothy D. Wilson. 2001. The illusion of external agency. *Journals of Personality and Social Psychology* 79:690-700.

Giles, Howard, Justine Coupland, and Nikolas Coupland. 1991. *Contexts of accommodation: Developments in applied sociolinguistics.* New York: Cambridge University Press.

Ginet, Carl. 1966. Might we have no choice? In *Freedom and determinism,* ed. Keith Lehrer, 87-104. New York: Random House.

———. 1980. The conditional analysis of freedom. In *Time and cause: Essays presented to Richard Taylor,* ed. Peter van Inwagen, 171-86. Dordrecht: D. Reidel.

———. 1983. A defense of incompatibilism. *Philosophical Studies* 44:391-400.

———. 1990. *On action.* Cambridge: Cambridge University Press.

———. 1995. Reasons explanation of action: An incompatibilist account. In *Agents, causes, and events,* ed. Timothy O'Connor. Oxford: Oxford University Press.

———. 1996. In defense of the principle of alternative possibilities: Why I don't find Frankfurt's argument convincing. *Philosophical Perspectives* 10:403-17.

———. 1997. Freedom, responsibility and agency. *Ethics* 1 (1): 374-80.

———. 2002. Reasons explanations of action: Causalist versus noncausalist accounts. In *The Oxford handbook of free will,* ed. Robert Kane, 386-405. New York: Oxford University Press.

Gladwell, Malcolm. 2005. *Blink: The power of thinking without thinking.* New York: Little, Brown.

Goetz, Stewart. 2005. Frankfurt-style counterexamples and begging the questions. *Midwest Studies in Philosophy* 29:83-105.

Goldberg, Gary, and K.K. Bloom. 1990. The alien hand sign: Localization, lateralization and recovery. *American Journal of Physical Medicine and Rehabilitation* 69:228-38.

Goldberg, Gary, Nathaniel H. Mayer, and Joseph U. Toglia. 1981. Medial frontal cortex and the alien hand sign. *Archives of Neurology* 38:683-86.

Gollwitzer, Peter M. 1990. Action phases and mind-sets. In *Handbook of motivation and cognition, Vol. 2*, ed. E.Tory Higgins and Richard M. Sorrentino, 53-92. New York: Guilford Press.

———. 1993. Goal achievement: The role of intentions. In *European review of social psychology*, ed. Wolfgang Stroebe and Miles Hewstone, 141-85. London: Wiley.

———. 1999. Implementation intentions: Strong effects of simple plans. *American Psychologist* 54:493-503.

Gollwitzer, Peter M., and Veronica Brandstätter. 1997. Implementation intentions and effective goal pursuit. *Journal of Personality and Social Psychology* 73:186-99.

Gould, Louis N. 1948. Verbal hallucinations and activity of vocal musculature. *American Journal of Psychiatry* 47:427-39.

Graham, George, and G. Lynn Stephens. 1994. Mind and mine. In *Philosophical psychology*, ed.

George Graham and G. Lynn Stephens, 91-109. Cambridge, MA: MIT Press.

Grahek, Nikola. 2007. *Feeling pain and being in pain*. 2nd ed. Cambridge, MA: MIT Press.

Green, Michael F., and Marcel Kinsbourne. 1989. Auditory hallucinations in schizophrenia: Does humming help? *Biological Psychiatry* 25:633-35.

Greenwald, Anthony G., Debbie E. McGhee, and Jordan L.K. Schwartz. 1998. Measuring individual differences in implicit cognition: The implicit association test. *Journal of Personality and Social Psychology* 74 (6): 1464-80.

Grunbaum, Adolph. 1953. Causality and the science of human behavior. In *Readings in the philosophy of science*, ed. Herbert Feigl and May Brodbeck, 752-80. New York: Appleton-Century Crofts.

———. 1971. Free will and the laws of human behavior. *American Philosophical Quarterly* 8:299-317.

Guzeldere, Guven. 1995. Is consciousness the perception of what passes in one's own mind? In *Conscious experience*, ed. Thomas Metzinger, 335-57. Paderborn: Schoeningh-Verlag.

Haggard, Patrick. 2005. Conscious intention and motor cognition. *Trends in Cognitive Science* 9 (6): 290-95.

Haggard, Patrick, and Sam Clark. 2003. Intentional action: Conscious experience and neural prediction. *Conscious Cognition* 12 (4): 695-707.

Haggard, Patrick, Sam Clark, and Jeri Kalogeras. 2002. Voluntary action and conscious awareness. *Nature Neuroscience* 5 (4): 382-85.

Haggard, Patrick, and Martin Eimer. 1999. On the relation between brain potentials and the awareness of voluntary movements. *Experimental Brain Research* 126 (1): 128-33.

Haggard, Patrick, and Helen Johnson. 2001. Attention and awareness: Attended and unattended stimuli enter conscious awareness at similar times. In *Action and visuospatial attention*, ed. Peter H. Weiss. Julich, Germany: FSZ.

———. 2003. Experiences of voluntary action. *Journal of Consciousness Studies* 10 (9-10): 72- 84.

Haggard, Patrick, and Benjamin Libet. 2001. Conscious intention and brain activity. *Journal of Consciousness Studies* 8 (11): 47-63.

Haggard, Patrick, Chris Newman, and Elena Magno. 1999. On the perceived time of voluntary actions. *British Journal of Psychology* 90:291-303.

Haji, Ishtiyaque. 1999. Moral anchors and control. *Canadian Journal of Philosophy* 29:175- 203.

———. 2002a. Compatibilist views of freedom and responsibility. In *The Oxford handbook of free will*, ed. Robert Kane, 203-26. Oxford: Oxford University Press.

———. 2002b. *Deontic morality and control*. Cambridge: Cambridge University Press.

Hallett, Mark. 2007. Volitional control of movement: The physiology of free will. *Clinical Neurophysiology* 118 (6): 1179-92.

Harris, Paul L., Tim German, and Patrick Mills. 1996. Children's use of counterfactual thinking in causal reasoning. *Cognition* 61:233-59.

Hasker, William. 1999. *The emergent self*. Ithaca: Cornell University Press.

Hebb, Donald O. 1949. *Organization of behavior*. New York: Wiley.

Heil, John, and Alfred R. Mele, ed. 1995. *Mental causation*. New York: Oxford University Press.

Held, Richard. 1961. Exposure-history as a factor in maintaining stability of perception and coordination. *Journal of Nervous and Mental Disease* 132:26-32.

Held, Richard, and Alan Hein. 1963. Movements-produced stimulation of the development of visually-guided behavior. *Journal of Comparative Physiological Psychology* 56:872-76.

Hilgard, Ernest R. 1965. *Hypnotic susceptibility*. New York: Harcourt, Brace & World.

Hobbes, Thomas. 1654. *The English works of Thomas Hobbes, Vol. 5*. Ed. William Molesworth. London: Scientia Aalen, 1962.

Hodgson, David. 1991. *The mind matters*. Oxford: Clarendon Press.

———. 2002. Quantum physics, consciousness, and free will. In *The Oxford handbook of free will*, ed. Robert Kane, 85-110. New York: Oxford University Press.

———. 2005. A plain person's free will. *Journal of Consciousness Studies* 12 (1): 1-19, with commentaries at 20-75.

———. 2007. Why I (still) believe in free will and responsibility. http://users.tpg.com.au/raeda/website/why.htm. Edited version published under the title Partly Free in *Times Literary Supplement*, July 6, 2007.

———. 2008. A role for consciousness. *Philosophy Now* 65:22-24.

Hoffman, Ralph. 1986. Verbal hallucinations and language production processes in schizophrenia. *Behavioral and Brain Sciences* 9:503-48.

Holland, Peter. 1993. *The quantum theory of motion: An account of the de Broglie-Bohm causal interpretation of quantum mechanics*. Cambridge: Cambridge University Press.

Honderich, Ted, ed. 1973. *Essays on freedom of action*. London: Routledge & Kegan Paul.

———. 1988. *A theory of determinism, Vols. 1-2*. Oxford: Oxford University Press.

———. 2002a. *How free are you?: The determinism problem*. 2nd ed. Oxford: Oxford University Press.

———. 2002b. Determinism as true, compatibilism and incompatibilism as false, and the real problem. In *The Oxford handbook of free will*, ed. Robert Kane, 461-76. New York: Oxford University Press.

Hook, Sidney, ed. 1958. *Determinism and freedom in the age of modern science*. New York: Collier-Macmillan.

———. 1959. *Psychoanalysis scientific method and philosophy*. New York: New York University Press.

Horgan, Terence, John Tienson, and George Graham. 2003. The phenomenology of first-person agency. In *Physicalism and mental causation*, ed. Sven Walter and Heinz-Dieter Heckmann, 323-40. Exeter, UK: Imprint Academic.

Hospers, John. 1950a. Meaning and free will. *Philosophy and Phenomenological Research* 10 (3): 307-30. Reprinted in *Introduction to philosophy: Classical and contemporary readings*, 3rd ed., ed. Louis Pojman, 388-97. New York: Oxford University Press.

———. 1950b. Free will and psychoanalysis. *Philosophy and Phenomenological Research* 20. Reprinted in *Readings in ethical theory*, ed. Wilfrid Sellars and John Hospers, 560-75. New York: Appleton-Century-Crofts, 1952.

———. 1953. *An introduction to philosophical analysis*. Englewood Cliffs, NJ: Prentice-Hall.

———. 1958. What means this freedom? In *Determinism and freedom in the age of modern science*, ed. Sidney Hook, 126-42. New York: Collier Books.

Hume, David. 1739. *A treatise of human nature*. Ed. L.A. Selby-Bigge. Oxford: Clarendon Press, 1960.

———. 1743. *An enquiry concerning human understanding*. Ed. L.A. Selby-Bigge. Oxford: Clarendon Press, 1955.

Hunt, David. 2000. Moral responsibility and avoidable action. *Philosophical Studies* 97:195-227.

Huxley, Thomas. 1898. *Method and result: Essays by Thomas H. Huxley.* New York: D. Appleton and Company.

Inouye, Tsuyoshi, and Akira Shimizu. 1970. The electromyographic study of verbal hallucination. *Journal of Nervous and Mental Disease* 151:415-22.

Jack, Anthony Ian, and Andreas Roepstorff. 2002. Introspection and cognitive brain mapping: From stimulus-response to script-report. *Trends in Cognitive Science* 6 (8): 333-39.

Jack, Anthony Ian, and Tim Shallice. 2001. Introspective physicalism as an approach to the science of consciousness. *Cognition* 79: 161-96.

Jahn, Reinhard, and Thomas C. Sudhof. 1994. Synaptic vesicles and exocytosis. *Annual Review of Neuroscience* 17:219-46.

James, William. 1884. The dilemma of determinism. *Unitarian Review.* Reprinted in *The will to believe and other essays in popular philosophy,* 145-83. New York: Dover, 1956.

———. 1890/1918. *The principles of psychology.* New York: Dover.

Jarrett, Christian. 2008. Mind wide open. *Psychologist* 21 (4): 294-97.

Jaspers, Karl. 1913. *Allgemeine psychopathologie.* Berlin: Springer.

———. 1963. *General psychopathology.* Manchester: Manchester University Press.

Jeannerod, Marc. 1994. The representing brain: Neural correlates of motor intention and imaginery. *Behavioral and Brain Science* 17:187-202.

———. 1997. *The cognitive neuroscience of action.* Oxford: Blackwell.

———. 1999. The 25th Bartlett lecture: To act or not to act: Perspectives on the representation of action. *Quarterly Journal of Experimental Psychology Section A* 52 (1): 1-29.

———. 2006. Consciousness of action as an embodied consciousness. In *Does consciousness cause behavior?* ed. Susan Pockett, William P. Banks, and Shaun Gallagher, 25-38. Cambridge, MA: MIT Press.

Jeannerod, Marc, Chloe Farrer, Nicolas Franck, Pierre Fourneret, Andres Posada, Elena Daprati, and Nicolas Georgieff. 2003. Action recognition in normal and schizophrenic subjects. In *The self in neuroscience and psychiatry,* ed. Tilo Kircher and Anthony David, 380-406. Cambridge, UK: Cambridge University Press.

Johnson, Susan. 2000. The recognition of mentalistic agents in infancy. *Trends in Cognitive Science* 4:22-28.

Johnson, Susan, Amy Booth, and Kirsten O'Hearn. 2001. Inferring the goals of a non-human agent. *Cognitive Development* 16:637-56.

Johnson, Susan, Virginia Slaughter, and Susan Carey. 1998. Whose gaze will infants follow? Features that elicit gaze-following in 12-month-olds. *Developmental Science* 1:233-38.

Kahneman, Daniel. 1973. *Attention and effort.* Englewood Cliffs, NJ: Prentice-Hall.

Kane, Robert. 1985. *Free will and values.* Albany: SUNY Press.

———. 1989. Two kinds of incompatibilism. *Philosophical and Phenomenological Research* 50:219-54.

———. 1995. Acts, patterns, and self-control. *Behavioral and Brain Sciences* 18:131-32.

———. 1996. *The significance of free will.* New York: Oxford University Press.

———. 1999. Responsibility, luck, and chance: Reflections on free will and indeterminism. *Journal of Philosophy* 96: 217-40. Reprinted in *Agency and responsibility: Essays on the metaphysics of freedom,* ed. Laura Ekstrom, 158-82. Boulder, CO: Westview, 2001.

———. 2002a. Introduction: The contours of contemporary free will debates. In *The Oxford handbook of free will,* ed. Kane, 3-41. New York: Oxford University Press.

———. 2002b. Some neglected pathways in the free will labyrinth. In *The Oxford handbook of free will,* ed. Kane, 406-37. New York: Oxford University Press.

———. 2002c. Free will: New directions for an ancient problem. In *Free Will,* ed. Kane, 222-48. Malden, MA: Blackwell.

———. ed. 2002d. *Free will.* Malden, MA: Blackwell.

Kant, Immanuel. 1781. *Critique of pure reason.* Trans. by Norman Kemp Smith. New York: St. Martin's Press, 1965.

―――. 1788. *Critique of practical reason (The Cambridge edition of the works of Immanuel Kant: Practical philosophy).* Trans. by Mary Gregor. Cambridge: Cambridge University Press, 1996.

Kaplan, David. 1989. Demonstratives. In *Themes from Kaplan,* ed. Joseph Almog, John Perry, and Howard Wettstein, 481-563. New York: Oxford University Press.

Kaplan, Leonard. 2006. Truth and/or consequences: Neuroscience and criminal responsibility. In *Does consciousness cause behavior?* ed. Susan Pockett, William P. Banks, and Shaun Gallagher, 277-99. Cambridge, MA: MIT Press.

Kay, Aaron C., S. Christian Wheeler, John A. Bargh, and Lee Ross. 2004. Material priming: The influence of mundane physical objects on situational construal and competitive behavioral choice. *Organisational Behaviour and Human Decision Processes* 95:83-96.

Kelley, Harold H. 1972. Attribution in social interaction. In *Attribution: Perceiving the causes of behavior,* ed. Edward E. Jones, David E. Kanouse, Harold H. Kelley, Richard E. Nisbett Stuart Valins, and Bernard Weiner, 1-26. Morristown, NJ: General Learning Press.

Kenny, Anthony. 1978. *Free will and responsibility.* London: Routledge & Kegan Paul.

Kim, Jaegwon. 1979. Causality, identity, and supervenience in the mind-body problem. In *Midwest studies in philosophy, Vol. IV,* ed. Peter A. French, Theodore E. Uehling, Jr., and Howard K. Wettstein, 31-50. Minneapolis: University of Minnesota Press.

―――. 1984a. Epiphenomenal and supervenient causation. *Midwest Studies in Philosophy* 9:257-70. Reprinted in *Supervenience and mind,* Kim, 1993b.

―――. 1984b. Concepts of supervenience. *Philosophy and Phenomenological Research* 9:153-76. Reprinted in *Supervenience and mind,* Kim, 1993b.

―――. 1987. 'Strong' and 'global' supervenience revisited. *Philosophy and Phenomenological Research* 48:315-26. Reprinted in *Supervenience and mind,* Kim, 1993b.

―――. 1989. The myth of nonreductive materialism. *Proceedings and Addresses of the American Philosophical Association* 63:31-47. Reprinted in *Supervenience and mind,* Kim, 1993b.

―――. 1990. Supervenience as a philosophical concept. *Metaphilosophy* 21:1-27. Reprinted in *Supervenience and mind,* Kim, 1993b.

―――. 1991. Dretske on how reasons explain behavior. In *Dretske and his critics,* ed. Brian McLaughlin, 52-72. Oxford: Basil Blackwell. Reprinted in *Supervenience and mind,* Kim, 1993b.

―――. 1992. 'Downward causation' in emergentism and nonreductive materialism. In *Emergence or reduction,* ed. Ansgar Beckermann, Hans Flohr, and Jaegwon Kim, 119-38. Berlin: De Gruyter.

―――. 1993a. The nonreductivist's troubles with mental causation. In *Mental causation,* ed. John Heil and Alfred R. Mele, 189-210. Oxford: Clarendon Press. Reprinted in *Supervenience and mind,* Kim, 1993b.

―――. 1993b. *Supervenience and mind: Selected philosophical essays.* Cambridge: Cambridge University Press.

―――. 1996. *Philosophy of mind.* Colorado: Westview Press.

―――. 1997. The mind-body problem: Taking stock after 40 years. *Philosophical Perspectives* 11:185-207.

―――. 1998. *Mind in a physical world.* Cambridge, MA: MIT Press/Bradford Books.

―――. 1999. Making sense of emergence. *Philosophical Studies* 95:3-36.

―――. 2005. *Physicalism, or something near enough.* Princeton, NJ: Princeton University Press.

Kircher, Tilo, and Dirk Leube. 2003. Self-consciousness, self-agency, and schizophrenia. *Consciousness and Cognition* 12:656-69.

Klein, Martha. 1990. *Determinism, blameworthiness and deprivation.* Oxford: Oxford University Press.

Knobe, Joshua, and Shaun Nichols, eds. 2008. *Experimental philosophy.* Oxford: Oxford University Press.

Knoblich, Günther, Frank Stottmeister, and Tilo Kircher. 2004. Self-monitoring in patients with schizophrenia. *Psychological Medicine* 34:1561-69.

Koestler, Arthur. 1978. *Janus: A summing up*. New York: Random House.

Kornhuber, Hans H., and Lüder Deecke. 1965. Hirnpotentialänderungen bei willkürbewegungen und passiven bewegungen des menschen: Bereitschaftspotential und reafferente potentiale. *Pflügers Arch* 284:1-17.

Kriegel, Uriah. 2009. *Subjective consciousness: A self-representational theory*. New York: Oxford University Press.

Kühn, Simone, and Marcel Brass. 2009. Retrospective construction of the judgment of free choice. *Consciousness and Cognition* 18:12-21.

Lackner, J.R., and M.F. Garrett. 1972. Resolving ambiguity: Effects of biasing context in the unattended ear. *Cognition* 1 (4): 359-72.

Lamb, James. 1977. On a proof of incompatibilism. *The Philosophical Review* 86:20-35.

———. 1993. Evaluative compatibilism and the principle of alternative possibilities. *Journal of Philosophy* 90:517-27.

Lambie, John A., and Anthony J. Marcel. 2002. Consciousness and the varieties of emotion experience: A theoretical framework. *Psychological Review* 109:219-59.

Lamont, Corliss. 1967. *Freedom of choice affirmed*. New York: Horizon.

Laplace, Pierre Simon. 1814. *A philosophical essay on probabilities*. Trans. from the 6th French ed. by Frederick Wilson Truscott and Frederick Lincoln Emory. New York: Dover, 1951.

Lau, Hakwan. 2007. A higher order Bayesian decision theory of consciousness. *Progress in Brain Research* 168:35-48.

———. 2010. Theoretical motivations for investigating the neural correlates of consciousness. *WIREs Cognitive Science* 2 (1): 1-7.

Lau, Hakwan, and David M. Rosenthal. 2011. Empirical support for higher-order theories of conscious awareness. *Trends in Cognitive Science* 15 (8): 365-73.

LeDoux, Joseph. 1996. *The emotional brain: The mysterious underpinnings of emotional life*. New York: Simon and Schuster.

Lehrer, Keith. 1960. Can we know that we have free will by introspection? *Journal of Philosophy* 56:145-57.

———. 1964. 'Could' and determinism. *Analysis* 24:159-60.

———. 1966. An empirical disproof of determinism. In *Freedom and determinism*, ed. Keith Lehrer, 175-202. New York: Random House.

———. 1968. Cans without ifs. *Analysis* 29 (1): 29-32.

———. 1976. 'Can' in theory and practice: A possible worlds analysis. In *Action theory*, ed. Myles Brand and Douglas Walton, 67-97. Dordrecht: D. Reidel.

———. 1980. Preferences, conditionals and freedom. In *Time and cause: Essays presented to Richard Taylor*, ed. Peter van Inwagen, 76-96. Dordrecht: D. Reidel.

Leibniz, Gottfried Wilhelm. 1898. *The monadology and other philosophical writings*. Trans. Robert Latta. London: Oxford University Press.

Lerner, Jennifer S., Deborah A. Small, and George Loewenstein. 2004. Heart strings and purse strings: Carryover effects of emotions on economic decisions. *Psychological Science* 15:337-41.

Levin, Michael. 1979. *Metaphysics and the mind-body problem*. Oxford: Oxford University Press.

———. 2004. A compatibilist defense of moral responsibility. In *Introduction to philosophy: classical and contemporary readings*, 3rd ed., ed. Louis P. Pojman, 425-36. New York: Oxford University Press.

———. 2007. Compatibilism and special relativity. *Journal of Philosophy* 104 (9): 433-63.

Levine, Lindsay R., Ezequiel Morsella, and John A. Bargh. 2007. The perversity of inanimate objects: Stimulus control by incidental musical notation. *Social Cognition* 25 (2): 267-83.

Lewis, David. 1966. An argument for the identity theory. *Journal of Philosophy* 63:17-25.

———. 1972. Psychophysical and theoretical identification. *Australian Journal of Philosophy* 50:249-58.

———. 1980. Mad pain and Martian pain. In *Readings in philosophy of psychology, Vol. 1*, ed. Ned Block, 216-23. Cambridge: Harvard University Press.

———. 1981. Are we free to break the laws? *Theoria* 47:113-21. Reprinted in *Philosophical Papers, Vol. II*, Lewis. Oxford: Oxford University Press.

———. 1995. Should a materialist believe in qualia? *The Australian Journal of Philosophy* 73:140-4.

Libet, Benjamin. 1979. Subjective referral of the timing for a conscious sensory experience. *Brain* 102:193-224.

———. 1981. The experimental evidence for subjective referral of a sensory experience backwards in time: Reply to P.S. Churchland. *Philosophy of Science* 48:182-97.

———. 1985. Unconscious cerebral initiative and the role of conscious will in voluntary action. *Behavioral and Brain Science* 8:529-66.

———. 1987. Are the mental experiences of will and self-control significant for performance of a voluntary act? *Behavioral and Brain Science* 10:783-91.

———. 1989. Conscious subjective experience vs. unconscious mental functions: A theory of cerebral processes involved. In *Models of brain function*, ed. Rodney M.J. Cotterill, 35-50. New York: Cambridge University Press.

———. 1992. The neural time-factor in perception, volition and free will. *Revue de Metaphsique et de Morale* 2:255-72.

———. 1993. The neural time factor in consciousness and unconscious events. In *Experimental and theoretical studies of consciousness* (Ciba Foundation Symposium), 123-36. London: John Wiley and Sons.

———. 1994. A testable field theory of mind-brain interaction. *Journal of Consciousness Studies* 1:119-26.

———. 1996. Neural time factors in conscious and unconscious mental functions. In *Toward a science of consciousness*, ed. Stuart Hameroff , Alfred Kaszniak, and Alwyn Scott, 156-71. Cambridge, MA: MIT Press.

———. 1999. Do we have free will? *Journal of Consciousness Studies* 6 (8-9): 47-57. Reprinted in *The Oxford handbook of free will*, ed. Robert Kane, 551-64. New York: Oxford University Press, 2002.

———. 2001. Consciousness, free action and the brain. *Journal of Consciousness Studies* 8 (8): 59-65.

———. 2002. The timing of mental events: Libet's experimental findings and their implications. *Consciousness and Cognition* 11:291-99.

———. 2006. The timing of brain events: Reply to the 'Special Section' in this journal of September 2004, ed. Susan Pockett. *Consciousness and Cognition* 15:540-47.

Libet, Benjamin, Anthony Freeman, and Keith Sutherland, eds. 1999. *The volitional brain: Toward a neuroscience of free will*. Thorverten, UK: Imprint Academic.

Libet, Benjamin, Curtis A. Gleason, Elwood W. Wright, and Dennis K. Pearl. 1983. Time of conscious intention to act in relation to onset of cerebral activity (readiness-potential): The unconscious initiation of a freely voluntary act. *Brain* 106:623-42.

Libet, Benjamin, Dennis K. Pearl, David E. Morledge, Curtis A. Gleason, Yoshio Hosobuchi, and Nicholas M. Barbaro. 1991. Control of the transition from sensory detection to sensory awareness in men by the duration of a thalamic stimulus. The cerebral time-on factor. *Brain* 114:1731-57.

Libet, Benjamin, Elwood W. Wright, Curtis A. Gleason. 1982. Readiness-potentials preceding unrestricted 'spontaneous' vs. pre-planned voluntary acts. *Electroencephalogr Clin Neurophysiology* 54 (3): 322-35.

Lieberman, David A. 1979. Behaviorism and the mind: A (limited) call for a return to introspection. *American Psychologist* 34:319-33.

Llinas, Rodolfo, and Urs Ribary. 1993. Coherent 40-Hz oscillation characterizes dream state in humans. *Proceedings of the National Academy of Sciences USA* 90:2078-81.

Locke, Edwin A., and Amy L. Kristof. 1996. Volitional choices in the goal achievement process. In *The psychology of action: Linking cognition and motivation to behavior*, ed. Peter M. Gollwitzer and John A. Bargh, 365-84. New York: Guilford Press.

Locke, Edwin A., and Gary P. Latham. 1990. *A theory of goal setting and task performance.* Englewood Cliffs, NJ: Prentice-Hall.

Locke, John. 1689. *An essay concerning human understanding.* Ed. Alexander Campbell Fraser. New York: Dover, 1959.

Lycan, William. 1987. *Consciousness.* Cambridge, MA: Bradford Books/The MIT press.

———. 1990. Consciousness as internal monitoring. In *Philosophical perspectives, Vol. 9,* ed. James Tomberlin, 1-14. Atascadero: Ridgeview.

———. 1996. *Consciousness and experience.* Cambridge, MA: Bradford Books/The MIT Press.

MacKay, Donald G. 1973. Aspects of a theory of comprehension, memory and attention. *Quarterly Journal of Experimental Psychology* 25:22-40.

Macrae, C. Neil, Galen V. Bodenhausen, Alan B. Milne, Luigi Castelli, Astrid M. Schloerscheidt, and Sasha Greco. 1998. On activating exemplars. *Journal of Experimental Social Psychology* 34:330-54.

Macrae, C. Neil, and Lucy Johnston. 1998. Help, I need somebody: Automatic action and inaction. *Social Cognition* 16:400.

Malenka, Robert C., Ronald W. Angel, Bethany Hampton, and Philip A. Berger. 1982. Impaired central error-correcting behavior in schizophrenia. *Archives of General Psychiatry* 39:101-7.

Malcolm, Norman. 1968. The conceivability of mechanism. *Philosophical Review* 77:45-72.

Mandler, George. 1975. *Mind and emotion.* New York: Wiley.

———. 1985. *Cognitive psychology: An essay in cognitive science.* Hillsdale: Lawrence Erlbaum Associates.

Manschreck, Theo C. 1986. Motor abnormalities in schizophrenia. In *Handbook of schizophrenia, Vol. 1: The neurology of schizophrenia,* ed. Henry A. Nasrallah and D.R. Weinberger, 65-96. Amsterdam: Elsevier.

Marcel, Anthony J. 1983. Conscious and unconscious perception: Experiments on visual masking and word recognition. *Cognitive Psychology* 15:197-237.

———. 2003. Introspective report: Trust, self-knowledge and science. *Journal of Consciousness Studies* 10 (9-10): 167-86.

———. 2005. The sense of agency: Awareness and ownership of actions and intentions. In *Agency and self-awareness,* ed. Johannes Roessler and Naomi Eilan. Oxford: Oxford University Press.

Marcel, Anthony J., and E. Bisiach, eds. 1988. *Consciousness in contemporary science.* Oxford: Clarendon Press.

Matson, Wallace. 1987. *A new history of philosophy, Vol. 1.* New York: Harcourt, Brace, Jovanovich.

Matsuhashi, Masao, and Mark Hallett. 2006. The timing of conscious thought into action. *Clinical Neurophysiology* 117 (suppl. 1): S96.

———. 2008. The timing of the conscious intention to move. *European Journal of Neuroscience* 28:2344-51.

Matthews, Gary. 1996. Neurotransmitter release. *Annual Review of Neuroscience* 19:219-33.

McCann, Hugh. 1998. *The works of agency: On human action, will and freedom.* Ithaca: Cornell University Press.

McClure, John. 1998. Discounting causes of behavior: Are two reasons better than one? *Journal of Personality and Social Psychology* 74:7-20.

McGuire, Philip K., G.M.S. Shah, and Robin M. Murray. 1993. Increased blood flow in Broca's area during auditory hallucination in schizophrenia. *Lancet* 342:703-6.

McKenna, Michael. 2003. Robustness, control, and demand for morally significant alternatives: Frankfurt examples with oodles and oodles of alternatives. In *Moral responsibility and alternative possibilities: Essays on the importance of alternative possibilities,* ed. David Widerker and M. McKenna, 201-18. Burlington, VT: Ashgate Publishing.

Mele, Alfred R. 2009. *Effective intentions: The power of conscious will.* Oxford: Oxford University Press.

Mellor, C.S. 1970. First rank symptoms of schizophrenia. *British Journal of Psychiatry* 117:15-23.

Meltzoff, Andrew N. 1995. Understanding the intentions of others: Re-enactment of intended acts by 18-month-old children. *Developmental Psychology* 31:838-50.

Melzack, Ronald, and Warren S. Torgerson. 1971. On the language of pain. *Anesthesiology* 34:50-59.

Metzinger, Thomas, ed. 1995. *Conscious experience.* Paderborn: Ferdinand Schoningh.

Mill, John Stuart. 1860. *On liberty.* Oxford: Blackwell, 1947.

———. 1865. *An examination of Sir William Hamilton's philosophy.* Ed. John M. Robson. Toronto: Routledge & Kegan Paul, 1979.

Miller, George. 1956. The magical number seven, plus or minus two: Some limits on our capacity for processing information. *Psychological Review* 63:81-97.

Mischel, Walter. 1973. Toward a cognitive social learning reconceptualization of personality. *Psychological Review* 80:252-83.

Mlakar, Janez, Jose Jensterle, and Christopher D. Frith. 1994. Central monitoring deficiency and schizophrenic symptoms. *Psychological Medicine* 24:557-64.

Monterosso, John, Edward B. Royzman, and Barry Schwartz. 2005. Explaining away responsibility: Effects of scientific explanation on perceiving culpability. *Ethics and Behavior* 15 (2): 139-58.

Moore, G.E. 1912. Free will. In *Ethics,* Moore, 84-95. Oxford: Oxford University Press.

Moskowitz, Gordon B., Peter M. Gollwitzer, Wolfgand Wasel, and Bernd Schaal. 1999. Preconscious control of stereotype activation through chronic egalitarian goals. *Journal of Personality and Social Psychology* 77:167-84

Muraven, Mark, and Roy F. Baumeister. 2000. Self-regulation and depletion of limited resources: Does self-control resemble a muscle? *Psychological Bulletin* 126: 247-59.

Muraven, Mark, Dianne M. Tice, and Roy F. Baumeister. 1998. Self-control as limited resource: Regulatory depletion patterns. *Journal of Personality and Social Psychology* 74: 774-89.

Nagel, Thomas. 1974. What is it like to be a bat? *Philosophical Review* 83 (4): 435-50. Reprinted in *Mortal Questions,* Nagel. Cambridge: Cambridge University Press, 1979.

———. 1986. *The view from nowhere.* New York: Oxford University Press.

Nahmias, Eddy, Stephen Morris, Thomas Nadelhoffer, and Jason Turner. 2004. The phenomenology of free will. *Journal of Consciousness Studies* 11 (7-8): 162-79.

———. 2006. Is incompatibilism intuitive? *Philosophy and Phenomenological Research* 73 (1): 28-53. Reprinted in *Experimental philosophy,* ed. Shaun Nichols and Joshua Knobe, 81-104. Oxford: Oxford University Press, 2008.

Neely, Wright. 1974. Freedom and desire. *Philosophical Review* 83:32-54.

Neisser, Ulric. 1967. *Cognitive psychology.* Englewood Cliffs, NJ: Prentice-Hall.

Nichols, Shaun. 2004. The folk psychology of free will: Fits and starts. *Mind and Language* 19 (5): 473-502.

———. 2006a. Folk intuitions on free will. *Journal of Cognition and Culture* 6 (1-2): 57-86.

———. 2006b. Free will and the folk: Responses to commentators. *Journal of Cognition and Culture* 6:305-20.

———. 2008. How can psychology contribute to the free will debate? In *Are we free? Psychology and free will,* ed. John Baer, James C. Kaufman, and Roy F. Baumeister, 10-31. New York: Oxford University Press.

Nichols, Shaun, and Joshua Knobe. 2007. Moral responsibility and determinism: The cognitive science of folk intuitions. *Nous* 41: 663-85. Reprinted in Knobe and Nichols 2008, 105-26.

Nielsen, Kai. 1971. *Reason and practice: A modern introduction to philosophy.* New York: Harper & Row.

Nietzsche, Friedrich. 1914. *Beyond good and evil: Prelude to a philosophy of the future.* London: T.N. Foulis.

Nisbett, Richard E., and Lee Ross. 1980. *Human inference: Strategies and shortcomings of social judgment.* Englewood Cliffs, NJ: Prentice-Hall.

Nisbett, Richard E., and Timothy D. Wilson. 1977. Telling more than we can know: Verbal reports on mental processes. *Psychological Review* 84:231-59.

Novemsky, Nathan, Jing Wang, Ravi Dhar, and Roy F. Baumeister. 2007. The interaction of ego-depletion and choice. Manuscript submitted for publication.

Nozick, Robert. 1981. *Philosophical explanations.* Cambridge, MA: Harvard University Press.

Obhi, Sukhvinder S., and Patrick Haggard. 2004. Free will and free won't: Motor activity in the brain precedes our awareness of the intention to move, so how is it that we perceive control? *American Scientist* 92 (July-August): 358-65.

O'Connor, Timothy. 1994. Thomas Reid on free agency. *Journal of the History of Philosophy* 32:605-22.

———. 1995a. Introduction. In *Agents, causes and events: Essays on free will and indeterminism,* ed. Timothy O'Connor, 3-12. Oxford: Oxford University Press.

———. 1995b. Agent causation. In *Agents, causes and events: Essays on free will and indeterminism,* ed. Timothy O'Connor, 173-200. Oxford: Oxford University Press.

———. 1996. Why agent causation? *Philosophical Topics* 24:143-58.

———. 2000. *Persons and causes: The metaphysics of free will.* New York: Oxford University Press.

———. 2002. Libertarian views: Dualist and agent-causal theories. In *The Oxford handbook of free will,* ed. Robert Kane, 337-55. New York: Oxford University Press.

Owens, D.G. Cunningham, Eve C. Johnstone, and Christopher D. Frith. 1982. Spontaneous involuntary disorders of movement. *Archives of General Psychiatry* 39:452-61.

Page, Monte M. 1969. Social psychology of a classical conditioning of attitudes experiment. *Journal of Personality and Social Psychology* 11:177-86.

Papineau, David. 2002. *Thinking about consciousness.* Oxford: Oxford University Press.

Peacocke, Christopher. 1999. *Being known.* Oxford: Clarendon Press.

Pereboom, Derk. 1995. Determinism al dente. *Nous* 29:21-45.

———. ed. 1997. *Free will.* Cambridge: Hackett Publishing.

———. 2000. The explanatory irrelevance of alternative possibilities. In *Free will,* ed. Robert Kane, 111-24. Malden, MA: Blackwell.

———. 2001. *Living without free will.* New York: Cambridge University Press.

———. 2002. Living without free will: The case for hard indeterminism. In *The Oxford handbook of free will,* ed. Robert Kane, 477-88. New York: Oxford University Press.

Perenin, M.T., and Y. Rossetti. 1996. Grasping without form discrimination in a hemianopic field. *Neuroreport* 7:793-97.

Perez-Alvarez, Marino. 2008. Hyperreflexivity as a condition of mental disorder: A clinical and historical perspective. *Psicothema* 20 (2): 181-87.

Perlovsky, Leonid. 2010. Consciousness: A scientific possibility of free will. Cognitive science and mathematical models of the mind. *Sci Topics.* http://www.scitopics.com/Conscious-ness_a_scientific_possibility_of_free_will_Cognitive_science_and_mathematical_models_of_the_mind.html

Perry, John. 1979. The problem of the essential indexical. *Nous* 13 (1): 3-21.

———. 2010. Wretched subterfuge: A defense of the compatibilism of freedom and natural causation. *Proceedings and Addresses of the American Philosophical Association* 84 (2): 93-113.

Pettit, Philip. 2001. *A theory of freedom: From the psychology to the politics of agency.* Cambridge: Polity Press.

Pink, Thomas. 2004. *Free will: A very short introduction.* Oxford: Oxford University Press.

———. 2009. Free will and consciousness. In *The Oxford companion to consciousness,* ed. Timothy Bayne, Axel Cleeremans, and Patrick Wilken, 296-300. New York: Oxford University Press.

Pinker, Steven. 2002. *The blank slate: The modern denial of human nature.* New York: Viking.

Pockett, Sue. 2004. Hypnosis and the death of "subjective backwards referral." *Consciousness and Cognition* 13:621-25.

———. 2006. The neuroscience of movement. In *Does consciousness cause behavior?*, ed. Susan Pockett, William P. Banks, and Shaun Gallagher, 9-24. Cambridge, MA: MIT Press.

Pockett, Susan, William P. Banks, and Shaun Gallagher, eds. 2006. *Does consciousness cause behavior?* Cambridge, MA: MIT Press.

Polger, Thomas, and Owen Flanagan. 1999. Explaining the evolution of consciousness: The other hard problem (presented at *Toward a Science of Consciousness II*, April 1996, Tucson, Arizona). Online version, 1999. http://homepages.uc.edu/~polgertw/Polger-SSPP1997.pdf

Popper, Karl. 1982. *The open universe: An argument for indeterminism.* London: Hutchinson.

Popper, Karl, and John Eccles. 1977. *The self and its brain.* Berlin: Springer Verlag.

Posada, A., Nicolas Franck, Nicolas Georgieff, and Marc Jeannerod. 2003. Anticipating incoming events: An impaired cognitive process in schizophrenia. *Cognition* 81:209-26.

Posner, Michael, and Charles R.R. Snyder. 1975. Attention and cognitive control. In *Information processing and cognition: The Loyola symposium*, ed. Robert Solso, 205-23. New York: Psychology Press.

Priestley, Joseph. 1788. *A free discussion of the doctrines of materialism and philosophical necessity: In a correspondence between Dr. Price and Dr. Priestly.* London. Reprinted in *Priestly's writings on philosophy, science, and politics*, Joseph Priestly, ed. John Passmore. New York: Collier, 1965.

Preston, Jesse, and Daniel M. Wegner. 2005. Ideal agency: On perceiving the self as an origin of action. In *On building, defending, and regulating the self*, ed. Abraham Tesser, Joanne V. Wood, and Diederik A. Stapel, 103-25. Philadelphia, PA: Psychology Press.

Prinz, Wolfgang. 1997. Explaining voluntary action: The role of mental content. In *Mindscapes: Philosophy, science, and the mind*, ed. Martin Carrier and Peter K. Machamer, 153-75. Pittsburgh, PA: University of Pittsburgh Press.

Ravizza, Mark. 1994. Semi-compatibilism and the transfer of non-responsibility. *Philosophical Studies* 75:61-94.

Raz, Joseph. 2006. *Engaging reason: On the theory of value and action.* Oxford: Oxford University Press.

Reid, Thomas. 1788. *Essays on the active powers of the human mind.* Cambridge, MA: MIT Press, 1969.

———. 1895. *The works of Thomas Reid, D.D., Vols. 1 & 2.* 8th ed. Ed. Sir William Hamilton, Edinburg: James Thin. Reprinted with an introduction by H.M. Bracken. Hildeshein: George Olms Verlag, 1967.

Ridley, Matt. 2003. *Nature via nurture: Genes, experience, and what makes us human.* New York: HarperCollins.

Roediger III, Henry L., Michael K. Goode, and Frank M. Zaromb. 2008. Free will and the control of action. In *Are we free? Psychology and free will*, ed. John Baer, James Kaufman, and Roy F. Baumeister, 205-25. New York: Oxford University Press.

Rolls, Edmund T. 1999. *The brain and emotion.* Oxford: Oxford University Press.

———. 2004. A higher order syntactic thought (HOST) theory of consciousness. In *Higher-order theories of consciousness*, ed. Rocco J. Gennaro. Amsterdam & Philadelphia: John Benjamins.

———. 2005. *Emotion explained.* Oxford: Oxford University Press.

Romanes, G.J. 1895. *Mind and motion and monism.* Longmans, Green & Co.

Rosenthal, David M. 1984. Armstrong's causal theory of mind. In *Profiles: David Armstrong*, ed. Radu Bogdan, 79-120. Dordrecht: D. Reidel Pub. Co.

————. 1986. Two concepts of consciousness. *Philosophical Studies* 49 (3): 329-59. Reprinted (with minor revisions) in Rosenthal 2005a, 21-45. All references to reprinted version.

————. 1991a. The independence of consciousness and sensory quality. In *Consciousness: philosophical issues 1*, ed. Enrique Villanueva, 15-36. Atascadero, CA: Ridgeview Pub. Co. Reprinted in Rosenthal 2005a, 135-48.

————. ed. 1991b. *The nature of mind*. New York: Oxford University Press.

————. 1993a. Higher-order thought and the appendage theory of consciousness. *Philosophical Psychology* 6 (2): 155-67.

————. 1993b. Multiple drafts and higher-order thoughts. *Philosophy and Phenomenological Research* 53 (4): 911-18.

————. 1993c. State consciousness and transitive consciousness. *Consciousness and Cognition* 2 (4): 355-63.

————. 1993d. Thinking that one thinks. In *Consciousness*, ed. Martin Davies and Glyn W. Humphreys, 197-223. Oxford: Basil Blackwell. Reprinted in Rosenthal 2005a, 46-70.

————. 1994. The identity theory. In *A companion to the philosophy of mind*, ed. Samuel Guttenplan, 348-55. Oxford: Basil Blackwell.

————. 1997. A theory of consciousness. In *The nature of consciousness: Philosophical debates*, ed. Ned Block, Owen Flanagan, and Guven Guzeldere, 729-54. Cambridge, MA: MIT Press.

————. 2001. Introspection and self-interpretation. *Philosophical Topics* 28 (2): 201-33. Reprinted in Rosenthal 2005a, 103-31. All references to reprinted version.

————. 2002a. The timing of conscious states. *Consciousness and Cognition* 11 (2): 215-20.

————. 2002b. Persons, minds, and consciousness. In *The philosophy of Marjorie Grene*, ed. Randall E. Auxier and Lewis E. Hahn, 199-220. Chicago: Open Court.

————. 2002c. Consciousness and mind. *The Jerusalem Philosophical Quarterly* 51 (July): 227- 51.

————. 2002d. Explain consciousness. In *Philosophy of mind: Classical and contemporary readings*, ed. David Chalmers, 406-21. New York: Oxford University Press.

————. 2003. Unity of consciousness and the self. *Proceedings of the Aristotelian Society* 103 (3): 325-52. Reprinted (revised and expanded) in Rosenthal 2005a, 339-63. All references to revised and expanded version.

————. 2004a. Being conscious of ourselves. *Monist* 87 (2): 161-84.

————. 2004b. Varieties of higher-order theory. In *Higher-order theories of consciousness*, ed. Rocco J. Gennaro, 17-44. Amsterdam: John Benjamins.

————. 2005a. *Consciousness and mind*. New York: Oxford University Press.

————. 2005b. Consciousness, interpretation, and higher-order thought. In *Psychoanalysis as an empirical, interdisciplinary science: Collected papers on contemporary psychoanalytic research*, 119-42. Vienna: Verlag der Vsterreichischen Akademie der Wissenschaften (Austrian Academy of Sciences Press).

————. 2008. Consciousness and its function. *Neuropsychologia* 46:829-40.

Rosenthal, Robert, and Lenore Jacobson. 1968. *Pygmalion in the classroom*. New York: Holt, Rinehart, and Winston.

Roskies, Adina, and Shaun Nichols. 2008. Bringing moral responsibility down the earth. *Journal of Philosophy* 105 (7): 1-18.

Ross, Peter. 2006. Empirical constraints on the problem of free will. In *Does consciousness cause behavior?*, ed. Susan Pockett, William P. Banks, and Shaun Gallagher, 125-44. Cambridge, MA: MIT Press.

Russell, Paul. 2002. Pessimists, pollyannas, and the new compatibilism. In *The Oxford handbook of free will*, ed. Robert Kane, 229-56. New York: Oxford University Press.

Ryle, Gilbert. 1949. *The concept of mind*. New York: Barnes & Noble.

Sacks, Oliver. 1987. *The man who mistook his wife for a hat and other clinical tales*. New York: Harper and Row.

Sanz, Angel S. 2005. A Bohmian approach to quantum fractals. *Journal of Physics A: Mathematical and General* 38:6037.

Sanz, Angel S., and F. Borondo. 2007. A quantum trajectory description of decoherence. *The European Physical Journal* 44:319-26.

Sarkissian, Hagop, Amita Chatterjee, Felipe De Brigard, Joshua Knobe, Shaun Nichols, and Smita Sirker. 2010. Is belief in free will a cultural universal? *Mind and Language* 25 (3): 346-58.

Sass, Louis A. 1992. *Madness and modernism: Insanity in the light of modern art, literature and thought*. New York: Basic Books.

———. 1998. Schizophrenia, self-consciousness and the modern mind. *Journal of Consciousness Studies* 5:543-65.

Sass, Louis A., and Josef Parnas. 2003. Schizophrenia, consciousness, and the self. *Schizophrenia Bulletin* 29 (3): 427-44.

Schacham, Saya, and Randall Daut. 1981. Anxiety or pain: What does the scale measure? *Journal of Consulting and Clinical Psychology* 49:468-69.

Schachter, Stanley, and Jerome Singer. 1962. Cognitive, social, and physiological determinates of emotional state. *Psychological Review* 69 (5): 379-99.

Schlick, Moritz. 1939. *The problems of ethics*. Authorized translation by David Rynin. New York: Prentice-Hall.

———. 1966. When is a man responsible? In *Free will and determinism*, ed. Bernard Berofsky, 54-62. New York: Harper & Row.

Schmeichel, Brandon J., Kathleen D. Vohs, and Roy F. Baumeister. 2003. Intellectual performance and ego depletion: Role of the self in logical reasoning and other information processing. *Journal of Personality and Social Psychology* 85:33-46.

Schooler, Jonathan W. 2000. Consciousness, meta-consciousness, and the role of self-report. Plenary Address, Towards a Science of Consciousness, Tucson, AZ.

———. 2001. Discovering memories of abuse in the light of meta-awareness. *Journal of Aggression, Maltreatment, and Trauma* 4:105-36.

———. 2002a. Establishing a legitimate relationship with introspection: Response to Jack and Roepstorff. *Trends in Cognitive Science* 6:372-73.

———. 2002b. Re-representing consciousness: Dissociations between consciousness and meta-consciousness. *Trends in Cognitive Science* 6:339-44.

Schooler, Jonathan W., and Charles A. Schreiber. 2004. Consciousness, meta-consciousness, and the paradox of introspection. *Journal of Consciousness Studies* 11:17-39.

Searle, John. 1990. Consciousness, explanatory inversion, and cognitive science. *Behavioral and Brain Sciences* 13:585-642.

———. 1992. *The rediscovery of the mind*. Cambridge, MA: MIT Press/Bradford Book.

———. 2000. Consciousness, free action and the brain. *Journal of Consciousness Studies* 7 (10): 3-22.

———. 2001a. *Rationality in action*. Cambridge, MA: MIT Press.

———. 2001b. Free will as a problem in neurobiology. *Philosophy* 76:491-514.

Sellars, Wilfrid. 1963. *Science, perception, and reality*. London: Humanities Press.

Shapiro, Deane H. 1982. Overview: Clinical and physiological comparison of meditation with other self-control strategies. *American Journal of Psychiatry* 139:367-74.

Shatz, David. 1985. Free will and the structure of motivation. *Midwest studies in philosophy, Vol. 19*, ed. P. French, 451-82. Minneapolis: University of Minnesota Press.

———. 1997. Irresistible goodness and alternative possibilities. In *Freedom and moral responsibility: General and Jewish perspectives*, ed. Charles H. Manekin and Menachem H. Kellner, 13-51. College Park: University of Maryland Press.

Shiffrin, Richard M., and Susan T. Dumais. 1981. The development of automatism. In *Cognitive skills and their acquisition*, ed. John R. Anderson, 111-40. Hillsdale, NJ: Lawrence Erlbaum Associates.

Shiffrin, Richard M., and Walter Schneider. 1977. Controlled and automatic human information processing: Perceptual learning, automatic attending, and a general theory. *Psychological Review* 84:127-90.

Shoemaker, Sydney. 1968. Self-reference and self-awareness. *Journal of Philosophy*. 65 (19): 555-67. Reprinted with slight revisions in *Identity, cause, and mind: Philosophical essays*, Shoemaker. Cambridge: Cambridge University Press, 1984.

———. 1986. Introspection and the self. *Midwest Studies in Philosophy* X: 101-20. Reprinted in *The first-person perspective and other essays*, Shoemaker, 3-24. New York: Cambridge University Press, 1996.

———. 1990. First-person access. *Philosophical Perspectives* 4:187-214.

Shore, David I., Charles Spence, and Raymond M. Klein. 2001. Visual prior entry. *Psychological Science* 12:205-12.

Sie, Maureen, and Arno Wouters. 2010. The BCN challenge to compatibilist free will and personal responsibility. *Neuroethics* 3 (2): 121-33.

Sirigu Angela, Elena Daprati, Sophie Ciancia, Pascal Giraux, Norbert Nighoghossian, Andres Posada, and Patrick Haggard. 2004. Altered awareness of voluntary action after damage to the parietal cortex. *Nature Neuroscience* 7:80-84.

Skinner, B.F. 1971. *Beyond freedom and dignity*. New York: Vintage Books.

Slote, Michael. 1980. Understanding free will. *Journal of Philosophy* 77:136-51.

———. 1990. Ethics without free will. *Social Theory and Practice* 16 (3): 369-83.

Smilansky, Saul. 1990. Van Inwagen on the 'obviousness' of libertarian moral responsibility. *Analysis* 50 (1): 29-33.

———. 2000. *Free will and illusion*. Oxford: Clarendon Press.

Smith, Edward E., and John Jonides. 1998. Working memory: A view from neuroimaging. *Cognitive Psychology* 33:5-42.

Smith, Eliot R., and Frederick D. Miller. 1978. Limits on perception of cognitive processes: A reply to Nisbett and Wilson. *Psychological Review* 85:355-82.

Snyder, Mark, Elizabeth D. Tanke, and Ellen Berscheid. 1977. Social perception and interpersonal behavior: On the self-fulfilling nature of social stereotypes. *Journal of Personality and Social Psychology* 35:656-66.

Söllner, Thomas, and James E. Rothman. 1994. Neurotransmission: Harnessing fusion machinery at the synapse. *Trends in Neuroscience* 17:344-48.

Sommers, Tamler. 2007. The illusion of freedom evolves. In *Distributed cognition and the will: Individual volition and social context*, ed. David Spurrett, Harold Kincaid, Don Ross, and G. Lynn Stephens, 61-75. Cambridge, MA: MIT Press.

Soon, Chun Siong, Marcel Brass, Hans-Jochen Heinze, and John-Dylan Haynes. 2008. Unconscious determinants of free decisions in the human brain. *Nature Neuroscience* 11 (5): 543-45.

Sosa, Ernest. 1984. Mind-body interaction and supervenient causation. *Midwest Studies in Philosophy* 9:271-81.

Spence, Sean A. 1996. Free will in the light of neuropsychiatry. *Philosophy, Psychiatry, and Psychology* 3 (2): 75-90.

Spencer, Steven J., Steven Fein, Connie T. Wolfe, Christina Fong, and Megan A. Duinn. 1998. Automatic activation of stereotypes: The role of self-image threat. *Personality and Social Psychology Bulletin* 24:1139-52.

Sperry, Roger. 1983. *Science and moral priority*. New York: Columbia University Press.

———. 1991. In defense of mentalism and emergent interaction. *Journal of Mind and Behavior* 12 (2): 221-46.

Staats, Peter, Hamid Hekmat, and Arthur Staats. 1998. Suggestion/placebo effects on pain: Negative as well as positive. *Journal of Pain and Symptom Management* 15 (4): 235-43.

Stace, Walter T. 1952. *Religion and the modern mind*. New York: Lippincott. An excerpt of which is reprinted in *Introduction to philosophy: Classical and contemporary readings*, 3rd ed., ed. Louis P. Pojman, 382-87. New York: Oxford University Press.

Steele, Claude. 1997. A threat in the air: How stereotypes shape intellectual identity and performance. *American Psychologist* 52 (6): 613-29.

Steele, Claude, and Joshua Aronson. 1995. Stereotype threat and the intellectual test performance of African Americans. *Journal of Personality and Social Psychology* 69 (5): 797-811.

Stephens, G. Lynn, and George Graham. 2000. *When self-consciousness breaks: Alien voices and inserted thoughts*. Cambridge, MA: MIT Press.

Sternberg, Eliezer. 2010. *My brain made me do it: The rise of neuroscience and the threat to moral responsibility*. Amherst, NY: Prometheus Books.

Sternberg, Saul, and Ronald L. Knoll. 1973. The perception of temporal order: Fundamental issues and a general model. In *Attention and performance IV*, ed. S. Kornblum. New York: Academic Press.

Stillman, T.D., E. Sparks, Roy F. Baumeister, and Dianne M. Tice. 2006. What makes freedom? Situational factors that influence ratings of free will. Manuscript in preparation.

Stirling John D., Jonathan S. Hellewell, N. Quraishi. 1998. Self-monitoring dysfunction and the schizophrenic symptoms of alien control. *Psychological Medicine* 28:675-83.

Strawson, Galen. 1986. *Freedom and belief*. Oxford: Oxford University Press.

———. 1994a. The impossibility of moral responsibility. *Philosophical Studies* 75 (1-2): 5-24.

———. 1994b. *Mental reality*. Cambridge, MA: MIT Press.

———. 2000. The unhelpfulness of indeterminism. *Philosophy and Phenomenological Research* 60:149-56.

———. 2002. The bounds of freedom. In *The Oxford handbook of free will*, ed. Robert Kane, 441-60. New York: Oxford University Press.

———. 2004. Free agents. *Philosophical Topics* 32 (1-2): 371-403.

———. 2010. *Freedom and belief*. Rev. ed. Oxford: Oxford University Press.

Strawson, P.F. 1959. *Individuals: An essay in descriptive metaphysics*. London: Methuen.

———. 1962. Freedom and resentment. *Proceedings of the British Academy* 48:1-25. Reprinted in *Free will*, ed. Gary Watson, 59-80. Oxford: Oxford University Press, 1982.

Swinburne, Richard. 1986. *The evolution of the soul*. Oxford: Clarendon Press.

Taylor, Richard. 1966. *Actions and purpose*. Englewood Cliffs, NJ: Prentice-Hall.

———. 1992. *Metaphysics*. 4th ed. Englewood Cliffs, NJ: Prentice-Hall. (First ed., 1963.)

Taylor, Shelley E. 1989. *Positive illusions*. New York: Basic Books.

Tegmark, Max. 1998. The interpretation of quantum mechanics: Many worlds or many words? *Fortschritte der Physik* 46:855-62.

———. 1999. The importance of quantum decoherence in brain processes. *Physics Review E* 61:4194-206.

Thalberg, Irving. 1989. Hierarchical analyses of unfree action. In *The inner citadel: Essays on individual autonomy*, ed. John Christman, 123-36. Oxford: Oxford University Press.

Tomberlin, James E., ed. 2000. *Action and freedom*. Boston: Blackwell.

Trakakis, Nick. 2007. Whither morality in a hard determinist world? *Sorites* 19:14-40.

Tye, Michael. 1995. *Ten problems of consciousness*. Cambridge, MA: MIT Press.

Underwood, Geoffrey. 1979. Memory systems and conscious processes. In *Aspects of consciousness: Psychological issues*, ed. Geoffrey Underwood and Robin Stevens, 91-121. London: Academic Press.

———. 1982. Attention and awareness in cognitive and motor skills. In *Aspects of consciousness: Psychological issues*, ed. Geoffrey Underwood and Robin Stevens, 111-143. London: Academic Press.

Unger, Peter. 2002. Free will and scientiphicalism. *Philosophy and Phenomenological Research* 65 (1): 1-25.

Van Duijn, Marc, and Sacha Bem. 2005. On the alleged illusion of conscious will. *Philosophical Psychology* 18 (6): 699-714.

Van Gulick, Robert. 2000. Inward and upward: Reflection, introspection, and self-awareness. *Philosophical Topics* 28:275-305.

———. 2001. Reduction, emergence and other recent options on the mind/body problem: A philosophical overview. *Journal of Consciousness Studies* 8 (9-10): 1-34.

Van Inwagen, Peter. 1974. A formal approach to the problem of free will and determinism. *Theoria* 24:9-22.

———. 1975. The incompatibility of free will and determinism. *Philosophical Studies* 27:185-99. Reprinted in *Free will*, ed. Gary Watson. New York: Oxford University Press.

———. 1978. Ability and responsibility. *The Philosophical Review* 87:201-24.

———. 1983. *An essay on free will.* Oxford: Clarendon Press.

———. 1989. When is the will free? In *Philosophical perspectives Vol. 3*, ed. James E. Tomberlin, 399-422. Atascadero, CA: Ridgeview.

———. 1990. Response to Slote. *Social Theory and Practice* 16 (3): 385-95.

———. 2000. Free will remains a mystery. *Philosophical perspectives 14: Action and freedom*, ed. James E. Tomberlin, 1-19. Oxford: Blackwell. Reprinted in *The Oxford handbook of free will*, ed. Robert Kane, 158-77. New York: Oxford University Press, 2002.

Vargas, Manuel. 2005. The revisionist guide to responsibility. *Philosophical Studies* 125:399-429.

———. 2006a. Philosophy and the folk: On some implications of experimental work for philosophical debates on free will. *Journal of Cognition and Culture* 6 (1-2): 240-54.

———. 2006b. On the importance of history for responsible agency. *Philosophical Studies* 127 (3): 351-82.

———. 2007. Revisionism. In *Four views on free will*, ed. John Martin Fischer, Robert Kane, Derk Pereboom, and Manuel Vargas, 126-65. Oxford: Blackwell. (Responses to critics, 204-219.)

———. 2009. Review of Alfred R. Mele's *Effective intentions: The power of conscious will.* Notre Dame Philosophical Reviews (9): http://ndpr.nd.edu/news/24156-effective-intentions-the-power-of-conscious-will/

Velleman, David. 1989. Epistemic freedom. *Pacific Philosophical Quarterly* 70: 73-79.

Velmans, Max. 1991. Is human information processing conscious? *Behavioral and Brain Sciences* 3:651-69.

———. 2003. Preconscious free will. *Journal of Consciousness Studies* 10 (12): 42-61.

Vezér, Martin Alexander. 2007. On the concept of personhood: A comparative analysis of three accounts. *Lyceum* 9 (1): 1-15.

Vohs, Kathleen D., and Roy F. Baumeister. 2006. *Does depletion promote passivity? Self-regulatory resources and active coping.* Manuscript in preparation.

Vohs, Kathleen D., Roy F. Baumeister, Brandon J. Schmeichel, Jean M. Twenge, Noelle M. Nelson, and Dianne M. Tice. 2008. Making choices impairs subsequent self-control: A limited resource account of decision making, self-regulation, and active initiative. *Journal of Personality and Social Psychology* 94 (5): 883-98.

Vohs, Kathleen D., and Ronald J. Faber. 2007. Spent resources: Self-regulatory resources availability affects impulse buying. *Journal of Consumer Research* 33:537-47.

Vohs, Kathleen D., and Todd F. Heatherton. 2000. Self-regulatory failure: A resource-depletion approach. *Psychological Science* 11:249-54.

Vohs, Kathleen D., and Jonathan W. Schooler. 2008. The value of believing in free will: Encouraging a belief in determinism increases cheating. *Psychological Science* 19:49-54.

Von Cranach, Mario, and Klaus Foppa, eds. 1996. *Freedom of decision and action: A problem of nomological psychology.* Heidelberg: Asanger.

Wallace, R. Jay. 1994. *Responsibility and the moral sentiments.* Cambridge, MA: Harvard University Press.

Waller, Bruce. 1990. *Freedom without responsibility.* Philadelphia: Temple University Press.

———. 2004. Virtue unrewarded: Morality without moral responsibility. *Philosophia* 31 (3-4): 427-47.

Walter, Henrik. 2001. *Neurophilosophy of free will.* Cambridge, MA: MIT Press.

Watson, Gary. 1975. Free agency. *Journal of Philosophy* 72:205-20. Reprinted in *Free will*, ed. Gary Watson, 96-110. New York: Oxford University Press, 1982.

———. ed. 1982. *Free will.* New York: Oxford University Press.

———. 1987. Free action and free will. *Mind* 96:145-72.

———. 1996. Two faces of responsibility. *Philosophical Topics* 24:227-48.

Waugh, Nancy C., and Donald A. Norman. 1965. Primary memory. *Psychological Review* 72:89-104.

Wegner, Daniel M. 2002. *The illusion of conscious will.* Cambridge, MA: Bradford Books, MIT Press.

———. 2003. The mind's best trick: How we experience conscious will. *Trends in Cognitive Science* 7 (2): 65-69.

———. 2004. Precise of *The illusion of conscious will. Behavioral and Brain Science* 27 (5): 649-59; discussion 659-92.

———. 2005. Who is the controller of controlled processes? In *The new unconscious,* ed. Ran Hassin, James S. Uleman, and John A. Bargh, 19-36. New York: Oxford University Press.

———. 2008. Self is magic. In *Are we free? Psychology and free will,* ed. John Baer, James Kaufman, and Roy F. Baumeister, 226-47. New York: Oxford University Press.

Wegner, Daniel M., and John A. Bargh. 1998. Control and automaticity in social life. In *Handbook of social psychology,* 4th ed., ed. Daniel T. Gilbert, Susan T. Fiske, and Gardner Lindzey. Boston: McGraw-Hill.

Wegner, Daniel M., and Thalia Wheatley. 1999. Apparent mental causation: Sources of the experience of will. *American Psychologist* 54:480-91.

Weisberg, Josh. 2001. The appearance of unity: A higher-order interpretation of the unity of consciousness. In *Proceedings of the 23rd Annual Conference of the Cognitive Science Society,* ed. Johanna D. Moore and Keith Stenning, 1117-21. Mahwah, NJ: Lawrence Erlbaum Associates.

Weiskrantz, Lawrence. 1986. *Blindsight.* Oxford: Oxford University Press.

———. 1997. *Consciousness lost and found: A neuropsychological exploration.* New York: Oxford University Press.

White, Gregory L., Sanford Fishbein, and Jeffrey Rutstein. 1981. Passionate love and misattribution of arousal. *Journal of Personality and Social Psychology* 41 (1): 56-62.

Whyte, Lancelot. 1978. *Unconscious before Freud.* New York: Basic Books.

Wicklund, Robert A., and Jack W. Brehm. 1976. *Perspectives on cognitive dissonance.* Hillsdale, NJ: Lawrence Erlbaum Associates.

Widerker, David. 1995a. Libertarian freedom and the avoidability of decision. *Faith and Philosophy* 12 (1): 113-18.

———. 1995b. Libertarianism and Frankfurt's attack on the principle of alternative possibilities. *Philosophical Review* 104 (2): 247-61.

———. 2002. Responsibility and Frankfurt-type examples. In *The Oxford handbook of free will,* ed. Robert Kane, 323-34. New York: Oxford University Press.

Wiggins, David. 1973. Towards a reasonable libertarianism. In *Essays on freedom and action,* ed. Ted Honderich, 31-61. London: Routledge & Kegan Paul.

Williams, Lawrence E., and John A. Bargh. 2008. Experiencing physical warmth promotes interpersonal warmth. *Science* 24 (322): 606-67.

Wilson, David L. 1976. On the nature of consciousness and physical reality. *Perspectives in Biology and Medicine* 19:568-81.

———. 1993. Quantum theory and consciousness. *Behavioral and Brain Science* 16:615-16.

———. 1995. Seeking the neural correlate of consciousness. *American Scientist* 83:269-70.

———. 1999. Mind-brain interaction and violation of physical laws. *Journal of Consciousness Studies* 6 (8-9): 185-200.

Wilson, Timothy. 2002. *Strangers to ourselves: Discovering the adaptive unconscious.* Cambridge, MA: Belknap Press of Harvard University Press.

———. 2003. Knowing when to ask: Introspection and the adaptive unconscious. *Journal of Consciousness Studies* 10:131-40.

Wilson, Timothy D., and Nancy Brekke. 1994. Mental contamination and mental correction: Unwanted influences on judgments and evaluation. *Psychological Bulletin* 116:117-42.

Wilson, Timothy D., Samuel Lindsey, and Tonya Y. Schooler. 2000. A model of dual attitudes. *Psychological Review* 107 (1): 101-26.

Wilson, Timothy D., and Jonathan W. Schooler. 1991. Thinking too much: Introspection can reduce the quality of preferences and decisions. *Journal of Personality and Social Psychology* 60 (2): 181-92.

Wilson, Timothy D, and Julie I. Stone. 1985. Limitations of self-knowledge: More on telling more than we can know. In *Review of personality and social psychology Vol. 6*, ed. Phillip Shaver, 167-83. Beverly Hills: Sage.

Winkielman, Piotr, Kent C. Berridge, and Julia L. Wilbarger. 2005. Unconscious affective reactions to masked happy versus angry faces influence consumption behavior and judgments of value. *Personality and Social Psychology Bulletin* 31 (1): 121-35.

Wittgenstein, Ludwig. 1958. *The blue and brown books*. Oxford: Basil Blackwell.

Wolf, Susan. 1980. Asymmetrical freedom. *Journal of Philosophy* 77:151-66.

———. 1981. The importance of free will. *Mind* 90 (359): 386-405.

———. 1990. *Freedom and reason*. Oxford: Oxford University Press.

Wood, Ledger. 1941. Determinism: Free will is an illusion. *Philosophy* 16:386-89.

Wyma, Keith. 1997. Moral responsibility and the leeway for action. *American Philosophical Quarterly* 34:57-70.

Zagzebski, Linda. 2002. Recent work on divine foreknowledge and free will. In *The Oxford handbook of free will*, ed. Robert Kane, 45-64. New York: Oxford University Press.

Zahavi, Dan, and Josef Parnas. 1998. Phenomenal consciousness and self-awareness: A phenomenological critique of representational theory. *Journals of Consciousness Studies* 5:687-705.

Ziehen, Theodor. 1899. *Introduction to physiological psychology*. Translation C.C. Van Liew and Otto W. Beyer. New York: Macmillan.

Zimmerman, David. 1981. Hierarchical motivation and the freedom of the will. *Pacific Philosophical Quarterly* 62:354-68.

Zuriff, Gerald E. 1985. *Behaviorism: A conceptual reconstruction*. New York: Columbia University Press.

Index

Aarts, Henk, 133n17, 165
absolute agency, 27
action initiation. *See* consciousness;
  conscious will; Libet
Adam, Charles, 175n9
adaptive unconscious, 4, 99, 109–115,
  122, 125, 126–127, 128, 133n18, 139,
  151, 168, 171–174; difference
  between Freudian unconscious and,
  109–110. *See also* consciousness;
  automaticity
agent-causal libertarianism, 3, 16–29,
  141–142, 170; argument against,
  29–41, 59; coherence of, 30, 56n8;
  and our folk-psychological
  intuitions, 79, 85–86; on the function
  of consciousness, 142–144, 170; and
  mental causation, 29–41, 55, 59;
  negative constraint on, 20, 46;
  positive constraint on, 20, 46; and
  quantum-mechanical uncertainty,
  38–41; and the rejection of atomistic
  physicalism, 16, 24–25. *See also*
  introspective argument for free will;
  libertarianism; mental causation
agentive experience. *See* sense of
  agency; subjective feeling of
  freedom
Albert, David, 41
alien hand syndrome, 219–221, 258n5
alternative possibilities (or could-have-
  done-otherwise) condition, 66,
  72–75, 78; classical compatibilist
  approach to, 67–72; compatibilist
  denial of, 72–78; folk-psychological
  intuitions about, 79–82, 85; and
  PAP, 75–78, 94n25. *See also* character
  examples; conditional analysis;
  Frankfurt-style cases
Amsel, Abram, 167

Andersen, Holly, 211–212
Andersen, Susan M., 135n33
Anscombe, G.E.M., 64
apparent infallibility of consciousness.
  See consciousness
apparent spontaneity of intentional
  states. *See* intentional states
apparent transparency of
  consciousness. *See* consciousness
Armstrong, David M., 34, 57n10, 154,
  156, 233
Aron, Arthur, 119, 121, 127
Aronson, Joshua, 133n17, 135n27
Audi, Robert, 67, 72, 94n24
Aune, Bruce, 67, 93n19, 130n1
Austin, J.L., 93n16
authentic agency, 68, 93n17
automaticity, 4, 99, 106–108, 111,
  115–124, 126, 129; empirical
  findings related to, 116–124; and the
  HOT theory, 164–166. *See also*
  consciousness; adaptive
  unconscious
automatism, 100, 102, 132n5, 247
auto-motive goal-directed model,
  123–124, 128, 165–166. *See also*
  automaticity
Ayer, A.J., 2, 60–62, 64–65, 67,
  91n4–91n5, 92n12, 130n1

Baars, Bernard, 168, 171–174
Baer, John, 176n24
Bandura, Albert, 123
Banks, William P., 125, 196, 213n10
Barbosa, G.D., 41
Bargh, John A., 4, 9, 98, 102, 106, 107,
  111, 115–118, 119–120, 122–124,
  126–127, 128, 133n13, 133n17,
  134n22–134n23, 134n25–134n26,
  135n28, 135n33, 136n35, 136n37, 149,

About the Author

Gregg D. Caruso is Assistant Professor of Philosophy and Chair of the Humanities Department at Corning Community College, SUNY. He previously taught philosophy at Brooklyn College and was a Writing Fellow at John Jay College of Criminal Justice. He received his B.A. from William Paterson University and his MPhil and PhD from The Graduate Center of The City University of New York. He is the author of several journal articles and book chapters on, among other things, free will and consciousness and is an Assessing Editor for the *Journal of Mind and Behavior*.